Unmasking the State

Unmasking the State

Making Guinea Modern

MIKE MCGOVERN

The University of Chicago Press
Chicago and London

Mike McGovern is associate professor of anthropology at the University of Michigan. He is the author of *Making War in Côte d'Ivoire*, also published by the University of Chicago Press.

The University of Chicago Press, Chicago 60637
The University of Chicago Press, Ltd., London
© 2013 by The University of Chicago
All rights reserved. Published 2013.
Printed in the United States of America

22 21 20 19 18 17 16 15 14 13   1 2 3 4 5

ISBN-13: 978-0-226-92509-7 (cloth)
ISBN-13: 978-0-226-92510-3 (paper)
ISBN-13: 978-0-226-92511-0 (e-book)
ISBN-10: 0-226-92509-9 (cloth)
ISBN-10: 0-226-92510-2 (paper)
ISBN-10: 0-226-92511-0 (e-book)

The University of Chicago Press gratefully acknowledges the generous support of the Frederick W. Hilles Publication Fund of Yale University toward the publication of this book.

Library of Congress-Cataloging-in-Publication Data

McGovern, Mike.
  Unmasking the state : making Guinea modern / Mike McGovern.
    pages. cm.
  Includes bibliographical references and index.
  ISBN-13: 978-0-226-92509-7 (cloth : alk. paper)
  ISBN-10: 0-226-92509-9 (cloth : alk. paper)
  ISBN-13: 978-0-226-92510-3 (pbk. : alk. paper)
  ISBN-10: 0-226-92510-2 (pbk. : alk. paper)
  [etc.]
  1. Guinea—Politics and government—20th century. I. Title.
  DT543.8.M35 2013
  966.52'03—dc23
                                                    2012019394

♾ This paper meets the requirements of ANSI/NISO Z39.48-1992 (Permanence of Paper).

Any large-scale account of human action has to involve both "history" and "sociology": a narrative of the collective subject's passage through time and an analysis of how that subject is constituted. The former is often regarded as a "dynamic" dimension and the latter as a "static" one. And while it can be readily conceded that they are *just* dimensions, aspects of what is concretely a complex, undecomposable unity, the problem stubbornly remains of how to write about either without the distortion of not simultaneously writing about the other.

—J. D. Y. Peel

Marginals stand outside the state by tying themselves to it; they constitute the state locally by fleeing from it. As culturally "different" subjects they can never be citizens; as culturally different "subjects" they can never escape citizenship.

—Anna Lowenhaupt Tsing

Zusammen gestohlen aus verschiedenem diesem und jenem

—Beethoven, autograph to String Quartet in C♯ minor, opus 131

For Margaret and Thomas McGovern

CONTENTS

Note on Orthography / xi
Acknowledgments / xiii

PART I : THE GRAMMAR AND RHETORIC OF IDENTITY

ONE / Competing Cosmopolitanisms / 3

Iconoclasm as a Cosmopolitan Idiom / 5
Uncanny Iconoclasm / 8
Jouissance and the Search for Purity / 12
Ethnogenesis: Two or Three Things I Know about It / 14
Iconoclasm and Ethnogenesis in the Context of Competing Cosmopolitanisms / 19
The Chapters / 20

TWO / The Tactics of Mutable Identity / 27

Insecurity, Migration, and Fluidity of Identities / 31
The Koivogui-Kamara Corridor and the Question of Ethnicity / 39
Clanship and Ethnic Mediation / 52
Who Was "Malinke" in 1921? / 55
Living with Violence, Binding Insecurity / 60

Interlude I: Togba's Sword / 63

THREE / Autochthony as a Cultural Resource / 65

Autochthony as a Cultural Resource / 67
The Politics of Sacrifice / 70
The Significance of Oaths and Ordeals / 80

FOUR / The Emergence of Ethnicity / 85

Space, Landscape, and Production: Loma Rice Farming / 87
Land Tenure and Cash Crops / 89
The Logic of Ethnicized Territory / 93
Mise en Valeur and Ethnicity / 100
Mamadi's Story / 106

FIVE / Portable Identities and the Politics of Religion along the Forest–Savanna Border / 111

Portable Identities / 114
Iconoclastic Precedents / 123
Monotheism and Modernist Anxiety / 133
Northern–Southwestern Mande Links and Their Denial / 137

PART II : REVEALING AND RESHAPING THE BODY POLITIC

Interlude II: Bonfire / 143

SIX / Personae: Demystification and the Mask / 147

Changing Notions of Personhood in Modernist Political Discourse: Personae, Masks, and Mystification / 152
Contradictory Cosmopolitanism: Marxism and the Modern Person / 160
Modernist Anxiety and Double Double Consciousness / 164

SEVEN / Unmasking the State: Making Guinea Modern / 167

Demystification, the Forest Region, and the Guinean Nation / 170
Demystification: An "Inside Job"? / 179
The Cultural Politics of Catching Up: A Comparison / 184
A Convergence of Reasonings / 191

EIGHT / Performing the Self, Performing the Nation / 195

The Aesthetics of Discretion and the State / 196
Aestheticization, Folklorization, Re-presentation / 208
A Sociology of Ambition / 219
Surviving Authoritarianism / 225

CONCLUSION / Double Double Consciousness in an African Postcolony / 227

The First Legacy: Denigration into Ethnic Solidarity / 228
The Second Legacy: Embattlement into National Solidarity / 231
Violence, Marginality, and Divided Consciousness / 233

*Appendix 1 / List of Kɔkɔlɔgi/zu and their dominant clans,
according to Beavogui/Person / 237*
Appendix 2 / Agricultural Production in Giziwulu, 1999 / 241
Notes / 245
Works Cited / 275
Index / 289

NOTE ON ORTHOGRAPHY

Loma terms are written using a combination of International Phonetic Alphabet (IPA) and French orthography.

Consonants: For the implosive "b," I have retained the French "gb" (instead of the IPA ß). For the voiceless labiovelar stop, I have retained the French "kp." However, for the voiced velar fricative, I use the IPA gamma symbol ("γ") rather than the French "gh."[1]

Vowels: "a," "e," "i," "o," and "u" all occur in Lomagui, and are pronounced as in Spanish or according to IPA conventions ("a" as in "bat"; "e" as in "say"; "i" as in "meet"; "o" as in "know"; and "u" as in "glue."

In addition, there are two more vowel sounds in Loma, for which I have used IPA conventions: "ɛ" as in "met"; and "ɔ" as in "not."

I have written Loma words using the definite article, which, in Lomagui, is the suffix "i" or "gi." Plurals are formed by adding the suffix "ti" to the end of the definite article.

The text also uses a number of terms from the northern Mande languages, namely Maninkakan. Plurals in Maninkakan are formed by adding the suffix "lu" (sometimes "nu") to a word, though in the literature, the Bamanakan pluralization, formed with the suffix "w," is more common.

---

1. In the southern Guinean dialects of Lomagui, the sound that I render as "nγ" often sounds more like a nasalized glottal stop. However, the velar fricative sound does sometimes come through, so I have decided to use the "nγ" orthography. In northern Loma dialects, this sound is often dropped altogether, especially from the beginning of words (e.g., "nγazanui" = "azanui" ("woman"), or "nγalui" = "alui" ("moon").

ACKNOWLEDGMENTS

> I was told about the case in Texas, but it had happened in another state. It has a single protagonist (though in every story there are thousands of protagonists, visible and invisible, alive and dead).
>
> —Jorge Luis Borges

So begins Borges's parable "The Ethnographer." In considering my own debts as an ethnographer, I admire his prescience. There are thousands of protagonists in the pages that follow, and it is a pleasure to have the opportunity to thank a few here.

The research was funded at various points by many institutions. The finished product would have been impossible without their help. I thank Emory University, which was always generous both with fellowship and ancillary support; the SSRC International Dissertation Research Fellowship, which funded research in 1997; the SSRC-MacArthur Peace and Security in a Changing World fellowship, which supported research in both England and Guinea between 1997 and 1999; a Fulbright-Hays fellowship, which supported my research in Guinea in 2000–2001; and a Harry Frank Guggenheim Dissertation Writing Fellowship, which underwrote my writing during 2003. A sabbatical leave and a Yale MacMillan Center Faculty Research Grant allowed me to return for much of the 2008–2009 academic year to undertake the research that led to chapter 8 of this book.

In Guinea, I would have accomplished nothing without the help of my Guinean colleagues and friends in Macenta Préfecture and in Conakry. Alamako Onepogui, Pepe Bilivogui, and Aboubacar "Banks" Kourouma worked alongside me at different moments as research colleagues and earned my unending gratitude. Jacques Onivogui was my first French teacher in Guinea and has remained an indispensable guide. Professor Galema Guilavogui facilitated my research at every step and generously shared his thoughts with me about Loma history both when he served as Secretary General of the University Gamal Abdel Nasser and when he served as Minister of National Education. Ambassador Tolo Beavogui, also a historian who has served his country in diverse ways, shared his expertise with me in conversation and correspondence. My friends in Conakry, especially Dr. Serge Mara and Vaba Guilavogui, helped my wife Susan and me in numerous ways. Other friends in Conakry, including El Hadj Tafsir Thiam, Ousmane Barry, Kim Maggio, Gaby Sanoussi, and Martin and Kadi Hartney, also made our time in the capital enjoyable and profitable. I thank M. Cissé and M. Kaba at the National Archives and Dr. Sylla at the Bibliothèque Nationale for their generous help. Among my debts to Guinean intellectuals, perhaps none surpasses that to Facinet Beavogui, the brilliant and thorough historian of the Loma-speaking region. I never had a chance to meet him before his untimely death, but I feel as if I have shared many conversations with him about Loma history and culture.

In the forest region, I must start in N'Zerekore with my old friend Alain Koivogui, friend and palm wine–drinking companion. Thanks also to the Bakoly family. In Macenta Préfecture, I thank Gile, Mao, Chinois, Pepe and Doyen Bilivogui, and on the women's side of the family, Loopu Kalivogui, Kulubo Bilivogui, Fanta Kalivogui, and Ouidoh Pivi. On the other side of the village, I thank Bala Pivi, Nyankoye and Parisien Pivi, and Siaka Bilivogui. The late Pokpa Kalivogui and Foromo Kalivogui facilitated my stay. During the research, Oua Bilivogui, Siaka Bilivogui, N'Zolea Bilivogui, Pascal Pivi, Siba III Kalivogui, and Duogi Pivi were of enormous help. In my second research site, Avit Beavogui and the late Elisabeth Onivogui were my hosts, teachers, and friends during a crucial period in my research. Finally, in the Guekedou area, I relied heavily on the hospitality and assistance of Eddie Keturakis and Khadiatou Diallo. Dominique Millimounou and the team he assembled were fantastic and incredibly hard-working.

Back home, my thanks go to my mentors and colleagues who have saved me from many errors, though I have stubbornly insisted on forging ahead with some of my more idiosyncratic interpretations. Parts of this book started life as a portion of my very long Ph.D. dissertation, and my committee went far beyond their professional obligations in making sure it was as good a document as I could manage. Ivan Karp, my advisor throughout, was an unending source of ideas, citations, and engaged criticism. His death in 2011 means that he did not see this book come into being, but nearly every page bears some mark of his influence. Cory Kratz has, since my first semester of graduate school, read my work with tremendous attentiveness. Many manuscript pages have come back to me with as much of her writing on them as my own. Like Ivan, she has pushed me to situate my analysis not only in relation to the regional literature, but also in comparison to works from across the continent. Eddy Bay single-handedly convinced me of the importance of addressing the issues that now underpin the historical angle of this study, and has consistently challenged me to keep gender in the foreground and to clarify what I meant when I wrote about ethnicity. Bruce Knauft brought a refreshing Melanesianist perspective to his generous engagements with my material and helped save me from the "curse of the OK."

Over the years of working on this project, I have met and learned from many others, both professors and students. I thank especially my co-Guineanists. Chris Hayden gets top billing here: he sent books from France, shared many archival documents, and has always read my work carefully, providing collegial and constructive critiques. Nicole Anderson, Lacey Andrews, Alexis Arieff, David Berliner, Graeme Cousens, Becky Furth, Tim Geysbeek, Odile Goerg, Siba Grovogui, Doug Henry, Christian Højbjerg, Jean-Hervé Jézéquel, Lansine Kaba, Fred Lamp, Claude Rivière, Ramon Sarró, and Jay Straker all helped in important ways at different times. I must especially single out James Fairhead and Melissa Leach for sharing with me some tremendous documents from their vast collection, including the Seymour and Ash narratives from the 1860s, which they were then annotating along with Tim Geysbeek.

In addition, thanks to Mariane Ferme, Caspar Fithen, Lans Gberie, Will Reno, Paul Richards, Rosalind Shaw, and Susan Shepler for bouncing ideas around from the Sierra Leone side; to Warren d'Azevedo, Jeanette Carter, Stephen Ellis, Comfort Ero, Svend Holsoe, Byron Tarr, and Mats Utas from the Liberia side; Joanna Davidson, Eric Gable, and Marina Temudo from Guinea Bissau; and Mary Jo Arnoldi, James Brink, and Rod McIntosh from the Malian side.

My colleagues at Yale have been consistently challenging, stimulating, and supportive. Barney Bate, Kamari Clarke, Narges Erami, Erik Harms, Marcia Inhorn, Bill Kelly, Kwame Onoma, Rod McIntosh, Catherine Panter-Brick, Doug Rogers, Jim Scott, Shivi Sivaramakrishnan, Helen Siu, David Watts, and Libby Wood deserve special mention, as do my inspiring graduate students Susanna Fioratta, Mike Degani, Adrienne Cohen, and Samar Al-Bulushi. Stacey Maples of Yale's Beinecke Library has become my indispensible cartographer. Chapter 2's argument has been significantly clarified and improved by his work. Among those who have shaped my intellectual horizons generally and this project in various ways are Sealing Cheng, Ken George, Peter Geschiere, Yvan Guichaoua, Katrin Hansing, Doug Holmes, Wendy James, Peri Klemm, Julie Livingston, Greg Mann, Peter Mark, Donna Murdock, Polly Nooter-Roberts, David Parkin, Al Roberts, Sunanda Sanyal, Dan Smith, Krista Thompson, Bob White, and Luise White. Rob Leopold and the late Bill Siegmann contributed more to this work than I could enumerate here. I especially thank Rob for his astute reading of the manuscript. He saved me from plenty of mistakes, small and large. I am sorry that Bill, like Ivan, could not see this fruition of our many conversations.

As this work moved toward life as a book, I benefited enormously from the kind solicitude of David Brent, my editor at the University of Chicago Press. Priya Nelson has also been wonderfully responsive and helpful. Two anonymous reviewers provided encouragement and constructive critique that definitely improved the book. Thanks to them.

There are those family and friends without whom this project never would have happened. Thanks to Matthew Dwyer, Kim Eadie, Brian Keizer, Tim Merello, Jerry Neumann, Rachel Norwood, Jason Pronyk, and Lupe Salazar for friendship and encouragement. My in-laws, Don and Genie David, have been extremely supportive and also braved the long trip to Conakry, Labe, and beyond.

The final and deepest thanks are to my two families. My family of choice, Susan, Theo, and Delia, has been involved with every step of the development of this project. From graduate coursework at Emory to archival work in Provence to a year in England, Susan and I logged many frequent flyer miles and many hours on the phone. Every moment of my fieldwork was shared with her, as was almost every moment of the book's long gestation. Our children have leavened the stresses of work with the joys of life together, and I think this has made for a better book.

My parents, Margaret and Thomas McGovern, have supported my intellectual growth since my childhood, sacrificing time, energy, and money to do what was best for my education rather than their own comfort. They could never have expected that my intellectual and personal energies would become directed toward understanding a small corner of West Africa, but they can hardly doubt that those energies have been channeled by the discipline, self-motivation, and excitement they instilled in me and the intellectual training they always supported. This book is dedicated to them.

PART ONE

The Grammar and Rhetoric of Identity

ONE

Competing Cosmopolitanisms

This is a book about iconoclasm and ethnogenesis—that is, about the attempt to destroy objectionable objects and the coming into being of new ethnic identities. Each acted on the other in the region of West Africa that came to be known as the Republic of Guinea. They were, to use the somewhat pretentious academic phrase, mutually constitutive. In this book I argue that seemingly unrelated factors, including slash-and-burn agriculture, the existence of inherited clans with special relations to totemic animals, and the presence or absence of professional oral historians, played crucial roles in this process. Above all, it was the imposition of state power on the formerly decentralized region where each three or four villages had been a law unto themselves that set into motion the reciprocal development of iconoclasm and ethnogenesis in the rainforest–savanna frontier zone I write about.

There are four such states relevant to the story I tell in the following pages. The first was that of the Almamy Samory Touré, a late-nineteenth-century conqueror and proselytizer whose state encompassed much of the region that was to become *Guinée forestière* and more specifically, Macenta Préfecture (map 1). The second was the French colonial state. The third, and most important for this story, was the government headed by Sékou Touré from independence in 1958 to his death in 1984. After Guinea alone among French colonies chose immediate and complete independence in September 1958, his government built policy out of an ideological commitment to state-socialist modernism and Pan-Africanist valorization of precolonial history and culture. The fourth state that enters the story obliquely is that of the post-socialist government of Lansana Conté, an army colonel who took power in a coup d'état one week after Touré's death in 1984, and who held on to it, as Touré had done, until his death in 2008. Not much of

Map 1. Map of Guinea

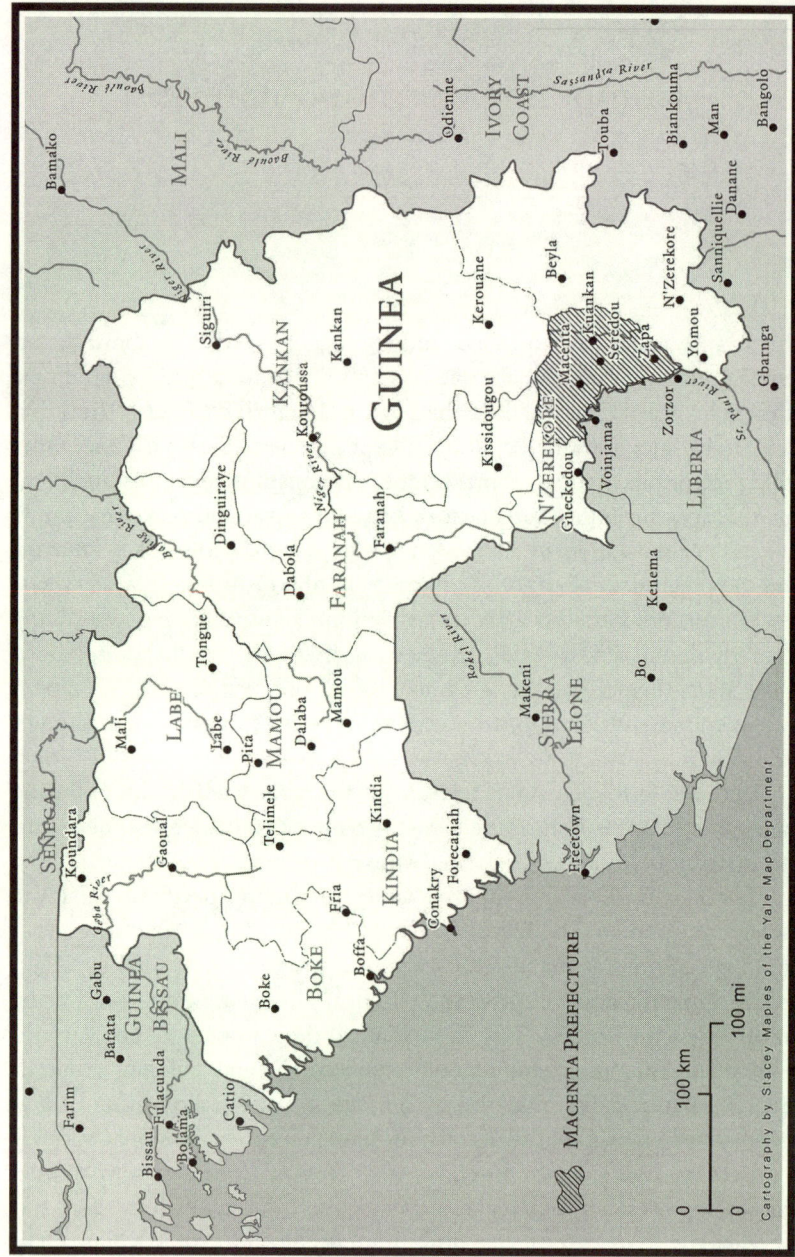

this book is about the Conté period, but because almost all of the research for it was conducted during the Conté years, there are occasional references to it. This book, a historical ethnography of the socialist period in Guinea, will be followed by a later book that focuses on the legacy of socialism under conditions of postsocialist governance in the 1990s and 2000s.

Iconoclasm as a Cosmopolitan Idiom

> [T]he revolution is devoted to acting on the people so that they come back to themselves [*pour qu'il revienne à lui-même*], to their personality, to their originality.... (Touré 1969, 351)

The "Demystification Program" was launched almost immediately after Guinea claimed its independence from France in a referendum.[1] It specifically targeted all forms of precolonial cultural practice deemed backward or primitive, and it focused to a large degree on the polytheistic periphery of a country that had become about 80 percent Muslim and 10 percent Christian by the end of colonialism. Demystification teams including soldiers and representatives from the Ministry of Culture went from village to village, forcibly collecting masks and figurines and burning most of them while taking a few to display in national and regional museums, and recruiting young people to perform the initiation dances that they simultaneously outlawed. The Guinean state demanded several transformations of the country's peripheral inhabitants, including the choice of a monotheistic religion.[2]

As newly independent Guinea embraced socialism in the early 1960s, national elites embraced several forms of cosmopolitan practice and discourse that hailed Guinea's arrival on the international scene. Yet these cosmopolitan idioms were not, themselves, without contradictions and ambivalences. Scientific socialism held out the promise that countries like Guinea could vault forward in the political economic queue, but only if they acknowledged and then renounced their alleged backwardness. Pan-Africanism, by contrast, allowed African countries to embrace African histories and cultures denigrated by Eurocentric ideologies, but it offered mostly intangible benefits to a country seeking rapid economic development. In this context, Guinean state elites mobilized a third cosmopolitan form that partially resolved the contradictions within and between transnational Marxism and Pan-Africanism. Iconoclastic sweeps aimed at eradicating religious "fetishism" and social "mystification."

While I am interested in the ways the Demystification Program was ex-

Figure 1. "We prefer liberty in poverty to opulence in slavery." From *L'action politique du Parti Démocratique de Guinée en faveur de l'émancipation de la Jeunesse guinéenne.*

perienced by speakers of Lomagui in the region where I conducted fieldwork, this book takes Demystification as a window on the logics, dynamics, and internal contradictions of a postcolonial socialist state.³ Why did eradicating polytheism become one of a fledgling country's first policy initiatives? Why was the program prosecuted with such ferocity—beating and publicly humiliating elders, exposing men's sacred objects to women, who were supposed to be rendered infertile or die as a result? Why was it announced a total success about once a year, only to be started over the next?

To get at that set of questions, I will begin with a brief ethnographic vignette and then suggest three possible frames for interpreting it. The frames do not exist in a zero-sum relation to one another, but each one (in my mind at least) adds further nuances to the others. The effect, I hope, will be one of increasingly subtle and complex interpretation. In the end, I don't intend to offer a single interpretive frame that accounts for all of the phenomena involved in Demystification—in fact after twenty years of trying to understand this iconoclastic movement, I still find it perplexing, so will not pretend to that type of mastery.

I begin with a story that I have been mulling over for many years. I was in my second fieldwork site, beginning to settle in after a month or two. Having spent fifteen months in an isolated, ethnically homogenous Loma-speaking[4] village of about 1,200 inhabitants, I was now working in a small, ethnically heterogeneous town of 8,000 people about 40 km away.

I was speaking with an elder Loma man, and we were talking about the history of his town, including current relations between the two main ethnolinguistic groups who lived there, the Loma (understood to be the original inhabitants of the area) and the Manya (one of the two biggest ethnic groups in the country but understood to be relative newcomers in this region). As we were talking, an older man walked by at a distance. He greeted my interlocutor in Maninkakan (a Northern Mande language), and we responded in kind. The elder Loma man talking with me said, "You see him? He and I were initiated into the men's secret society together. In the sacred forest, everything took place in the Loma language. He spoke Lomagui perfectly. Today, he is a Muslim elder and would deny that he was ever initiated. If you greet him in Lomagui, he will pretend not even to understand you. You should try it the next time you see him. And yet, he has the same cicatrizations on his back as me."[5] I did indeed try a few days later, and he responded to my Loma greeting with the roughly equivalent response in Maninkakan.

For Loma speakers, the bonding that takes place between initiates secluded for months or even years in the forest is one of the strongest social ties that exists,[6] and it cuts across all other solidarities created by kinship, marriage, religious, or even ethnic relations. What troubled my Loma informant and many other Loma people I knew well was what they perceived to be the hypocrisy of this sort of personal erasure—a form of iconoclasm at the individual level. That full immersion into Islam required a renunciation of secret society membership was well understood. The same was true for serious converts to Protestant (though not necessarily Catholic) Christianity. Most Loma speakers who did not convert to a world religion might not have valued this choice, but they understood it. What they did not understand was why embracing a world religion would entail such a thoroughgoing attempt to efface past actions that were easily verifiable by those who had been there to witness the events. Why, they asked, pretend not to even know the greetings in a language one once spoke fluently and continued to hear spoken every day?

I would like to take this small everyday case as a starting point for thinking through the complexities of iconoclasm at the everyday level of village life. I believe that if we can untangle some of the complications involved in such a story of personal iconoclastic self-making, we will be able to understand something new about the history and sociology of this postcolony. To understand the kind of state postcolonial Guinea was and what it aspired to be, it helps to understand the reasons why iconoclasm became a privileged tool in the state's arsenal for shaping new socialist citizens. Understanding iconoclasm in Guinea may also give some new critical purchase to the broader discussion of iconoclasm as practice and ideology.

Uncanny Iconoclasm

Guinea's Demystification Program prompts three questions:

1. Why do some objects become so objectionable to iconoclasts that they "require" their own eradication?
2. How does this process work, even when the objects in question have never been seen by those who find them offensive, and they will in fact have to be viewed for the first time in order to destroy them?
3. What accounts for the particularly strong affective component in iconoclastic movements such as the one in Guinea?

To try to answer the first question, "Why do some objects become so objectionable to iconoclasts that they 'require' their own eradication?" I turn to W.J.T. Mitchell. Mitchell's work is important precisely because of his ability to bring clinically precise thinking to the phenomenon of the power of images. This power is perfectly intuitive at the same time that it is extremely difficult to explicate. Mitchell's framework for unraveling this problem draws on both Marx and Freud, but uses them as jumping off points toward his own original framework. In his 2005 collection of essays, entitled *What Do Pictures Want?* he interrogates the power of images to bring out in us what we might think of as the "exorcist" and "adoricist" reactions described by Luc de Heusch (1971) for possession practices in Africa.[7]

Mitchell asks about the source of the "surplus value of images," first by asking how techniques such as cloning destabilize our notions about "the thing itself" (and consequently, as if in mirror image, any simple notions of the relationship between the thing and its image). Secondly, he asks about the interrelationships of those aura-laden images, the totem, the idol, and the fetish. He quotes Lévi-Strauss quoting McLennan, "fetishism is totemism minus exogamy and matrilineal descent"(2005, 99)—an absurd equation that nonetheless insightfully points to the place where Marx's preoccupation with use and exchange values crosses Durkheim's distinction between mechanical and organic solidarities.[8] For them, as for Freud, what distinguishes the fetish is its lack of social usefulness.[9] For Mitchell, ever interested in iconoclasm, this is what distinguishes the "iconoclastic hostility" trained on the fetish from the "curatorial solicitude" aimed at the totem (100).

He writes that there are four ways of relating to a libidinal object: love, desire, friendship, and *jouissance*:

> What happens to the four ways of relating to a libidinal object when an image or picture is involved? An exact correspondence emerges between these relations and the standard array of sacred icons and iconic practices: love belongs to the idol, desire to the fetish, friendship to the totem, and jouissance to iconoclasm, the shattering or melting of the image. When a picture wants love, or more imperiously, when it demands love, but does not need it or return it, but looms in silence, it becomes and idol. . . . When it asks to be shattered, disfigured or dissolved, it enters the sphere of the offending, violent or sacrificial image, the object of iconoclasm, the pictorial counterpart to the death drive, or the ecstatic shattering of the ego associated with the orgasm. When it is the object of fixation, compulsive repetition, the gap between articulated demand and brute need, forever teasing with its fort-da of lack and plenitude, its crossing of drive and desire, it is the fetish. . . . Finally there is friendship . . . and its proper image type, the totem. (Mitchell 2005, 74)

Mitchell's magisterial treatment of the power that images have over us brings together Marxist and Freudian notions of the fetish, the anthropological and Freudian notions of the totem, and an intellectual history of iconoclasm. He imposes order on our hunches about the work of iconoclasm. We can only begin to make sense of it by paying close attention to both the implicit theories of society that accompany the classification of differing images, and then by paying equally close attention to the affective (even libidinal) economies that overlay these same theories.

Bruno Latour's writings supplement Mitchell's formulations in several ways. He has insightfully stated about the religious fetish or idol:

> The only one who is projecting feelings onto the idol is the iconoclast with a hammer, not those who should be freed, by his gesture, from their shackles. The only one who believes is him, the fighter against all beliefs. . . . Belief, naïve belief, might be the way for the iconoclast to enter into contact, violent contact, with the others. It is not a state of mind, not a way to grasp statements, but a *mode of relations*. (1997, 67)

As Latour rightly notes, there is something about this iconoclastic posture, both accusatory and slightly desperate for making contact, that seems to characterize young men. In this desire to instantiate a mode of relations, iconoclasm seems to serve almost the same purpose for citizens of the new postcolonial cosmopolis as the incest prohibition serves for isolated corporate communities as described by Lévi-Strauss (1969). It is a prohibition that prescribes other forms of contact, exchange, and sociality. And indeed, if we look at the personnel involved in most iconoclastic undertakings, we find that they are overwhelmingly young men. Latour underlines "the extravagant belief that the iconoclast wishes to impute to them [the would-be naïve believers]," as well as insisting on iconoclasm's modernist flavor. The iconoclast thus transubstantiates the fetish. However, by accusing those who use the fetish of belief (in his view, naïve belief), he in fact attributes to it powers that it may never have had in the eyes of its actual users. At the least, the iconoclast mistakes a metaphor for the thing itself. In this context the iconoclasts[10] bring a zeal and a naïve sincerity to their own practice that they project onto those they figure as "behind," "backwards," and "fetishistic."

We are, I hope, fumbling toward the beginnings of an answer to the first question, which was why images have the power to provoke humans in the way they have done for millennia. Less well understood, I think, is the answer to my second question, why the knowledge of an image rarely if ever seen by the iconoclast would provoke the iconoclastic reaction. In Guinea, the foci of iconoclastic attention were not golden calves, but objects (masks, figurines, staffs of office) used only by initiates in settings spatially and temporally removed from the sight even of members of the same village of the opposite gender or too young to be initiated, let alone the wider national population. Here we should perhaps talk about the *image of the offending image*. Michael Taussig (1999) has drawn our attention to the political potency of secrecy and the ways in which it draws defacing reactions similar to iconoclasm. He has also noted the perverse effect of iconoclasm in such settings, namely the "awkwardness to iconoclasm, paradoxically privileging its target by virtue of ridicule" (1999, 27).

Is it correct to say that such objects provoked via their role as parts of an "open secret"? As an alternative system of meaning-making and of political sovereignty? Yes, certainly.[11] But I don't think this can account fully for some of the ardor with which iconoclasm in Guinea, or many other places, has been undertaken. To begin to answer my third question, why does iconoclasm provoke such strong emotional reactions, we need to dig deeper into this rich vein of self-contradictory material. I propose that we take a brief detour, namely to consider Freud's notion of the uncanny.

In his essay "The 'Uncanny,'" Freud begins by giving us the etymology of the German word "heimlich" which, although it has come to mean "homely," has a history of two uses: "on the one hand it means what is familiar and agreeable, and on the other, what is concealed and kept out of sight." He continues, linking the uncanny to the compulsion to repeat, and arguing, "every affect belonging to an emotional impulse, whatever its kind, is transformed, if it is repressed, into anxiety" ([1917] 1995, 143). He further describes the play of "irrational" beliefs, such as those characterizing what he calls animism. The uncertainty about whether we have really surmounted our ancestors' backward beliefs, and the struggle to repress our animist past, result in anxiety. They also cause the uncanny feeling we have when such repressed beliefs return to consciousness. "Unheimlich is the name for everything that ought to have remained . . . secret and hidden but has come to light" (125). Thus, "the animistic beliefs of civilized people" (142) always risk rising back up to the surface.

This, I think, gives us a new vantage point on the vignette of the Loma and the Manya elders. It helps to explain how the concerns of a modernizing state might coincide with the concerns of some of its citizens, including those with a shallow monotheistic pedigree who nonetheless wanted to lay claim to the respect, prestige, and dignity that had come to accompany forms of religious piety that were valorized locally, nationally, and globally. Taken together, Freud's insights about the uncanny, Latour's about the iconoclast, and Mitchell's about the anxiety created by what he calls the "surplus value of images" suggest that the iconoclast is, as often as not, trying to purge some uncanny impurity from himself, even though the drama may be played out in the sacred groves or places of worship of others.

I should be clear here in stating that the analysis in this book is not psychoanalytic, and the reader will be hard pressed to find Freud mentioned in the remaining pages. The dynamic identified by Freud as the religious element of the uncanny is largely the same one Donald Donham (1999) describes as Ethiopian modernists' desire to "cut history off at the pass." Donham's analysis of the 1975 Ethiopian revolution makes no mention of Freud and I could easily do the same here. However, one advantage I see in at least invoking Freud is the fact that it emphasizes that the anxieties about civilization, progress, and modernity that Marxists and zealous converts to world religions in Guinea or Ethiopia experienced are nearly identical to those of the twentieth-century European bourgeois Freud described. Indeed, what is striking to me in looking at the Demystification Program in comparative perspective is that it shares so many elements of an enactment we might find on most any continent where those most invested in the project of modernity invariably fear that "we have never been modern" (Latour 1993; cf. Wald 1995) Elements of the bedrock modernist faith that underpins Marxism and of the residues of colonial racism bring modernist anxiety into relief in settings like newly independent Guinea, but they might easily be found many other places too.

Jouissance and the Search for Purity

Still, I don't think we can be satisfied with an explanation that simply ends with the pat statement—it's all a matter of projection. Recent converts, like new nations and their civil servants, may have some characteristic forms of anxiety that borrow from and improvise out of the grammar of the already anxious undertakings of colonization and proselytization. Yet I am not satisfied with an argument that stops here, and not only because of reservations about the applicability of some of these categories of analysis in West African settings.[12]

The point I want to return to is that the particular fantasy structure of iconoclasm is linked to the uncanny sense of matter out of place, but matter that is too intimately connected to oneself to be simply brushed aside. As Arjun Appadurai has noted in his *Fear of Small Numbers* (2006), it is precisely in those instances where there is a high level of intimacy, of intermarriage, of physical, emotional, and cultural proximity, that rejection is *most* likely—not least—to turn toward a logic of extirpation.

In another context (Côte d'Ivoire), I have explained the fantasy of xenophobic politics by looking at the ways that charismatic religious figures link Christian prophetic rhetoric to the politics of autochthony (McGovern 2011). As Geschiere (2009) has described, autochthony is an ideology of nativeness that has been invoked from ancient Greece to contemporary Europe, Africa, and North America in order to justify the partition of political rights. Autochthonous "owners of the land" claim the right to exercise political preeminence and to limit or deny political rights to newcomers. The fact that many autochthones or their ancestors were themselves once newcomers rarely undercuts the confidence with which they wield autochthonous rhetoric. Like Guinean iconoclasm, this imaginary solution of sending everyone back to their "proper" places participates in a similar logic of extirpating that which is uncannily internal to the individual or the community, yet which no longer squares with the individual's/community's sense of itself. It is not incidental that most of the charismatic movements in Côte d'Ivoire were also preoccupied with eliminating witchcraft, that most uncanny instance of "matter out of place." Although Loma speakers have no belief in witchcraft and grant sorcery only very limited importance,[13] many other Guineans do have highly developed notions about witchcraft and sorcery, and these have sometimes been attributed to the activities of the power associations.

The other thing that links iconoclasm and xenophobic politics is that in the exterminating violence that accompanies these moves toward self-mastery, ownership, and purification, there is often a perverse joy involved—*jouissance* (Barthes 1973) is probably the most apt term. We have already touched on some of the reasons why recent converts to monotheism could feel a degree of anxiety about the polytheistic residue that might indeed have been a part of their own biography. This is, as it were, the itch. Yet we are left with the question of why it feels so satisfying to scratch that itch. This question becomes more pressing when we consider the ferocity, the frenzy, and the compulsiveness that accompany so many iconoclastic undertakings around the world. This may help to explain why Guinean Demystification began anew year after year, announcing itself as a success, then returning again to start the unfinished work over.

In chapter 5, I describe how the Demystification Program built upon a preexisting idiom of destruction of "idols" as a central step in the conversion to world religions. This precedent combined with Marxist idioms of unmasking the ideological supports of unjust economic relations, and of leveling economic disparities (cf. Fitzpatrick 2005). In chapters 6, 7, and 8, I discuss how Demystification also bridged the distance between Marxism and Pan-Africanism by simultaneously outlawing and folklorizing the same objects, and then exporting this authentic (but surpassed) chapter of Guinea's history via the world-renowned dance troupe, *Les Ballets Africains*. This allowed Guinean modernists to purge the uncanny traces of the past. At the same time it signaled to both the "backward" periphery and the general population the outlines of the banned cultural content and what was

Ethnogenesis: Two or Three Things I Know about It

So far, I have discussed the analysis put forward in the second half of the book—in chapters 6 through 9. The first half of this book takes fine-grained ethnographic and historical materials to show how the modern conception of ethnicity came into being in postcolonial Guinea. I focus specifically on Macenta Préfecture, which is home to a Loma-speaking majority and a minority that speaks Mandekan (Greenberg 1955). Loma speakers, like other speakers of Southwestern Mande languages, are known for their Poro men's and Sande women's power associations, more commonly called secret societies. In the forest region of Guinea, most of Liberia, and most of Sierra Leone, all boys are initiated into the Poro society and all girls into the Sande society. These are classic "rites de passage" (van Gennep [1960] 1980), bringing the initiate into adulthood after a period of seclusion in a sacred grove located in the forest near the village where non-initiates and all members of the opposite gender are prohibited. They are also the first of a series of interconnected societies, each controlling different powers such as the ability to treat snake bites, to help infertile women conceive a child, or to control lightning. I call all of these institutions power associations rather than secret societies in this book, as I think that more accurately describes their most salient characteristic.

I explain Loma categories for understanding personhood and power, built around the potentially dangerous life force known as *manye*, which is channeled and controlled through the use of *sale*, a term that can mean medicine, talisman, or mask, and the power associations that control knowledge of particular forms of *sale* within a system of cultivated discretion. Each of these categories has its analogue among the Northern Mande languages, which I group together as Mandekan in this book. Potentially dangerous life force is called *nyama*, powerful medicine or objects are called *basi* or *daliluw*, and the analogues of the Southwestern Mande Poro society are the Northern Mande *Komo, Jo,* and *Korɛ* societies. Despite, or perhaps because of these similarities, speakers of the Northern and Southwestern Mande languages have come to think of themselves as fundamentally different from one another. It is this process of separation, hardening, and distanciation that I refer to as ethnogenesis.

This process of ethnogenesis was both a cause and a result of the iconoclastic movement I describe in the second half of the book. I argue, however, that it is impossible to understand how and why the Demystification Program took place as it did unless we understand the details of rural swidden (slash-and-burn) rice farmers' lives. Consequently, the first half of the book consists of classical ethnography that describes rural agricultural sociology, the forms of ritual and kinship relations that constitute localized political power and legitimacy, and the *moyenne durée* history of population movements. At each step of the way, however, I analyze the way these practices were not timeless custom but were in fact interacting with a series of polities that aimed to encompass them, from precolonial Muslim empires to the French colonial state to the socialist state of Sékou Touré's Parti Démocratique de Guinée (hereafter PDG).

My argument is inspired by some of the best ethnographic works on the region, including those by Berliner (2005, 2007, 2010), Sarró (2009, 2010) and Højbjerg (2007, 2010). Sarró (2010) crystallizes this line of argument in his wonderful essay, "Map and Territory: The Politics of Place and Autochthony among Baga Sitem (and their Neighbours)." He describes the ways that villagers operating according to the old "rules" that privileged ethnic ambiguity and fluidity but maintained strict hierarchical political relations between early settlers of a territory and relative newcomers found themselves surprised by a new set of rules. Changes to the law under colonial and especially postcolonial governments privileged new kinds of relations to land, and often rewarded those who entrepreneurially moved into fertile zones to cultivate cash crops or to do other forms of work (commerce, transport, cutting and selling timber) that were part of the cash economy. Under such pressures, also described by Geschiere (2009) and Geschiere and Nyamanjoh (2000) in other settings, the logics of authochthony and ethnicized territory suddenly became attractive or even a matter of survival from the point of view of beleaguered "owners of the land." As one man said to Sarró (2010, 243), "the problem was that they, the Baga landlords, had been too generous: they had given land and shelter to too many strangers and now the strangers thought that they could 'stand up' instead of 'remaining seated.'" Berliner's and Højbjerg's essays in the same volume (2010) clarify further how the recognition of the inherently creole origins of maroon societies can sometimes serve as the springboard of nativist discourses of identity when those same groups see themselves as threatened by an outside group. The core of this story is one of fluid ethnolinguistic distinctions that became hardened, of contemporary social and political divisions cast backward in historical time and narrated as age-old incommensurable differences.

This is a story that also has a great deal in common with the analysis of

Zomia in Southeast Asia put forward by James Scott (2009). When writing my Ph.D. dissertation on this topic, I had already been greatly impressed by the ways that Edmund Leach's (1954) analysis of Kachin and Shan relations in highland Burma resembled much of what I had seen and heard in Guinea's southeastern rainforest corner. Like highland Burma, this is an area where kinship, marriage alliance, and political hierarchy are all connected to one another. Wife-givers are preeminent, and wife-receivers are supposed to be their political clients. At the same time, such hierarchies are crosscut by various forms of reciprocity as well as by the attempts by subalterns to improve their stations, whether by ruse or by force.

What I had not realized until Scott's *The Art of Not Being Governed: An Anarchist History of Upland Southeast Asia* (2009) was published was that the resemblances went much deeper than "mere" structures of kinship and marriage alliance. The deeper kinship between the West African rainforest region and the Southeast Asian highlands that Scott (after van Schendel) calls Zomia is one of maroon societies. In both cases, these multiethnic, polyglot societies held themselves together on the one hand by sometimes effective, sometimes not so effective norms of kinship and marriage relations. Beyond that, they are societies formed out of a commitment to carving tiny islands of autonomy out of an encompassing environment of violence and depredation.[15]

The product of some five hundred years of depopulation and destabilization as the result of the intervillage warfare spurred and encouraged by the Atlantic slave trade, the towns and micro-chiefdoms of the area that became Macenta Préfecture were typically comprised of a mixture of a successful war chief and some fearless young men, a large number of refugees of various ethnolinguistic origins, captives, and a few traders. These traders had usually negotiated the protection necessary to ply their wares along the dangerous bush paths that linked fortified towns, often built at the top of hills and surrounded by rampart walls whose remnants can still be seen in the area (Person 1968). The founder's cults found in Southeast Asia (Tannenbaum and Kammerer 2003) are similar to the complex of village settlement and strategic sacrifice described in chapter 3. Similarly, though written in parallel, my account of agricultural practice, state intervention, and ethnogenesis is remarkably similar to that described by Scott for highland Southeast Asia (2009). Indeed, it would be accurate and fair to the ethnographic particularities of the West African forest–savanna frontier zone I describe to call it a West African Zomia.[16]

It is in this context that a politics and aesthetics of discretion have become central to the institutional life of the societies of this rainforest belt.

As many others (d'Azevedo 1962b; Bellman 1984; Ferme 2001; Murphy 1980, 1981) have also argued, the ownership and management of knowledge, and the ability to remain discreet in disbursing it, are central preoccupations of people in Loma and neighboring Kpelle, Mande, Gola, and other societies in this region. What I call "discretion" has more often been termed "secrecy." I find the latter term misleading, both because the rules of discretion are often applied with equal strictness to knowledge and comportments that are not at all secret, and at the same time to other elements of social and political life at the village level that are, at most, open secrets. I describe and analyze this politics and aesthetics of discretion at greater length elsewhere (McGovern 2004), and in summary form in chapter 8.

The intersection of political, philosophical, and aesthetic concerns around this complex of discretion/secrecy has attracted not only the attention of states that have tended to treat "secret societies" they did not control as an a priori threat, but also the attention of more philosophically oriented anthropologists. Building upon the superb regional ethnography of secrecy mentioned above, some of my close colleagues (Berliner 2002, 2005, 2007; Højbjerg 2002a, 2002b, 2007), like some anthropologists working elsewhere (Whitehouse 2000, 2002) have developed sophisticated analyses of the cognitive aspects of religious reflexivity and transmission. I do not take up that line of argument here, partly because they have done such a thorough job of it, but also because my own interests are somewhat different. The attempts by the Guinean state to destroy Loma speakers' ritual objects and perhaps by proxy to eliminate the parallel system of religious-political secrecy and autonomy are one instance of a wider phenomenon that is my core interest. That is, how do the agents representing states, and especially socialist states, work to constitute that state's legitimacy and effective rule? And how do the putative targets of this rule react to these attempts?

For understanding this, I find that it is especially fruitful to work "from the margins of the state" (Das and Poole 2004), where effective rule is most fragile and where coercive attempts to impose state law tend to erode the state's legitimacy. Many Loma speakers fled for long or short periods of time into Liberia, where the other half of the Loma-speaking population lives and where they were free to pursue their religious lives as they pleased.[17] At that level, it is not surprising that the practices of the Poro and Sande societies continued after the twenty-six-year ban was lifted. What interests me more is the way that the power associations, already centuries old at the time of Guinean independence, became subjects of state rhetoric and policy. This policy operated in such a way that the rhetorical and indeed dramaturgical construction of secrecy (and its unmasking) became a central trope of the state's self-definition. At the same time, it caused Loma speakers to qualitatively change their own politico-religious practices, sometimes transforming discretion into true secrecy, as when whole villages sent their ready-to-be-initiated young men or women across the border in the middle of the night to simply become adults in the "normal" Loma way.

Secrecy exercises a complex epistemological and ethical sway in descriptions such as this one, that deal with information that may be subject to laws of "that which must not be spoken." This is one reason why I do not write much of what I know about how certain events took place at the village level, but try in almost all cases to draw my own descriptions of Demystification from what is already available in the public record.[18] I can say that whatever I have included here also squares with what I understand to be accurate on the basis of my participant observation research.

The state interventions epitomized by the Demystification Program were thus an important part of the process of reshaping and hardening ethnic identities that have come to seem self-evident. The West Africa literature also throws up many comparable examples to show that the ways that polytheistic and polyglot groupings of mostly Mande people became "Loma" or "Manya" is not an isolated dynamic. Jean-Loup Amselle's 1990 *Logiques métisses* is the best known of these works. Amselle dissects the seemingly self-evident and quite different ethnic categories of Fulbe and Bamana in order to show us how, in the areas of Mali, Guinea, and Côte d'Ivoire where he works, people have frequently jumped over the line separating one ethnic group from another. Sometimes these switches had to do with religious practice, sometimes with livelihoods, other times with migration; but in every case, the elaborate tango of mutual constitution and distinction from an intimate other is central to the dynamic. Other works, including Furth (2005) and van Bruijn and van Dijk (1997) specify the related dynamics from within the seemingly monolithic ethnic bloc of "The Fulbe."

Because of their longstanding experience of outside interference and pillage, the people in area I write about were and remain profoundly skeptical of claims by encompassing states that they could or would do anything beneficial for them. The armies of the nineteenth-century Muslim empire-builder Samory Touré had pillaged and enslaved them as other warlords had done before. The French who followed first conquered the region by force, then extracted corvée labor, and expropriated women, grain, and livestock according to their whims. When the socialist government also expropriated farmers' crops to feed people in the towns, forced families to relinquish their teenagers to participate in cultural festivals, and banned the very initiations and masquerades that the youngsters were forced to perform as folklore, people in Macenta and the surrounding area (known as *La Région forestière*, its inhabitants known as *Forestiers*) were not much surprised.[19]

In this context, as in the Southeast Asian one described by Leach (1954) and Scott (1998, 2009), there has been a tension between the usefulness of negotiable identities and those that claim to be historically deeper and more legitimate, using the rhetoric of modernist states and world religions. The vignette of the two elders already tells us something about how formerly fluid identities became increasingly fixed over time in Macenta Préfecture. I want to go beyond that somewhat familiar story of hardening ethnic identities to talk about how this process took place in twentieth-century Guinea. My claim is that the Demystification Program was intimately linked to this process, as both cause and effect of the creation of newly distinct identities out of a formerly shifting set of points on a cultural continuum where people cultivated potential axes of relatedness rather than shutting them down.

Iconoclasm and Ethnogenesis in the Context of Competing Cosmopolitanisms

The competing cosmopolitan frames provided by Marxist and Pan-Africanist ideologies assigned very different values to precolonial African cultures and practices. Pan-Africanism identified African precolonial cultures as the source of specifically African genius and particularism, and it insisted that there are African social, political, and economic bases on which to build a distinctive modernity. Scientific socialism, on the other hand, insisted upon a single path to modernity. Although socialism identified problems of exploitation within European modernity, it did not hesitate to treat non-European societies with Eurocentric disdain.[20]

Every non-European Marxist and socialist government had to make its own peace with this contradiction. I argue in this book that in Guinea, the working solution to this problem was to parse the precolonial cultural practices of the people of Guinea into those that could be deemed wholesome and those that were identified as noxious. The experience of conversion to world religions, very recent for some Guineans, provided a template for this process of sorting, validating, and erasing.

In this way, iconoclasm can be understood as making a claim for equal membership in a world of nations. Newly independent countries like

Guinea knew themselves to be denigrated by others, including the erstwhile colonizers. Iconoclasm provided a solution to the desire to eradicate the embarrassing residue of premodern backwardness from the body politic. Sékou Touré made frequent calls for Guineans to "come back to themselves," to reclaim an authentic precolonial self that had been terribly deformed by the experience of colonialism. Despite this he partook in the often anxious undertaking of eliminating embarrassing traces of precolonial backwardness. Those who practiced African religions in Guinea were not embarrassed by their alleged barbarity. As Latour would predict, only the modernist iconoclasts seem to have been fully convinced of the peasants' belief. However, Forestiers did come—and it happened rather quickly— to understand that being a full citizen of the young nation entailed the necessity of being embarrassed by such practices and finding some cherished or useful objects objectionable. Their practices, experienced imaginatively through the eyes of others, became beliefs.[21] This experience of seeing oneself through others' eyes when those others may themselves experience themselves through the eyes of yet another imagined outside gaze is what I call "double double consciousness." This term, adapted from DuBois' discussion in *The Souls of Black Folk* ([1903] 1994) is one of the foci of the second half of the book.

The Chapters

I imagine three types of readers for this book. One group may be most interested in the kind of rural ethnography that constitutes the first half, and which has become increasingly rare in academic anthropology. The second group, more interested in the anthropology of the state and the study of cultural policy, especially those of socialist states, might skip the first half of the book and go directly to the second. My ideal reader will read the whole, and I try to make the case that full understanding of either half of the book will come only from understanding how the dynamics described in each half work on one another. For those who may still be unconvinced, I sketch the contents of the remaining chapters here.

Part 1: The Grammar and Rhetoric of Identity

The next four chapters lay out the building blocks of social and political identities, showing the ways they acted on one another. The last chapter in the section addresses the ways that their articulation also played a central role in shaping the dynamics that culminated in the Demystification Project. These chapters tack between village-level micropolitics and the regional idioms of kinship, autochthony, and clan affiliation to show the different ways that people along this section of the West African forest–savanna frontier maintained high levels of social and cultural flexibility that aided them in negotiating situations of endemic insecurity caused by the intervillage raiding spurred by the Atlantic slave trade. By so doing, they help to explain why the politics of ethno-religious identity took the particular twists and turns they did, and how techniques for managing unpredictability and insecurity changed during the colonial and socialist postcolonial periods. These transformations led to a distinctive type of ethnogenesis that was the result of many of the same dynamics that led toward an iconoclastic "solution" to the contradictions rising out of these changes. By doing this, these chapters set the scene for understanding the Demystification Program, the focus of part 2.

Chapter 2 introduces the grammar of micropolitics within this portion of the Upper Guinea Coast and describes the ways in which recurrent population movements characterized the region in the nineteenth century. Drawing on the work of Bledsoe, d'Azevedo, Jackson, Kopytoff, and Murphy, as well as my own fieldwork, the chapter shows how ethnic identity was fluid and negotiable through the idiom of totemic clans common to multiple ethno-linguistic groups. The chapter also introduces the principle of autochthony as the ultimate basis of political legitimacy, showing how it, too, was often renegotiated through the establishment of fictive kinship relations and rewritten genealogies. The picture that emerges is one of considerable movement, fluidity, and negotiability that continued through much of the twentieth century, as individuals and whole villages remained mobile, fleeing first colonial forced labor and taxes and later the domination of the socialist state.

Chapter 3 explains two institutions that underlie Loma conceptions of socio-political legitimacy: autochthony and the relationship between mother's brothers and sister's sons. Loma villages and all the land within them are understood to belong to the descendants of the village's first settler, often figured as a hunter who found a good place to live while hunting in the bush. This village founder enters into a relationship with the area's earth and water spirits (*inegiti*), from whom he receives permission to settle in the area. All subsequent settlers borrow land from him, just as he borrowed it from the earth spirits. The relationship between this first settler and the second man who joins him in the village is figured as one between a wife-giving mother's brother (*kekɛ*) and a wife-receiving sister's son (*daabe*). While the autochthonous uncle enjoys political preeminence and can in principle revoke rights to the land he has lent, he is beholden to his nephew, who performs sacrifices on his behalf to the earth spirits. All subsequent arrivals in the village enter into a *kɛkɛ–daabe* relationship with a resident host with whom they enter into a reciprocal relation. Political legitimacy and hierarchy are thus enacted on a quotidian basis by the performance of sacrifices of one individual or group for another. Such ancestral sacrifice both renews the relations among the living, the ancestors, and the earth and water spirits at the same time that they perform the hierarchical relationship between first (or earlier) settlers and their later arriving clients, nephews, and sacrificers.

Chapter 4 describes the process that began shutting down the possibilities for renegotiating one's identity under adverse circumstances in the area that became Guinea's forest region. First, competition for colonial-era chieftaincies between 1918 and 1925 led the rather bewildered French authorities to split chieftaincies into halves "belonging" to the two language groups resident in the area, Loma and Manya. This novel basis of political legitimacy was amplified by the socialist government, which introduced land tenure laws granting durable rights to anyone—including migrating "strangers"—who put land to uses the government deemed rational. While the politics of land tenure and chieftaincy began hardening identities around claims to land ownership or legitimate authority, a second factor, conversion to Islam or Christianity, operated to further fix once-fluid identities in place. To become Muslim was to *be* ethnically Manya, just as to become Christian or continue to practice Forestier religion was to *be* Loma. While the French introduced Roman Catholic proselytisation to Guinea, they also granted Muslims a significantly higher "civilizational" status than polytheists. This bias was continued and extended by the Touré government after independence, and Demystification was the primary vehicle for forcing Guineans to choose a world religion.

Chapter 5 explores the search for and mobilization of a usable past in the construction of a postcolonial Guinean nation that had inherited arbitrary colonial boundaries. It explores both the content of the new state-sponsored history, narrated as if the unfolding of the present were presaged by past glory, and also its form. Analyzing the institutions and practices of history-making along the forest–savanna frontier, I argue that the form as much as the content of historical narration determines its political uses and potentialities. The chapter also analyzes several iconoclastic movements that took place in Guinea in the late precolonial and the colonial periods, which served as precedents to the later Demystification Program. This chapter forms the bridge between the chapters of part 1, which show the process of ethnogenesis taking place within a variety of encompassing state settings, and those of part 2, which emphasize the process of nation-building, with the dynamics of ethnogenesis moving to the background.

Part II: Revealing and Reshaping the Body Politic

The chapters in part 2 focus on the Demystification Program and the individuals who undertook Demystification and related policies of the socialist state. While the chapters in part 1 set the scene for understanding the micropolitical dynamics into which Demystification intruded, the second half of the book explores questions surrounding the work that Sékou Touré and his civil servants saw themselves doing in the social, cultural, and political fields. This was a project of full-blown social engineering, and these chapters show many of the potentialities and perils of such an ambitious undertaking.

Chapter 6 begins with a consideration of Marcel Mauss's essay, "A Category of the Human Mind: The Notion of Person, the Notion of Self" (1985), in which Mauss sketches a history of the person. It is notable that the Latin *persona* denoted a "mask." The chapter considers the relations between persons and objects and the ways they have been considered politically problematic in a variety of historical settings, often leading to iconoclastic attempts to purge these offending elements. The chapter explores the crucial role played in Demystification by Forestier modernists—the teachers, administrative cadres, and self-consciously modernist youth from the forest region who aided in attempts to eradicate what they considered nefarious and backward practices in their own towns and villages.

Chapter 7 places the Guinean Demystification Program within the broader cultural and political context of an ambitious modernist state's attempts to effect radical social change. It shows how the state's formulation of proper political participation was far-reaching and in many ways classically modernist. This chapter looks at the government's legal and administrative attempts to radically alter gender relations in marriage, school, and the workplace, its work at policing public morals, and its attempts to turn agricultural practices on their heads. Enlarging on the interrelation between nation-building and ethnogenesis, it shows how several of the state's social engineering projects played out within a rhetoric of ethnic distinction. While Demystification was aimed overwhelmingly at the nation's "backward" Forestier polytheists, attempts to eradicate distinctions between noble and servile descent took place in a context of the government's attempts to undercut the legitimacy of the ethnic Fulbe (Fulani) nobility.

Chapter 8 enters the second half of the central paradox of Demystification by exploring the instantaneous folklorization of the very practices that had just been outlawed. I begin by tracing the meanings and uses of discretion by Loma speakers. I argue for an understanding of discretion as a key technique for managing political and ontological insecurity, rather than the fetishization of secrecy it has usually been misunderstood as being. Having shown how systematically Loma-speaking adults work to shape children and adolescents into discreet individuals, I hope to show the reasons why Demystification was so troubling to Guinea's Foresters, even if their consternation was not exactly that of people whose secrecy had been shattered. Next, drawing on interviews, and photographic and textual documentation, the chapter describes the Guinean state's construction of one of the most influential and far-reaching "culture industries" on the African continent. Having created *Les Ballets Africains*, the national folkloric troupe that was many Europeans' and North Americans' introduction to African dance and music, the Guinean state underwrote a series of other professional musical and dance troupes, acting as patron to such famous musicians as Bembeya Jazz and Salif Keita. The ambivalence felt by many Guinean families toward this culture industry was even more pronounced in the forest region, on whose (outlawed) traditions many of the performances were based. Foresters thus found themselves as simultaneous objects of derision and fascination, and cast as the foils in a kind of national morality play. Despite the negative stereotypes that were thus elevated from interregional prejudice to national cultural policy, many Guinean Foresters found themselves interpellated (Althusser 1971) by this modernist ideology in complex ways. I return to the issue of discretion in analyzing the "sociology of ambition" in revolutionary Guinea, and show how Forester intellectuals may have fared better than any other group during the socialist period, despite the abuse they sometimes endured. Their ability to keep a low profile may have been instrumental to their ability to rise within the system of socialist cadres without drawing the unwanted attention that sent so many of their colleagues from other parts of Guinea into exile or to their deaths in Camp Boiro.

Starting from DuBois's concept of double consciousness—"this sense of always looking at one's self through the eyes of others"—the Conclusion returns to the mutual constitution of the Loma "people" and the Guinean state, and Loma speakers as both members of a newly hardened ethnic group and as citizens of a proudly independent nation. Loma speakers thus understood and understand themselves as the "others' others," a group whose objectification as primitive was a necessary foil to creating modern Guinean national identity, even while that nation was itself considered "second class" by many non-Africans. They are thus extremely well placed to critique the symbolic as well as the physical violence involved in making modern Guineans, at the same time that they derive considerable pride from their Guinean identity. I draw on my fieldwork to show how finely drawn this double-sided experience became under the circumstances of the Liberian war, when Liberians of Loma, Kpelle, and other Forestier ethno-linguistic groups came over the border, and proved to be at least as different from Guinean Forestiers as Guineans from other ethno-linguistic backgrounds. Looking at Guinea's success in navigating the civil wars of the 1990s without getting drawn in, I suggest that the productive tension between national and ethnolinguistic identity was one of the factors that helped Guinea to avoid civil war.

TWO

The Tactics of Mutable Identity

> Can one know more or less precisely where the different people of the forest region of Upper Guinea and the surrounding regions come from? Posed in this way, the question remains dubious: in effect, to ask where the Kpelle, Kono, Mano, Loma, Kissi, Lele, Dan, etc. used to be means that one considers them as having existed in their present form if not since time immemorial then at least since some long-ago epoch. In fact, the populations that we studied in 1946–47 were simply the result of a mixing together of people, either in their present locations or in other regions from which a migration brought them into the forest region, pushing others ahead of them in part, and mixing together with them in an equal part. (Germain 1984, 19)[1]

Chapter 1 argued that iconoclasm can be understood as making a claim for equal membership in a world of nations in a context where newly independent countries like Guinea knew themselves to be denigrated by others, including the people of the erstwhile colonizing countries. It was thus part of a process of enacting and embodying nationhood that prompted selection from a relatively fixed menu of choices: Modern nations have passports, flags, national anthems, stamps, and currency; they claim seats at the United Nations and other international organizations; and they aspire to send teams to the Olympics or the World Cup. This chapter and the next address the ways that ethnogenesis—the coming into being of qualitatively new ethnic identities—became a process that was intimately linked to the other aspects of Guinea's colonial and postcolonial nation building.

The substantive focus of this part of the book is the play between ethnic assimilation and differentiation on the part of Loma and Manya speakers in the area that has become Macenta Préfecture. While both groups now present their ethnic, linguistic, and religious differences as primordial, this interpretation of history is not supported by the facts. As late as 1945, there is documentary evidence that both Loma speakers and the peripheral Mandekan speakers[2] living among and next to them shared largely interchangeable polytheistic ritual and cultural lives.

On the linguistic front, it is clear that in the period since c. 1500, when Loma- and Manya-speaking populations were in or near their present locations, the Northern and Southwestern Mande languages had already separated. We can thus talk about populations with many shared cultural traits yet speaking distinct languages. What is equally clear is that in the context of persistent slave raiding (as late as 1906) and the major population movements it occasioned, there was considerable intermingling amongst these language groups, and in the contact zones (e.g., Macenta), most people were probably multilingual, as they are today.[3]

With a similar ritual/religious life but different languages, we can see how the question of ethnic distinction might become a preoccupation for Loma speakers, Manya speakers, and the states that governed them. I address the issue in this chapter with some detailed analysis of the settlement history of Macenta Préfecture and parts of Lofa County, in the context of previous historical work on migrations and settlement histories of the wider region. I argue that by using the institutions of translatable clan names and power association membership, (proto) Loma and Manya speakers were able to switch ethnic identities, a hypothesis supported by the fact that such dynamics still operate today.

The question remains why the narrative of primordial difference is so appealing to most members of both language groups today if it is true that there has been so much intermingling. The answer to this question is complex and is intimately linked to the dynamics that occasioned Demystification in Guinea. The process of amplifying differences allowed peripheral Mandekan speakers living in the forest–savanna frontier region to pretend to a heritage and a history of Islamic practice that were fictional but which nonetheless carried great prestige in Guinea in the 1960s and 1970s. Conversely, it offered Loma speakers undisputed title to the privileges accruing (in principle) to first-settling landowners. Such claims, however, did not always bring the expected benefits. Peripheral Mande are still treated like second-class citizens in subtle ways by Maninka from such historical centers of Islamic learning as Kankan,[4] and Loma speakers found that the inalienable political and land tenure rights that should have been attached to autochthonous identities were often disregarded by the socialist state.

These frustrations did not cause Loma and Manya speakers in Macenta Préfecture to drop their identitarian claims, but rather added an element of bitter stridency to them. Especially from the 1990s onward, these claims of identity have been used to justify a series of increasingly violent attempts at asserting political dominance. This tendency, which includes one large-scale massacre and numerous smaller ones in the region, has been intimately linked to the violence of the Liberian war, and especially the fighting in Lofa County, where the war took on an ethnicized slant,[5] and where even during times of peace, villages have undertaken ethnic cleansing.

As I argue later in the chapter, both West African and foreign scholars have often operated according to an implicit model of enduring ethno-linguistic difference that I characterize as the "oil-and-water thesis." The assumptions of this model are that contemporary ethno-linguistic groups map onto what we imagine to have been similarly differentiated groups in the past. As Germain (an exception to this tendency) argues in the epigraph to this chapter, much of the scholarship on the region implies that scholars "consider [contemporary ethnic groups] as having existed in their present form if not since time immemorial then at least since some long-ago epoch" (1984, 19). Thus groups such as "the Loma" are imagined to be invaded, penetrated, or infiltrated by "the Malinke."[6] This fits well with the embattled politics of identity currently in play.[7] However, I argue throughout this chapter that the historical materials (scattered as they are) do not support this thesis. Because of the ways that interethnic difference is now invoked in a context of land disputes, planned ethnic cleansing, and intermittent clashes, the subject has pressing contemporary significance.

This argument is not novel in the context of anthropological studies of ethnicity. From Fredrik Barth's 1969 collection of essays on ethnicity onward, most anthropologists and many historians have characterized ethnicity as a kind of social process. While most have moved away from a focus on the content of ethnic ideologies and toward process, scholars like Barth (1969) and Mafeje (1971) have also been criticized for taking an *overly* instrumentalist approach, as if ethnicity were nothing more than a strategy for accumulation, covered by a veneer of false consciousness. As scholars of East Africa have argued, ethnicity is a complex interaction of factors: ecological, economic, cultural, aesthetic, rhetorical, and political (Galaty 1982, 1993; Klumpp and Kratz 1993; Parkin 1978, 1991; Southall 1956, 1970; Spear and Waller 1993). In his introduction to a collection of essays on Maasai ethnicity, Spear writes:

> However derived, ethnicity remains a powerful ideology for identity formation and social action. That is precisely why leaders seek to invent and invoke it, and why followers are so often willing to kill and die for it. It is thus im-

portant to understand the power of symbols embedded in myth, language, and social behaviour that sustain social identities, for it is this very power that makes ethnicity so effective once such loyalties are evoked. (1993, 16)

In this chapter I shall not address the mobilization of symbols and rhetoric to political ends; that is one objective of the second half of the book. However, it is my goal to historicize the interaction of Loma speakers and Manya speakers in such a way that the oil-and-water thesis becomes untenable. In Africanist literature, francophone anthropologists and historians have done much to "deconstruct" the naturalized ethnic differences assumed in the savanna region (Amselle 1990; Amselle and M'Bokolo 1985; Bazin 1985; cf. Chretien and Prunier 1989). In many cases, this work has focused on the shifting boundaries between Fulbe and Northern Mande groups who, like the East African Maa and Bantu groups, are presumed to be nomadic pastoralists and sedentary farmers respectively. As those authors have shown, language, religion, and livelihood have formed shifting constellations over time, and in many cases only began to take on more fixed characteristics in the last century.[8]

There has been little work of the same kind done for the forest–savanna frontier region, especially where Northern and Southwestern Mande speakers meet. Some of the best scholars working on this area (e.g., d'Azevedo 1994–95; Fairhead and Leach 1996; Jackson 1974; Massing 1978–79, 1985; Person 1968) offer much suggestive material, but few have made a concerted effort to take on the assumptions of both local actors and scholars operating within the oil-and-water idiom.[9] In this chapter my brief is to present enough of the history of population movements, chiefdom settlements in the Macenta region, and census materials on ethnolinguistic and religious identity to throw that model into serious doubt. In the second half of the book, I revisit this subject and show how the fragile construction of ethnoreligious identity in this area emerged hand-in-hand with the imposition of state power, and how this relationship spawned undertakings such as the Demystification Program.

In the context of the precolonial slave-raiding insecurity that characterized the area that became Macenta Préfecture, maintaining small autonomous spaces was essential to the survival of people living along the forest–savanna frontier. This chapter enumerates some of their tactics, including the translation of clan identities and ethnicity. These were part of the repertoire of everyday practices that made up a strategy for creating autonomous spaces.

It is important to enter here into some detail about the long-term population movements through the region and the settlement history of the area that became Macenta Préfecture. The next section describes the movements of Kamara (Diomande) lineages and other migrants into the forest region. Rather than remaining "Malinke" (the umbrella term the French colonizers used to describe all Northern Mande speakers in Guinea), many became Loma over the years.

Insecurity, Migration, and Fluidity of Identities

The fact that the Central West Atlantic region experienced several hundred years of persistent insecurity (c. 1500–1900) meant that populations were tremendously mobile. Some moved as refugees, others as soldiers, still others as captives. There were still others who, especially during periods of stability, traveled as traders and Islamic clerics. The history of insecurity in the region is thus intimately tied to the histories of population movements and the interactions of different ethnolinguistic groups.

We may look to the linguists to help us explain the degree of relatedness of different languages in the region. In this regard, we are aided by the fact that, excepting the southeastern corner of Liberia, all the African languages spoken in Guinea, Sierra Leone, and Liberia belong to one of two groups within the Niger-Congo language family. These are the Mande and the West Atlantic (Greenberg 1963). Each of these may be further split into two main subgroups, the Mande into the Northern and Southwestern groups,[10] and the West Atlantic into the Mel subgroup and Pulaar, the only member of the Northern West Atlantic group spoken widely in the three-country region. Below is a simplified diagram.

Armed with this information, we can take an initial cut through the history of the region. Linguists have attempted to date the split between some of these languages. Welmers (1958) has estimated that the Northern and Southwestern Mande languages separated some 2,500 years ago. At this time, it appears that the entire coastal area of what is now Liberia,[11] Sierra Leone, and Guinea was probably sparsely populated by people speaking a proto-Mel language or languages. These, the ancestors of the present-day Gola, Kissi, Sherbro, Temne, Limba, Baga, and Nalou, probably lived in the one- to two-hundred-mile-wide strip along the coast. To the northeast, reaching toward the savanna, were Northern and Southwestern Mande speakers. Further north still were the ancestors of the Fulbe, Wolof, and Serer. Map 2 is a schematic diagram of this state of affairs.

These dates are approximate, given current evidence. However, linguists, archaeologists, and historians (Hair 1967; Brooks 1993; Jones 1981;

Table 1. West African languages in Upper Guinea Coast region

Mande languages (also includes Soninke)		West Atlantic languages (also includes Wolof, Serer)	
N Mande	SW Mande	Pulaar (Fulani)	Mel
Soso (Soussou)	Loma (Toma)		Kissi
Bamana[a] (Bambara)	Landoγo (Loko)		Gola
Maninka (Malinke)	Mende		Sherbro
Kuranko	Bandi (Gbande)		Temne
Koniyanke	Kpelle (Guerze)		Banta[b]
Dyula			Limba
Manya			Baga
Kono			Nalou
Vai			
Dama[c]			

[a] Bamanakan, Maninkakan, Kurankokan, Koniyankakan, Dyulakan, and Manyakan share over 90 percent lexical similarity (Bird 1970).
[b] A Mel language related to Sherbro and Temne now extinct. Former Banta speakers have mostly adopted Mende (Migeod 1926, 203; Richards personal communication 2002).
[c] A language closely related to Vai and Kono, now extinct. Former speakers of Dama according to Dalby (1963) have mostly adopted Mende.

Person 1961; Rodney 1970; Welmers 1958) agree on the general outlines of this situation. Over the next 1,500 years (c. 500 BCE–1,000 CE), the Southwestern Mande languages took on separate and distinct forms, as did the various Mel languages.

From this point onward, we have a clearer picture of the chronology involved as a result of three sources: Arabic-language chronicles from the Sahelian educational centers such as Timbuktu; oral sources that chronicle the major battles, population movements, and rises and falls of empires in the region; and, as of the late fifteenth century, the writings of Europeans, who were arriving on the coast. As other scholars have analyzed this material, I offer a précis here.

Yves Person (1961) argued that the linguistic and archeological evidence suggest that Mande speakers moved southwestward in the thirteenth to the eighteenth centuries. Certainly we know that with the defeat of Soumaoro Kanté, leader of the Soso, by Sundiata Keita, leader of the Maninka, in 1235, the Soso moved westward. One fraction of the Northern Mande group, the Kono-Dama-Vai,[12] probably began moving southward towards the coast of what is now Liberia shortly after this (c. 1350–1400). Probably during this same time, other clans who would later become the Kpelle, Loma, Bandi and Mende, and Landoγo were moving into the Konian highlands and some of the adjacent forest. As Loma speakers say, *Veatiɛ ta yezu*,

Map 2. Map of Upper Guinea Coast region, c. 500 BCE

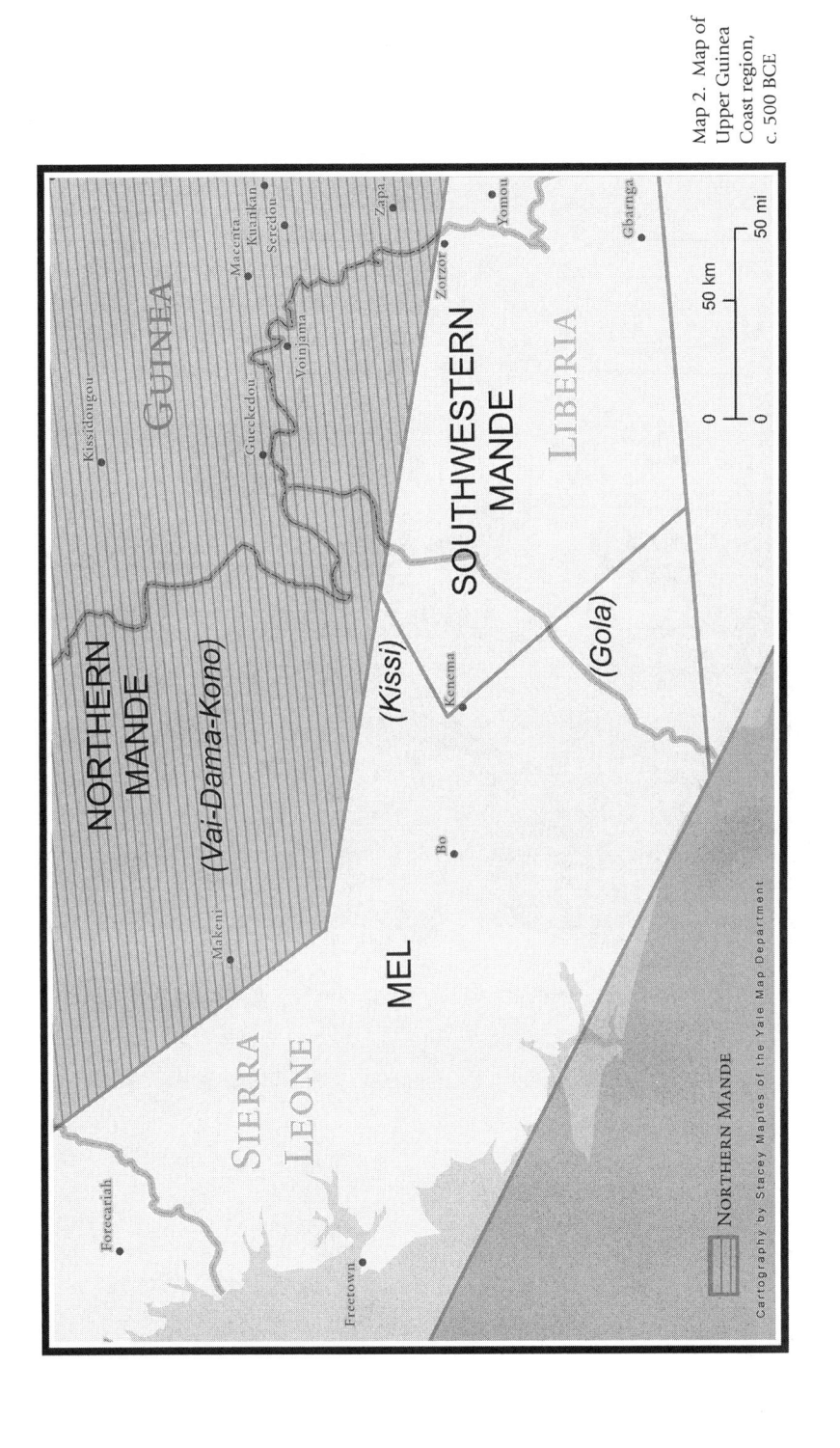

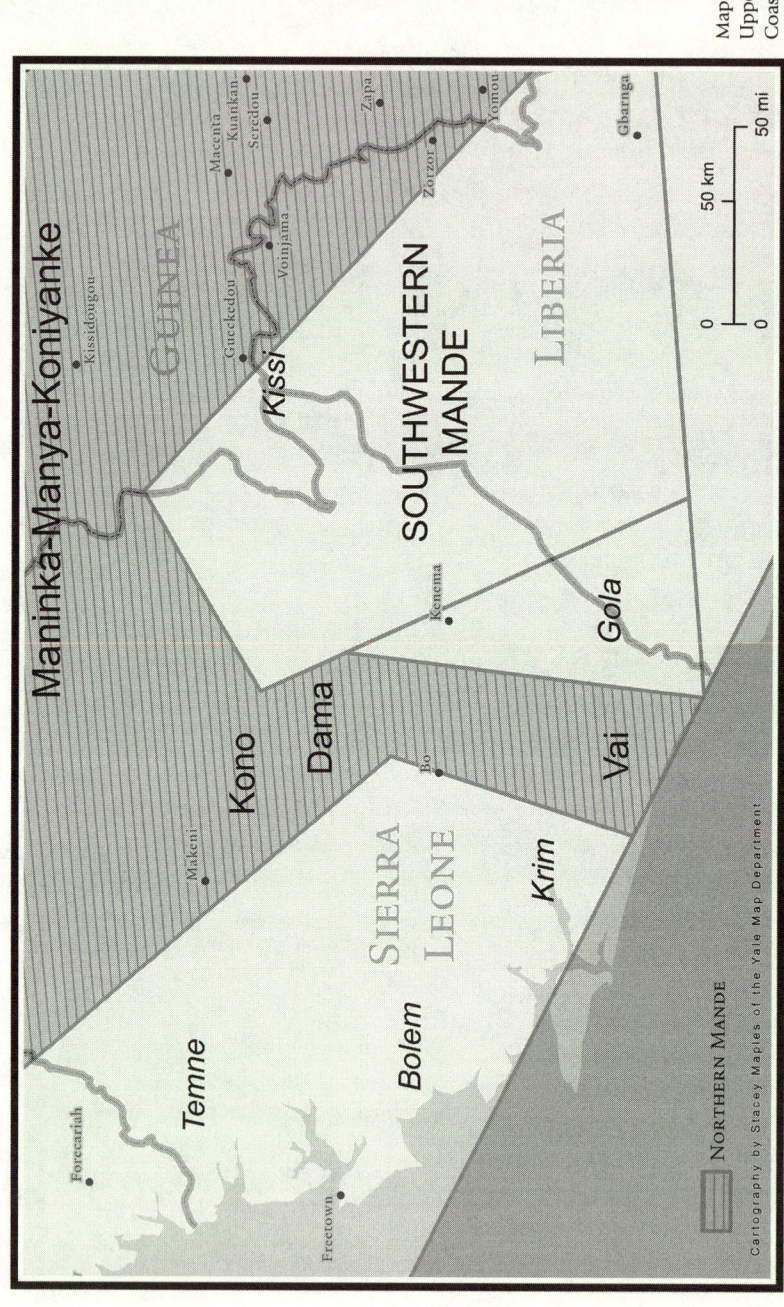

Map 3. Map of Upper Guinea Coast, c. 1400

Cartography by Stacey Maples of the Yale Map Department

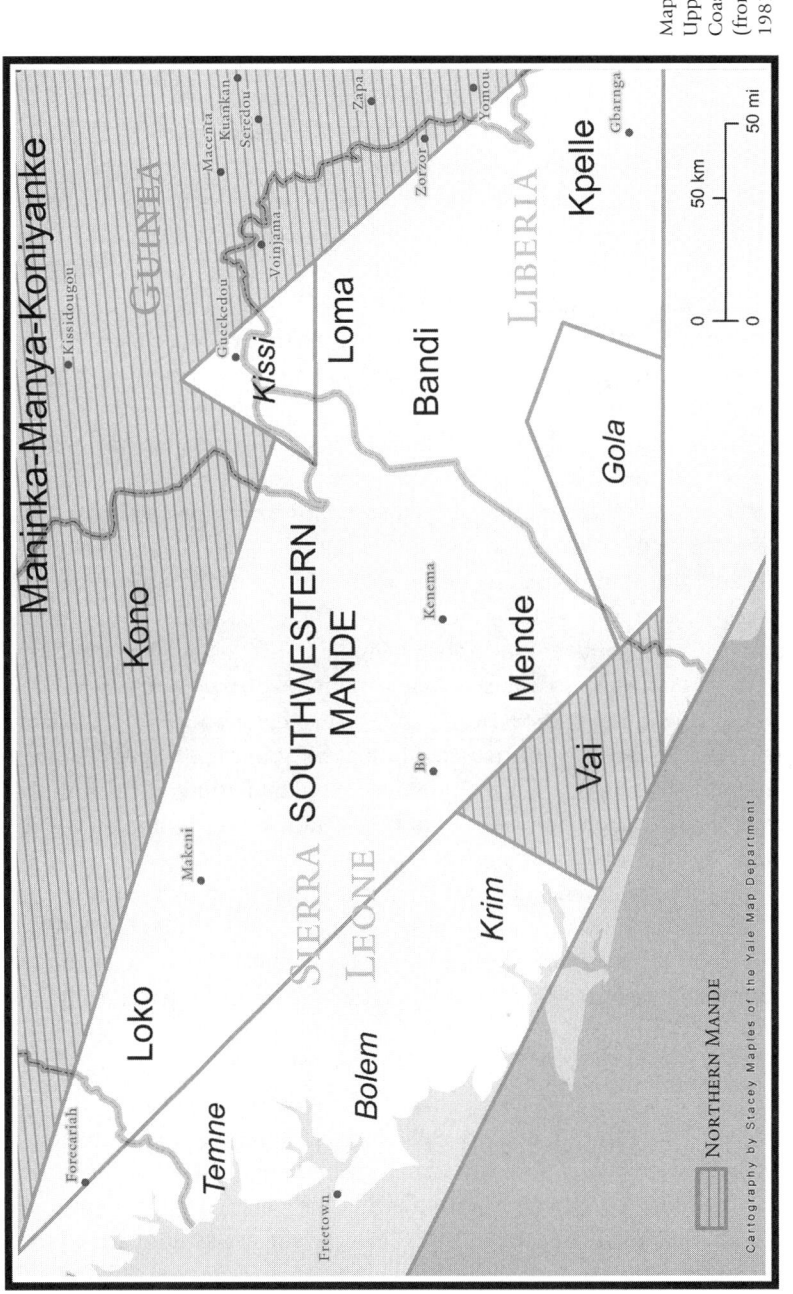

Map 4. Map of Upper Guinea Coast, c. 1550 (from Jones 1981)

tilè lèzu ("people move [migrate] downward, they don't move upward"). The direction "downward" means toward the sea, the same northeast-to-southwest axis followed by the three major rivers that transect the Loma-speaking territory.[13]

By 1400, it is clear that Kono-Dama-Vai speakers had descended in some numbers towards the coast, effectively separating the Kissi- and Gola-speaking populations from their nearest Mel language-speaking neighbors, the Sherbro, Temne, and Limba. At this same time, Fulbe people began inhabiting the mountainous range that came to be known as the Futa Jallon. This movement pushed the Soso westward toward the coast, and consequently pushed the Baga and Nalou to the edge of the Atlantic. These Mel speakers were thus isolated from their former Temne and Limba neighbors, creating three islands of Mel speakers, separated by columns of Mande-speaking populations that had reached the coast. This state of affairs is schematized in map 3.

The last step in this series of movements is the best documented, because it occurred as many of the first European explorers and traders arrived on the coast. Yet there is little agreement among scholars about the actual meanings of the related oral, written, and linguistic evidence. This period concerns the Mani invasions of the mid-1500s, and the military confederation known as Hondo. In 1668, Olfert Dapper, a Dutch physician and armchair geographer-ethnographer, compiled his *Description of Africa* from available published accounts as well as testimony from Dutch traders resident in Africa. Using the term "Cumba" interchangeably with "Mani," he writes: "The year 1515 is when the Cumbas burst into the Capez country to enrich themselves by pillage. But attracted by the fertility of the soil, they decided to accustom themselves, and chased the Capez from all the places where they decided to establish themselves" (1686, 249).

My principal interest in this regard is in understanding the importance of this set of movements in the emergence of the Kpelle-Loma-Bandi-Landoγo-Mende groups that today make up the core of the Southwest Mande language-speaking group. What seems to be one result of these sixteenth-century movements (which certainly continued thereafter) is that the mass of southwest Mande-speaking people pushed westward toward the coast of present-day Sierra Leone. This movement, which cut the Mel-speaking Kissi off from the Mel-speaking Gola, is represented in map 4.

The question for both historians and ethnographers has been who were the Mani, or Mane or Cumba, as they were also called? First, it seems that scholars of the area have given insufficient weight to a simple fact: in Northern Mande languages, the suffix "nka," "nke," or "nko" (as in

Maninka, Diallonke, or Kuranko) simply means "the people of." Thus, the Mani and the Maninka are, in their own language, the same people. What, exactly, it meant to be Maninka in that particular place and time is a more complicated question, yet we can say with some confidence that the Mani were at least in part Northern Mande speakers, related to today's Maninka or Malinke. Most analysts (Person 1961; Abraham 2001), drawing on sixteenth- and seventeenth-century sources like Dapper (1668) and Fernandes (1951), have suggested that the invading force was comprised of a Northern Mande military elite[14] and a rank-and-file population made up of some other ethnic group. This seems plausible, but who were these foot soldiers, and what is their relation to the populations of the region today? All the available evidence suggests that their identities were fluid, allowing negotiation of the relations among language, ethnicity, and territory.[15]

In his essay on the settlement of the region, Warren d'Azevedo (1962a) paid close attention to Europeans' accounts of the Hondo and Kondo confederacies: two multi-ethnic confederations based in the town of Bopolu from the 1600s to the 1800s, in a heavily forested part of the Gola-speaking region of what is now Liberia.[16] The spoils of local warfare here, as in the Loma-speaking region, were slaves and control of the trading route between the savanna and the ocean. Seventeenth-century Hondo appears to have occupied approximately the same region as the Nineteenth-century Condo confederacy. About Hondo and its neighbors, Dapper wrote:

> They are called Galaveys because they originated among the Galas [Golas], and having been chased out of their country by the people of Hondo, they came to live in the land of the Veys [Vai—to the south]. Beyond this great forest, near the confines of Hondo and Manoë [the Manos], live the Galas, who obey a governor whom the king of Manoë sends there. Hondo is next to this forest and further to the northeast than the land of the Galaveys. In the province of Hondo is enclosed one called Dogo. Next to the Hondos are the Conde-Quojas [Kono], that is the "high Quojas" whose language differs from the Quojas of the coast [Vai] as German does from Dutch. (1686, 253)[17]

The Southwestern Mande populations, none of whom are identified by their present-day ethnonyms in the sixteenth- and seventeenth-century sources, were a major fraction of the groups identified as the "Hondo," "Dogo," "Folgia," and also the "Mani." That this history has not been clearly traced has much to do with anachronistic readings of history. Yves Person, whose voluminous research on the region put him in a perfect position to recognize these historical, linguistic, and cultural links for what they were, touched on this interpretation, but then seemed to be overcome by his Maninkophile obsessions in which all roads led to the Konian highlands, and surmised that "if [the Mano] had any share in the Mane adventure, it could only be as part of the Sumba cannibal hordes along with other Mande peoples such as the Kpele [Kpelle], the Toma [Loma], the Gbunde or Mendi, and the Kru peoples" (1971, 678).[18]

The forest–savanna frontier at the time was similar to that described by Bazin (1974) for the Segou state (in present-day Mali) in the early nineteenth century: young men gathered around a strong leader in order to save themselves from slave-raiding. With their arrival, the ranks of military recruits swelled, further strengthening the political-military machinery of an already powerful town or confederation (like Bopolu/Hondo). Consequently more young men (with their families) came from yet further away, seeking security and further strengthening the polity and its army. Ethnolinguistic identity would probably have taken second place to the flexibility required for survival.

The written historical record from the mid-1500s onward indicates that the last four-hundred-fifty years in the Upper Guinea Coast region has been characterized by an alternation between large-scale wars such as the Mani invasions, causing major and rapid population movements, and periods of relative peace, in which occasional raids or flare-ups would nonetheless have helped to keep the memory of insecurity alive. The continuous information we have from the mid-nineteenth century onward indicates that the forest–savanna frontier region experienced major tumult from roughly 1860 to 1910, succeeded by a period of relative peace from 1910 to 1990, which has again been succeeded by a period of regional warfare, tumult, and forced migration during the 1990s and 2000s.

The social consequences were intense personal insecurity and extensive interethnic mixing. When the Atlantic slave trade was abandoned by the English in 1807, and then by the French and Americans, the system of production (i.e., raiding) in this region actually intensified.[19] Holsoe (1977) describes how those nations that continued to trade in slaves (the Portuguese and Spanish, for instance) demanded entire boatloads of slaves together, as opposed to the ten or twenty slaves they were formerly willing to buy at each small barracoon along the coast. They did this so as to escape detection by the British navy's vessels, whose job it was to intercept slavers and liberate their captives. Accounts by my Loma-speaking informants (as well as Beavogui's [1991]), indicate that many late-twentieth-century Loma elders' parents and grandparents were captured and enslaved during this period, and all sources agree that slave raiding was still common as late as

1906. By this point, captives were destined toward the internal slave trade, but conditions of insecurity were similar regardless of the destination of the war captives.

During these dangerous years in the late precolonial period, flight to safety followed by the deployment of one's social capital were the means of survival. As Caroline Bledsoe has written: "during periods of military strife in the Central West Atlantic region, political allegiance involved attaching oneself to a powerful patron who could offer protection from marauding groups seeking captives and booty. Various degrees of subordination (slavery, pawnship, clientship and so on) were the price of safety" (1980, 145).

I have elsewhere described the situation of contemporary Liberian refugees settling in Guinean Loma-speaking villages, sometimes invoking the bonds forged by previous generations of migrants and refugees (McGovern 2004, 2012). What we see in the refugee situation is the importance of the tactics of mutable identity in the region today. This situation gives us a sense of the dialectical, tactical nature of claims about identity. Such maneuvering was also a part of the historical dynamic, in which people who operated in uncertain and violent circumstances used power association membership, clan membership, marriage alliance relations, and networks of personal contacts to negotiate their relations to others. I shall now describe some of these dynamics, starting with the links among clan identity and settlement history in the area that became Macenta Préfecture.

The Koivogui-Kamara Corridor and the Question of Ethnicity

Lebiyaɣa e Musadu bhaoni. (It is respect that made Musadu prosper.)

—Loma proverb

Here we take the broad historical sketch I have just presented and narrow our focus to the contemporary Loma-speaking heartland in Macenta Préfecture, Guinea, and Lofa County, Liberia. It is in this section that I raise questions about the assumptions underlying the oil-and-water model of ethnic identity. I rely heavily on the work of Facinet Beavogui, the Loma historian who did many years of research in the Loma-speaking region. In his 1991 doctoral thesis, he goes to some lengths to detail the settlement history of the region. By putting his material into the wider historical context I have outlined above, I come to different conclusions. I show that the Loma-speaking "corridor" between the Makona River to the northwest and the Ziama mountains to the southeast shows the traces of a surprisingly homogenous migration by people of the Kamara and Koivogui clans, who are the dominant landowners in almost every chiefdom of this corridor.[20] Kamara and Koivogui are the Manya and Loma versions (respectively) of the same clan.[21] Meanwhile, the Loma-speaking chiefdoms on either side of this corridor are far more heterogeneous in terms of dominant clans. These facts lead to my interpretation that the "Koivogui-Kamara corridor" is the product of a relatively recent migration/conquest by non-Muslim, Maninkakan-speaking, Kamara lineages, some of whom "became" Loma over the past two hundred years, while others retained their Manya ethnicity.

Loma precolonial political organization was made up of two types. To the north of the Ziama mountains, most political units (known as *zuti*, pl.) were small, consisting of a handful of villages and their satellite, slave-run farming hamlets. The southern part of the region, from the Ziama Mountains to the Diani river (and in some cases, slightly to the east of it), consisted of seven confederations: Vekema, Bhilu, Woima, Ziama, Akai, and two Kpelle confederations (one called Niankan, the other, Briama). These seven territories were known as *kɔkɔlɔgiti*.[22] The term *kɔkɔlɔgi* refers, literally, to the Loma word for the piece of thick bark used to carry an ember from one hearth to light another. Loma custom surrounding this act is fairly elaborate. As my Loma host once told me, "when you come to take fire from someone else's hearth, you never ask. It is considered bad luck. Fire has the power to destroy life." The *kɔkɔlɔgiti* are ranked in the order that I have written them above, and exist in a relation of older brother to younger brother.[23]

The concept of *kɔkɔlɔgi* operates at multiple levels at once. In the first village history I ever collected, I was told:

> The *kɔkɔlɔgi*, literally the bark used to carry embers from one house to another, is the source of light and civilized cooking and warmth. This was what symbolized the power that reunited the federations. It [the *kɔkɔlɔgi*] was made by the last Loma people in the Kerouane region, the Kourouma and Kamara. (Giziwulu, October 31, 1998)

Many village and confederation histories, when explaining the hierarchical order of the federations, repeat some version of the following story:

> The diviner Manabula said the federations would be great if they took seven pairs of shoes, put a rock on top of them in a stream leading into the Veaa [Via] river [near Bokeza, in present-day Liberia]. This was the symbol of the

kɔkɔlɔgi. This stack remains there today; it rises when the water rises, is never submerged, and never sinks into the mud. This is a symbol of their unity. During the tribal wars, none of Bhilu's [one of the kɔkɔlɔgi's] satellites fought among themselves. (Bayema, November 6, 1998)

One of the confederation's goals was to stop intervillage raiding among the member kɔkɔlɔgiti:

> When all seven representatives [of the kɔkɔlɔgiti] came, they worked toward a judgment to help finish the war [actually intervillage raiding]. The question they posed was, "What will we do if we are attacked after having put down our weapons?" The decision was that if anyone broke the truce, all the others would unite against them, would burn the village to the ground, and would exterminate all their kin. This finished the fighting, through the agency of the kɔkɔlɔgi. (Giziwulu, October 31, 1998)

At the same time, the movement of the kɔkɔlɔgi from region to region, starting to the northeast in Kerouane and heading toward the Via river, seems like an explicit reference to the dissemination of the Poro power association.[24] In his study of the Poro society among Liberian Mano speakers, Harley (1941) claimed that the Poro's sacred fire was passed from the Loma to the Kpelle, and from the Kpelle onward to the Mano, just as in village life live embers are passed from one household to another on the thick piece of bark. Note also the fact that the original carriers of the kɔkɔlɔgi are said to have been Kourouma and Kamara, two Northern Mande clan names equivalent to the Loma Bhawogi and Koivogui, respectively, but given to me in their original Northern Mande forms (even in Giziwulu, a village that did not allow Manya speakers to stay overnight). Beavogui cites the kɔkɔlɔgi's source as Musadu, the town in the Konian highlands that many Loma speakers and Kpelle speakers consider to be the source of their own clans. Korvah (1995) also cites this town in his history of Bonde chiefdom. The Loma proverb quoted at the beginning of this section refers elliptically both to Musadu's ritual importance and to its status as an economic center.[25]

Finally, this same movement "downward" toward the sea, appears to be the movement of populations, gradually moving from the northeastern savanna of the Manding heartland toward the region's rainforest. According to Beavogui (1991), this route is called *zalabhaloe*, or "the route of the lion," by some Loma-speaking elders. It seems the story of the kɔkɔlɔgiti

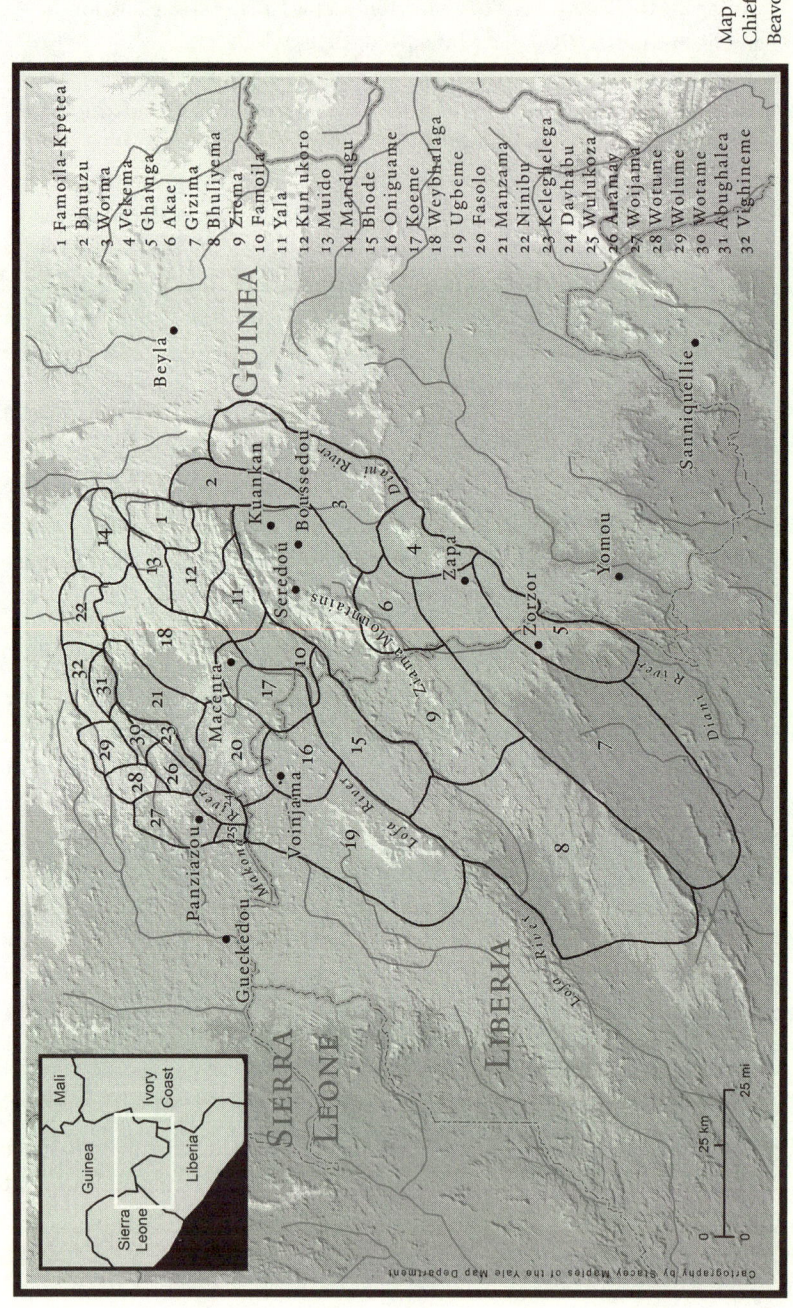

Map 5. Loma Chiefdoms. From Beavogui 1991.

condenses all three of these movements (creation of political alliance, extension of the Poro, and migration). This convergence may point us toward more significant interpretations, as I suggest below.

The specificities of settlement histories in this the region present more precise evidence about these movements. Consider map 5, based on Beavogui 1991.[26]

Beavogui attempted to identify the late precolonial polities. The entire list, with annotations and dominant clans for each chiefdom/confederation appears as Appendix I.

In studying the map and the histories Beavogui gives of the settlements of most of the chiefdoms there listed, a clear pattern emerges. Today's Loma-speaking region is crossed by four major natural boundaries. Each runs diagonally from the northeast to the southwest. In the south, the Diani River (called the St. John's in Liberia) roughly marks the southeastern limit of Loma-speaking territory. To the northwest of the Diani run the Ziama mountains, steep and craggy hills covered with forest that are considered by most Loma speakers to separate Northern from southern Loma speakers. To the north of these mountains runs the Lofa River, from which the north-westernmost county of Liberia takes its name. Finally, to the north of this lies the Makona River. Only a small percentage of Loma villages exist to the northwest of this river, although judging from place names further northwest (in what is today Kissi-speaking country), Loma speakers may once have extended further in that direction.

In his *kɔkɔlɔgi*/chiefdom map (map 5), Beavogui lists thirty-two chiefdoms. He cites a ruling clan for twenty-eight of them, two more are Kpelle chiefdoms, and I have added the ruling clans of one other (Akae). This map of clan dominance describes a remarkably clear pattern. The Loma-speaking territory is most usefully split into three regions.[27] From the Diani to the Ziama mountains, the homeland of the southern Loma speakers bounded by Kpelle-speakers to the south and Koniyanke-speakers to the northeast, the dominant clans are quite mixed: Guilavogui, Pivi (equivalent to Onivogui), Bilivogui, Grovogui, Beavogui. To the north of the Makona River, in the northernmost Loma-speaking region, the situation is similarly mixed: chiefdoms are dominated by Guilavogui, Onivogui, Zumanigui, and Beavogui clans. However, in the area bounded by the Ziama mountains to the south and the Makona River to the north (which has the Lofa River running through its middle), there is an unmistakable pattern. Of fourteen chiefdoms listed, Beavogui gives the dominant clans for thirteen. Of those thirteen, four (Ugbémɛ/Wubomai, Yala, Famoila, Famoila-Kpetea) "belong to" the Koivogui. Four belong to the Kamara

(Mandugu, Muidu, Kunukɔrɔ, Oniguamɛ). Three belong to the Koivogui and another clan (Fasalɔ, Koemɛ, Ninibu), and two (Weybhalaga, Manzama) were settled first by Loma clans (Weybhalaga by Guilavoguis, Manzama by Zumaniguis) but later experienced significant influxes of Kamara migrants who controlled some villages at the time of colonial conquest. In short, every one of the chiefdoms acknowledges sole or shared Koivogui/Kamara dominance.

The pattern becomes significant in light of the fact that that Kamara and Koivogui are in fact the peripheral Northern Mande (Manya/Koniyanke) and the Loma variants of the same clan. Both respect the leopard as their totemic familiar. Switching between Kamara and Koivogui identities, as I describe in the next section, was easy and can still happen today (though rarely). In the present context where religion and ethnicity map onto one another, the switch typically happens when a Loma speaker converts to Islam, and thus takes the Northern Mande equivalent of his or her Loma clan name as a family name.[28]

This evidence presents a consistent picture: between the Ziama mountains and the Makona River, all thirteen chiefdoms whose dominant clans are identified by Beavogui are "owned" in part or whole by Koivogui/Kamara lineages. While completely different clans (Onivogui, Beavogui, and Zumanigui) predominate north of the Makona, only one chiefdom shows any Koivogui domination, and it is Keleγelega chiefdom, along the banks of the Makona (i.e., directly adjacent to the "Koivogui/Kamara corridor").[29] Ostensibly, Koivogui clans crossed the river here and made slight inroads into the northernmost Loma-speaking region. Similarly, in the south, it was only in Woima where Beavogui found any Koivogui influence (though I understand Woima to "belong" to the Bilivoguis), and in the south, Kamaras only penetrated as far as Kwanga, the seat of the area that became known as Buzie.[30] Generally, this southern region is dominated by Bilivogui, Grovogui, Beavogui, Guilavogui, and Pivi (Onivogui) clans.

What should we make of this information? All commentators on the settlement of the Loma-speaking region agree that successive waves of Southwestern Mande-speaking immigrants moved from the present-day regions of Kerouane and Musadu southwestward into the forest region now inhabited by Loma speakers (Beavogui 1991, 2001; Germain 1984; Massing 1978–79, 1985). Furthermore, most agree that there were successive waves of Northern Mande invaders arriving from the northeast. In his article, "Who were the Vai?" Adam Jones suggests, "The Kamara factor deserves further investigation" (1981, 177), a challenge taken up by Massing especially in his article, "The Mane, the Decline of Mali, and the Mandinka Expansion towards the South Windward Coast" (1985).[31] He recounts the founding of Musadu (also called Misadu and Musdaougou) by Feren Kamara, a leader of the polytheistic Kamara Diomande who lived on the southern fringes of the Northern Mande world c. 1550. One of Feren Kamara's seven son's (Fala Wubo) is explicitly acknowledged as the founder of Wubomai chiefdom, the major Loma-speaking political unit in northern Lofa County, Liberia, and part of the Kamara-Koivogui corridor. Moreover, Massing links Feren Kamara to the passage of the kɔkɔlɔgi throughout what is today the Loma-speaking region: "In each of the traditions of the kokolo, there usually follows a list of the clans who received it; all of them, however, quote Fanggama (Feren Kamara?) as founder. The kokolo appears to have been an alliance sealed by sacred oath to avoid warfare and to respect the traditions and customs of the original inhabitants, in particular their sacred sites of animist ancestor worship" (1985, 44).

This dynamic of conquest, migration, and acculturation has parallels in neighboring regions. A 1995 report by the Land Tenure Center on a village in neighboring Yomou Préfecture focuses on a Kpelle-speaking majority and its Koniyanke-speaking minority that parallel the Loma-Manya relation. In describing the settlement history of the village and each of its clans, they note:

> The Komara come from Sosabala (in the Konikoro district of Beyla). They installed themselves first successively and temporarily in Pela and Lakpara [neighboring villages] before coming to Nonah. Marabouts, the Komara nonetheless accepted *tattouage* [Poro/Sande initiation] in order to better integrate themselves into Kpelle life. This is how the Nonamou [the village's land-owning clan] accorded them the management of a vast area of cultivation within Nonah's territory. (Diallo et al. 1995, 14)

This passage shows the process of assimilation in play, as the Komaras accepted power association membership which led in turn to more permanent land-use rights. The authors imply that because the Komaras were Northern Mande and marabouts, they would "normally" not have accepted initiation into the power associations, but that they did so for instrumental purposes (in order to solidify their claims on land use). This is most likely an anachronistic reading of the contemporary ideology of identity backwards in time. In fact, there is little evidence to suggest that simply because these peripheral Northern Mande speakers were "marabouts" coming from the north that they would not have been familiar with, or possibly even members of, similar power associations.[32]

Returning to Macenta, we see that the present situation of clan dominance in the Loma-speaking region shows a great deal of heterogeneity in the northern and southern regions. It seems likely that such heterogeneity obtained across the region until a period during the sixteenth and seventeenth centuries, when Kamara Diomande moved southwestward from the area around Kerouane and Musadu, through Diomandou (in Maninkakan, lit. "Diomande town"), and down a "Kamara/Koivogui corridor" between the Ziama mountains and the Makona River (see map 6).

In the context of the fact that this corridor is surrounded by the heterogeneous political geography to the north and south, and the fact that all ethnic groups in the region acknowledge the important migrations/conquests of the Kamara Diomande from the savanna toward the sea, the homogeneity of this corridor appears to be the result of a massive and relatively recent migration of these non-Muslim Northern Mande speakers. There is nothing unusual in this migration per se, except for its notable homogeneity. What is most important in this situation is the relation between the Kamara and the Koivogui who, together, dominate so much of this region. Although they now consider themselves to be very different people—with different languages, different ethnicities, different religions, and different connections to the region's history and politics, I argue in this book that they were essentially the same group of people when they came into the region that is now Macenta Préfecture and Lofa County.

A perfect example of the translatability of clan identities comes from the Wubomai chiefdom mentioned above. Though Fala Wubo's father is known to have been of the Kamara clan, Fala Wubo and his descendants, who still lay claim to autochthonous political legitimacy in northern Lofa County (Korvah 1995), have simply switched from Kamara to Koivogui clan affiliation. The process has been eased somewhat by the deformation of Feren Kamara's name. In Korvah's account of Wubomai's history, it appears as Fali Kama (Currens 1974, 12). Massing notes versions from Foligama to Fonigama to Fanggama (1985, 43–44). In the process of migration, conquest, and assimilation, it appears that members of the Diomande Kamara lineage, speaking Mandekan but sharing a similar culture with the people among whom they settled, changed their clan names to the Loma equivalents, began speaking Lomagui, and "became" Loma.[33]

Map 6 gives another version of the chiefdom map we have been studying. In all the chiefdoms where Koivoguis and Kamaras were the dominant or one of the dominant clans, I have distinguished between the two groups. They are thoroughly intermixed. One might expect those chiefdoms further north (and closer to the Northern Mande core populations)

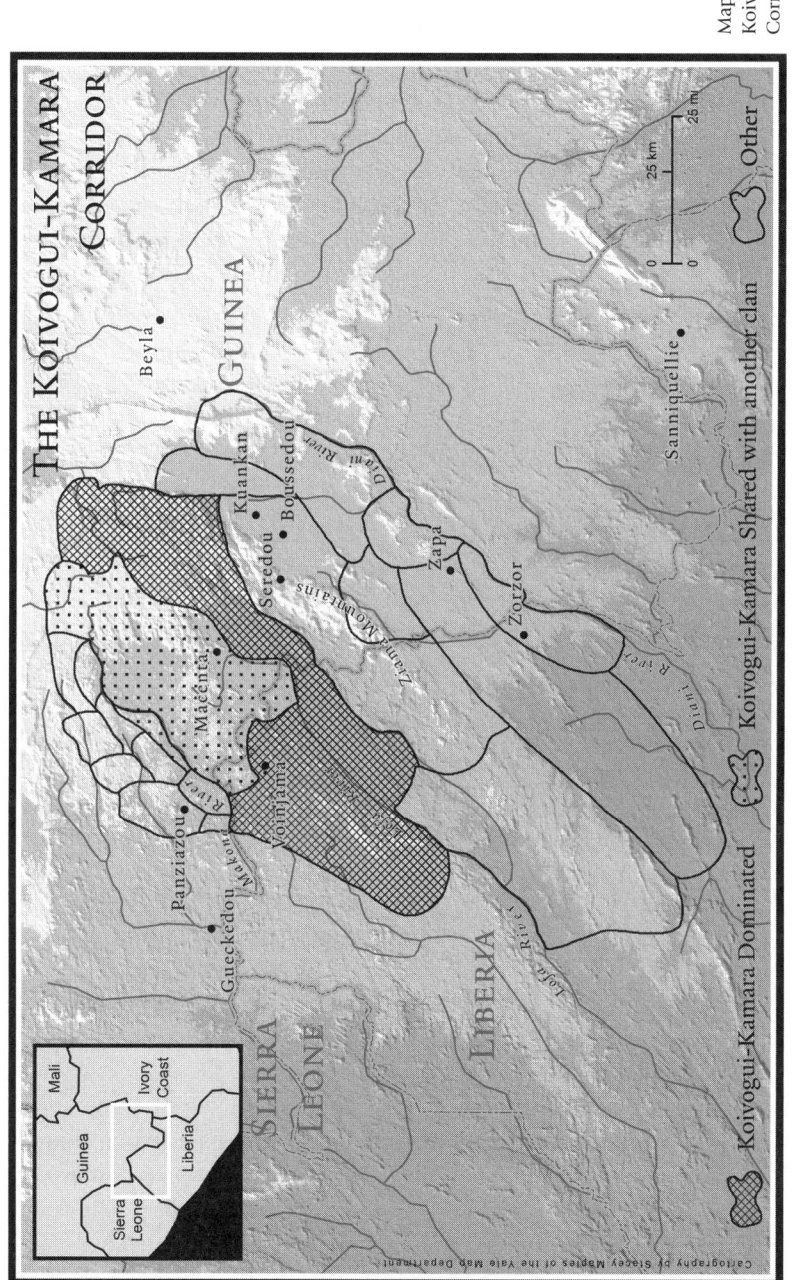

Map 6. The Koivogui-Kamara Corridor

to be dominated by Kamara (ostensibly "still" Manya), and those further south to be dominated by Koivoguis (those, according to my argument, who had assimilated into Loma society and "become" Loma), but this pattern is barely recognizable. Indeed, the rate of assimilation within each chiefdom probably resulted from a set of micropolitical factors particular to the setting. Only by looking at the bigger picture of settlement history can we recognize the fact that two groups who acknowledge one another as being "the same" by virtue of their shared clan totem; who both recognize the fact they have come from the area to the northeast and have pushed southward over the last two to four hundred years; and who as of 1920 were at least 85 percent non-Muslim and involved in the same cultural system organized around membership in various power associations such as the Komo and Poro—moved into this region in a series of waves of migration and conquest. Yet the preeminent historian of the Loma people (Beavogui) either missed this point or chose not to highlight it. And he is not alone. Most of the literature on the region takes it as a self-evident fact that Loma people and Manya people are easily distinguished. Consider the following passages:

> They [the Loma] have occupied their present area of settlement in southeast Guinea and northwestern Liberia for at least 400 years, and for almost just as long, have disputed their territory with other Mande people such as the Koniyanke. (Højbjerg 2002a, 59)

> During the eighteenth and nineteenth century, Malinke lineages from the Konian, the plateau between the Milo and Sankarani Rivers, began to infiltrate the Toma, to a greater or lesser extent. (Massing 1978-79, 51)

> Wherever Mande groups settled among host societies, they attempted to preserve their social and cultural mores. (Brooks 1993, 73)

There are many others like them. I call the model implicitly underlying these accounts the "oil-and-water thesis." According to the assumptions of this unstated model, at point A in the distant past, there are two different groups of people, speaking different languages, coming into contact. At point C, in the contemporary period, the two groups continue to speak different languages and to consider one another to exhibit self-evident cultural and religious differences. The intuitive assumption is that during period B—the intervening two to four centuries—these "different" ethnolinguistic groups maintained their separate identities and statuses passed down (patrilineally) as portable, immutable identities. Thus, those who are Loma today are presumed to be the descendants of those who were Loma three or seven or fifteen generations before, and likewise for those who are Manya today. I believe this assumption is often incorrect and generally misleading. The shift I suggest we make is subtle, but it has far-reaching consequences. Rather than connect points A and C with a straight line, we might be better served by imagining a zig-zagging one. Many individuals in this region shifted their ethnic/linguistic/religious identities at least once over the generations.

The crux of this dynamic is that during periods of relative stability, warlords who controlled an area sought to legitimate their rule. The only widely accepted currency of symbolic domination was a claim to autochthony. My examination of village and chiefdom histories around Macenta shows that many current "landowners" in fact usurped territorial control by force, often just 100–150 years ago (McGovern 2012; cf. Murphy and Bledsoe 1987). Whether a dominant clan's autochthony was real or fictional, it could not be claimed by anyone who embraced the identity of the newcoming ethnic group. Thus Loma-speaking communities made their peace with conquerors who were sometimes Loma speakers, sometimes Manya speakers, by requiring them to assimilate to local culture and language, if they wanted to weave themselves into "autochthonous" genealogies.[34] Newcoming warlords thus gained legitimate political authority in return. The notion of portable, unchanging ethnic identity is implausible in this context, given the material and cultural dynamics that were in play.[35]

It is the underlying oil-and-water assumption that leads Massing, in an otherwise excellent interpretation of the southern expansion of the Diomande Kamara from the Konian highlands into the forested zone of what is now Sierra Leone, to state, "The Mane were of Mandinka rather than Southern Mande stock" (Massing 1985, 21). In this case, as in the writings of Adam Jones, P.E.H. Hair, and Yves Person, historians have been keen to determine whether the Mane invaders chronicled in the mid-sixteenth century along the coast of present day Liberia and Sierra Leone (Dapper 1668; Donelha [1625] 1977) were "really" Northern or Southwestern Mande speakers. To phrase it another way, were the invaders Mani(nka)? Or were they the proto Men(d)e? Each ethnonym bears obvious resemblances to the "Mani" or "Mane" invaders noted by European sources on the coast in the mid-1500s. My suggestion is that this very question is misplaced. Undoubtedly, at that point the Northern and Southwestern Mande languages were well distinguished from one another. Yet most of the evidence points to the fact that pre-Islamic Northern Mande and Forestier societies were far more similar than different. The area in question extends southwestward some 150 km from the southern edge of the Konian highlands into the forest of what is today northwest Liberia. Commenting on Olfert Dapper's 1668 text, Massing writes that "the fact that the account asserts that Hondo was ruled by many and diverse princes makes me believe that a precursor of the Condo confederacy was already in existence in the 17th century" (1985, 49).

I agree with Massing that Hondo appears to be an earlier version of the Condo multicultural warlord state, but I would also extend the analogy backward to the Mani invasions. Dapper's account is the most detailed of the early European texts in terms of situating the polities of the interior, and the location he gives for Hondo (and the neighboring "Dogo," "Konde-Kquoja," and "Manoë") is probably the area from which the Mani invaders began their sweep southward and then up the coast. As Massing notes, this is an exercise that necessarily starts with educated guesses and ends in speculation, but it seems clear that in the area where Loma-speaking populations live today, the descriptions going back to the 1500s indicate a consistent mixture of warfare and ethno-linguistic heterogeneity.

It seems likely that at any given moment during this period (c. 1500–1900), there would have been some people of Northern Mande origin who would have been considered strangers, outsiders, or invaders by their Southwestern Mande-speaking hosts, and others at various points along the way to becoming assimilated to the culture, language, and ethnic identity of their hosts. Prior to the colonial period, all the available evidence indicates that Northern Mande-speaking people were incorporated into Southwestern Mande societies by switching languages, changing easily translated clan names, joining power associations that crossed ethnic boundaries, and entering into marriage alliances. Consider the following passage from the "Journal of the Journey of George L. Seymour to the Interior of Liberia," written in 1858:

> The Booseys [Loma] and Mandingoes [Manya] are mixed up in this city, as are Pesseys [Kpelle] and Booseys near the city of Solong. This connection of different tribes is controlled by the influence of domestic ties; for they intermarry to a considerable extent, which has a powerful check on their disposition to war. (Anderson, Sims, and Seymour 2003, 194)

Fairhead and Leach write of the area directly to the north of present-day Macenta:

> While linguistic identity would always have carried some significance, Kissidougou's history affirms the centrality of clan, lineage and power-association politics which cross-cut linguistic divides.
>
> Identity in relation to language and origin (ethnicity) acquired greater significance from the colonial period when early administrators mapped out ethnic boundaries, when anthropologists mapped out ethnic cultures, and when historians sought to map out ethnic origins. (1996, 114)[36]

Many contemporary historical accounts (including Beavogui 1991) combine the presentist point of view—that the Manya and Loma consider one another eternal enemies and radically different—with accounts of historical competition between two opposed groups. There is little evidence to suggest that the two map onto each other directly, and this seems an anachronistic interpretation. I have written elsewhere about the history of warlord conflicts in the region, which were not ideologically motivated (on the basis of ethnic, political, religious, or any other identity), but opportunistic (McGovern 2011, 2012; cf. Reno 1998; Richards 1996, 2004). We must now ask what happened when a warlord gained control of a region and a period of relative peace settled in.

To work our way out of the assumptions entailed by the oil-and-water thesis, we need to consider the *moyenne durée* dynamic of the gradual assimilation of conquerors by the people they have conquered, and of migrants by their hosts. As soon as we entertain this model, it becomes more difficult to talk about a group of Loma people who were involved in an age-old struggle with another well-defined ethno-linguistic group; of one discrete group penetrated by another; or of newcomers "preserv[ing] their social and cultural mores" (Brooks 1993, 73). In fact, at any given moment between c. 1500 and 1900, some Loma speakers were most likely fighting among themselves; some Loma speakers were fighting against Manya-speakers and other groups (such as the Kpelle); and some people of Manya origin who had *become* Loma were probably also fighting against various outsiders, some of whom also might eventually *become* Loma. In the chapters that follow, I describe and analyze both the motivations and the dynamics behind this complicated micropolitical maneuvering, emphasizing especially the importance of the state in providing groups with new kinds of claims about identity and political rights. It is an explanatory framework that fails the test of parsimony, but it may account for more of the historical and sociological facts than other lines of analysis. The rest of the chapter describes some of the mechanisms by which such assimilation operated.

The region along the forest–savanna frontier was a cultural crossroads, especially in the context of the kinds of intervillage warfare fuelled by the Atlantic slave trade. The specter of persistent insecurity this fighting introduced made fluidity of identity a necessary strategy for managing constantly changing situations. Even today, Loma-speaking elders regularly talk about relatives and ancestors who were caught up in this tumult in the late nineteenth and early twentieth centuries. Some were enslaved and taken away, some were killed, and others had been enslaved elsewhere, becoming members of Loma families.[37] Others openly acknowledged the history of their families' changed ethnicity. The strategies available to Southwestern Mande-speaking people for dealing with insecurity seem to have been twofold: try to maximize knowledge in the esoteric arts of war and self-protection, and keep open options for flight and negotiating new situations and identities. In this context, ethnicity, language, and religious practice all had to remain open to immediate compromise and change.

Clanship and Ethnic Mediation

> Even though the Tomas pretend not to have any shared origins with the neighboring peoples, each one establishes a sort of assimilation between his honorable [clan] name and that of the strangers who respect the same prohibition, and they often translate their name by that of the stranger. For example, a *Koivogui*, whose *Niei*[38] is the leopard calls himself *Kamara*, because the Malinkes who have this *diamu* have the leopard as their *tana*. (Gamory-Dubourdeau 1925, 315)

Michael Jackson, in an article entitled, "The Structure and Significance of Kuranko Clanship" (1974), describes Kuranko speakers' strategic uses of clan membership.[39] Clan identity, he emphasizes, constitutes an "'ideology of identities,' not of behaviour. . . . [I]t becomes imperative that we begin considering clanship as a 'way of thinking about social organization that may be more or less metaphorical'" (Jackson 1974, 397). He goes on to describe how members of a Kuranko clan (such as the Mara) may recognize an affinity to members of other clans within other ethnic groups (he cites the Mara as linked to the Maninka Konde, the Temne Bangura, the Mende Mala, and the Yalunka Samura). He writes, "such 'related' clans often share the same totem (*tana*)" (401). Along the forest–savanna frontier, it is typical for people to recognize their affinities with those who share the same totem, regardless of ethnic origin. Table 2 lists the Loma totemic

Table 2. Loma totemic clan names with Manya/Koniyanke equivalents, where applicable

Clan name	Animal	Manya/Koniyanke equivalent
Koivogui	leopard	Kamara
Guilavogui	dog	Traore, Dole[a]
Beavogui	antelope[b]	Keita
Bilivogui	goat	Bayo, Cisse, Kourouma[a]
Sampogui/Zoumanigi	catfish	Koroma, Kamara—Semamfilasi lineage[a]
Pivi/Onivogui/Onepogui	red-winged sparrow/all birds	Soumaoro, Kamara—Fen Semenesi lineage[a]
Falivogui	crocodile	Bamba
Coyavogui	monkey	Conde
Soropogui	"small rice-eating bird with white neck"[c]	Conde
Goepogui	gazelle	Kane, Soumaoro
Gouavogui/Bhawogui	Cotton tree	Kourouma
Dopavogui	red deer (*Tragelaphus scriptus*)	Mara, Kane
Grovogui/Golovogui	chimpanzee	Kamara[a]
Tero	chicken	
Seevogui	elephant	
Inapogui	mouse	Kamara—Fen Blemasi lineage[a]
Kpakpavogui—*kpakpagi* plant		
Sovogui	horse	Kamara—Masenesi lineage[a]
Koevogui	snail	
Koropogui	caiman	
Sedepogui	?	
Kalivogui	snake (all)	
Tupui/Tupuvogui	viper	
Solopogui/Soropogui	sparrow	
Pamavogui	iguana	
Kebawogui	Kebai plant	
Foniwogui	Fonio	
Sakuvogui	tortoise	
Towaoro	antelope	

[a] As noted in Person 1968, 1:576–79.
[b] Only one source claims that the Beavogui's totem is a hippopotamus (Beavogui 1973). Since many clans have secondary totems this may be the animal to which the author refers.
[c] Adam 1951, 95.

clan names, as well as their Manya equivalents. As I have argued in regards to the settlement history of the "Kamara-Koivogui corridor" of the central Loma-speaking region, it is fairly common for people to switch situationally between the different clan names, and thus ethnicities.[40]

Similarly, Jean Suret-Canale (1963) noted the translatability of various clan names throughout the eastern half of Guinea, given in table 3.

Table 3. Interchangeable clan names

Malinke [Maninka]	Toma [Loma]	Guerze [Kpelle]
Traoré (totem-dog)	Guilavogui	Honomou/Zogbelemou
Cissé (totem-bird)	Onivogui	Gomou
Camara (totem-leopard)	Koivogui	Loulemou (Dore in Kono)
Kourouma (totem-turtle)	Sakouvogui	Hamouteamou
Soumaoro (totem-sparrow)	Soropogui	Haba

Moreover, Jackson notes:

Except in the case of the ruling clans, Kuranko genealogies are shallow (they seldom trace descent through more than three ascending generations). This "genealogical amnesia" may be one reason why Kuranko have been able to assimilate "strangers" so easily into the local community and disguise or idealize the nature of descent origins. The principles of local group attachment often override the principles of descent affiliation. (1974, 402)

This is exactly the case with Loma speakers (cf. Leopold 1991, 99). Jackson goes on to state:

The adoption of clan totems is a way of affirming social solidarity by an act of choice. . . . These structuring principles [of clanship] must, in my view, be understood against a historical background of continual population movement, of territorial dispersal and fragmentation, of inter-tribal mixing. . . . It is not that hospitality, protection, or assistance are automatically established on this basis, rather that familiarity and inclusiveness are always *possible*. (1974, 407–11; my emphasis)

Jackson's analysis applies perfectly to the Loma-speaking region. In other words, the clan (*gē*) idiom may be invoked in a particular situation where one person wants to define, or even *create*, a relationship to another person. As one Loma man told me, his paternal grandfather, a Maninka of the Keita clan, transformed himself into a Beavogui, and none of his descendants has ever gone back. He embraced his hybrid heritage and said that like some other Beavoguis, his family came from Fouala, near the Guinea–Côte d'Ivoire border (some 150 km to the east of today's Loma-speaking region).

This process also went in the opposite direction. Most Loma speakers who converted to Islam in the twentieth century simply switched their names to the Northern Mande equivalent. The reasons for the change could be more indirect, too. As former civil servant and ambassador Tolo Beavogui specified:

> All of the early colonial translators [in the forest region] were Bambara soldiers. . . . It is for this reason that for all the first military recruits in Macenta, all the family names were Malinkisés.[41] . . . I have seen the list in Macenta, and they all have family names like Kourouma; voila, because the Bambaras came and "you, you have which totem—*I dyamun?*—which totem? What do you not eat?" Thus they gave the equivalent [name]. (Beavogui, December 13, 2008)

In the area that became Macenta Préfecture as elsewhere, ethnicity is an idiom of both affinity and difference, in this case mediated through clan affiliation. Ethnicity may be invoked, claimed, or assumed, depending upon a particular situation (Chretien and Prunier 1989; Galaty 1993; Klumpp and Kratz 1993; Sow 1989). At certain moments it is construed in a more literal and at other times in a more metaphorical way. In the context of strategies of assimilation and relationality, it is important to underline the distinction Jackson makes between "the principles of local group attachment [and] . . . the principles of descent affiliation" (1974, 402). Until very recently along the forest–savanna frontier, the former trumped the latter, as Jackson notes for the area of Sierra Leone some 150 km to the northwest of Macenta. More recently, however, the ideology of identity has shifted, with both Loma and Manya speakers claiming longstanding, fixed differences of culture, language, and religion. In the following section, we begin to explore the history behind such claims.

Who Was "Malinke" in 1921?

> In the mixing of races provoked by the wars, it is almost always the vanquished Toma who has imposed his language on the victorious Malinke. . . . Thus, while a large proportion of the Malinke in contact with the Tomas speak the latter language, a lot fewer of these speak Malinke. (Lieutenant Faivre, *Monographie du secteur Toma*, 1908, quoted in Beavogui 1991, 63)[42]

Doing archival work in Conakry, I came upon the scattered results of censuses undertaken by the French colonial administrators throughout Guinea. They seemed to indicate that in Macenta, although someone (census takers, translators, interviewees?) recognized ethno-linguistic differences between Loma speakers and Manya speakers (called "Toma" and "Malinké," respectively), a surprisingly small percentage of the Manya speakers had converted to Islam by 1921—in fact only about 15 percent. The picture looked like this. In 1921, about 22 percent of the population of Macenta *Cercle* was identified as "Malinke." In Macenta town, 44 percent of those Malinke were identified as Muslims, and in the rest of the cercle, fewer than 16 percent of those identified as Malinke were said to be Muslim. My argument about the Koivogui-Kamara corridor would lead to the following interpretation: Many of the non-Muslim Malinke families in the rural areas were probably on their way to *becoming* Loma.[43] Some might move on after a short stay, and be replaced by newer arrivals, while others stayed on and intermarried, most often with Loma-speaking women. Their children would grow up speaking both Lomagui and Maninkakan, and would participate in the local ritual life, initiating their children into the village's power associations,[44] sometimes introducing ritual innovations from the north.

Early on, the French were interested in ascertaining both the ethnolinguistic identity and the religious affiliation of their recently conquered subjects. As time went by, they either became less interested in these labels, or sophisticated enough about the complexities surrounding self-ascribed identities that they no longer found them useful. By the 1931 census, there are no longer categories for religious affiliation, and by the 1956 census, Guineans are no longer listed by ethnicity. However, some of the early material is intriguing. In 1908, the first French census of the sector that would become Macenta Préfecture counted 27,276 inhabitants. This number rose to 80,420 by 1921 (at a 14.99 percent annual growth rate), to 105,944 in 1931 (a 3.17 percent a.g.r.), to 121,816 in the 1956 census (a 0.60 percent a.g.r.), and to 193,109 in 1983 (a 2.17 percent a.g.r.). By 1996, the postsocialist government of Guinea listed Macenta's population at 281,053 (a 3.50 percent a.g.r.). Macenta Cercle/Préfecture's population has accounted for between 3.34 and 4.91 per cent of the national population over the 75-year period, 1921–96.[45]

The 1908 census indicates a radically reduced population. The reasons for this appear to be twofold. First, this was the year that the French completed their violent conquest of the Loma-speaking area, which culminated in the siege and destruction of Bousseme (called Boussedou in Maninkakan and also by the French) in 1907 and Koyama in 1908. According to Loma-speaking elders, thousands of Loma speakers left the territory that was becoming French Guinea and sought refuge with their relatives in the area that eventually became Lofa County, Liberia.

In the three districts (of present-day Macenta Préfecture) designated

"Mandougou," "Kounonkoro," and "Bouzié," the officers counted a total of 9,690 Malinkés and 2,730 Tomas. Of all these, 1,380 people were listed as "Musulmans," and 11,040 as "Fétichistes." Assuming that all of the Loma speakers were identified as "Fétichistes"[46] (this is the case in all the censuses that specify ethnicity and religion simultaneously), 1,380 of 9,690 of the Malinké were designated Muslim. This is only 14.24 percent of the Manya-speaking population.

Two further points bear emphasis. First, the three districts listed sat at the northeastern limit of the region that became Macenta Préfecture, and, as the figures indicate, 78.01 percent of the population was identified as Malinké. This preponderance was the result both of the area's geographic placement (directly on the forest–savanna frontier) and the fact that these Manya had assisted the French in their battles against Samory in the 1890s and against the Loma in the period 1905–8 (Person 1968, 525; Massing 1978–79; Beavogui 1991). Thus, while many Loma speakers fled French brutality and reprisals for their intransigence, the Manya speakers had already begun reaping the benefits of their cooperation. There is no reason I can discern why any of the Manya interviewed might have felt direct or indirect pressures to claim fétichiste as opposed to Muslim affiliation. Indeed, given the fact that there were already some Muslims throughout the area, it is reasonable to assume that some pressure to convert to Islam (for which there is clear evidence several decades later) might already have begun. Given all these factors, the figure of an 86 percent non-Muslim Manya-speaking population is very significant.

Another part of the 1908 Macenta census covered the two kɔkɔlogiti of Koima [Woima] and Vekema (the area where I did much of my fieldwork ninety years later). Although the numbers here look suspiciously round (in Koima: 4,500 Toma, 350 Guérze [Kpelle], 150 Malinké. In Vékéma: 10,000 Toma, 1,800 Guérze, 200 Malinké), they indicate only five Muslims in Koima (ostensibly of the 150 Malinké, thus 3.3 percent), and ten Muslims in Vekema, or 5 percent of the Malinké. Given that these Malinké were a small minority of the overall population (these confederations lie at the southeastern corner of the Loma-speaking heartland), they may have felt more pressure to assimilate, and the lower incidence of Islamic identification is not surprising. The figures from 1908 are found in table 4.

In 1921, the population had grown dramatically from 1908, ostensibly because many of those who had left Guinea for Liberia had returned. Indeed, colonial officers' reports from the period state this fact explicitly. The ratio of Malinké/Toma in the regional population had changed radically. While Malinkés accounted for 53.57 percent of the area's population

Table 4. Ethno-religious census figures, 1908

	Mandougou, Kounonkoro, and Bouzié	Koima	Vékéma
"Toma" (ostensibly all "fétichiste")	2,730 (22% of total)	4,500 (90% of total)[a]	10,000 (83% of total)[b]
"Malinkés fétichistes"	8,310 (67% of total)[c]	145 (3% of total)	190 (1.6% of total)
"Malinkés musulmans" (Muslim Manya)	1,380 (11% of total)[d]	5 (0.1% of total)	10 (0.08% of total)

[a] Guerzes (Kpelle) made up another 7 percent of total.
[b] Guerzes made up another 15 percent of total.
[c] 86 percent of Malinkes thus being fétichiste.
[d] 14 percent of Malinkes thus being Muslim.

Table 5. Ethno-religious census figures, 1921

	Macenta town	Macenta rural	Macenta overall
Toma, Guerze, Kissi	86	62,884	62,970
Malinkés Fétichistes	802 (56%)	13,478 (84%)	14,280 (82%)
Malinkés musulmans	632 (44%)	2,477 (16%)	3,109 (18%)

(14,613 of 27,276) in 1908, that proportion had shrunk to 21.62 percent (17,389 of 80,420) in 1921. In other words, almost all of the increase in the population over the intervening thirteen years had come in the form of Loma speakers, adding further credence to the claim that many Loma had returned from Liberia. Of 17,389 Malinké, 3,109 (17.88 percent) are listed as Muslim, a steady increase from 1908's 14.24 percent, but still a small minority.

The ratio of Muslims to fétichistes is even more striking if one compares urban and rural populations. The 1921 census specifies that Macenta town, the administrative seat, was home to 632 "Malinkés musulman" and 802 "Malinkés non musulman" (while 1,434 of the town's 1,581 inhabitants were Malinke, only 86 Toma living there). Thus 44.07 percent of the Mandekan-speaking population was Muslim, and they included such specified groups as "Indigènes sachants lire et écrire" ("natives who know how to read and write"), "Tirailleurs" ("African troops"), and "Eleves à l'Ecole rurale" ("students"). All of the Malinke listed in these three categories were said to be Muslim. However, in the undifferentiated mass of the hinterland population, the proportions are quite different. Not only are the ethnic ratios turned upside down, but the religious ratios, too. Of 15,955 Malinke living outside Macenta town, only 2,477, or 15.52 percent of them, are listed as Muslims, very close to the 1908 figure of 14.24 percent.

As many authors have emphasized, colonial censuses are often flawed (Anderson 1991, 163; Appadurai 1996, 114; Cohn 1987, 224). Nevertheless, it is worth noting that even with a large margin of error, they indicate, consistently and over several decades (i.e., via information collected by different colonial officers probably using different methods), that the majority of so-called "Malinkés" in the Macenta region were not Muslim. This fact has been confirmed by my interlocutors during fieldwork, though usually with some uneasiness. An unexpected form of triangulation comes from the fact that the techniques of gathering census material in francophone West Africa changed significantly over time. In this context, it is even more suggestive that the percentage of Islamized rural Malinke remained almost constant.

A final point of contrast comes from the Guekedou 1921 census material. There, of the 540 "Malinkés" noted, all 540 are said to be Muslim. Given that Guekedou is the closest town to Macenta, a mere 60 km away, where Kissi speakers, another group of "fétichiste" Forestiers, lived together with a Malinke minority, why should the numbers be so different? I would argue that once the Muslim community becomes large and concentrated enough, there is strong pressure placed on other members of the kin-occupational-ethnic community to claim a unified ethno-religious identity. By 1921, Guekedou's Malinke had consolidated some sort of unitary identity (quite possibly in dialogue with the introduction of colonial census-making) that caused them to appear 100 percent Islamized. In the cases where censuses skew the reality on the ground, we usually expect their objectifying influences to cause people to espouse "modern" monotheistic identities.[47] This was clearly not the case in the Macenta area in the first part of the century. By the 1960s, the process of espousing a unified religious identity was finished in the Macenta region. To be Manya was to be Muslim, and in the vast majority of cases, to be Muslim was to be (or to become—see chapter 3) Manya. However, by 1921, this process had not yet played itself out in the Macenta region as it apparently had done in Guekedou.

Although Northern and Southwestern Mande ethnic identities are often portrayed as primordial and radically different in Macenta Préfecture, there are many people of mixed Loma-Manya parentage, called *Toma Manian*. They are an intermediate group, rather despised by the Loma speakers, and generally assimilated to the wider group of Muslim Mandekan speakers resident in the préfecture. However, on the basis of the settlement histories, census material, and oral testimonies, I would argue that over the last several centuries, this is how many people who now consider themselves to be "pure" Loma also came into the region. Sometimes evading coerced Islamization or slave raiding to the north, arriving in successive waves from the northeast; at other times inserting themselves by force as conquerors, bringing variations of Mande cultural formations with them but eventually just disappearing into the mix, such immigrants transformed themselves over several generations from Manya to "Toma-Manian" to Loma. At different periods, it might have taken a generation, at others three or four generations, to make this switch from Toma-Manian to "pure" Loma. A crucial factor in this process is the shallow genealogies maintained by Loma speakers. They are almost always three to four generations deep. This is the same regional dynamic Jackson notes among the Kuranko, and that Murphy and Bledsoe (1987) note among Kpelle speakers of Liberia as facilitating the recalibration of identities. Today, it seems, the clock has stopped, and people are frozen in their present identities.

Living with Violence, Binding Insecurity

A major ritual preoccupation of Northern and Southwestern Mande-speaking people is to control flows—of potentially dangerous energy (Lomagui: *manye*/Mandekan: *nyama*), potentially dangerous persons, or powerful knowledge—often through the institution of the power associations.[48] There are limits to the efficacy of strategies for binding strangers' dangerous potentialities. As the Loma-speaking area has become encompassed by modern states in the last one hundred years, people have lost much of their ability to control outsiders' access to the region, the land, and to the wealth it contains.[49] In the realms of kinship, marriage, and religion, they have found that many of their erstwhile Manya-speaking clients have reneged on their obligations to their hosts/uncles/wife-givers. Under different circumstances, like those of precolonial migration and warfare, these same newcomers might have found it preferable to assimilate to Loma language, culture, and identity, but the context of the modern state has often made it preferable to claim monotheistic, "Malinké" identity.

In the struggle to control dangerous flows, Loma speakers have sometimes enlisted colonial and postcolonial states to assist them, usually with disappointing results. One of the prime experiences of twentieth-century modernity for many Loma speakers has been the diluted efficacy of social idioms like clan translatability that had created micropolitical networks of stability, even during periods of warfare. Loma speakers have become first frustrated, later angry, over what they regard as the most profound betrayal imaginable: Manya-speaking strangers underlining their difference from their hosts *and* attempting to dominate them politically. The next two chapters explore different ways that this tension has played out over the last one hundred years in the area that became southern Macenta Préfecture. The ultimate consequence has been a shift from the process of assimilation I have described in this chapter[50] to a hardening of distinct identities. This shift is both cause and effect of the breakdown of stranger-host reciprocity in the Macenta area, and it constitutes the foundation upon which the edifice of state-sponsored iconoclasm such as the Demystification Program was built. Without understanding the gradual shift from a series of techniques and strategies tending toward assimilation to a parallel set of practices stressing difference and civilizational hierarchy, it remains very difficult to explain why the socialist state became involved in such a far-reaching iconoclastic policy so soon after independence.

In this chapter I have hoped to do two things: First, to demonstrate that while people living in the area that became Macenta Préfecture had differing origins and now consider themselves to be different, there is no straight line connecting these two moments. In fact, for most of the period c. 1500–1900, the distinction between Loma and Manya was probably very fluid, as the epigraph to this chapter suggests. Many of those people who consider themselves Loma or Manya today may well have been the opposite at some point in the recent past, and their various ancestors may have switched back and forth several times. This is especially true between the Koivogui and Kamara clans that came to dominate much of the central Loma-speaking region of Macenta Préfecture and Lofa County. The following chapters examine the ways that difference was manufactured and hardened, often through a series of unintended consequences related to the imposition of state authority.

Secondly, we should remember that these fluid, situationally negotiated identities operated in a specific context: that of endemic violence and insecurity fuelled by the European trade in slaves. Loma speakers, Manya speakers, and their other neighbors had to maintain an ability to attach themselves to and assimilate into multilingual, multiethnic communities with a largely shared culture. The case of the region that became Guinea, Liberia, and Sierra Leone suggests that violent disruption may be a key factor in determining the angle at which seemingly opposed principles intersect. Rather than think of violence as only destructive of existing order, we may also find that instances of disruption and insecurity have contributed to the emergence of new systems. This is an observation made long ago by Marx with regard to the birth of European capitalism.[51] It may have been insufficiently applied to the understanding of the pasts of African societies that were integral in their own right to the development of the modern capitalist world system.

INTERLUDE I

Togba's Sword

"Did you hear? They stole Togba's sword. Took it to Conakry."
"Togba? N'Zebela Togba, the great Loma war chief?"
"Yes, him."
"Who is 'they'?"
"You know, there is an old man, Foromo, who has these things."
"Yes, I know him. I've seen all of Togba's things in his house."
"Well, it was his *daabenui*."
"His nephew?! Who, one of the Bilivoguis?"
"No, no. It was a Manya."
"A Manya nephew? What happened?"
"Well, they caught up with him in Conakry. He was trying to sell the thing."
"Sell it? How could he?"
"I don't know."
"So, they got it back?"
"Yes."
"And what did they do to the Manya?"
"Well, nothing. It was his *daabe*, wasn't it?"

THREE

Autochthony as a Cultural Resource

This chapter summarizes the interrelated ideals and practices surrounding kinship and marriage alliance in Macenta,[1] and then focuses on the concept of autochthony and its uses in the Loma-speaking area. While the analysis continues to situate the Macenta material in a regional context, I rely primarily on my fieldwork data.

The last chapter argued that the differences—today naturalized—between Northern and Southwestern Mande-speaking people have a tenuous basis in historical fact. Subsequent chapters will show just how important colonial and postcolonial states were in manufacturing and articulating civilizational difference. Indeed, the instrumental use of history was central to the legitimation of the postcolonial Guinean state and to the ways that it constructed Guinea's Forestiers as useful others.

From the precolonial period to the present, there were well-defined rules governing the interactions between newcomers and "autochthonous" residents in the territory that became Macenta Préfecture. Many of them were organized through the kinship idiom of relations between mother's brother and sister's son, known in Lomagui as *kɛkɛ–daabe*. The *kɛkɛ–daabe* relation has a much broader set of connotations and is the master idiom of social relations amongst Loma speakers. This relation is one of hierarchical complementarity (Leopold 1991), in which the *kɛkɛ*, who is in principle uncle, host, autochthon, wife-giver, and political patron, is superior to his *daabe*, who is nephew, guest, more recent arrival, wife-receiver, and political client. This relationship of hierarchy is crosscut by two different types of complementarity. First, in the sparsely populated forest region of Guinea, Liberia, and Sierra Leone, labor rather than land was the limiting factor on agricultural production, and so in many regards wealth was measured in people (Bledsoe 1980; Guyer and Belinga 1995). This made wives, children, resident strangers, and other clients valued members of a "big person's" household. Secondly, a further relationship between *kekɛ* and *daabe* is that between *sacrifiant* and *sacrifiteur*.[2] The political potency of autochthony rests upon the successful enactment of a repertoire of sacrifices to ancestral spirits (*goveiti*) and autochthonous earth and water spirits (*inegiti*). While the social and political benefits of successful sacrifice accrue to the *kekɛ*, they can only be performed by his *daabe*.

This chapter engages the *kekɛ–daabe* relation inasmuch as it relates to the politics of autochthony. It is thus the facet of *kekɛ* first settler and *daabe* newcomer that is relevant here.[3] I introduce the rules organizing these interactions while showing the ways that they are often subverted and manipulated in practice. Even the breaking of rules often has its own unstated norms. This becomes one of the central problems of the book. I have argued already that in many respects Loma and Manya speakers originated from the same region, practiced the same religion, and subscribed to the same overarching complex of ideas about the person and society. While there are specific rights and responsibilities accruing to autochthones and hosts, in reality many putative autochthones are in fact recent arrivals (McGovern 2012). Even in this context of social plasticity, a large proportion of Manya speakers have flouted the rules of stranger-host relations in such a way as to bring the usually unspoken rules of autochthony to the forefront of political action.[4] The ways that such rules have been broken (rather than bent, or tied into knots) has much to do with the intervention of the colonial and socialist states.

In Macenta and the wider region, the principle of autochthony structures stranger-host relations as well as hierarchies between lineages and clans. Loma speakers' strategies for increasing their wealth-in-people build on the principle of autochthony, which distinguishes *zukenuiti* (owners-of-the-land) from *mawɛɛiti* (newcomers). Firstcomers are considered to own the land, and they derive their political power from this ownership. Newcomers become clients, borrow land, and increase the firstcomers' wealth-in-people. This idealized schema is often complicated by the fact that many so-called landowning lineages are themselves relative newcomers to an area, and landowner status is used as much to legitimize actually existing power hierarchies as vice versa (Murphy and Bledsoe 1987).

Autochthony in this area (as elsewhere) is a social idiom or principle that seems simple in its definition and clear in its application, yet is constantly shifting and reinvented (Geschiere 2009). Like clan identities that criss-cross ethno-linguistic boundaries, autochthony is stable in its instability. As Geschiere (2009), Jackson (2006), and others have emphasized, autochthony is often trumpeted most loudly when supported least well in fact. Scholars of nationalism have made a similar point in their arguments that nations are actively created, not passively inherited from primordial sources (Anderson 1991; Chatterjee 1993; Gellner 1983; Hobsbawm 1990; Hroch 1985). This is a quintessentially anthropological insight (though anthropologists have no monopoly on it), epitomized in the term "fictive kinship." The term acknowledges the constructedness of many putative kinship links in face-to-face societies, but insists that they are no less potent for that. In this chapter, I suggest the term "fictive autochthony" to describe a similar process of constructing identities. While the assertion that such fictive but nonetheless socially significant idioms exist is sweet music to the ears of most sociocultural anthropologists (we too live a fantasy of demystification), it is not the what but the how that has held my attention. Autochthony and the affiliated idioms of kinship and marriage alliance are social idioms. They have thus provided means for people to live with uncertain and violent circumstances and touch almost every corner of life in Loma-speaking villages.

Autochthony as a Cultural Resource

Siazia nu lɛ tɛɛ loga. (A person on the move raises no chicken.)

—Loma proverb

Autochthony—as an ideal, a rhetoric, a set of practices—is a foundational notion in Loma social and political life. It underlies kinship and marriage alliance, and is also foundational to land tenure and ethnic identity. It is the concept that links these topics together and allows one to stand in for another.

Autochthony is a two-way process. There is an overarching symbolic order that can be brought to bear on the negotiation of micropolitical struggles in a village or territory. Describing that symbolic order is my interest here, and I will sketch some of its uses and consequences. But micropolitical struggles themselves can sometimes spawn new forms of identity and consciousness, and even alter symbolic systems. Although we will only look at one side of that dynamic, it is worth emphasizing that these movements between levels are not necessarily synchronized. While there is an interplay between the symbolic-rhetorical and the material-instrumental levels, the dynamic as it develops in one direction may frankly contradict the dynamic moving in the other.

Autochthony as it is enacted and experienced, however, works through practices and objects that combine these levels. The brief interlude that preceded this chapter, entitled "Togba's Sword," might have passed barely noticed, an enigmatic tangent to the discussion of history and politics. To most Loma speakers, it would have been shocking. The object stolen, a nineteenth-century steel sword, probably of European manufacture, was wrapped in decrepit leopard skin. It was not too striking an object when I first saw it, but its revelation to me had been ceremonious. Its importance lay in the fact that it condensed an entire nexus of relationships between spirits and humans, the living and the dead, a territory and those who inhabited it. It was the insignia of lineage identity for the chiefly lineage of the town and the surrounding kɔkɔlɔgi. It was also one of the most powerful objects in the region for sealing agreements by oath. Finally, as I remarked in passing, because N'Zebela Togba had become the designated resistance hero of the Loma, his sword represented the martial prowess and honor of anticolonial struggle for the entire Loma ethnic group.[5] Such an object's theft by a *daabe* "nephew" put one of the rules governing *kɛkɛ-daabe* relations—that the nephew can take any object from his uncle without asking—to the ultimate test. I explain below some of the routes by which such an object achieved its heightened significance.

We begin with the description of Loma speakers' attachment to their land. Such descriptions almost always make reference—implicitly or explicitly—to the contrast between the Loma attitude and that of their Northern Mande neighbors to the places where they live. In reference to the proverb cited as the epigraph to this section, "A person on the move raises no chicken," Akoi Zoumanigi (a Loma speaker himself) writes:

> *L'aventure* [mobility] is a phenomenon that the Loma generally do not appreciate. For him, one must not isolate [i.e., abandon] the ancestors' tombs. An adventurer has little or no chance to be present at the burial ceremonies of his relatives who die far from him. This attitude of the Loma is verified by the fact that the only préfecture [in Guinea] from which he originates (Macenta) has its administrative center occupied by other ethnicities [Manya]. (1989, 24)

The term *l'aventure* has one source in the quest for specialized knowledge and wealth that has long been described as part of the strategies of striving of people throughout the Upper Guinea Coast region.[6] The term also refers to the need for cash introduced by colonial conquest and the imposition of head or house taxes. This caused Loma speakers (especially men) in both Guinea and Liberia to leave their villages in order to work on plantations, seek employment as cooks and servants, and to join the army. Commenting on the ramifications of this process,[7] Gamory-Dubourdeau wrote in 1925:

> Their [the Loma's] attachment to the soil and to the ancestral customs is remarkable and if, now, young people emigrate voluntarily within Guinea, it is always just temporarily. The money needed to pay bridewealth amassed, they come back to their valleys to live next to the tombs of their fathers. (1925, 290)

In the 1990s as I conducted fieldwork, Loma speakers frequently referred to their attachment to the graves of their ancestors. This is a topic I shall address immediately below, but it is worth noting here the antithesis of the stereotyped "rooted" Loma: the "uprooted" Manya. Dozens of times, when Loma speakers wanted me to know what was most essential about "The Loma," they emphasized their links to the soil and to their ancestors' graves. Many times, they pointed out the absence of this constancy among "the Manya." Manya speakers were frequently described in Lomagui as *ziazia* and in French as *nomades*.[8] The former term literally means "walk-walk," and carries the pejorative connotation of someone who cannot stay put. The proverb already cited says, *Siazia nu lɛ tɛɛ loga*, or literally, "A walk-walk person does not chickens raise." A related proverb has it that, *Zowei ziaziaga nyoun nyoun na kɔtɛ kadha loya* ("The ritual specialist [*zowei*] who moves around ends up losing his power"). This admonition refers to a *zowei ziaziaga*, or a *zowei* who is constantly traipsing about rather than staying put in his village where the sources of his esoteric power lie.

What, then, are the sources of such power, and how do they relate to the notion of autochthony? Autochthony is the relation of a particular territory with a defined group of persons with rights in that territory. Every Loma person inherits two identities at birth: the father's totemic clan (*gē*) and his patrilineage (*burude*).[9] I have described the clans in chapter 2. Their main characteristic is that they share a special relationship with a totemic animal or plant that all members must avoid harming or eating. Sociologically, they are significant both because they facilitate interethnic assimilation and because the totemic clan is the largest social group practicing marriage exogamy,[10] but they have no direct effect on a person's status as autochthon or stranger.

Patrilineal descent groups are the other major unit of Loma collective action, and I call them lineages in this book. They are shallow unilineal corporate groups whose members recognize direct descent along the male line from a named ancestor. As Leopold (1991) notes, such genealogies rarely name more than two generations of deceased ancestors before jumping to the "original" ancestor (if that ancestor has not already been named). Leopold describes one nine generation-deep genealogy given to him (with difficulty) by some members of a landowning lineage, but adds that its recitation offered " no apparent social reward" to the one elder able to produce it (1991, 100). Schwab recounts two similar Loma genealogies, casting doubt on them (1947, 21–22). In many African societies, including Loma speakers' Northern Mande neighbors, reciting genealogies provides abundant social rewards, and genealogies are central to people's struggles for power and legitimacy. If genealogical reckoning is not central to Loma politics, which lineage practices *do* offer Loma elders an "apparent social reward"?

The Politics of Sacrifice

In many ways, the most important thing that Loma lineages do together is to perform sacrifices (*salaɣaiti*), which brings us back to autochthony. For it is in the realm of corporate sacrifices (as opposed to the recitation of genealogies) that Loma descent groups assert particular claims to legitimate authority, territorial control, and group identity. Such claims may apply to a realm as limited as a village quarter (*kwi*), or one as large as a chiefdom (*zu* or *kɔkɔlɔgi*). The realm of sacrifice is the site where Loma speakers can make claims about the relations among three distinct but inextricably linked groups: the living, the ancestors, and the earth and water spirits of a given territory. Consider the organization of Giziwulu as it was described to me when I first arrived:

> Yelibala Gbaogbao [deceased] was the founder of the village. He was the father of Gbaouy [deceased] and of Pokpa Kalivogui [living], who is the village's *taakenui* (landowner). The village is divided into thirteen *kwiti* (quarters). Each but one belongs to a specific clan. Anyone else settling there will be their *daabenui*.[11] (T.K., November 4, 1998)

The speaker went on to list each quarter and the lineage to which it belonged, ending with the center of the village, which belonged to every resident.

As this account indicates, well-established lineages in Loma villages are associated with a *kwi* (quarter). Quarters can be quite small, with only 20–25 inhabitants in four or five houses,[12] or they can reach 100–150 inhabitants living in thirty houses. In Giziwulu, the Koivogui clan was particularly small, numbering only twenty-three people, and the two Pivi quarters held fewer than thirty people each. The Kalivoguis were undisputed autochthonous landowners of the village and kɛkɛ to everyone else, while the Bilivogui were their *daabenui*, and consequently were the *taalaabe* or village nephews. In the account, the reader will have discerned a vagueness in distinguishing between clan and lineage, and such ambiguity is common in Loma village life. Loma speakers often say, for instance, "The village of Boussedou belongs to the Beavoguis," or "The kɔkɔlɔgi of Woima is for the Bilivoguis." What they mean is that a specific lineage (or sometimes a group of related lineages) of the Beavogui or Bilivogui clan is the recognized landowner of the territory known as Boussedou or Woima. An unrelated Beavogui arriving from a distant village would *not* gain special privileges in Boussedou on the basis of his clan identity.

The ambiguity inherent in these descriptions is not accidental. Loma speakers cultivate such ambiguity, and it is the basis of much strategic manipulation in everyday life. The hypothetical Beavogui, having arrived in Boussedou where another lineage of the (numerous and widely dispersed) Beavogui clan were landowners, would probably cultivate the fiction that he was somehow distantly related to the landowners, and over the course of a few generations, if he and his descendants were good citizens in the village, such a fiction might be tolerated by most people, most of the time. The social field in which such a working fiction would be rejected is that of sacrifice.

There are many types of Loma sacrifice, but I will focus on two here. One operates at the lineage level. Leopold notes that while in everyday contexts lineages (*burude*) and quarters (*kwi*) are often conflated, quarters contain many people (wives and strangers) who are not members of the lineage. He writes, "The collective action and social identity of a lineage emerges only in the field of ritual and affinal relations" (1991, 119). *Doing* a sacrifice is the most direct kind of statement that Loma speakers make about who they *are*, because sacrificial relations assert privileged contact between the living and the *goveiti*, or the ancestors.

In Giziwulu, like other Loma villages, there were three potential sites for lineage sacrifice. One was the tomb of a founding ancestor (*kaba*). In the modern era, this was typically a raised dais of cement in the middle of a *kwi*. Houses were loosely arranged around the tomb, and if it was not exactly the geometric center of the quarter, it was the ritual and social center.[13] These modern tombs were an improvisation on precolonial tombs. These ancestral tombs, also located at the center of a *kwi*, are typified by large flat stones laid over the grave site(s) of one or several lineage ancestor(s), and a series of large (1 to 1.5 meters long) flat stones partially buried in the ground around the tombs, sticking up vertically from the ground. The tomb is considered to be the home of an ancestral *govei*. During the socialist period, it was made a crime to bury people inside a village, and all people were supposed to be buried in designated graveyard sites outside the village. This was how most Loma speakers were buried already (only important male founders would be buried in the village), but it put an end to the possibility of (legally) creating new politically and ritually significant ancestral gravesites. From the time of the socialist state's Demystification push, some sacrifices were forced underground.

A second site for sacrifices was the *kpakpagi*, or lineage sacrificial shrine. This type of shrine resembles the protective sacrifice that hangs over the entrance to many villages. The *kpakpagi* (fig. 2) is suspended from a goal post–shaped wooden superstructure, and liana vines hang from the center, wrapped around the shrine objects, which can include a regime of palm kernels, stones, or precolonial iron money (*koli*).

Lastly, there are occasionally shrines kept inside the house and propitiated by lineage heads. These are called *salaɣaiti*, or "sacrifices," and are objects to which sacrifices are offered. In the house where my wife and I lived in Giziwulu, the lineage elder kept his *salaɣai* in an adjacent room, and would come to propitiate it once every two or three months. It was a bundle of liana vines, each one a corkscrewed strand about a meter long, bound together in a tight cylinder about 50 cm diameter. This *salaɣai* was kept with the lineage's dagger, the other ritually powerful object representing lineage unity that I describe below. Unlike the ancestral tomb or the fixed shrine, this *salaɣai* was portable. However, it was only ever used in the one room of the house, which otherwise went unoccupied. To my understanding, this *salaɣai* served the same function as a *kpakpagi* lineage shrine for my hosts' lineage, whose (still living) lineage elder was the first family member to migrate to Giziwulu, thus depriving them of the possibility of an ancestral tomb.

The organization of village space, and its inherent links to the practice of ancestral sacrifice, spawned several types of tension in Giziwulu. As I noted above, there was unanimous agreement in Giziwulu that the Kalivogui clan were the village's landowners. It was also agreed that the Bilivogui were the village's *taalaabe*, the village's second family who performed sacrifices for the village as well as for the Kalivogui landowners.

The oral history cited above recounted, however, that there were two Bilivogui quarters, and six Kalivogui quarters, corresponding to eight dif-

Figure 2. *Kpakpagi* sacrificial shrine. From Gaisseau 1954.

ferent lineages within the two clans. Indeed, there was just one lineage among the Kalivoguis and one among the Bilivoguis that were landowner and *taalaabe* lineages. This left five Kalivogui lineages and one Bilivogui lineage without the kinds of ritual or political prerogatives that accrued to their clanmates. Tensions among these lineages usually remained sub rosa, but they did emerge from time to time. The members of the two Bilivogui lineages rarely interacted socially, and although they farmed adjacent swathes of the village's territory, they rarely joined one another's collective work groups. The relations among the village's Kalivogui lineages were close, whether because or in spite of the fact that they were all descended from seven brothers. The landowning Kalivogui lineage retained fairly undisputed political and ritual preeminence.[14]

Nevertheless, tensions did arise, and I describe one typical argument among Kalivoguis over rights to land use below. In this dispute, the two adversaries made explicit reference to the ancestral soil and its ability to mete out supernatural justice on wrongdoers. But such tensions could also arise in more mundane fashion. While I was living in Giziwulu, there was a *faawungi* (village moot or court case) just about every other morning. Such meetings took place most of the time in a quarter adjacent to mine, presided by an elder of the Teru lineage, a group with no claim to firstcomer status. The head of the Teru lineage was a cantankerous but powerful man who had served in the French colonial army, yet maintained a persona of staunch traditionalism. He was one of the few people in the village who openly opposed my presence there, and most importantly, he was a powerful *zowei* whose quarter housed the Poro enclosure behind it, at the edge of the forest.

The head of the landowning Kalivogui lineage, meanwhile, was universally acknowledged as the legitimate landowner of the village, and his son was the village chief. However, the elder Kalivogui was near ninety years old, infirm, and rarely left his bedroom. The Teru elder had capitalized on this situation and had shifted the place of village business to the space in front of his own house. Teru was feared by most everyone in the village, though not well liked. The proximity of the Poro enclosure next to his house reminded the reticent of his implied ability to enforce his will on others, though many complained bitterly that under no circumstance should village business be conducted in his quarter.

Consequently, the elder Kalivogui's son, who was the village chief, was forced to walk across the village to the Teru quarter in order to attend to business that in principle he was supposed to initiate and organize. While Teru was forceful, gruff, and intelligent, the chief was weak and uncharismatic. The usual complementary balance between frontstage and backstage regions (Goffman 1959) that Murphy (1981, 1990) has described for Kpelle and Mende communities was shattered. Landowners, who usually enjoy unchallenged front stage support and exercise a modicum of authority as the public face of elder male authority, are in most instances guided by the powerful backstage elders of the Poro society. In this case, Teru had moved to consolidate both forms of influence, and he did so by shifting the locus of village business away from the Kalivogui founder's tomb—the normal center of male public discussion—towards his own *kwi*.

As Murphy and Bledsoe describe for the neighboring Kpelle, there is a regional semiotics of burial linked to the politics of sacrifice, through which people *perform* hierarchy and identity, and assert authority. In one case they describe, a chief's younger brother had founded a new village that had begun to develop the political and economic weight needed to justify becoming the seat of an independent chiefdom. However, when the younger brother died, his elder brother blocked his burial in the new village:

> [B]y making sure that Sia [the younger brother] was buried at the headquarters-village of the lineage, Kana [the chief and older brother, who survived Sia] recreated the outward signs of political solidarity in the lineage. Had Sia's followers managed instead to bury him in the new territory, they would have created a potential ritual argument for independence. Their offerings at Sia's grave could later be interpreted as confirming that Sia's establishment of the village was the pivotal event in the founding of a new territory. (Murphy and Bledsoe 1987, 134)

This instance of the failure of Sia's followers to establish a new polity is the exception that proves a significant rule. It highlights the fact that burial is an important first step in a two-part process of asserting political prerogatives: first, burying a significant figure in the village, and second, performing lineage sacrifices to him, thus transforming him into the founding ancestor of a new lineage, and a focal point of political identity and legitimacy for his descendants. This process of turning an offshoot village into a ritually (and thus politically) freestanding site is one way that new villages and new lineages start. Like the process of lineage schism described by Turner ([1957] 1996), such processes are always contested.

Burials are always indicative of a Loma person's status and the circumstances of his or her death (Leopold 1991).[15] Burying a person in the village is a political act, and in Giziwulu, there was only one Kalivogui and one Bilivogui tomb.[16] These tombs are central to conceptions of autochthony and space. Because they become privileged sites of sacrifice, they crystallize the relations among the aspects of the visible and invisible world whose interaction gives autochthony its potency: earth spirits, ancestral spirits, and living humans.

This became clear to me through an undertaking that shifted the village's political and ritual focus back to the landowners' quarter: the refurbishment of Giziwulu's road. This road was first cleared in 1960, at the behest of the eldest living male in the landowning Kalivogui lineage, the ninety-year-old elder who was father of the village chief whose authority had been usurped by his rival, Teru. Between 1960 and 2000, the road had degraded to the point where it was largely impassable. After I had completed a year's fieldwork in Giziwulu, I returned to the U.S. to teach for a semester, and upon returning to Guinea, the elders of the village asked me to "go in front of" the village in negotiating a deal to have the road re-cleared, graded, and outfitted with three bridges that would make it passable even in the rainy season.

Discussions of this work involved the whole village, and the numerous meetings about it took place in the landowning Kalivoguis' *kwi*, with many participants sitting on the tomb of the village founder[17] and others sitting on the porches of all the surrounding houses. This discussion had to take place there not only out of respect for the original road work that the elder Kalivogui had commissioned forty years prior, but also because the work automatically called up ritual questions surrounding the reshaping of the soil, all of which belonged (at least in ritual terms) to the landowners. They were the only lineage qualified to make the necessary arrangements with the earth spirits that could facilitate or destroy the project.

The landowning Kalivogui lineage and their Bilivogui sacrificers had a special sacrificial spot on the mountain beside the village. During times of crisis or change, only they could sacrifice to the landowning ancestors and the mountain's *inegiti* earth spirits on behalf of the entire village, and they had to do so in preparation for the road work. In fact, those of us involved in collecting the money from each villager for the work had a great deal of trouble getting people to pay up before the sacrifices had been performed and people knew whether they had been accepted. Had they not met with a positive response (signified by a sacrificed cock ending his final death throe on his back), it is likely the project would have ceased.

Periodic sacrifices to a significant mountain or stream next to a village are common to most Loma villages (Schnell 1949, 4), as Loma speakers often consider such places to be the "homes" of both a village's *goveiti* (ancestral spirits) and *inegiti* (earth/water spirits). These sacrifices were targeted along with masquerades and other forms of "fétichisme" by the socialist government in its Demystification Program.[18] Perhaps the most fascinating account of such a sacrifice is that by Game Guilao, a Catholic Loma speaker who lived in France from the 1950s. The account, published in 1967 in *Esprit*, the French Catholic socialist journal, is entitled "La mort des fétiches," or "The Death of the Fetishes," and describes a village sacrifice on a mountain in Macenta Préfecture in 1961, while the Demystification Program is raging. Guilao, who is visiting Macenta from France, declares that the work of Demystification is already a fait accompli: "The degradation is very advanced, the game is disorganized, and each one backs away, not because he has found other things to do, but out of fear of being ridiculous and being called backward" (1967, 238).[19]

For Guilao, this is an event formerly of ritual and now just culinary importance; the last gasps of a dying animism that is about to be replaced by "a new wind [that] had whispered in [the Loma's] ears and rendered them attentive" (1967, 243). The new wind, he implies, was not just Sékou Touré's modernism but the Christianity that Guilao himself had embraced. History has not followed the course Guilao predicted; during the period of my research, the majority of Loma speakers continued to brush off monotheism. One also doubts the accuracy of his interpretation of his fellow Loma speakers' states of mind during the sacrifice. For Guilao, like the modernist elites in Conakry who had decreed the Demystification Program, the glitches in the sacrificial enactment would surely mark the death knell of these "backward" practices.[20]

The performance of such sacrifices at the turn of the twenty-first century indicated their continuing importance. One reason such sacrifices have not been easily abandoned is because they serve a political as well as a "religious" function. Just as Beavogui (1998) described the ways that the Poro men's association has adapted itself to the political interests and necessities of the day, sacrifice also works to align past ideals and present needs—many of them tied up in village micropolitics. As Guilao mentions, the sacrifice commemorated Massawoi. This name is a shortened form of "Massa Koi(vogui),"[21] or "Koivogui, the chief." By making Massawoi the primary ancestor honored in the chiefdom's sacrifice, his descendents asserted their autochthonous status and continuing political authority.

Many researchers who have worked in the area have noted that the region now inhabited by Southwest Mande speakers is littered with abandoned village sites (Fairhead and Leach 1994; Ferme 2001, 23–26; Schnell 1949, 4; Schwab 1947, 30). Giziwulu had, some 200 meters outside the edge of the contemporary village, several *kabati* grave sites of the type that normally lie at the center of a lineage quarter. This, I was told, was the site of the old village, which had been attacked and razed during the mid- to late-nineteenth-century slave-raiding wars. The modern village was founded at the very end of the nineteenth century, shortly before the French conquered the region. Relocating the village after a period of exile required the reestablishment of a working relationship between the autochthonous lineage and the local ancestral and earth spirits.[22]

It is only the elders of the autochthonous landowning (*zukenui*) lineage that have the ability to communicate with the *inegi* earth and water spirits of a place, and they do so through sacrifice. This sacrifice is performed by their *daabenui*. They sacrifice both to the *inegiti* and to the ancestors of the autochthonous lineage. Ultimately, it is this triangular relationship, among autochthonous lineage head, the spirits of his lineage ancestors, and the *inegi* earth and water spirits, that gives landowning lineages their authority. During my fieldwork in Giziwulu, I witnessed a series of "village sacrifices" in which the village renewed the liana *bɔlɔwɔlɔgi* braid surrounding the village and the *kpakpagi* town sacrifice that hung over the main entrance. These powerful objects were meant to protect the village from both physical and invisible attack, and their renewals were presided over by representatives of the landowning Kalivogui lineage. Giziwulu's inhabitants told me that the sacrifices would keep ill-intentioned living actors (witches) or invisible ones (angry ancestors, destructive *inegiti*) from killing men by causing them to slip and fall from palm trees, women by difficulties in childbirth, and children by unexplained sudden illnesses.

Loma speakers go to great lengths to ensure that these relations between landowners and the invisible world are amicable and productive. In one village, I was told:

> The founder was named Gbana. He had a farm here where he grew cotton and cola nuts. He decided to build a village on the site of his farm. So that the village would be prosperous, they built the first mud daub house, and had a totally nude woman live in it for seven days. Luti-Koolu was her name. . . . The ceremony that consecrated the construction of the village is called the *tamakingi* (seclusion of the woman for seven nights). Every time the woman who has performed this ceremony dies, another woman performs it. (A.G, November 8, 1998)

The elaborateness of some of these rites points to an important aspect of Loma cosmology. Land is owned and not owned. It is inalienable from those who originally inhabited it, namely the *inegiti* spirits. Landowners' autochthonous authority derives from their ability to negotiate a successful relationship with the *inegiti*. Autochthonous landownership is in principle an inheritance, but even this seemingly fixed status is more an accomplishment than an essential quality. It is achieved primarily through sacrifice.²³ As Fortes (1987, cf. Leopold 1991, 106) has argued, identity derives from both knowing and showing. In this respect, Loma sacrifice is similar to Fortes's description of sacrifice among the Talensi. He writes that sacrifice "is a special ritual procedure for establishing or mobilizing a relationship of mutuality between the donor (individual or collective) and the recipient; and there is generally, if not always, an implication of mutual constraint, and indeed of actual or potential mutual coercion in the act" (Fortes 1987, 296). Identity here is supremely performative, and the living and the dead constitute each other mutually in the performance. A landowner who cannot gain the cooperation of *inegiti* and ancestral spirits will have misfortunes such as bad deaths visit his village, and will see it diminish in size. From lineage to village to chiefdom sacrifices, Loma sacrifice (both to *goveiti* and *inegiti*) constitutes a nested structure of identity claims instantiating and asserting corporate social identity. It is through sacrifice that people negotiate and enact political claims to legitimate (autochthonous) authority that often go unstated in everyday life.

To say that these sacrifices are a nested set should not obscure a crucial distinction between lineage sacrifice in general and a landowning lineage's sacrifices to the *inegiti*. Even the landowning elder who has amicable relations with the *inegiti* in the present knows that such relations could change at any moment. The *inegiti* are famously capricious. After all, they ostensibly existed in their places before the first human settler arrived, and they could continue on if the village disappeared. This situation contrasts with that of lineage ancestors. While they are able to affect the living with good or bad luck—even spiteful retribution for having been ignored—if their descendants disappear, they will, too. This is the mutually coercive relationship to which Fortes refers: The living wish to secure the good will and assistance of the spirits of the dead. At the same time, they are likely—in Loma sacrifice as in most of Africa—to remind the ancestors that if the living do not prosper, there will be no one left to propitiate the ancestors. Landowners are in a weaker position in relation to the earth and land spirits, and thus the accomplishment of productive relations with them is all the more impressive.

If asked directly, many Loma speakers say that the invisible world resembles the world of the living, reproducing its hierarchies and other social relations. This anthropomorphized (not to say Durkheimian) explanation is not incorrect. Yet we may also say that the world of the living resembles the spirit world. In his thesis on Loma religious beliefs, Keletigui Guilavogui writes:

The spirits are the genies who have been the first to occupy the territory. The founding ancestor of a village had to give them gifts in order to obtain the right of settlement. All his descendants do the same. The genies, as opposed to the ancestors, are fixed in specific places or objects that men must approach in order to communicate with them. Wherever a genie may be, one addresses oneself to it. It is not omnipresent. (1987, 25)

Inegiti (which Guilavogui calls "genies" in this passage) are thus rooted in particular places, and their authority derives from the fact that they have preceded humans in those places. They are autochthonous in relation to village founders and their descendants, just as those founders are autochthonous in relation to later arrivals to the village. To bypass the protocol implied by these relations is to court danger. In principle at least, it could bring destruction on a village. Loma understandings of the invisible world thus serve as a model for the organization of autochthonous claims among the living. As we have already seen, however, reality often wreaks havoc with the kind of neat cosmological systems beloved of academics and their chosen informants. Whether Loma firstcomers derive their political authority from the system of religious beliefs or vice versa becomes a chicken-and-egg question, but we are interested here primarily in the ways that the two play off each other. To see that, we shall look at one crisis point where the two worlds meet and autochthony is enacted.

The Significance of Ordeals and Oaths

Loma juridical processes are based on the assumption that complainants in a court case will be tempted to lie in order to support their claims, and that witnesses, too, are unlikely to be impartial. Consequently, it is necessary to find technical means of moving beyond verbal testimony. In North American society, we use polygraph tests and DNA evidence to prove and disprove the claims people make in court. Loma speakers have two primary techniques for discovering contested truths: divination (which I will not discuss here),[24] and the use of ordeals and oaths, which call upon the agency of the invisible world to make the truth evident.

Tests could include an ordeal[25] or use of a *tekpelɔgi* or *kpelɛgi* ("swear"; cf. Speed 1991) on which people make public oaths. *Kpelɛgiti* are either ritual objects or an ancestral weapon. Like Togba's sword described in the interlude above, these are lineage heads' insignias of office, usually a *wibowai* (European knife/sword) or a spear once owned by an ancestor in the precolonial period. Such objects condense the relationship between a living lineage head and his ancestors, and in the case of landowning lineages are symbols of autochthony.[26] Neel writes, "Among the tests, there is one that consists of eating a white cola nut that has been placed on a gris-gris; another test called *sale loba*, a vegetable poison boiled in a turtle soup; and one called *goneregui*, another poison that is said to have the ability to cause the belly of the guilty to swell up" (Neel 1913, 473).

These tests and oath-taking objects seem to vary in their details across the region, but most are made of iron or steel, combined with some detachable substance (that is ingested by the oath-taker), which can include earth, sweat, or a cola nut. In all cases, the efficacy of the medium derives from its contact with an object or person representing the authority of the lineage, its ancestors, and their relation to the soil; the nexus of autochthonous reference.

In a village near Giziwulu, the process was described to me thus: the appropriate social unit produces its ritual object of corporate identity—usually a sword, knife, or spear. In a case between two individuals, this may be a lineage object, or in more global cases (over land-use rights and territorial limits, for instance), it may be a village or chiefdom object, that is, the lineage object of the village or chiefdom's landowning lineage. This object serves as the *kpelɛgi* for the case. Then the *daabe* of the lineage washes his forehead, elbows, and knees with water, catching this water in a calabash and placing it next to the *kpelɛgi*. The water is thus rendered ritually powerful first by the infusion of the *daabe*'s "body dirt" (Fortes 1987), from these three ritually powerful parts of his body, and second, by its proximity to the object that symbolizes the corporate identity of the lineage (the *kpelɛgi*). The person or persons taking the oath drink the water and are told that if they are lying they will fall ill and die. The result makes the truth manifest.[27]

One use of *kpelɛgi* in Giziwulu was related to the road renovation work. After a month or two, the project soon ran into numerous small problems, resistances, and delays that threatened to bring it to a standstill. Although it had been the village that had asked me to help them with this undertaking, many of the village's leading figures had backed away from the work, and some even appeared to be opposed, though in public they insisted they were behind the project.[28] The main actor in the village who convinced me to keep pushing ahead with him for the completion of the work (and the collection of the money from the villagers, who had agreed to pay 20,000 francs—then worth about fifteen dollars—for every inhabitant over fifteen years old) was the village secretary. This left the two of us as the ostensible heads of the project (even though I had since moved to my second research site) and thus lightning rods for criticism and dissatisfaction. The secretary had a high school education and was the chief's right hand, especially in dealings with the government, since he could read and write and the chief could not. As the work slowed, people in the village started to accuse the secretary (and me, as I later found out) of stealing their money, and several, being of an unforgiving nature, had threatened to kill him. As time went on, he recognized that his own brothers had begun acting suspiciously toward him and took quick action.

Without making any accusations toward his kinsmen, the secretary invited them to his house, where he produced his lineage's ancestral sabre. He also produced a chicken, and proposed that they all take an oath of lineage solidarity over the animal, which they reluctantly agreed to do. His *daabe* cut the chicken's throat over a lineage sacrifice (*salaγai*), then gave the animal to the secretary's wife to cook. Several hours later, when the meal was prepared, he called his brothers and other lineage mates to eat the meal, and the brothers all made excuses or had left the village. When they refused to eat the meal, he told me that his suspicions had been confirmed. He told me that from that point on, he knew that he must not eat or drink anything with his brothers. If they had eaten the meal, he said, they knew that if they tried to poison him or harm him in some other way, they would immediately die. Even the intention of doing him harm could make them ill. Their refusal had made their bad intentions evident but had simultaneously provided the secretary with a degree of protection. The brothers knew that not eating the sacrificed chicken was highly unusual, and that if any harm were to befall the secretary, they would be blamed. The secretary had neutralized one group of his enemies in the village, at least to the extent that they feared an "impartial" investigation of any mishap that befell their brother.

Another common use of a *kpelɛgi* involves disputes over land-use rights. Such disputes make the most explicit links between the principle of autochthonous rights in land use and the set of esoteric responsibilities attached to them. I was present in Giziwulu when an important village elder became involved in an intractable land dispute with a relative. This man was from one of the Kalivogui lineages in the village and was my neighbor. He was a powerful *zowei*, head of a *kwi* in the village, and a relatively prosperous farmer. In this case, we see the use of the type of oath that Neel called *goneregui* above. The effective ingredient was nothing less than the disputed soil itself. My notes read:

Autochthony as a Cultural Resource / 83

6/25/99 Not much happened yesterday, except some interesting commentary on oaths.... The men, however, had clearly gone to the oath-taking of V. Kalivogui in a land dispute between him and another Kalivogui [the oath took place on the disputed parcel, more than an hour's walk from the village]. He would drink some of the earth in question, mixed into water. I asked, what would happen? I was told the land was now his until/unless he had lied, in which case he would fall ill and die. I asked, if he admits his lie early on, could he be exonerated? Very difficult, P. said. He would probably die no matter what. But couldn't he also die of natural causes? I asked. Yes, P. said, but the *kpεlεgi's* death had its own special sign: the belly would start gradually to swell until it became enormous, virtually touching the ground. All medical treatments would do no good, and eventually, the guilty party would die. A kind of African Pinocchio. He said he had seen it in one land dispute between a man from the village and one from Balagolaye. The latter took the oath, and after a few months started getting the swollen belly. He recanted his story and asked forgiveness of his adversary and the earth, but within a year or so was dead.

I asked about what the agent was in all these punishments. Loma people always talk about it being *the earth* that does this or that. I asked, is it the soil itself, or the earth spirits, *jinn*, the ancestors, or something else? I even further defined my question, saying, "OK, is it something chemical or biological in the composition of the soil—something *physical*, or is it something *mystical*?" They laughed at the stubbornness of my Western dichotomizing, but agreed that the punishment was mystical, giving half-hearted support to the agency of "earth spirits." But they really and truly voted for simple *earth* as a simultaneously physical and mystical entity.

Interestingly, the elder died over the course of the next six months, while I was back in the U.S. When I returned and was told that he had died, I remembered the conversation about the oath. I asked, as casually as I could manage,

"Well, what did he die of?"

"Oh, he was sick for a while," a friend said.

"Sick with what? Did he have any symptoms?"

"Stomach problems. His belly was all swollen."

I couldn't believe what I was hearing, and when I reminded my friend about the oath and its supposed effects on whichever party had lied, he became annoyed.

"No, that wasn't it at all," he said. "V. was telling the truth, and no matter what other people say, it wasn't the oath that had killed him. Probably some kind of stomach cancer, or something." I dropped the subject. I later found that there were factions who (as my friend's defensive response indicated) believed that V. had been struck down by his own lie in combination with the agency of the *kpelɛgi*.

Kpelɛgi objects, on which Loma speakers swear oaths, are thus crystallizations of all the factors that come together to form the Loma conception of autochthony. They bring together the three agents I have noted above as working in tandem to constitute lineage, village, and chiefdom authority: living humans, ancestors, and earth spirits. The relations between the living and the dead are most clearly condensed in the object of the lineage *wibowai*, or precolonial knife, sword, or spear. Because the object typically belonged to the apical ancestor from whom the lineage takes its name and identity, it links the living and the dead, and as in the case of the village secretary, it makes an explicit demand of all lineage mates to live and work cooperatively for the growth and success of the lineage.

Other types of *kpelɛgi*, such as the soil incorporated in the last example, bring together the living and the earth spirits in a contest of legitimacy. The earth spirits, it is implied, know who first struck a deal with them, and thus they know who is the legitimate claimant by virtue of his relation to the person who initially enticed their acceptance through sacrifice. The death of V. is a particularly clear example of the stakes involved in playing with the "real" autochthonous order of things in a Loma village. Even though some in the village defended his memory, others pointed to his death as a clear example of the retribution that follows automatically from disrespecting "the earth"—the proper orderly relations between humans and earth spirits, as they have negotiated legitimate rights in land use.

Yet it must be emphasized again that the principle of autochthony, while fixed and historically given in principle, is available to many types of reformulation. "Fictive autochthony," as I call it, has allowed conquerors (some Loma, some Manya, but in any case strangers) to legitimate their control of a territory after the fact. This legitimation rests on the invisible world's ostensible acceptance of the "new autochthon's" sacrifices. Cases like that of V. are instances of failure that are essential to the continuation of the ideological system of autochthonous rights. Those sacrifices and oaths made by conquerors that do not result in sickness and death are the underpinning for the construction of a new micropolitical order in the village. This is not, however, a threshold crossed once and then fixed for good. Periodic challenges might cause a conqueror and his descendants to "prove" again, through sacrifice and oaths, that they maintain the good will of the earth and ancestral spirits. Identity in this as in other realms of Loma life is not given but accomplished through social work and performance.

FOUR

The Emergence of Ethnicity: Ethnicized Territory and Conversion to World Religions in the Colonial Period

My focus in this chapter is the birth of a notion of ethnicized territory in the Macenta area of Guinea. By ethnicized territory, I mean to say a notion—novel in this region—that ethnolinguistic identity and specific parcels of territory were organically linked. Rather than the mosaic of relations between first-coming and later-arriving individuals and lineages described in the last chapter, this new logic of autochthony and political hierarchy posited whole ethnic blocs as being either autochthonous or foreign. Though this shift is a product of identifiable state policies and rural Guineans' reactions to them, it is now part of the common sense of Loma speakers' conceptions of politics and ethnicity, and it is treated as always having existed. Under the new dispensation that I found in Macenta Préfecture while conducting fieldwork in the late 1990s, the system of ancestral sacrifice and kɛkɛ–daabe relations described in the last chapter regulated relations among Loma speakers, while Loma speakers attempted (often unsuccessfully) to apply the logic of ethnicized territory to their relations between themselves and Manya speakers.

I begin by giving an outline of Loma agriculture and land tenure norms, then focus on the material and political contexts of new forms that were imposed upon them. I then turn backward to describe two transformative moments in the history of Loma land tenure: the establishment of colonial canton chieftaincies and their renegotiation in the late 1910s and early 1920s,[1] and the changes in land tenure laws introduced by the socialist government after independence in 1959. These transformations were introduced by the state (first colonial, then socialist) for reasons that had little to do with the micropolitics of ethnic identity in the forest region. However, the unintended consequences they produced were central to hardening Loma and Manya identities in the area, and laid the foundation for the political economic divisions that fed into the development of Loma speakers' resentments and growing sense of unified ethnic identity.

This chapter explores the ways that local micropolitical dynamics interacted with those of the states that encompassed the Macenta region. One of the major arguments of this chapter is that socialist policies designed to erase centuries-old disparities between noble and servile populations in the Fulbe and Maninka areas that contained some 70 percent of the Guinean population had major and largely unforeseen effects in the forest region, where they hardened and polarized ethnic identities. This process is intimately linked in both its intended and unintended consequences to the state's iconoclastic attempt to do away with the religious practices and masquerades of the forest region.

Land tenure and use thus provide a concrete instance of the ways that the state comes to constitute the terms in which the local is discussed, and vice versa. Much recent writing on state, transnational, or cosmopolitan spheres (Cheah and Robbins 1998; Ferguson and Gupta 2002; Gupta 1995; Gupta and Ferguson 1997; Lefebvre 1991; Scott 1998) asserts (often only implicitly) that state power, even when it works in counterintuitive ways and through unexpected networks, is oriented by state elites' intentionality. The remaining chapters in this book do not deny the significance of intentionality, but following the work of recent francophone studies of African politics (Bayart 1993; Bayart, Ellis, and Hibou 1999; Chabal and Daloz 1999; Mbembe 2000), they emphasize that the negotiation of rule that Mbembe calls "commandement" is often characterized by the attempt to manage disorder and unintended consequences as much as intentional projects.[2]

In the present era of IMF/World Bank interventions, international arms and drug smuggling networks that involve Africa, and "complex humanitarian emergencies," African rulers and ruled have increasingly found themselves aligned together in attempting to manage their relations with outside actors to their own advantage. The use of "disorder as a political instrument" (Chabal and Daloz 1999; MacGaffey 1991; MacGaffey and Bazenguissa-Ganga 2000) at both elite and subaltern levels suggests that the attempts described in this book—of a strong socialist state to impose itself on its citizens—look increasingly like artifacts of a quaint historical period. Despite this, the significance of unintended consequences of both colonial and postcolonial policies in Guinea shows that there is historical continuity alongside innovation. But this is jumping ahead. We must return to the village.

Space, Landscape, and Production: Loma Rice Farming

Before looking at the ways that land tenure and use in Macenta changed over the course of the twentieth century, we should have some sense of how Loma speakers cultivate the land. The basic techniques of dry land rice cultivation have remained constant throughout the twentieth century and probably go back several centuries. Growing rice is central to Loma speakers' identity and their economy. The agricultural production of Giziwulu's farmers for the year 1999 is detailed in Appendix 2. The importance of rice in the economy of Giziwulu and other villages like it in Guinea's forest region only grew during my 1997–2001 fieldwork period as the world price of coffee plummeted to less than half what it was at the time of the survey. Upland rice is typically cultivated on hills (some quite steep, exceeding 45 degrees), although the terrain usually varies within one field. Using only machetes and axes,[3] they clear spaces averaging slightly less than one hectare. The area cleared may range from young fallow, five or six years old, up to ancient forest that has not been cultivated in living memory. In my own survey of Giziwulu's farmers, 21 percent of men's farms were cultivated in primary forest.

To get a fuller sense of the varieties of agricultural practice in a southern Loma-speaking village in the 1990s, we may follow Sibabwe and Akoi, two brothers in Giziwulu, as I did during my fieldwork.[4] The first year I knew them, they cultivated a joint farm. This farm, located some 17 km (2 1/2 hour walk) from the village, was in the *Goɛ* (primary forest) at the outer edges of Giziwulu's vast territory. In fact, as they planned to start clearing space for a rice field, the two brothers found that several men from a Kpelle village some five kilometers further away had begun clearing an adjacent area. Although they lived much closer than the Giziwulu people to the area they were clearing, the land was part of Giziwulu's territory, and the brothers informed them that they had no right to the land because they had not come to Giziwulu to ask permission of the *Tiɣizamayati* (owners of the land). The Kpelle farmers, all young men, told Sibabwe and Akoi, both middle-aged men, to leave them alone and tend to their own fields.

As the young men continued, the brothers actually left the field they had started clearing, and waited. When all of the heaviest work[5] was finished on this illegitimate field, the brothers brought a complaint in Giziwulu against the men of the neighboring village, explaining how they had cleared an area without permission, how Sibabwe and Akoi had informed them that they were not entitled to farm that land, and how the young men had insolently continued. As they expected, the ruling between the elders of the two villages went in Giziwulu's favor, and they reclaimed the field, some two hectares in size.

The next year, they had a choice. Old-growth forest typically supports two consecutive years of intensive rice farming. The harvest from this big field had been very good, but the time spent walking out to the field was costly, and it meant that they had spent many nights sleeping in a nearby hamlet, away from the village. Sibabwe, especially, did not mind this so much, because he was friendly with the family who lived, full-time, in this hamlet and was well provided by his host, who usually had at least two raffia palms producing palm wine at any given time. Akoi, however, did not want to farm again so far from the village.

The process was especially arduous because both men had recently split from their wives, so that when the time came for the women's portions of the rice-growing cycle (sowing, weeding, harvesting), they had to hire a women's collective work group. Not only did this require money and the provision of food for all the workers, the brothers also could not be 100 percent sure that they would receive the help they needed when they needed it. A wife who participated in a work group would work, in rotating order, on the field of each member. Even if she might want to skip one of the group's agreed work days, a woman who had benefited from the work of her mates risked disapproval, fines (levied by the head of the group), and most importantly, the risk that others would refuse to support her in the next round of work. The same groups, hired by someone (like the two brothers) who could not make these kinds of reciprocal moral claims on each member, could be much less reliable. The fact that each day of work on this field also entailed five hours of round-trip walking made their field an especially tough sell, and several delays (in weeding and harvest) during the first year's agricultural cycle had diminished the field's yield.

Consequently, Sibabwe and Akoi made farms the next year much closer to home. By this time, Akoi was living with a different woman, and they agreed to work together. They would make one big field together, and Akoi would clear a smaller, individual field for her. These fields were side-by-side on land that the family had farmed before, only a twenty-minute walk from the village. They were the closest rice fields I saw to the village during my research (the average field was a forty- to sixty-minute walk from the village). The same year, I cleared and planted a garden nearby, in a swamp area bisected by a stream. I sometimes worked with Akoi, clearing his field, which had lain fallow for ten years.

I also worked with his brother, Sibabwe, who was working a plot some two kilometers away, a forty-minute walk from the village. This area was seven-year regrowth and relatively easy to clear. Sibabwe had chosen a plot directly behind his coffee plantation, and he also had an adjacent grove of bananas and a raffia palm tapped for wine, so his entire agricultural sphere lay within a contiguous patch of about two hectares. This was unusual for men in the village, who often had coffee plantations, cocoa plantations, raffia palms, and rice fields each in a different place. In the intensive period from December to April, during which they cleared, felled trees, burned the dried brush, then re-burned it, Giziwulu men focused their energies on their rice field(s). The rest of the year, they went from site to site in the bush, tending to particular plantations or other productive activities, like climbing palm trees and cutting down regimes of palm kernels in order to make oil.

The period of women's work in the rice cultivation cycle is longer, though somewhat less intense.[6] Sowing rice in April and May, they weed between July and September, and may harvest at various times from September through early December. Women usually intercrop Loma rice fields with vegetables like corn (*gbazi*), okra (*kpasagi*), hot peppers (*kizɛgi*), manioc (*malakwi*), and eggplant (*boboi*). They cultivate separate gardens with some other crops, including tomatoes (*worukone*), squash (*kpili*), and onions (*yavai*). Women also take over year-old rice fields that need little clearing, sometimes to plant a second, low-yield rice crop, or more often to plant a field of peanuts (*tɛnɣagi*) or beans (*toway* or *nyiibe*).

This overview gives the reader a passing familiarity with the kinds of practices and decision-making involved in contemporary Loma speakers' farming. In the next section we shall see how some of these practices came into being, as cash crops were introduced by the French colonial regime in the 1920s, for instance. We will also place these practices, taking place in hundreds of villages in Macenta Préfecture, into the broader context of the politics surrounding land tenure, usage, and political control over territory in the region.

Land Tenure and Cash Crops

Loma speakers divide space into the civilized area of the village, the liminal sacred forest surrounding most Loma villages, and the bush (*dɔboizu*), consisting of cultivated spaces, fallow, and forest that has not been cultivated in living memory.[7] Prior to about 1920, this cultivated area was made up entirely of rice fields intercropped with garden vegetables. What was once an undifferentiated space of rice and vegetable cultivation has, since about 1930, become increasingly split into two distinct spaces: a near ring consisting of small cash crop plantations, and a more distant ring of rice fields. The introduction of cash crops (especially coffee) by the French colonial administration catalyzed important changes in Loma speakers' conceptions and practices surrounding land tenure.

In Loma villages, all land belongs to the first-settling lineage in perpetuity, and although it is split into parcels and subdivided again and again, in principle the land remains the property of the landowners. Loma peasants have typically been land-rich and people-poor. Because labor was the limiting input in agricultural production, landowners were often in the position of recruiting new settler-clients to their territory. The violence of intervillage raiding that continued into the first years of the twentieth century caused major population movements and placed such "clients" in a relatively powerless position. However, the other side of this equation, landowners' need for wealth in people, evened the power differential significantly. This interplay is elegantly captured in Leopold's (1991) usage of the term "asymmetrical complementarity."

Frequent and often violent displacements in the past made landowner status negotiable, but the rules governing land tenure remained clear, and any Loma farmer can describe them today: Land belongs, in the first and the last instances, to the village's *zukenui* landowning, first-settling lineage, which typically also supplies the village's administrative chief. Customary divisions over time allow land to be divided by lineages that have been granted use rights by the *zukenuiti* and that have cleared and cultivated that land over a period of generations. This de facto ownership gives such lineages the right to loan land to newcomers who subsequently become their own stranger-clients, although the host lineage should always present the newcomer to the head of the *zukenui* lineage as a courtesy. Because rice cultivation continues to be practiced predominantly on a rotating, slash-and-burn basis, this notion of use rights remains intact. Individual members of a lineage plant fields within the lineage's customary territory, but, after one or at most two years, they leave the spot to allow it to regenerate itself as fallow. A farmer may come back to a plot he has already cultivated (especially if it was he who first felled the old-growth hardwood trees on the plot),[8] or it may be cultivated next by a different member of the lineage. Despite the loose system of rights to use this land, no one would ever claim to own the land except the *zukenui* landowners, who consecrate this right through their sacrificial relationship with the village's earth and ancestral spirits.[9]

The most important wrinkle in this system applies to instances of fruit-bearing trees. As in other parts of Africa (Berry 1975), trees belong to individuals and are inheritable property. In principle, the ground in which they are planted does not belong to the tree owner. In practice, however, planting trees on a plot of land typically cements the tree owner's de facto ownership of the land in which they are planted.[10]

Loma speakers have long harvested and sold the cola nuts (*tuuli*) that grow in this rainforest area,[11] and most Loma men can tell you who planted a particular cola tree and when. Like other trees, cola trees are personal property inherited by a man's sons. Raffia (*kili*) and oil (*dooi*) palms are also planted and owned by particular men for the palm oil and palm wine they produce.[12] Raffia must be planted in wet, swampy areas, and men who harvest palm wine typically have palm tree nurseries in the swampy areas of their family land, transplanting trees as they grow and cultivating them for the seven to ten years necessary before they will become viable wine-giving trees. These trees are also personal property, belonging to men, and inheritable, though palms have a far shorter lifespan than cola trees, which can live at least seventy-five years.

With the French administration came the introduction of coffee and cocoa plantations. I discuss the system of production below, but should describe here some of the changes that took place with regard to the spatial arrangement of the plantations. Loma men often planted some coffee or cocoa trees piecemeal, close to the village, when they were first introduced

Figure 3. *Koli* precolonial iron money. Photo by author.

by the French. As the colonial administration increased its presence in the forest region,[13] the demands for taxes became stricter. In the first years after their conquest, the French accepted taxes in the local *koli* or *guinze* currency.

Before long, the tax was payable only in colonial currency or in kind. One of the means of gaining the required funds was growing cash crops. In the Macenta area, this usually meant coffee, first introduced in Guinea in 1919 and distributed generally in 1935, with 525,000 plants given to local farmers. Between 1937 and 1945, Guinea's annual coffee production averaged one hundred tons, and it increased after the war (Beavogui 2001, 170). Loma farmers began planting small plantations of coffee trees to pay taxes and to buy consumables like imported pots and plates, factory-made cloth, fish hooks, and industrial wire for making traps.

These plantations laid bare an incipient contradiction in Loma understandings of land tenure. While no one "owns" land in a Loma village except the landowning lineage, those lineages that have lived in a village for several generations acquire de facto rights to the land they habitually farm.[14] The planting of fruit-bearing trees, like coffee, is generally accepted by Loma speakers to turn weak lineage or individual rights into solid individual rights. The trees belong to the planter and are inheritable by his sons. This applies equally to coffee and cocoa, introduced in the colonial period, and to cola. In principle, this is men's work, although in practice there are women today who have banana plantations of their own. Banana plants, while usually replanted in the same place using offshoots from the existing plants, die each time a bunch of bananas is cut from them. In over fifty life-history interviews with women, I found that none owned coffee, cocoa, or cola trees, although Leopold states that in Liberia, "Both men and women plant forest tree crops such as kola, banana, pineapple, orange and avocado" (1991, 49).

With the planting of cash crops, Loma farmers built upon an aspect of Loma land tenure that hinted at individual rights to land. Plantations were not only integral to Loma-speaking farmers' insertion into the cash economy but also introduced personal, quasi-inalienable landownership in a way that fragmented land into small parcels. This dynamic is central to the oppositions between Loma speakers and Manya speakers over the last fifty years.[15] We shall see below how the emergence of individually owned parcels combined with other factors in such a way that it became a vehicle for interethnic distinction and competition.

The Logic of Ethnicized Territory

> Our [French] occupation has brought the creation, in the villages, of a new office, that of *Zuutigi* (corruption of the Malinké word *Dugutigi*, village chief). The Tomas, in effect, seeing us arrive as the protectors of their Malinké enemies, showed for a long time a justified mistrust given that we were surrounded by employees and interpreters from the enemy race. They carefully dissimulated their real organization and presented as the chiefs of the communities straw men, people of little consequence. (Gamory-Dubourdeau 1925, 328)

We now have a picture of a tension within Loma land tenure norms that was made more acute by the colonial introduction of cash crops. At about the same time that the French introduced coffee plants into the Macenta area (1919), there was another important consequence of colonial policy. This grew out of the institution of canton chieftaincies and the way that French administrators chose to legitimize certain claims to chieftaincy over others in the Macenta region. Competition arose between those defined as Loma and Manya between 1918 and 1925, as the French instituted indirect rule through the use of the territorial unit of the *canton*.[16] As Ramon Sarró has written about the Baga-speaking region on Guinea's coast:

> Whatever the intentions behind the creation of the cantons, in reality, French colonial administration created an ideal situation for some sectors of the population to claim "autochthony" (or other similar concepts) and chase away or despotically subordinate the strangers of their canton. I am not claiming that before the French administration, subordination did not exist or that strangers were not perceived as strangers. I am only arguing that the French supported the opposition between natives and strangers and provided a whole set of strategies to legitimate it. One such strategy was preferring "customary" chiefs to strangers and forcing people to legitimate their candidacies to chiefdoms by proving their links with chiefly native lineages. (Sarró 1999, chapter 4)

In the area that became first the Cercle de Macenta and later Macenta Préfecture, a similar struggle took place over the rents available to canton chiefs under the colonial system. The variables of migration, mutable identities, landowner status, and autochthony that I have presented in previous chapters converged in competition over these chieftaincies. In Macenta like the coastal region Sarró describes, these variables had combined in a variety of ways over the course of the precolonial era. Though they certainly changed over time, we can reconstruct a picture of their interaction in the last decades of the nineteenth century, as I have tried to do on the last two chapters.

What Sarró argues, and I argue is also true in Macenta, is that with the introduction of the new colonial administrative units and the shifts in land tenure practices, the same variables recombined in ways that promoted ethno-linguistic distinction. In precolonial times, autochthony connected particular lineages to particular territories. Many times these lineages were of heterogeneous ethnolinguistic background (cf. Murphy and Bledsoe 1987). Even clan identities were no reliable predictor of autochthonous or landowning statuses.[17] In short, the flexible politics of autochthony and landowning privilege operated at the level of Big Men and their descendant lineages, and to the extent that clan or ethnolinguistic identity were relevant to local political situations, it was primarily in terms of negotiating productive relations as newcoming clients. These negotiations were ad hoc and had little to do with ethnolinguistic identity.

The French administration operated according to a different logic, partly because the logic of portable ethnic identities that crosscut local claims to autochthony was what they encountered in most other parts of the Guinean territory. In the Futa Jallon or the Maninka heartland, it did matter whether you were from a blacksmith clan or a noble one, and this held wherever you might settle. At the same time, the relation between speaking a language (Pulaar or Maninkakan, for instance) and being a member of a cultural/civilizational group (the French tended to use the term "race" where the English might have used "tribe") was more naturalized in most other parts of the territory. While this ideology of identity asserted homologous relations between language, ethnicity, and territory, the historical reality in many parts of the Northern Mande/Fulbe world was closer to that I have described for the forest region, with considerable intermixing and translation of identities through clan affiliation (Amselle 1990; Bazin 1985). I am arguing here that in the forest region, the ideology as well as the reality of portable identities was weak, and that this had specific political consequences in the context of encompassment by a state that operated through a system of indirect rule that required "legitimate" chiefs for each territorial unit. What would be the measure of legitimacy, and who would define it?

The colonial system of administration worked in Guinea by offering compensation through surplus extraction. Canton chiefs not only had the ability to take a share of the taxes they forcibly collected on behalf of the colonial state, they also were entitled to other perquisites, including the use of forced labor on immense farms and a share of the rice, oil, livestock, and other goods collected for the colonial administrators. Most Loma speakers' accounts of the colonial period describe colonial officials turning a blind eye to canton chiefs' (and work-gang leaders') abuses and exactions as long as they produced the desired results. This policy left individual French administrators technically blameless while the system of incentives for their African intermediaries and henchmen promoted violent extraction.

Controlling canton chieftaincies was thus a lucrative enterprise based on frank coercion. We should remember that, according to Loma elders, slave-raiding warfare in the Macenta area was ongoing until the 1906 French conquest. Powerful warlords built walled war towns that stood as autonomous mini-polities, even if few of them outlasted the lives of their leader. These polyglot towns grew both by raiding neighboring villages and towns for slaves and by welcoming those who arrived as refugees, begging protection and promising their allegiance before their villages were destroyed. The shift from warlord to canton chief was a rather smooth one in terms of local understandings of power, status, and modes of extraction. As with the precolonial competition among warlords in the region, the competition for canton chieftaincies was fierce. Such competition was enacted through a string of ever-shifting alliances among the powerful. Seeking competitive advantage through alliances with the powerful was the operative logic in the precolonial period along the forest–savanna frontier, as in other sections of the territory that became Guinea. Documents in the colonial archives in Conakry and Dakar give a sense of Guineans' understanding of the importance of controlling canton chieftaincies. Among the documents involving Guineans addressing the colonial administration, issues surrounding cantonal politics (chiefs' behavior toward their subjects, canton boundaries, legitimacy of existing chiefs, succession struggles) outnumber the documents concerning all other topics combined.[18]

In the Macenta area, Manya leaders such as Kekoura Kaman Kamara of Kwanga[19] allied themselves with the French. Perhaps they decided early on that it would be impossible to resist the Europeans' stronger firepower, but the decision was certainly also motivated by a desire to use the alliance so as to gain the upper hand over their Loma-speaking hosts and neighbors. The Samorian period (c. 1865–98) had produced mixed results for these non-Islamicized Manya chiefs. Samory recognized his ethno-linguistic links to his fellow Koniyanke/Manya living slightly to the southwest of his own natal village, but he also retained an allegiance to the Loma who were not only closely related in ethno-religious terms but also the people of his mother's family. The destabilized situation that prevailed around Macenta as Samory's empire began to falter in the 1890s gave Loma-speaking chiefs the opportunity to reassert their domination over territories that had recently been wrested away from them by Manya-speaking chiefs. Thus Kwanga was burnt to the ground several times in this period.

The French enlisted Kekoura's help, most notably in the two attacks/sieges of the neighboring Loma village of Bousseme (Guilavogui 1968). Manya traders also apparently acted as spies for the French in other southern Loma villages that continued to hold out against colonial conquest (Beavogui 1991, 377–78). Once these areas had been forcibly "pacified," the French rewarded their Manya allies with many canton chieftaincies (Kolibirama,[20] Mandugu/Ninibu, Kunukoro, Koadu/Koodu, Dulama, and Ziama/Buzie). Beavogui writes that the encompassment of Loma-speaking territories by Manya-controlled cantons "poisoned, moreover, the political atmosphere of the *cercle*, and reinforced the sentiment of the Loma that they had been reduced to the status of the Manyas' slaves, with the benediction of the Whites" (1991, 382). Beavogui's interpretation here echoes the 1925 estimation of Gamory-Dubourdeau, quoted in the epigraph to this section.

At this point something fascinating and unexpected happened. In the precolonial system of bringing symbolic and brute power into line with one another, Loma speakers would have had two choices: revolt, or grumble for a while then begin the slow process of accommodating themselves to power, and power to themselves. The latter could have taken several routes, including migrating away from this area and starting from zero as newcomers in a neighboring, Loma-speaking territory. Alternatively they could have started the several generations–long process of assimilating powerful overlords into the community through intermarriage, thus establishing good relations with the Manya rulers who might eventually be transformed into Loma autochthones.

Instead, in 1918, the entire village of Kolega, the traditional seat of the landowning lineage of Ninibu chiefdom, marched to Macenta town to meet the French *commandant de cercle*. Ninibu, a Loma-speaking precolonial chiefdom, had been annexed by the Manya-speaking chief of neighboring Mandugu chiefdom with French acquiescence. These Loma villagers protested their poor treatment at the hands of the Manya-speaking chief, and asked for the return of their own, autonomous chiefdom (Beavogui 1991, 382). The *commandant de cercle*, accepting the version presented by his interpreter (who happened to be the brother of the Manya-speaking chief), sent the villagers home and jailed their chief (382).

This typical episode in cantonal politics took another turn. The people of Ninibu allied themselves with those of a nearby chiefdom, Weybhalaga, who had an identical complaint. This time, they traveled to Conakry, bypassing the *commandant de cercle* in Macenta. The complaint was organized by one Game Guilavogui, "a [Loma-speaking] former cook who had accompanied several *commandants de poste* outside of [Guinea]" (Beavogui 1991, 383). Guilavogui, along with the chief of Ninibu, presented their problem to the lieutenant governor of Guinea and received a favorable response as well as an investigation of the colonial officer involved.[21] Beavogui (1998) has credited Guilavogui with facilitating the birth of "Loma nationalism," a term which might overstate the case. However, this is clearly a turning point in the history of the region.[22]

As a result of these protests, the French chose to adopt the logic of partition. Consequently, Kolibirama, Kunukoro, and Dulama chiefdoms were each split into a Manya half and a Loma half (1919); Mandugu and Ninibu were given separate status (Mandugu ruled by a Manya chief, Ninibu by a Loma one—1919); Koodu and Koadu were separated (1922), becoming ethnically Loma and Manya respectively. Finally, in 1925, Buzie (Manya) and Ziama (Loma) became separate cantons (Beavogui 1991, 380–90).

There are some straightforward interpretations we can draw from these events. Manya-speakers had gained a political advantage by aligning themselves with the French at the moment of colonial conquest. This was anything but an innovation. In the world of regional warfare and slave raiding, every war chief sought his own advantage through strategic alliances, and many of these were interethnic in nature. The mass of the evidence indicates that the precolonial Loma-speaking region was indeed settled, conquered, and politically organized on the basis of a historical succession of such alliances and conquests. Through the use of clan translatability, marriage alliance, power association membership, and the adjustment of shallow genealogies, conquerors assimilated into the local society and thus aligned physical and symbolic domination by becoming *zukenui* owners of the land. In many cases it appears that this process consisted of assimilating large numbers of Manya conquerors and migrants who, over time, "became" Loma autochthones.[23]

Thus, it is not the fact that the French rewarded their Manya allies after the battles of conquest that "created" ethnic difference in the Macenta area. That moment in the area's power politics was still legible through local idioms of managing domination and change. Paradoxically, it was at the moment when disgruntled Loma elders approached the colonial administrators to demand an easing of chiefly depredations that the process of Manichean distinction began. When, in 1919, the French lieutenant governor agreed to the logic of partition, the subsequent cantonal splits in Koodu/Koadu (1922) and Ziama/Buzie (1925) became inevitable. Controlling cantons had become a struggle defined by the logic of ethnolinguistic identity in a way that it had never been before. Beavogui states the case strongly:

> This partition of Buzie [canton, in 1925] closed the series of administrative reorganizations according to ethnic criteria. Up to 1945, there would be no other notable modification inciting so much passion as that from the period 1918–1925, which would contribute to the reaffirmation of the coherence of a Loma [identity] in the Macenta region. These liberation struggles [within canton politics] would in fact constitute the fundamental factor in the birth of a real Loma "nation" in Guinea. They would aid the Loma to become aware of their collective personality and to form a unified block against the Manya. (Beavogui 1991, 390)

I view the sources of ethnic distinction in this region to be more numerous and more complex than a simple struggle to control the benefits of canton chieftaincies (including the politics of religion). One should also be careful not to assign too much importance to this period, given that these struggles for partition began in 1918, and canton chieftaincies were abolished only thirty-nine years later, one year before Guinean independence. It is not so much that the politics of indirect rule "created" ethnic difference in Guinea as that it gave it a new language and logic. Beavogui presents an interpretation congruent with Gamory-Dubourdeau's—that "the Tomas, in effect, seeing us arrive as the protectors of their Malinké enemies, showed for a long time a justified mistrust given that we were surrounded by employees and interpreters from the enemy race" (1925, 328). It seems that this was an important moment in the emergence of a process that moved toward an encompassing logic of ethnicized territory. Still, I would offer a note of caution. It is clear that the French interpreted the situation in Macenta cercle in terms of competition between clearly defined ethno-linguistic blocs.[24] It is also clear that after a decade or more of interaction with the French administration, *some* Loma speakers may have come to share this view of local cantonal politics. In this regard, it is certainly significant that the spokesman for the Loma chiefs in Conakry was a Loma speaker employed by French colonial administrators.

We cannot derive from these two facts, however, the conclusion that ordinary Loma speakers in the 1906–18 early colonial period had come to see the local political situation in terms of self-evident ethnicized territory and interethnic competition. The interpretation that Loma cultural nationalism was born (ex nihilo) at this moment seems to flirt with anachronism. By referring to the "birth" of a Loma nation, Beavogui admits indirectly that such a consciousness of ethno-linguistic identity was not primordial. I would propose that we consider the possibility that both ways of seeing political-territorial competition—in terms of ethnicized territory, and in terms of conquest and the gradual realignment of identities, existed side-by-side during the c. 1920–60 period.[25]

What was unquestionably new was that ethno-linguistic identity had for the first time in this region become linked to durable, well-marked, and recorded territorial boundaries. Although I have emphasized how the identities of people moving across space were malleable, we might also frame the problem in a different way: As people moved, the space they called their own and were able to defend—their autochthonous territory—changed shape. In some cases it grew, in others it moved, in some it shrank or even disappeared. From the 1918–25 period onward, such territories acquired fixed boundaries, recorded in reports, drawn on maps, and affiliated with recorded ethno-linguistic identities.[26] Needless to say, this affected the way people thought and worked in an agricultural society.

Macenta cercle would thereafter remain fragmented on the basis of the logic of partition, in which each canton was judged to have a majority Loma or Manya population, and was thereafter recorded as "belonging" to one ethnolinguistic group or the other. While the French ushered in these effects at the level of cantonal boundary-reckoning, they simultaneously introduced cash crops. Plantation parcels required individualized fragmentation of collective farmland at the village level. Formerly negotiable territory thus began to be fixed and fragmented at two levels simultaneously in the period around 1920. At the canton level, ethnolinguistic identity had become the basis of the fragmentation. At the level of particular villages' cultivated space, fragmentation took place as a result of the crops planted (either rotating slash-and-burn upland rice or fixed tree crops), and ethnicity did not necessarily enter the equation. That would change with the advent of the socialist regime, which introduced policies that contributed to the fragmentation of territory along ethnic lines even *within* villages.

While many Loma farmers today develop modest plantations of cash crops such as coffee alongside their upland rice production, Manya-speaking planters in the Macenta area have often become more specialized. Some Manya speakers living amongst Loma speakers have developed large plantations, often paying Loma-speaking contractual workers to do some or all of the farm labor, and buying rice for their families with the proceeds of their cash crop production. Such a commoditization of agriculture is almost unheard-of among Loma-speaking farmers. The next section discusses the ways that Touré-era land tenure policies favored plantation owners, but it must be noted that it was the colonial introduction of cash crops that began the process of a two-track land tenure system within Loma villages: 1) rice cultivation on rotating plots within alienable territories whose de facto rights of use belonged to long-settled village lineages, and 2) inalienable personal ownership of fruit-bearing trees and de facto control of the ground on which they were planted.

Mise en Valeur and Ethnicity

One of the major programs in social engineering undertaken by the government of Sekou Touré's Parti Démocratique de Guinée (PDG) during the 1960s and 1970s was its attempt to eradicate relations of landownership and of production that it characterized as "feudal." This initiative resulted in far-reaching changes in land tenure laws. The Touré government first declared that all land belonged to the state, and thus to each of its citizens, and then declared that anyone who was making approved use of a piece of land acquired de facto rights to it. One scholar of shifting land tenure norms in Guinea and their social consequences has written:

> After independence the Land Nationalization Law of 20 October 1959 awarded rights over all land to the state. Private property was renounced by the Touré regime, though family and communal usufruct rights were recognized. . . . Furthermore, under the First [Touré] Republic, land and permanent use rights were granted to some who favored the ruling elite, to communal work groups, and to the state. (Fischer 1994/95, 2)

The 1959 law was reiterated and strengthened by further laws passed in 1962, 1974, and 1983.[27] These laws defined the central theory of *mise en valeur*:

> It is once again recalled that the land is the exclusive property of the Guinean State,[28] and that it cannot be definitively ceded to any person. The enjoyment, according to the provisions fixed by the Government, belongs to whoever puts it to use for rational exploitation [*met en valeur pour une exploitation rationelle*]: buildings, plantations, farms, etc. (237/PRG du 2 mai, 1983, quoted in Diallo et al. 1995, 37–38)

This rule of mise en valeur (lit. "making productive" but usually rendered in English as "land to the tiller") land tenure primarily targeted other parts of the country, where feudal relations had existed between a hereditary nobility and a class of unfree people variously called "ex-captives," "serfs," or "slaves" by the state and in the literature (Derman and Derman 1973; Suret-Canale 1969). During the colonial period, ex-captives had been granted freedom in legal but not necessarily practical terms, and their lives were little changed.[29] The socialist government aimed to radically equalize these social classes in the Fulbe and Maninka regions, and changes in land tenure laws thus gave ex-captives durable use rights over the land they farmed. To the extent that this was possible in a society that had renounced private ownership of land, the mise en valeur law was a kind of land redistribution program in much of the country.

In the forest, however, these laws allowed people who had formerly been "strangers" to claim de facto ownership of whatever land they had "borrowed" under the traditional system of land-use rights. Loma principles of autochthony emphasize that it is the first-settling lineage that enjoys special relations with the land through their maintenance of esoteric relations with the area's earth, water, and ancestral spirits. Forestiers would have been the first to agree with the socialist state that land could not be parceled, bought, and sold. They would simply have disagreed about who had the authority to decide its disposition and according to which criteria. As one research project discovered about the landowning lineage in a Forestier village just south of Macenta Préfecture, "The Nonamou [landowning lineage] cannot sell land. The fact that they don't can be explained by the relationships that exist between the living, the dead, and future generations in local land tenure conceptions" (Diallo et al. 1995, 20).

The change imposed by the state on prevailing customary land tenure practices was compounded by the state's definition of what counted as mise en valeur. As Fischer notes, it "consists of only such activities as construction, development of irrigation infrastructure, and plantation agriculture" (1994/95, 7). The swidden, mobile techniques used in Forestier upland rice cultivation thus became classified as lacking in "valeur," a point emphasized by the language in the 1983 law, in which approved practices are called "[mise] en valeur pour une exploitation rationelle." Forestier rice agriculture thus becomes classified by implication as "irrational exploitation (use)," an attitude, documented at length by Fairhead and Leach (1996),[30] that the Guinean state has directed at peasant farmers. The denigration of Loma religious lifeways carried out in the Demystification Program was thus paralleled by laws that classified their agricultural techniques as irrational and then offered such "misused" land to outsiders willing to grow cash crops or irrigated paddy rice.

Nonetheless, Loma speakers today describe a situation in which Loma-speaking newcomers continued to respect the pre-socialist rules governing land access. After all, within a generation or two, if their relationship with their adopted village continued happily, they could easily acquire de facto rights to land and would have the same ability as any autochthon to plant cash crops or anything else there. Their descendants would thus typically "become" autochthons. The process had been the same for Manya speakers and other non-Loma strangers, although it might have taken somewhat longer.

Under the socialist government, however, Manya-speaking strangers were now in a different position. While the colonial system had provided them with advantages, first rewarding them with control of land for their military cooperation and then using the logic of partition to give them unchallenged political control over those areas where they were in the majority, the socialist land tenure laws gave them a new and unexpected advantage. They could (in theory, and like anyone else) walk into any Forestier village, find a plot of unfarmed land, and start clearing it, laying claim to it by the rules of mise en valeur. Still, the social and micropolitical realities surrounding agricultural practices made such a bold move unlikely. Claude Rivière describes the typical (slower) progression in this way:

> The process of infiltration and rural colonization . . . follows a well-known schema:
> 1. Arrival of the Dioula-Malinke[31] [traders] for trade in coffee, palm nuts, cola nuts.
> 2. Seasonal [contract] farm labor by Malinke farmers, brought in by the traders and chosen from among their relatives.
> 3. Request, by these Malinke, of a farming plot from the Guerze [Kpelle] village chief, after two or three years of seasonal wage labor.
> 4. The thriving of the coffee trees quietly planted by the Malinke in the forests, and preferential purchases of this Malinke coffee by the traders [who had brought them into the region] who come through during the harvest period.
> 5. Jealousy of the former [Forestier] landowners toward these newcomers, often more powerful politically and economically than the autochthones.

In Toma villages, the Toma-Manian, that is to say those Malinke who speak Toma, infiltrated sometimes since the invasions of Samory, have ended up taking the posts of [political] command, as the Koniyanke-Malinke have done in the Guerze country. (Rivière 1971, 85–86)

Many Loma speakers described this process in the same terms: Manya-speaking men arriving, asking to use plots of land for a year to grow rice, and, within a year or two, having established a toehold, proceeding to plant coffee or other plantation crops *without permission*, using the state to back them if the dispute escalated. One author describes:

> The political option of the first [Touré] republic to consider land as the exclusive property of the state led certain [land] borrowers in Nonah and other areas to disregard the agreements specified at the time of the loan, and to plant fruit-bearing trees. The change of administrations [in 1984] and of political orientation pushed the customary owners of the usurped land to try to take them back. It is this that has been at the base of certain conflicts. (Diallo et al. 1995, 35)

While the national laws allowed anyone to plant unauthorized coffee or cocoa trees, doing so without explicit permission (and thus in contravention of the "traditional" land tenure norms) would entail a social price: the person who pursued such a course would underline his "strangerness," a risk that Loma speakers say growing numbers of Manya-speakers took during this period. This was an unprecedented move and could not have taken place outside the context of the mise en valeur laws. For the first time, Manya speakers living in mixed towns and villages could acquire durable land rights *without having to assimilate culturally to Loma society* in the ways I have described in earlier chapters. Although they continued to take Loma wives, they were under less and less pressure to acknowledge their wife-givers as political and social patrons, to become initiated into Loma power associations, or to learn to speak Lomagui. In other words, the state had minimized their incentives to "become" Loma. When the collision of the old and new systems resulted in minor conflicts, as both Loma and Manya speakers acknowledge it did, the fact that Manya speakers had "ended up taking the posts of [political] command" as Rivière noted (1971, 86), meant that they usually prevailed.[32]

The mise en valeur laws have had a variety of effects on local politics. As one Loma schoolteacher told me, Loma speakers have often ceded their towns and villages voluntarily, preferring autonomy and isolation over the possibility of cultural domination:

A Loma man will found a small village. If it is successful, it will grow, and after some time, a Manya trader will come there. Later, he will bring his family, and maybe another trader or two will arrive. Before long, they will not be satisfied to pray in their houses, and they will insist on building a mosque. The first week they start calling out the call to prayer from the mosque, the old [Loma] men will pack up their things and move out to their family hamlets in the bush. Over the years, some of these hamlets will also become small villages, and eventually, a Manya trader will move there, and the process begins again. (K.B., January 9, 1997)

The process has also made the Forestier reception of refugees somewhat less welcoming than it might have been. Diallo notes one Forestier village's list of rules for the reception of refugees. The villagers, undoubtedly remembering their loans of land to Manya speakers with the state as mediator, imposed strict rules on the borrowing of land:

The land we have given you [to house the refugees]—after that portion, anyone who wants to make a farm or do another kind of work must inform the president of the district before he does any work. Because that land has owners. If the owner-of-the-land accepts, we will give the parcel to the interested party so he can work. (Diallo et al. 1995, 46)

The main outcome of the mise en valeur policy was that the resulting conflicts over landownership became a flashpoint for interethnic tensions in Macenta Préfecture. When the Conté government changed the law and restored the rights of customary landowners,[33] these usually Loma-speaking landowners sought to take land back.

In interethnic disputes, there may no longer be a shared language for such settlements. The Manya speakers using land have, after all, often been there for twenty to forty years. The land may thus have been inherited several times, or even sold with a deed from the original land borrower/planter to a third party. Manya confronted with the claim that the land from which they make their living was taken by illegitimate means tend to claim no knowledge of the original transaction, and given the frequent lack of documentation, they claim their customary right is as great as the putative landowner's. Such a dispute resulted in a January 2000 clash in the Koniseredou Souspréfecture of Macenta. There, a land dispute over territory at the limit between a mostly Loma-speaking and a mostly Manya-speaking village grew until the Manya speakers killed six Loma speakers, and the Loma speakers responded by killing thirty-four Manya speakers.

In the aftermath of this clash, one newspaper report quoted a Manya-speaking man:

> "It's this problem of land that is the cause of our conflicts, and not a religious problem, as certain people like to claim," confides Mamadi Kourouma, a young man. "The Toma consider themselves the owners of all the land in Macenta [Préfecture], because they were the first to settle here. They never respect the [territorial] limits between us. That is what provokes these palavers all the time, here and there throughout the prefecture." (Gamalo 2001)

This man has captured perfectly the rhetoric of ethnicized territory. From a presentist point of view, individuals had come to achieve quasi-ownership of land through the Touré-era principle of mise en valeur or through post-socialist land purchases. From the "traditional" Loma perspective, the land in an area will always belong to its first settlers, who can revoke land-use rights at will, though this would not normally happen once a lineage or individual had farmed an area for an extended period.

The terms in which this man has phrased the problem, however, lie somewhere in between these two principles of land tenure. He says, "The Toma consider themselves the owners of all the land in Macenta, because they were the first to settle here. They never respect the [territorial] limits between us." The definition of land tenure in terms of ethnic identity is an artifact of the colonial policies of partitioning cantons according to majority population. In the precolonial system, first settler (or indeed conqueror transformed into "first settler") status passed from one important man to his patrilineal descendants. The ethnicity of the members of the lineage was irrelevant and could change over time. More obviously, the territorial unit of Macenta Préfecture is a twentieth-century introduction, created by the colonial and adopted by the postcolonial governments. The precolonial territorial units—chiefdoms (*zuti*) and confederations (*kɔkɔlɔgiti*)—were bisected by the arbitrary colonial frontier and simultaneously conglomerated into the territorial units of Macenta Préfecture and Lofa County, Liberia.

Not only were the notions that land tenure has to do with ethnicity ("The Toma consider themselves the owners of all the land") or with units as large as a préfecture ("all the land in Macenta") twentieth-century innovations, the idea that these two variables would be interlinked was an even more recent introduction. With the colonial-era partition of cantons according to ethno-linguistic identity came the first step in moving away from the micropolitical negotiation that brought effective domination into line with legitimating symbolic categories and their statuses (*zukenui*). By 2000, the Manya-speaking man I have quoted correctly points to an extension of this logic: by that point, people were talking about préfecture-wide rights accruing to one ethnicity, as opposed to more specific village- or chiefdom-wide rights. This development resulted from the rise of ethnicized politics in Guinea in the 1990s. The dream of a return to an originary (and it must be said, fictitious) purity of identity had arrived in Macenta.

Many of these developments, including the Koniseredou massacres and several others like them, took place during the period of my fieldwork in Macenta Préfecture. As a researcher, I was left with a nagging question. I was gathering an increasing number of descriptions by Loma speakers of Manya speakers being until quite recently bilingual (in Maninkakan and Lomagui), non-Muslim, and initiated into the Loma men's Poro power association or a close equivalent. Manya speakers tended to dodge any discussion of these issues, saying they didn't know anything about such things. Just as I had given up hope of any corroboration from the Manya side of the recent history of Manya conversion, I met Mamadi Traoré. Or perhaps I should say Mamadi Guilavogui.

Mamadi's Story

> After the *fétiches* were consigned to the funeral pyre, a rash of conversions to Islam took place, around 1961, starting first with the Toma-manian [Manya], then touching the pure Toma [Loma]. Among the Guerzé [Kpelle] and the Kissi, Christianity progressed at the same pace. (Rivière 1971, 307)

I have argued at length against the oil-and-water thesis that assumes language-ethnicity-religion have remained congruent over time. In this chapter, we have seen some of the factors contributing to the hardening of ethno-linguistic identities. Here, I want to focus on the way these elements converged in Macenta Préfecture and underline their material as well as cultural-political context. The types of zig-zagging I have described among ethnic, linguistic, and religious identities in the nineteenth century were very much in evidence in twentieth-century Macenta as well. Not only did Manya speakers "become" Loma, but the transformations worked in the opposite direction as well.

During my research in the mixed town of Pelema, I began to hear a story from some Loma speakers, uttered in the same resentful tone I had heard in Giziwulu's more ethnically homogenous setting but carrying a different bundle of implications: "They say they are Manya, but they're really

Loma, just like us." Even more surprisingly, several people claimed, "All these 'Manya' in town? If they're in their fifties or older, they were initiated in the same sacred forest as us. Now, they're great Muslims. If you greet them in Lomagui, they pretend not even to understand you."

This fit together with some of my own suspicions, particularly in the context of accounts I had heard of twinned Loma and Manya sacred power association groves in the nearby town of Kwanga (Sivilisu). However, it moved the date of Islamization for some of the Muslim Manya in the area much further forward than I had understood on the basis of their own (and most Loma speakers') accounts. In effect, some Loma speakers in Pelema were telling me that in the 1950s, many people who were now unambiguously Muslims and Manya were still in the ambiguous category the French had called "Malinkés fétichistes." Were most Manya speakers in mixed towns still "fétichiste" in the 1950s?[34] Why did they deny the fact only forty years later?

In Pelema, I had conducted life-history interviews with the village's women before the men. During this period, I often saw an elderly woman named Fatoumata, about eighty years old, who had a Manya clan name, was a Muslim, and clearly considered herself ethnically Manya. However, she spoke fluent Lomagui, and we always spoke to each other in that language. When I began doing life-history interviews with the village's men, I met her son. His name was Mamadi, and he later explained to me the fact that his family (on both his mother's and father's sides) were among those Loma who had converted to Islam during the colonial period and as a consequence of their conversion had "become" Manya. His mother had been born and raised Loma, but now was Manya. Unlike many of Pelema's Manya-speaking inhabitants, Fatoumata did not appear to feel any embarrassment at her hybrid background.

Mamadi's own life had followed a series of fascinating twists and turns. Born in 1940, he began school in 1950. In 1957, he had finished seventh grade and took a nationwide test for a spot in the *école des enfants de troupe* (military school) in Bingerville, Côte d'Ivoire. He was one of fifteen children selected and the only one from the forest region. He received his uniform and had made all his arrangements to travel to Côte d'Ivoire in 1958 when Guinea chose independence from France and the scholarship was revoked. At this time, Mamadi was in a quandary. His father was a member of the BAG (Bloc Africain de Guinée) that had opposed the vote for independence. Now that the Parti Démocratique de Guinée had won the vote and taken control of the newly independent government, a series of reprisals began against BAG supporters and their families, and Mamadi lost his opportunity to continue his education. Instead, he took a six-month course in shorthand, soon becoming the secretary to the préfet of Macenta. In 1962, he was recruited into the army, became a parachutist, and had training in both Germany and Egypt. Returning to Guinea, he served in the army first in Labe, in 1964 becoming the secretary of Colonel Kaman Diaby and acting as liaison between the colonel and Fodéba Keita, Minister of the Interior.[35] He later moved from the military to the civil service and was a high-level administrative assistant for the next twenty years.

During this time, he started several plantations back in Pelema. He described these plantations as being for his father, but as he was his father's only son it was understood that they would revert to him upon his father's death. He planted coffee, cocoa, and cola trees, and in the year I interviewed him had a yield of four long sacks of coffee and six of cocoa. At that time he was planning to plant four more hectares of bananas. These were sizeable plantations by Guinean forest region standards,[36] all the more so in Pelema, where the state had declared much of the land to be protected forest. They allowed him a modest but comfortable retirement. We never discussed any difficulties he might have had in obtaining legal rights to the land for his plantations, but presumably his literacy and his connections to the PDG had facilitated this process.

These aspects of Mamadi's history were fairly typical of mid-level functionaries from the postcolonial era. Rather than retiring to a villa he had built in Conakry, as many upper-level functionaries did, he had planned to retire to his natal village, and preparing plantations was one of the most sensible strategies (along with educating his children well so they could look after him) available to achieve this goal. From another angle, his trajectory was a classically Manya one. He had never grown rice but instead had gained access to land and planted cocoa, cola, and coffee—a "rational" mise en valeur that guaranteed his continuing access to the land. Over the years he had paid day-laborers to do the work of clearing the brush in the plantations and harvesting the fruits. When he sold the yield, he was able to buy rice and other foodstuffs for the household.

In this equation, it would seem clear where Mamadi stood. A Muslim, a Manya speaker, a cosmopolitan who had traveled widely inside and outside Guinea, and a plantation owner who did not cultivate rice, he was a classic Manya "type." The only catch was that he was Loma by origin. Mamadi mentioned his family's origins in the middle of our first conversation, almost as an aside. He indicated an area about one kilometer from the center of the present village and said it had been marked by seven baobab (*guei*) trees, one of which was still standing. His family, of the Guilavogui clan, was one of the lineages that had settled the small original hamlet before the contemporary town (founded by the French) had brought people together from several places.

Mamadi's grandfather had been the one to convert, he said, and in doing so, changed his name from Galakpaye Guilavogui to Mamadi Traoré. He was a blacksmith, and, as his namesake, Mamadi the grandson still had his blacksmith tools. Galakpaye's son had learned to be a mason and worked for both the colonial and the socialist regimes. Mamadi considered himself to be Manya, and after checking to be sure that no one was listening in on our conversation, he said that most of the long-settled Manya families in Pelema had similar histories of conversion and consequent ethnolinguistic shifts. Others had come more recently from places such as Kwanga, and he declined to comment on their backgrounds. During this first conversation, Mamadi acted as if his family's history were typical. The next time we spoke, cross-border attacks from Liberia into Guinea had started, targeting mostly Manya-speaking villages. That time around, he no longer wanted to discuss the topic of ethnicity.

Some of the material policies of the PDG government, such as changes in land tenure law, were based upon a socialist philosophy of equality. Perhaps the most important of the consequences (largely unintended) of the policies of the socialist government was the fact that it took away both the political and cultural incentives for Manya-speaking men to conform to the cultural norms of their adopted communities. In the realm of livelihoods, this hardened yet another formerly fluid distinction. Loma speakers were farmers, not traders, and Manya speakers living in the forest were traders and/or planters. This distinction allowed both groups to silence the memory that in the recent past, even if Manya-speaking men came initially as warriors or traders, within a few generations many of their descendants had probably been assimilated as Loma-speaking rice farmers.

In this chapter, I have tried to show the ways that ethnic identity, agrarian sociology, and political economy are intertwined. Such an analysis has been central to Africanist anthropology and history, in East (e.g., Galaty 1982; Kratz 1986, 1994; Southall 1970), Central (e.g., Prunier 1995; Taylor 1999), Southern (e.g., Vail 1991), and West Africa (e.g., Amselle and M'Bokolo 1985). Each one helps to determine the ways the others play out. Combined with the politics of religion and portable identities described in the next chapter, they combine to harden ethnolinguistic identities. These processes preceded French colonial rule but were also shaped by it, especially in the benefits attached to canton chieftaincy and the competition for those spots that ensued. The process continued to change and evolve after the colonial period as well. History, however, rarely moves along an even continuum, but in fits and starts. Almost immediately after independence, the PDG government undertook an attempt to "demystify" the entire Guinean nation from backward forms of religious practice. The program focused on the forest region more than anywhere else, and as a result it galvanized emergent processes of differentiation between groups: "Toma" from "Malinké," "fétichiste" from monotheist, traditional from modern, mystified from demystified. This process was informed by the history of conversion to world religions, and also by the ways that history was and is told by the different groups that came to share the Guinean polity.

FIVE

Portable Identities and the Politics of Religion along the Forest–Savanna Border

This chapter addresses the ways that Loma speakers and Manya speakers talk—or do not talk—about their histories and cultures. As such it provides a fulcrum for the book. The first four chapters laid out the key elements of cultural and political identity in this region and how they changed shape and configuration in interaction with colonial and postcolonial state policies. The last four chapters will focus on those policies, in particular the policy of Demystification. This chapter is a fulcrum because it makes explicit an element of the argument that runs throughout the book. It shows how cultural policies in Guinea were *products of* the sociological and micropolitical processes I have described. At the same time, agents of the state often treated those processes—classified as custom or tradition—as raw material to be shaped and transformed by modernist bureaucrats.

By emphasizing these dynamic and contentious micropolitical dynamics, I aim to show why allegedly inert custom was capable of provoking such strong reactions and passionate interventions during the first years of Guinean independence. I describe historical rhetoric, the sociology of telling history or maintaining secrecy, and the justifications sometimes given for iconoclastic movements that preceded Demystification. Each helps to explain both the "itch" that Forestier fétichisme represented and the particular forms that anti-fétichiste "scratching" took in Guinea in the early 1960s.

In creating a picture of the cultural crossroads that became Macenta Préfecture, I have discussed various aspects of the Loma socio-political scene. We should keep in mind, however, that separating such idioms as personhood, clanship, ethnicity, autochthony, and *kɛkɛ–daabe* relations from one another is only a heuristic device. Examining the mechanism of a watch, piece by piece, we may gain insight into how it works, but we understand that each piece is useless unless it is working in synchrony with the others. Similarly, in the second part of the book, entitled "Revealing and Reshaping the Body Politic," we will look at the ways the pieces presented in the first half work together, against, and alongside one another.

Each of the social idioms so far presented has shown itself to be paradoxical. Concepts such as autochthony have been both fundamental to establishing hierarchy, legitimacy, and effective power, and at the same time were achieved and constructed, which is not what they claimed to be. My argument has been that one reason for this state of affairs is that, in the context of longstanding warfare and insecurity, this has been a strategy for accommodating the radical upheavals accompanying warfare and for meeting the need for recreating society anew during peacetime.[1] Thus autochthony might really only be "autochthony," a working fiction established by those powerful enough to propose it and accepted by everyone else as long as the ancestors and earth spirits seemed to assent. For what else could people do? Gathered together with other refugees, their villages razed, some relatives killed in battle, others taken as slaves, they nevertheless had to grow rice, raise children, bury the dead. This is the process I have called "living with violence, binding insecurity" in chapter 2.

By placing some of the significant social principles of Loma life in historical context, we see how fluid they had to be in their application, but I have tried to show that they were not completely up for grabs, to be imposed or chosen willy-nilly. My interpretation of translatable clan identities, autochthonous status, and *kekɛ–daabe* relations is that they were intermediary social idioms that allowed the conquered to assert their own conditions on their conquerors once peace broke out. In return the conquered granted legitimacy and remained as part of the conquerors' wealth-in-people (for without wealth-in-people, no warlord could become a peacetime Big Man). Although this model brings historical dynamism and various forms of change into the analysis, it is an ideal typical explanation, a clarifying synthesis imposed by me on unruly lived realities. Like any other systematic description it has its fixities and blind spots.

It is to the greatest of those blind spots that we now turn, for the most significant development in the political life of the Macenta area since the independence era has been the rejection by the majority of Manya speakers of this system of "binding insecurity." Manya speakers, often more economically powerful than their Loma-speaking hosts, have increasingly sought political influence while rejecting the route of assimilation toward

Loma ethnicity and autochthony. This rejection is both cause and effect of the process of identity formation that spawned the Demystification Program, and its explanation necessitates the introduction of the colonial and postcolonial state into the analysis.

The state is as much a discursive effect—the distinction between society and state, or between local "insides" and an encompassing national "outside"—as it is a set of institutions or human agents (Mitchell 1991). The development of the Guinean state as a discursive effect was closely linked to a set of contested ideas about identity and modernity that implicated the realms of religion, history, landownership, gender, generation, and ethnicity. The mobilization of some of these categories could be the unintended consequence of state policies with other ends. Such was the case with the socialist introduction of mise en valeur land tenure laws and the effect they had of hardening ethnic identities. At other times, the policies appear to have grown out of the conscious attempt to create modern national subjects. This was the case with the Demystification Program.

Many of these topics connect in one way or another with concerns about religion. This is a sensitive topic that caused anxiety among Guinean modernists such as Sékou Touré. This chapter begins by discussing some of the sociocultural differences between Northern and Southwestern Mande societies that have nothing to do with religion. It then addresses the question of ethnogenesis. To do so, I look at some differences in practice and discourse among Manya speakers, whom I call "peripheral Northern Mande speakers." These Mandekan speakers converted over the course of the twentieth century to Islam, and they were those the French colonial administrators referred to as "Malinkés Fétichistes" in chapter 2. They worked hard during the twentieth century to "trade up" their identities toward the prestigious legacy of empire and monotheism claimed by the descendants of the Mali empire.

The chapter then introduces the topic of religious identity and sketches its connection to the politics and history of ethnicity in the Macenta region as well as the wider forest region. By sketching some of the history of Islamic-political movements in the region, we set the stage for understanding how religion interacted in a synergistic way with both ethnic and national identities in twentieth-century Guinea. Appeals to religion were an essential aspect of Manya speakers' refusal of Forestier modes of negotiating domination and legitimacy. At the same time, the refusal itself became part of a national dramaturgy of self-making of which the Demystification Program was only the most dramatic instance.

Portable Identities

I have argued that Northern and Southwestern Mande societies are far more similar than different. However, neither group in Guinea sees it that way. There are significant differences between the groups, the first being demographic. While Manya speakers as a subgroup of the wider "Malinke" umbrella ethnonym are less numerous than Loma speakers, when all speakers of Mandekan are grouped together, they make up some 30–35 percent of the Guinean population, while the Loma are only 3–4 percent. Even the wider group of mostly Southwestern Mande-speaking Forestiers make up only 10 percent or so of the national population. Consequently, Loma speakers and other Forestiers are a minority group in the Guinean national sphere, while Manya speakers are part of one of the two major ethnolinguistic blocs (Fulbe and Malinke) that together make up almost three quarters of the Guinean population.

A second important difference is that Northern Mande speakers have a history of centralized political states stretching back to the great medieval empires of Ghana and Mali. The latter, which flourished from the thirteenth to the sixteenth centuries, brought the Northern Mande of the region that now straddles the Republics of Mali and Guinea into contact with the Arabo-Islamic culture that accompanied the conversion of many Northern Mande elites to Islam. In the broad terms proposed by Fortes and Evans-Pritchard (1940), Northern Mande societies were members of "Group A," the state societies, while Southwestern Mande societies were part of "Group B," the stateless societies. As Horton (1976) argued, Fortes and Evans-Pritchard's assertion that stateless societies were organized around competition between segmentary lineages had to be further nuanced in order for it to account for the realities of various West African political systems. Horton proposed three types of "Stateless Societies in the History of West Africa," of which Loma speakers most closely resemble his "Type 3" society; multi-ethnic polities organized around fortified towns, in which the kinship basis of political power is crosscut by secret societies and the principal distinction becomes one of powerful landowners to relatively powerless newcomers. Horton's own model has been further refined by Murphy and Bledsoe (1987), taking into account the importance of matrilateral kinship ($k\epsilon k\epsilon$–$daabe$ relations, in the Loma setting) and of the "semantics of territory" that relate practices of burial and sacrifice to claims about autochthony and precedence.

Just as the typologization of the Loma political system requires a number of caveats, we should not simply class the Malinke as a "state society."

For in the period between 1500 and 1800, the Northern Mande region was more of an "imploded state society," and as I have argued in the first half of the book, the similarities between Northern and Southwestern Mande societies during this period seem to have far outweighed their differences. Nevertheless, the memory of states and early adherence (at least by a minority) to Islam became important symbolic resources for people of Northern Mande origins in their struggle to capture the postcolonial state, as Paulla Ebron has argued for the parallel case of the Gambia. She writes:

> [Gambia's Oral History and Antiquities Division] has "recovered" the history of Mande kingdoms, the heritage of the Mandinka, as deserving of the same respect as the European heritage of exploration and rule. It is history. And in this context, Mandinka culture takes on the authority of civilization, not the limitation of ethnic culture and custom. Its political heritage is expansive and developing, and it can thus inspire national politics, education and scholarship. . . . [N]ational history is a single story in which Mande kings prefigure later rulers and offer an origin to the independent nation. (Ebron 2002, 90–91)

In the context of attempts to capture the postcolonial state, the prestige of affiliation with precolonial empire was a potent resource (in Guinea as in the Gambia). Yet if we look hard at the underlying cultural basis of this logic, we are forced back upon questions about personhood, causality, and destiny. For what is it about the history of long-defunct empires that would confer special status on people who happened to speak the same language six hundred years later?[2] Loma speakers have relatively little sense of inherited identity, while Northern Mande speakers like the Malinke and Bamana typically have a strong sense of the interplay between inheritance and individual becoming, expressed as the interplay between the *tere*, or inborn destiny, and the *dya*, or shadow self (Dieterlen 1947, 28). While Loma speakers have a well-developed sense of the shadow self (*maavisigi*), I never found any evidence of a notion of what Fortes described as "prenatal destiny" (1959, 36) that would parallel the Northern Mande *tere*.[3]

When we pose the question of what is different between Loma- and Manya-speaking societies in the context of postcolonial state politics, we may thus be better served by asking questions about differences in notions of personhood, destiny, and identity than about typologized political systems, even though it is precisely the difference in political systems to which actors themselves make repeated reference in their (postcolonial) political rhetoric. This became a significant fact in the context of postcolonial politics in which individuals argued for their fitness to rule the Guinean nation both in terms of their personal qualities and in terms of the qualities of their lineages, clans, and ethnic groups. Northern Mande speakers have a well-developed theory of the relations between the group and the individual, inheritance and ambition, to which we now turn.

In their article on the Mande hero, Charles Bird and Martha Kendall (1980) examine the interrelations of the terms *fadenya* and *badenya* both in twentieth-century Mande culture and in the epic of Sundiata Keita, thirteenth-century emperor of the Mande empire (Niane 1965). The greatest Mande culture hero, Sundiata followed the trajectory of leaving home to pursue his fortune and then returning to revitalize his society. As Bird and Kendall write, "The hero, we will argue, is someone with special powers used to work against the stabilizing and conservative forces of his society; he is someone who, pursuing his own destiny, affects the destinies of others. He is the agent of disequilibrium" (1980, 13).[4] *Fadenya* (lit. "father-childness") particularly signifies a set of durable capacities, powers, and dispositions that a child inherits from his father. They refer to the means inherited from the father's line as "reputation" (1980, 14) and "birthright" (16). McNaughton goes further, calling it "inheritance" and "destiny" (1988, 14).[5]

Northern Mande speakers' memory of illustrious ancestors goes back hundreds of years and is consecrated by professional genealogist praise singers called *jelilu*. The histories recounted by *jelilu* are one of the primary ways that Northern Mande-speaking people talk to and about each other, simultaneously describing and evaluating present-day activities by reference to epics such as that of Sundiata. Anthropologist Barbara Hoffman writes:

> An essential component of [Northern] Mande discourse strategies is familiarity with and acknowledgment of [Northern] Mande history. Elements of that history are frequently foregrounded in social interactions: the simple act of greeting someone can be a reminder of that person's social history, for the end of a formal greeting is marked by the terse compliment of calling a person by the patronym, which can be understood as an abbreviation of longer histories consisting of the names of famous persons and places of the clan's social history. (2000, 21)

One manifestation of these inherited relations is the institution of *sanankuya*, or joking relations. Northern Mande speakers from villages hundreds of miles away who have never met can fall easily into the stylized forms of abuse determined by the joking relations between two totemic clans of which they are members. In Loma-speaking villages and chiefdoms, clans do stand in a hierarchical relation within a village or chiefdom. However, this relation has to do with the accepted order of arrival in the area and with the status that some lineages within clans acquire as landowners or as newcomers. The Loma ideology of identity links such hierarchies to territory and is not portable, as *sanankuya* relations are. Koivoguis may be superior to Guilavoguis in village X and subordinate to them in village Y, depending on the order of arrival, marriage alliances, and the general micropolitical setting.[6] This makes land tenure and marriage alliance (each articulated through the logic of autochthony) the effective idioms for defining hierarchy and sociality in Loma social relations.

During the period c. 1500–1900, Southwestern Mande-speaking peoples formed multi-ethnic confederations that provided a competitive advantage over neighboring (also multi-ethnic) confederations in the context of the slave raiding/warlord political economy that then prevailed (d'Azevedo 1962). They cultivated mutable identities so as to facilitate renegotiation of relations with powerful actors. This fluid set of claims surrounding autochthony could be instrumental in carving out small islands of autonomy in the face of encroaching states, but it was also inherently unstable, and a dominant Big Man or warlord could easily find himself dispossessed (and probably killed) within a few years of rising to prominence. This instability contributed to a situation that Fischer and Himmelheber described for the neighboring Dan:

> In this society, the individual was constantly threatened . . . if he was not in some way indispensable. A good-for-nothing, at the mercy of his chief, might be sold as a slave. . . . These threatening circumstances caused a drive for individual prominence within the community, as perfection in performance was one means of ensuring one's safety. The resultant emphasis on personal value has found expression in the specialization of all types of activity. As the Dan say, "It is not what you do that matters, but that you do it better than any other. Be the best blacksmith, or drummer, or carver, or dancer of a certain type of mask, or seducer of women, or even thief!" (1984, 4–5)

While this passage is intended by the authors to explain the brilliance of Dan art, it makes an interesting general point. The kind of individual striving through which Mande speakers seek to acquire the knowledge and *sale* that will help them become exceptional persons resembles Euro-American individual striving in many ways. However, as Fischer and Himmelheber point out, in the forest–savanna frontier region, the political-economic context was entirely different, and the development of exceptional skills and knowledge was essential to survival in a way contemporary North Americans might be hard-pressed to even imagine.

One example of the social differences between Northern and Southwestern Mande ideologies of identity exists in attitudes toward witchcraft. The category of sorcery is one that highlights the distinction I have made in the figure above. Patrick McNaughton's analysis of Mande blacksmiths pays close attention to the Komo society, controlled by blacksmiths and entrusted with the identification of sorcerers. The description he gives of "Mande" (by which he means *Northern* Mande) sorcery specifies:

> When the Mande contemplate malicious sorcery they distinguish two basic types of sorcerers, although the distinguishing characteristics are often blended in individuals. . . . The first type are called "sorcerers who eat people" *mogodun subagaw* or *mogo domu subagaw*. Such persons are said to be born with voracious appetites for human flesh. . . . Sorcerers of the second type do not devour people. Nor are they necessarily born into their avocations. Often they are capable of transforming themselves into other animals or entities, but their greatest sources of power are their mastery of the "science of the trees" and the extent of their repertoire of *daliluw*. (1988, 48)

The important distinction McNaughton makes here between inherited (often unconscious) and sought-after capacities is roughly equivalent to the distinction usually made in the anthropological literature between witchcraft and sorcery (Evans-Pritchard 1937; Middleton and Winter 1963). Over more than two years of fieldwork, I tried to locate a parallel distinction among Loma speakers, but with little success. The notion of witchcraft as an inherited predilection independent of the witch's will (and often his or her knowledge) was only weakly relevant to Loma speakers' conceptions of esoteric attack. While Loma speakers identify certain powerful people as "eaters" of children, this is an entirely voluntary, conscious behavior enacted with the kinds of acquired esoteric knowledge that McNaughton attributes to the second class of sorcerers. For Loma speakers, *matalai* (sorcery) is an egoistic act that destroys defenseless persons (children) so as to appropriate their life force.[7]

Significantly, the Northern Mande system that McNaughton describes involves the interplay of two dynamics: one that is inherited and beyond the actor's control, and the other voluntaristic. Other aspects of Northern Mande social organization, such as noble (*horon*), artisan (*nyamakala*), or slave (*jon*) status, joking relations between members of clans (*sanankuya*), and the putatively fixed genealogies of each person, are all portable identities that locate the Northern Mande person in relation to others. Against these fixed qualities, which Bird and Kendall call "inheritance," there is the striving to overcome one's destiny, by which Northern Mande people seek to surpass their inheritance.[8]

In recent literature on Northern Mande societies, there has been considerable discussion of the extent to which inherited statuses themselves are mutable (e.g., Conrad and Frank 1995; Hoffman 2000). For the present discussion, the point is that *in principle* they are inherited, portable identities and relations to other people. Among Southwestern Mande speakers like the Loma, such inheritable, portable statuses either do not exist or are much weaker. The witch's decision to destroy another person's life for his or her own benefit can never be a fait accompli in Loma society. Such capacities are acquired and are the result of big persons' desires for power and greatness (see Ferme 2001, 159–87, on Mende "big persons"). Both because those powerful enough to kill others are usually elders, and because their targets are often either young people or the babies and children of young parents, the dynamics of Loma sorcery resemble broader intergenerational tensions within this gerontocratic society (McGovern 2011; Richards 1996).

In trying to understand the ways that history and identity have been brought to bear on national politics in the postcolonial period, it may help to delineate a set of ideal-typical distinctions between Northern and Southwestern Mande cultural emphases. Here, the main question we should pose is, "to what extent is your destiny determined by the characteristics and deeds of your ancestors?" The answer, for Loma speakers, is very little. Like other Southwestern Mande speakers, Loma speakers have shallow genealogies as opposed to Northern Mande speakers' long genealogies. While there are great barriers to status mobility for Northern Mande speakers (for instance for a person of slave descent or blacksmith origins who wants to marry a person of noble background), there are few such barriers for Loma speakers. A Loma-speaking person inherits a totemic clan taboo, membership in a patrilineage, some degree of autochthonous rights in a particular place, and little else. The emphasis is strongly on becoming, while for Northern Mande speakers there is a dialectical relation between inheritance and becoming. A person named Doumbouya will be recognizable as coming from a blacksmith clan just as a person named Kouyaté will be recognizable as coming from a jeli clan anywhere from Guinea, to Côte d'Ivoire, to Mali, and on to Burkina Faso. No such information can be gleaned from the family name or other inherited mark carried by a Southwest Mande native speaker.

Having presented a stylized distinction between these two cultural orientations, I want to immediately qualify it and propose a more nuanced model that will bring us back to political competition in Macenta Préfecture in the context of the postcolonial state. Between the two (Northern and Southwestern Mande) cultural ecumenes, we may locate an interstitial transition zone where *jeliya* is present but practiced less, inheritance of occupational status such as midwife, healer, or blacksmith is an ideal but is detached from the strict rules of *nyamakala*,[9] and ethno-linguistic identity is relatively fluid. This is, in many respects, the picture Yves Person paints of the nineteenth-century Konian highlands the home of Samory Touré, the Koniyanke/Manya empire builder, and the place from which Loma and Kpelle speakers claim to have migrated some five hundred years ago. This zone, inhabited by the "peripheral Northern Mande" (Kuranko, Kono, Koniyanke, Manya, Mandingo, Jula), is on the northern side of the forest-savannah frontier. Its importance is sizeable, as Person (1968) went to great lengths to emphasize.[10] The dynamics I describe in the rest of this chapter have an underlying connection: from the Samorian period (c. 1870–98) onward, the people of this intermediate zone have struggled—first against, and later to lay claim to—the civilization and prestige of the "core" Northern Mande zone, ultimately turning three zones into two.

Table 6. Forest–savanna ethnogenesis

(pre-c.1870)	(c. 1870–1960s)	(1960s–)
"Core" N. Mande (Maninka/Bamana) >	"Core" N. Mande (Maninka/Bamana) >	
		Homogenized N. Mande (Maninka/Bamana Manya/Koniyanke/Kuranko)
↑↓↑↓↑↓	↑↑↑↑↑↑	
"Peripheral" N. Mande (Manya/Koniyanke/ Kuranko) >	"Peripheral" N. Mande (Manya/Koniyanke/ Kuranko) >	
↑↓↑↓↑↓	↑↓↑↓↑↓	
SW Mande (Loma/Kpelle/Loko Bandi/Mende)	SW Mande (Loma/Kpelle/Loko/ Bandi/Mende)	SW Mande (Loma/Kpelle/Loko/ Bandi/Mende)

Person (1968) describes the period of Samory's empire-building as a "*Dyula* revolution." During this period, relations shifted between the minority of Muslim *dyula* (traders) in the Koniyan highlands and their hosts, whom Person describes in the same terms as I have described the "Malinkés fétichistes" in chapter 2 (i.e., linguistically similar to the "core" Northern Mande, culturally similar to speakers of Southwestern Mande languages like Lomagui). The dyula, who had actively discouraged their hosts from converting to Islam or taking up long-distance trade, had been content to seek economic gain but eschew political influence. With Samory, however, they decided to wrest political control away from their hosts, partly in response to the insecurity caused by persistent internecine slave-raiding, which also disrupted long-distance trade. During Samory's rise to power, Islam became an increasingly strong justification of his fitness to rule, a rhetoric he probably borrowed from the Fulbe jihadists whose holy wars preceded his conquests by five to fifty years. I describe the careers of both the Fulbe jihadist Umar Tal and Samory Touré later in this chapter.

From this period onward, the lines between "savage" and "civilized" populations were drawn in the forest–savanna frontier region. Samory built one of the largest empires ever known to West Africa, forcibly converted thousands, built mosques, and established a network of Islamic schools in his territory. Those who wished to lay claim to the mantle of civilization (and to escape the possibility of being sold by him as slaves) were compelled to convert to Islam, and they looked more toward the north, and such centers of Islamic learning as Kankan, than to the south, and the Southwest Mande-speaking people with whom they had lived and intermarried for centuries. Samory, himself a pure product of this fluid frontier society,[11] set into motion the process that ultimately banished the interstitial third category of people who spoke Northern Mande languages but whose lives were culturally indistinguishable from those of their Southwestern Mande-speaking neighbors to the south. Koniyanke, Manya, and Kuranko people living on the southern periphery of the Northern Mande-speaking world were forced to choose between the two ideal types I initially described.

Stephen Ellis has described the ways these dynamics play themselves out in contemporary Liberia, where the same people I call Manya in this book are called Mandingos:

> Most histories written by Mandingo themselves, or told by them to others, describe the Mandingo as a section of the Malinke people, descendants of the ruling elite of medieval Mali, the great empire of the savannah whose

existence had such an influence on the history of West Africa until its decline in the sixteenth century. . . . But other Liberians sometimes give a different account of who the Mandingo are and where they come from. While there were certainly some powerful Mandingo chieftaincies in northern Liberia in the early nineteenth century, some people from Lofa County today suggest that part of the Mandingo who live in Liberia are in fact the descendants of forest-dwellers who were enslaved by the Malinke, the true aristocrats of the savannah, and who have, as a result of renouncing their original [autochthonous] birthright, lost their rights to regard the forest as their homeland. . . . The attitude in this matter of the core group of Malinke, whose heartland is in the modern [R]epublic of Guinea, is telling. The Malinke of Guinea enjoy considerable prestige throughout West Africa due to their descent from the ruling group of the medieval kingdom of Mali, but they themselves generally regard their Liberian offshoot with some disdain, referring to some of them as Konyanké, or 'people of the forest,' who have a long history of interaction with the forest peoples. (1999, 38–39)

As Ellis points out, these fine points of history and identity are not trivial to those involved. They are at the center of struggles that have led to large-scale massacres in Guinea's forest region and in Liberia's Lofa and Nimba Counties. They have been even more central to the history of Guinea in the postcolonial period than to Liberia, for reasons I describe later in this chapter. Ellis describes Maninka[12] people's disdain for peripheral Northern Mande like the Mandingo-Manya-Koniyanke-Kuranko. This has been a source of both tension and anxiety in the Guinean postcolony.

The situation along the forest–savanna frontier resembles the model of the African Frontier described by Kopytoff: "It is on such frontiers that most African polities and societies have, so to speak, been 'constructed' out of the bits and pieces—human and cultural—of existing societies" (1987, 3). He goes on to discuss the centrality along African frontiers of "ethnically ambiguous" marginal societies

that nestle in the interstices between "normal" societies and ethnicities . . . [and present] a mishmash of regional cultural traits. . . . The collective, "official" history that such a society tells about itself may be unitary and straightforward. But that is belied by the individual histories of its separate kin groups that show their ancestors coming from different areas and at different periods—as refugees from war or famine, or as disgruntled kin group segments, or as losers in the succession struggles of their kin group segments. (1987, 4–5)

Many aspects of Kopytoff's model apply to Guinea's forest–savanna frontier where Loma speakers and Manya speakers intermingle. Also applicable is his observation:

> If [frontier societies] are rare in the literature, it is because they are apt to be ignored by the anthropologist, who usually prefers for his fieldwork site the unambiguous heartland of a society to its uncertain peripheries. But that is only part of the reason. They are also rare precisely because they are short-lived social formations on the way, potentially, to becoming full-fledged societies. (1987, 5)[13]

And thus the social formation of the interstitial fétichiste southern periphery of the Northern Mande world came into being during the period of Mande southern expansion after c. 1400. By the 1960s, it had effectively disappeared. Some Manya had probably (especially along the Koivogui-Kamara corridor) become Loma, and others became Muslim and "Malinke," as Ellis (1999) describes. In chapter 2, we saw that even as late as 1921, some 80 percent of the "Malinke" living in Macenta Préfecture were still recorded as being fétichiste, just like their Loma-speaking neighbors. At the point where postcolonial prestige drew on claims to monotheistic and imperial legacies, peripheral Northern Mande speakers' fétichiste pasts were an embarrassing reminder of the many and profound links between Northern and Southwestern Mande societies.

We turn now to a brief historical excursus that introduces two of the most prominent theocratic empire-builders in the history of Guinea, then turn to two less well-known historical instances from the late colonial period. In presenting these four sketches, my primary intention is to show the deep reservoir of iconoclastic practice from which the Touré government drew when it decided that the Demystification Program would be one of its first undertakings.[14] These experiences informed (and sometimes happened at the same time as) the process of ethnogenesis I have described so far. They also helped to define notions of ethno-religious identity in ways that linked "Malinke-ness" to Islam and to stratified states,[15] and "Forestier-ness" to polytheism and acephalous political organization.

Iconoclastic Precedents

During his rise to power and his twenty-six-year rule, Sékou Touré claimed Almamy Samory Touré as an ancestor and appropriated the idiom of religious renewal as a source of political legitimacy. In the explicit analogy between the two, Samory Touré was the primary anticolonial hero of late nineteenth-century Guinea and a holy man. Sékou Touré was the primary anticolonial hero of mid-twentieth-century Guinea (and Samory's putative grandson). His program of political renewal, by analogy, was *like* a struggle for spiritual renewal. This is a complex discourse, and we shall only focus on a corner of it here; the part that helps shed light on the Demystification Program.[16]

Again, we must ask why, in the context of building a new nation from almost nothing, did it seem necessary to the PDG to eradicate masks? The most obvious answer, from the point of view of the state and the Muslim majority who made up most of the national elite, was that the process of political renewal might well resemble the process of religious renewal, and the process of religious renewal, leading to conversion to monotheistic faith, had always been accompanied in this region by iconoclasm. There is nothing unique in the iconoclastic history of Guinea and the surrounding area. Among monotheistic religions, it is only certain forms of Christianity that have remained consistently indifferent to the second commandment that demands: "Thou shall not make unto thee any graven image, or any likeness of anything that is in heaven above, or that is in the earth beneath, or that is in the water under the earth." Jack Goody describes how, in northern Ghana,

> Even the local autochthones were affected [by a movement of Islamic renewal among neighboring Muslims in 1917]; they use masks in the villages but not in the town. The very nature of the written Islamic canon meant that there always existed the possibility that some individual or group might come to power, locally or nationally, by claiming to go back to God's word and his ways which had been neglected by other commentators or by later followers. The new purists would insist upon a return to basics, to the aniconic fundamentals. (1997, 42)

In 1999, Christian converts in the village where I was conducting research took an iconoclastic approach to Loma ritual, cutting up *bolowologi* liana vines and burning *sale* esoteric medicines. As we shall see below, Muslims have done the same thing. The historical precedents for Demystification are crucial to understanding the ways that the idioms of conversion and iconoclasm have migrated back and forth between the political and religious realms in this region. What I am interested in showing is how the impetus to wipe the slate clean and to start from zero became an important way of thinking about history, cultural practice, and social change.

Each of the movements of renewal I describe below invoked the myth of purification. The ideology of these movements often refers to the process of "cleaning." The process of jihad aims first at cleaning and purifying the self, which might have taken on impure accretions and practices over time, and secondly at cleaning the socio-political field, which has allowed such impurities to emerge or which refuses to discard them in the first place. It is not coincidental that in the process of upland rice cultivation discussed in chapter 3, the Loma (wɛzewo, lit. "to make clean") and Mandekan terms for clearing a field are related to those for "cleaning." And indeed, when inhabitants of the (Muslim) savanna come to the (fétichiste) forest, they often refer to the darkness of the tree cover and the inability to see long distances. Similarly, Foresters who have traveled northward complain of the relentless sun and its heat in the unprotected savanna regions of Guinea and neighboring Senegal and Mali. Today the multilateral lending institutions use the metaphor of transparency in exactly the same way to define concealment and discretion as pathological. During the revolutionary period in Guinea, these terms were also very much in use. They built upon preexisting discourses of renewal from the region's political-religious history.

Sékou Touré inculcated in Guineans a sense of the radical break they had made with the past by choosing independence in 1958, and the fact that the nation was starting from scratch. Touré used the moment of decolonization (indeed the mythologization of that moment) as a site for bringing together two seemingly incompatible strains of thought. The first was the idiom of iconoclasm that had been central to many major political and cultural movements in the region during the nineteenth and twentieth centuries. The second was the will to start afresh and reengineer society in a rational way that James Scott has called "authoritarian high modernism." The combination of these two interwoven strands made Demystification not just possible but almost necessary. In tracing this historical trajectory, we turn first to Umar Tal.

El Hajj Umar Tal

Umar Tal was one of the most prominent jihadists and empire builders in West African history. The seat of his kingdom was in present-day Guinea, and his empire extended into present day Senegal and Mali. He built a large theocratic state in the mid-nineteenth century, and he used his army to conquer, convert, and destroy the fétiches of neighboring populations. Tal, a charismatic Tukulor[17] mystic, made the Hajj to Mecca from 1828 to 1830. He had recently been won over to the Tijani[18] order of Sufism during his stay in the Futa Jallon (the central mountainous range of what is now Guinea). He returned to his native Futa Toro in 1825 and spent three years making his way to the Middle East. On the way, he visited the recently established Fulbe Islamic theocracies of Masina[19] and Sokoto.[20] He spent three years in the Islamic holy lands and Egypt studying scriptures and Islamic interpretation with Mohammed al-Ghali, the leading representative of the Tijani faith in Medina and Cairo. During his ten-year trip home, he proselytized the Tijaniyya form of Sufism in the Islamic states of Bornu, Sokoto (where he contested the succession to Muhammed Bello's throne),[21] and Masina before returning to the Futa Jallon in 1841.

After a period of regrouping at home following his many years absence, Tal conceived and carried out a jihadist movement, based in Dinguraye, now in northeastern Guinea. Umar's jihad, which lasted from 1851 to his death in 1864, was first waged against the "pagans" of the mini-kingdom of Tamba, located directly to the east of Futa Jallon. He continued to expand his jihadist state from his base there, first to gold-rich Bure, then northward to eastern Senegal and Karta, finally eastward to Segou, the great infidel capital of the Bamana. One of El Hajj Umar's first acts upon entering Segou in 1860 was to destroy the pagan *Boli* shrines, an iconoclastic gesture that has come to stand for the imposition of monotheism in the Segou region.[22] In 1862 Umar attacked the neighboring Muslim state of Masina and died soon after.[23]

For the purposes of this chapter, what is most important to note is the fact that the Fulbe jihadists (including Tal) were among the first indigenous political leaders in West Africa to base their political legitimacy on a universalist doctrine. It was an ideology that was not modernist, as was Sékou Touré's Marxism, yet it shared a number of orientations, particularly that it validated education and literacy as sources of wisdom and the basis for legitimate leadership. This system emphasized acquired skills and knowledge over noble descent, and it signaled a shift in notions about personhood and power that presaged the modernist revolution to come in twentieth-century Guinea. It also tapped into structural tensions that existed in the region, such as those between elders and youth and between those of royal descent and the ambitious, competent slaves who sometimes usurped their positions.[24] An iconoclast, Tal's political ambitions and his religious vision were ultimately inseparable.

Almamy Samory Touré

There is evidence to suggest that social class played a role in the late eighteenth- to mid-nineteenth-century jihads in West Africa. Persons of modest birth but with significant charisma and theological expertise, like Shehu Usman and Umar Tal, were able to overthrow ruling lineages and build political legitimacy on a new basis. This legitimacy ultimately rested on the claims they made to Islamic piety, the destruction of local religious practices, and the installation of Islam.

The situation in the eighteenth- and early nineteenth-century Koniyan highlands seems to have been the inverse. Its inhabitants, called Koniyanke (lit. "people of the Koniya" highlands around Musadu and Beyla, in present-day Guinea), were peripheral Northern Mande (Mandekan-speaking polytheists). In the Koniyan highlands during the eighteenth and nineteenth centuries, Muslim Northern Mande Dyula traders[25] lived amongst and intermarried with the local Koniyan people. The Dyula made their living primarily through the trade in cola nuts, grown in the cool, southern rainforest and highly prized in the northern Sahel. Their lucrative trade also dealt in salt, gold, slaves, and cloth.[26] Dyula assured their safety through marriage alliances with their hosts.

Yves Person, in his massive *Samori: une révolution dyula*, argues that Muslim dyula and clerics not only did not proselytize their religion. They actively discouraged the Koniyanke from converting. He writes:

> A situation of equilibrium finally established itself. Traders or clerics, the Muslims, in the minority, are perfectly integrated in an animist society which reserves certain specialized functions for them and appreciates them within limits. . . . Their prestige is great despite their small numbers, but political power escapes them. . . . Numerous links, as neighbors, friends, and even husbands, united them with [the animists] so much that the idea of a holy war to convert them was profoundly foreign to the old Malinké Islam. . . . The result was that the Muslim minority, interested in preserving its monopoly on prestigious religion, was generally opposed to the conversion of their neighbors. Numerous anecdotes from the Kuranko, Koniyanke, and Forest regions describe marabouts who worked hard to dissuade the local landowning chiefs, their hosts, every time that they wanted to abandon animism for the prestige of the public prayer. (1968, 132–33)

In Person's work we find incredibly complex interrelations of ethnicity, language, and religion that simultaneously bound Northern Mande speakers together and separated them along the forest–savanna frontier. For Person, this serves only to set the scene for the hero of his story: Samory, a trader (but not a Muslim at this point), came to be trained as a warrior. Having found his forte, he eventually overthrew his erstwhile commanders and began to expand his rule with the backing of a growing army of professional warriors.

The original justification for military expansion was that, as a former merchant, Samory was interested in making the trade routes secure for his fellow dyula. This is the "Dyula revolution" from which Person's work takes its title. In other words, the Muslim dyula minority finally decided not only to monopolize the spheres of trade and monotheistic religion but also to grab political power from their hosts.[27] As the empire expanded, however, Samory's justifications shifted. In 1884, some twenty years after he began his conquests, he converted to Islam, and in 1886 he proclaimed his empire a theocracy, giving himself the Islamic title Almamy.[28]

Whether Samory's conversion was "sincere" or merely a ruse to build the legitimacy of his quickly growing empire is difficult to know. He learned to read the Qur'an, and throughout his subsequent conquests he built mosques and installed Qur'anic schools and teachers, destroying polytheistic shrines and forcing those under his rule to convert to Islam. Adding to his prestige as a righteous iconoclastic emperor, it so happened that Samory's empire was expanding at exactly the moment that the French were expanding their own empire into the West African hinterland from their bases along the coast. As a result of their bitter rivalry, his legacy in Guinea is that of an anticolonial resistance hero.

What the examples of Umar Tal and Samory Touré point out is the fluid interchange between the realms of the religious and the political in precolonial West Africa. Religion had become one of the bases for political contestation, much like genealogical reckoning of noble descent. Those who were shown to be in the right gained legitimacy, though the actual struggles for political control were more often military than exegetical. The Islamic injunction to convert polytheists (by force if necessary) and the tradition of jihad and movements of renewal within Islam's history lent themselves to the forms of political Islam that emerged in West Africa in the eighteenth and nineteenth centuries. One of the most interesting of the renewal movements to follow this precolonial tradition was the West African form of reformist Islam most often called "Wahhabism" that flourished from the 1940s onward in Guinea, Mali, and Côte d'Ivoire.

The Wahhabiyya

Muhammad ibn Abd al-Wahab founded the Wahhabi form of Islam around 1744 in what is now Saudi Arabia. Its original goal was to revive Islamic practice in the region, a practice that had been degraded, in Wahab's eyes, by the *bid'a* (innovations) introduced by Sufi sects. Wahab and his supporter, Muhammad ibn Saud, ancestor of the Saudi royal family, conquered most of the Arabian peninsula and promulgated their form of ascetic Islam.[29]

The form of Wahhabism that came to West Africa was related to, but by no means identical with, this one. Lansiné Kaba (1974) details the lives and ambitions of Wahhabist clerics who returned to West Africa, usually after having studied at the Egyptian religious university, Al-Azhar.[30] He shows how their religious practice and political (anticolonial) commitment were intertwined in the period from the 1940s onward. These reformers sought to eradicate what they perceived as the *shirk*, or heresies, of the predominant sects of Islam in the region—Qadiriya, Tijaniya, and Mouridiya—all of them Sufi. The saints, marabouts, and initiation into esoteric rites common to these Sufi sects are all unacceptable and blasphemous to Wahhabis.[31]

As with Umar Tal and Samory Touré, the Wahhabis' notions about the necessity for religious reform coincided with political changes in the region that charged such theological arguments with greater significance. In the case of the Wahhabiyya, their attempt to renew Islam came at the moment when francophone West Africans were debating the issue of decolonization. Particularly in Guinea, the religious idiom slid in and out of the symbolic repertoire of Sékou Touré and the PDG. Kaba writes:

> Given the importance of cultural issues in nationalism, one could see how Islam, the religion of the majority in Guinea and Soudan,[32] could be used for cultural nationalism and political mobilization. The similarity between the clothing style of the Wahhabi and that of the PDG supporters in Kankan and the analogy between the language of the Wahhabiyya and that of the same party were intended to express the symbolic return to Africanity and to a non-Western universalism. (1974, 15–16)

At the intersection of Wahhabist and anticolonial critiques there was a distress with a cultural landscape that had become dominated by the values and criteria of the colonial society. As Benedict Anderson (1991) has pointed out, the proselytizers of nativism are often those cosmopolitans who are, by their own standards, those most tainted by metropolitan malaise. This was true of the West African Wahhabi.[33] The irony is supplemented by the way that the cultural politics of Islamic renewal played out according to a series of local strategies. Most important among these is the way that Wahhabism became a form of youth politics, particularly through the West African Wahhabis' Subbanu movement.

The Subbanu, or educational wing of the Wahhabist organization, was based in Bamako and derived its name from the Arabic for "youth" (*al-subban*). It was inspired by the Egyptian group *Jamiyat al-Subban al-Muslimin*, which the Subbanu leaders had encountered during their studies in Egypt at the time of their Haj to Mecca (Kaba 1974, 140). In 1949, they opened an Islamic school in Bamako. Most of these young clerics who had made the Haj and studied at Al-Azhar in Cairo were fluent in French, a prerequisite for the bilingual education insisted upon by the colonial authorities. The French, who felt they were able to negotiate with (if not co-opt) the existing Muslim brotherhoods in the region, were anxious about the threat of "Pan-Islamism." In the 1940s and 1950s, they paid particular attention to links between the subjects of their West African colonies and the forces behind the emergent politics of decolonization in the Middle East.[34] Consequently, the Subbanu school was approved only briefly in Bamako, then shut down. In spite of official repression, the Subbanu educators gave evening seminars in the large, walled, family compounds of Bamako, Bouake (Côte d'Ivoire's second largest city and a center of Wahhabi proselytization), and Kankan (Guinea's second largest city and a historical center of Islamic scholarship in the region), drawing ever-larger crowds.

The Subbanu espoused many of the views the French feared they might, referring to many of the older Sufi imams and marabouts as "colonialist lackeys." According to Kaba,

> [Sufi] Mysticism thus becomes synonymous with shrewd mystification and exploitation. . . . Given that religion had turned into a business and religiosity into a profession, it was inevitable, they argued, that ignorance and superstition were promoted as norms and that the masses gave their souls and wealth to mystics-turned-charlatans, soothsayers, and charm makers. The Wahhabi felt it necessary, consequently, to demystify those who were committing wrongs and making profit in the name of Islam.
>
> Members of the reform movement who acquired European education expressed their criticism against Marabutism in terms of class conflict. To them, Sufism seems to be a dysfunctional system of thought and practices, hence non-Islamic, because its ultimate aims are the emergence of a special category of Muslims. (1974, 113–16)

We see here many of the elements of the idiom of cultural "renewal" that was to take hold in the immediate post-independence period (1959–62) and that fed into the Demystification Program. There is a striking kinship between Kaba's locutions about "shrewd mystification and exploitation" and Sékou Touré's denunciation of "marabouts who exploited the believers. Fétichistes who lived off of the ordinary people's mystification" (1982). The Wahhabi emphasized youth avant-gardism, reeducation, and "reconversion"—demystification as the cure for traditional exploitation—and the search for an alternative, non-Eurocentric form of modernity.

Also important to note is the amalgamation of Marxist and Islamic reformist idioms in Kaba's description, a mix that remained the cornerstone of Sékou Touré's politics for twenty-six years. These young men, dissatisfied with the way that Islam was practiced and controlled by the Sufi brotherhoods in West Africa, put a great emphasis on the "proper" education of the local Muslim population. Part of their dissatisfaction with the brotherhoods was purely theological, and part of it was socio-economic, as they decried the exploitation of the illiterate by the marabout "charlatans." However, a large portion of their opposition to the marabouts was political, as they objected to what they perceived as the elder clerics' and the brotherhoods' complicity with the colonial regimes. As Kaba describes, the young Wahhabist clerics' theological, educational, and political programs were interlinked and culminated in their demand for independence.

While Muslim renewal movements have called for iconoclastic destruction in other settings, this does not seem to have been a major part of their concerns in mid-twentieth century Guinea, Mali, and Côte d'Ivoire. We should not fail to see, however, the contiguity between the Subbanu movement's desire to reorient religious and secular learning and the concern with destroying fétiches. At the same time that the Subbanu movement was pursuing change in the educational and clerical areas, a more overtly iconoclastic movement was active along Guinea's coast.

The Baga

At about the same time that the Wahhabiyya gained momentum in the West African Sahel, Guinea's coastal Baga-speaking region underwent the iconoclastic sweep of Aseku Sayon, a Maninka Muslim cleric, in the period around 1953 (Sarró 1999, 2009; cf. Berliner 2002, 2005; Lamp 1996). This cleric's critique was two-pronged, like that of the Wahhabis: simultaneously opposed to the "traditions" of paganism and superstition espoused by the elders and to the "innovations" of the colonial culture. This was primarily a youth movement, and the destruction of the status quo was a massive blow against gerontocratic hierarchy in rural Baga society.[35]

The Baga Islamic revival was characterized by the destruction of masks and other objects associated with local rituals. This area was as yet only sparsely Islamicized, and the proselytizers had come to turn "pagans" (*kafir*) into Muslims. This presupposed their abandoning ancestral shrines, sacrifices to earth and water spirits, the rites of initiation and fecundation, and the dancing of the *D'mba*, more commonly known as the Nimba, a mask often six feet tall (Lamp 1996). This movement, undertaken spontaneously by zealous Muslims in the period immediately before Guinean independence, was a template for the socialist state's post-independence Demystification Program, as Lamp notes.

The preceding descriptions give the reader a sense of the combinations of religious (but also political) rhetorics of renewal that played themselves out between 1850 and 1958 in the region that became Guinea. Arguments about religious interpretation and justifications of forcible conquest mutated, one into the other. The upheavals of French colonial penetration, conquest, and administration were crucial catalysts in this process, but they were by no means determinative of the strategies and objectives of Samory Touré, the Wahhabists, or the Baga proselytizers. The challenge posed by the rapid and total French military conquest and the changes it ushered into Guinean society probably forced many Guineans to think about the issue of religious/political renewal as a matter of urgency. As Geertz has written about the spread of Islam in Morocco and Indonesia:

> Western intrusion produced a reaction not only against Christianity (that can easily be overemphasized) but against the classical religious traditions of the two countries themselves. It was not European beliefs and practices, whose impingement upon either Moroccan or Indonesian spiritual life was tangential and indirect, toward which the doctrinal fire of the scripturalists was mainly directed; it was maraboutism and illuminationism. Externally stimulated, the upheaval was internal. (1968, 65)

In 1958, acceding to independence before any other francophone West African territory, Guinea had to come to terms with these issues, building upon the examples of its own regional history and that of the fledgling state of Ghana, independent just one year before Guinea. This was the context of the Guinean government's attempts to shape a modern sensibility in its formerly French subjects, newly minted as Guinean citizens. This shift, all the more abrupt given Guinea's Marxist orientation and the consequent importance of grass-roots political participation, required that the state create a new type of political actor. This project, with all its internal contradictions, was the key impetus behind the state's violent imposition of the Demystification Program. The focus on eradicating the traces of a "backward" paganism seems less idiosyncratic when we put it in the context of one of the primary models of radical socio-political renewal available to the postcolonial Guinean governing elite: the history of West African Islamic movements of renewal.[36]

Monotheism and Modernist Anxiety

The cause that galvanized politics in 1950s Guinea was decolonization (Cooper 1996; Kaba 1989). Revolutionary leaders such as Sékou Touré portrayed themselves as holding a vanguard position in the march toward a new, egalitarian order (Touré 1959, 1966, 1967). As with similar modernist movements around the world, the people who paid the price of national "progress" were often internal minorities (Scott 1998, 2009; Steedly 1993; Tsing 1993). Transformed from bumpkins into enemies of progress and national unity, they found themselves the object of violent social engineering. While Forestiers like the Loma were accused of performing human sacrifices (this was a central trope in the stereotype of Forestier savagery), it was Forestiers themselves who became a kind of national sacrificial offering to the gods of modernity. In retrospect it seems that Guinea's elites believed that the destruction of the sacred forest and the folklorization of its masquerades would clear the way for a collective national leap forward into modernity.

Donham (1999, 2002) has used the case of the Ethiopian revolution to reflect on the ambiguities of the Marxist upheavals that took place in poor, agrarian nations in Africa. While Marxist theory promises a radical equalization among those who participate in workers' revolutions the world over, it has nonetheless typically assigned countries like Ethiopia and Guinea the same backward status that capitalists and colonizers did. Donham describes the "emancipatory narrative offered by the Soviet Union as a kind of modernist trumping, one that promised to beat the West at its own game" (2002, 248). Yet such narratives did little to question modernist assumptions of a teleological trajectory from savage to civilized, technologically primitive to sophisticated, and superstitious to secular-scientific. It is not coincidental, Donham argues (1999), that the most eager converts to the rhetoric of Marxist revolution in the Maale villages where he worked were those modernists who had already converted to Christianity.

Both monotheist and Marxist modernists often subscribe to the narrative of developmentalism Karp (2002, 82) describes, which requires transformations in personhood in order for people to become productive modern citizens. It is this bittersweet contradiction that we need to keep in mind when thinking about the transition from the euphoric moment of decolonization to the initial ambivalences of the independent period. In the Guinean case, these contradictions appeared almost immediately in the realm of cultural politics, while they emerged later in other areas.

The urge to eradicate masquerades as a road to progress reminds us of the fact that progress is an imaginary construct that can only exist within a field of distinctions. There is no avant garde if there are no stragglers. No one is progressive except by comparison with those who are backward. As Knauft argues, "modernity is a geography of imagination that creates progress through the projection and management of alterity. . . . Notions of progress provoke paradoxes and creative struggles that highlight the power of imagination in the face of violent interactions, deferments, and disillusionments" (Knauft ed. 2002, 18–35).

Reflecting upon the imaginative work that is an integral part of notions of progress and modernity, it is easy to see that there are complex aspects of psychological and imaginative life involved that are probably beyond the competence of anthropologists to fully explicate. Nevertheless, this issue throws us back upon the question of interethnic relations between Loma speakers and Manya speakers, and where those relations fit into the larger, national rhetoric.

I have used the term "modernist anxiety" in the title of this section, and one of the areas that most directly touches on the motivations for Demystification is the religious facet of that anxiety. Although this book is far from psychoanalytic in its theoretical underpinnings, it is worth returning to Freud's writings on anxiety and its links to religion and belief, already mentioned in chapter 1. In his essay "The 'Uncanny,'" Freud maintains that "every affect belonging to an emotional impulse, whatever its kind, is transformed, if it is repressed, into anxiety" ([1917] 1995, 143). He further describes the play of "irrational" beliefs, such as those characterizing what he calls animism:

> We—or our primitive forefathers—once believed that these [animist] possibilities were realities, and were convinced that they actually happened. Nowadays we no longer believe in them, we have *surmounted* these modes of thought; but we do not feel quite sure of our new beliefs, and the old ones still exist within us ready to seize upon any confirmation. (148)

It is, he argues, the struggle to repress the animist past that results in anxiety, as well as the uncanny feeling we have when such repressed beliefs return to consciousness. Freud writes that "this uncanny is in reality nothing new or alien, but something which is familiar and old-established in the mind and which has become alienated from it only through the process of repression" (142). Placing this comment in the Guinean context, we are led to ask whether the uncanny mask of the savage Other does not derive its power from the very fact that it is the mask one wore only yesterday.

My presentation so far of the extensive cultural intermingling between Northern Mande and Southwestern Mande peoples in Guinea was not unmotivated minutiae. It is those recently converted Muslims described by Ellis (1999)—the Manya, Koniyanke, Kuranko, Mandingo—who have been at greatest pains to stress their difference from their pagan neighbors. Loma speakers and some Manya speakers admit that in fact such differences are often manufactured, and often quite recently. Sékou Touré himself, like Samory whom he claimed as an exalted ancestor, originated from this anxious peripheral zone. While Sékou was born into a Muslim family, Samory converted as an adult, and, in claiming his legacy, this was the source of some anxiety. This unspeakable facet of Samory's history stood as a testament to the fact that most peripheral Northern Mande speakers were until recently organizing their ritual lives around the same notions of personhood, esoteric forms of power, and the power associations like Komo, which so closely resemble the Loma Poro.

Such links have been effectively banished from the common sense of both Northern and Southwestern Mande speakers. If one were to borrow Freudian terms, one would say they had been repressed, an act that he argues must lead to anxiety. The very recent conversion of many Northern Mande speakers to Islam leads to the question: did anxiety about their polytheistic past lead Guinea's recent converts to lash out violently at their own recently abandoned practices? In this chapter I argue that Islam's universalizing and teleological logic exerted pressure on converts to renounce the past and wipe the slate clean.[37] The synergistic combination of religious and nationalist claims to legitimacy worked for some groups and against others in the postcolonial sphere of modernization and renewal. During this 1958–84 period, Sékou Touré's government often held the Samorian empire up as a model.

Touré's own origins as a Kuranko speaker from the Faranah region were directly implicated in his promotion of Samory Touré to the status of primary resistance hero and adoption of the model of the warrior-statesman-cleric. The disdain in which Kuranko and Koniyanke were still held at the moment of independence was one of the factors that seems to have limited Touré's appeal in core Maninka towns like Kankan. Sometimes described as an *arriviste* schemer even today by noble Maninka, he maintained a contentious relationship with the Northern Mande core, sometimes attacking the region's nobility as "feudal" and at other times pretending that all Mandekan speakers shared equally in the legacy of glorious precolonial empire.

One explicit example of the latter move can be found in the lyrics of the best-known record made by Guinea's best-known band, Bembeya Jazz. Founded in the Koniyanke town of Beyla in the heart of the Northern Mande periphery, the band came to serve as Touré's personal *jelilu* praise singers (although they played in the electrified, Cuban-influenced "jazz" style). Their most famous album remains *Regard sur le passé* ([1971] 2000). This record, with warrior-emperor Samory Touré's face on its cover, features a thirty-four minute, two-part praise song about Samory Touré, followed by a twenty-eight minute praise song about Sékou Touré entitled "Chemin du PDG" ("The Path of the PDG"). This record declares Samory's moral significance for postcolonial Guineans:

> Listen, son of Africa. Listen woman of Africa. Listen also, youth of Africa, tomorrow's hope. Listen all of you to a page from the glorious history of Africa. . . . Colonialism, to justify its domination, painted . . . Guinea's kings as savages. But, traversing the night of time, their history came to us by other means. . . . Proud Muslim [Samory], he had mosques constructed everywhere, and destroyed fétiches.

Finally, after describing Samory's arrest, imprisonment, and death in exile:

> They aren't dead, these heroes, and they will not die. After them, audacious pioneers took up the fight for national liberation, which, finally, triumphed under the direction of Ahmed Sékou Touré, grandson of this same Almamy Samory. On the 29th September of 1958 [when Guineans voted for complete independence] the revolution triumphed, definitively revenging that other 29th September 1898. Date of the arrest of the emperor of Wassoulou, the Almamy Samory Touré.

This passage typifies a key rhetorical strategy of the Touré era: creating a series of symbolic parallels between past and present, and particularly between Sékou Touré and Samory Touré. Samory, says the passage, is not dead and will not die. This is because of the immortality bestowed by the praise singer who writes the hero's name into History, and also because Sékou is presented as a kind of reincarnation of Samory.

Writing Samory into the trajectory of Mande emperors and then claiming him as a maternal grandfather, Touré actively sought to erase distinctions like those Ellis (1999) describes among different subsections of the Mandekan-speaking world. As in the Gambian case that Ebron describes, the history of empire was a cornerstone of Mandecentric political legitimization in the postcolonial period: "Its political heritage is expansive. . . . [N]ational history is a single story in which Mande kings prefigure later rulers and offer an origin to the independent nation" (Ebron 2002, 90–91). This has also been true in Mali and Guinea. This legitimacy comes both from a history of empire and of Islamization. Were it not for Samory's conversion to Islam, attempts to place him in the same category as ancient Mali's emperors would have been inadmissible to many in Guinea.

Northern–Southwestern Mande Links and Their Denial

Given the many similarities I have described between Northern and Southwestern Mande speakers, one may ask why each group rejects its affiliation with the other. As for peripheral Mandekan speakers like the Manya, I have noted the attempt to "trade up" their identity to that of the descendents of the Mali Empire. The anxiety that might be expected to accompany such a maneuver, combined with converts' zeal, seems to have resulted in the stridency with which they have asserted their difference from their Forestier hosts and neighbors.

Loma speakers who live in mixed towns say that most of the Manya speakers living among them were, as recently as the 1950s, initiated into the same power associations as the Loma. In mixed towns like Bofossou, Seredou, and Macenta town, informants describe most people speaking both languages, with differences between the two populations minimized. The primary distinction between the two groups was between newcomers and owners of the land. Newcoming Manya-speaking men typically cemented their relations with the resident lineages by marrying Loma women and becoming initiated into the power associations.

I interpret these interrelations described by informants as the most recent chapter in the settlement process described in chapter 2, in which I proposed a model of peripheral Northern Mande speakers moving southward into Loma territories in successive waves, gradually adopting Loma language and social practices, and "becoming" Loma. Some of those who arrived in the late nineteenth century may have been avoiding the forced Islamization that was taking place to the North. It was only the struggles over chieftaincy politics and more widespread Islamization in the region that short-circuited the former process of assimilation. From the late colonial period, Manya speakers began to find it advantageous to emphasize their differences from their hosts, rather than their similarities. This is both cause and result of the transformation of three ethnic categories into two that I have described in this chapter.

Several factors enter into the reckoning of local identities in the region that became Macenta Préfecture. Language, ethnic origins, cultural practices, forms of livelihood, and religion—each of these has its own history in the region, and the relations among them changed over time. By the mid-twentieth century, religion came to play a dominant role, and it continues to trump the other factors today in most instances. The foregrounding of religion has much to do with the region's interactions with colonial and postcolonial states. Islam became especially important to the legitimation of the state under Sékou Touré. He was explicit in connecting the moral world to the economic one. In his Manichean system

> one realizes the existence of two routes, two paths: the bad route and the good route; one realizes, thus, the existence of bad and good, and promises to stay on the good road, to stay on and follow strictly the good road, while asking God for his constant and generous aid to remain on this healthy path. (Touré 1977, 66)

Touré's "good route" required adherence to a world religion and to the creed of Touré's particular form of socialism. Manya speakers adopted this rhetoric, and we saw in chapter 4 some of the ways that differences in land use and tenure as they were engineered by the state helped to further differentiate "rational" Manya-speaking plantation owners from "irrational" Loma rice farmers.

It is more difficult to explain why Loma speakers themselves have accepted the oil-and-water model of identity.[38] While a degree of anxiety about religious heritage seems to motivate some Manya speakers, only a few educated Loma-speaking elites seem to share any such anxiety about whether their religious practices are modern or backward. More Loma speakers seem preoccupied with the material outcomes of ethno-religious claims, and Loma claims of radical Loma-Manya distinction have hardened as the political stakes of such claims have grown. Population density has risen to the point where land is becoming scarce for the first time in recorded or living memory. Demographic pressure seems to be more acute in the northern part of Macenta Préfecture than the south, but it has come to be seen as a general problem.

Loma speakers are sophisticated farmers and are well aware of the required fallow period for different plots of land. Because Loma agriculture is based on rotating slash and burn upland (dry) rice cultivation, it requires relatively more land per person. As communities have begun approaching the capacity of their villages' territory, they have become increasingly careful about the rules governing land tenure. Loma speakers have found it useful to join the more general logic of hardened ethnic categories. By first asserting their credentials as members of the *ethnically autochthonous* group and then Manya speakers' identity as *ethnic strangers*, they are able to evade the claims that Manya-speaking "nephews" can make on their Loma-speaking "uncles."

Drawing on Muslim Manya speakers' claims of difference, Loma speakers have agreed to a line of ethnic demarcation, stopping or at least slowing the process of assimilating outsiders. This moment might be the frontier tipping point Kopytoff describes for "short-lived social formations on the way, potentially, to becoming full-fledged societies" (1987, 5). With this shift, Loma speakers have muted discussions about who among them is "really" Loma; who is a firstcomer or a latecomer. They have displaced these tensions onto the field of ethno-religious difference.[39] All Manya speakers are strangers (by definition). By the same logic, all Loma speakers are autochthons. The field of autochthonous political legitimacy has shifted from the scale of localized lineages to that of ethnolinguistic groups. This is a dramatic historical shift, however quickly it has become naturalized as the common sense of people living in Macenta Préfecture. The naturalization of radical cultural difference between Forestiers and other Guineans was not, however, something that Loma speakers and Manya-speakers had to invent de novo. This was a drama of civilizational difference that had been staged, quite literally, by the socialist state. In the second part of the book, I turn to the Demystification Program and the related set of cultural policies promulgated by the Guinean state after independence in 1958. Demystification was both a result of and a crystallizing factor in the emergence of new ideas about culture, modernity, and ethnolinguistic identity in Guinea.

PART TWO

Revealing and Reshaping the Body Politic

INTERLUDE II

Bonfire

"Take me to the féticheur," said the administrator. The young translator ran off to consult with the group of elders that had come to meet the delegation just arrived from Conakry. The administrator didn't understand Lomagui, but he saw that the translator was pleading with them. As in the other villages, the prime féticheur, usually also the village's main blacksmith, must have refused to come out and acknowledge, much less greet, any group representing the state. The administrator waited. He had a list of names, if it became necessary to use it. The translator ran back.

"They say he has gone to visit his uncles in another village."

The administrator, who had memorized the names before entering the village, so as not to have to consult his list, walked briskly up to the village chief, the translator trotting behind him. He said, in French, "Take me to Moribah Onivogui's house now."

The men did not flinch, but the administrator saw their pupils grow in their dark, bloodshot eyes. The chief said something quickly to the translator.

"He says there are several Moribah Onivoguis in the village."

"The blacksmith. And tell him we go there immediately, or he will be *ligoté* and taken to jail." The command was translated, and the delegation set out for the old man's house. A child ran ahead, and as they arrived at the round house with its conical thatched roof, an old man was just walking away.

"Seize him and bring him back," the administrator said to the three soldiers accompanying them. They looked at each other for a moment, then complied, with obvious unease. The administrator had had problems with his military escort from the beginning. At first they had given him Loma soldiers, who, in situations like this, had systematically refused to follow orders. Their fear of these old men was so great that they preferred facing military prison, which is where the first contingent rested now. He had returned to Macenta for a group of Muslim soldiers from the savanna. These men were better trained and seemed to hold an arrogant disdain for the Loma villagers, whom they called cannibals and eaters of dogs. But when faced with orders like he had just given, it became clear that they, too, feared the power of the Loma féticheurs. Soon enough they would see.

"Are you Moribah Onivogui?" he asked. The old man, barefoot, wrinkled, with a wispy white goatee, but still powerful through his back and shoulders, nodded, looking him in the eye with hatred.

"*Ligotez* him." He ordered. The soldiers took the rope one of them was carrying, and while two of them pinned his arms behind him, the other wound the rope around his wrists, then his forearms, and finally around his upper arms, pulling them closer and closer together.

"Tighter," the administrator said. The soldier tugged at the rope, causing a resounding pop as one of the old man's shoulders came out of its joint. The soldier wound two more turns and the other shoulder popped out. Though the old man said nothing, he could not help wincing in pain.

"Let us now sit down in Old Moribah's hut and have a little talk." The translator said a few words, and the elders ducked their heads inside, followed by the old féticheur, the soldiers, and finally the administrator and his translator. The old men stood around the single room waiting for the administrator to choose his spot to sit. He saw a stool and seated himself on it. He motioned to the packed mud platform with a mat on top of it.

"Tell Moribah and the chief to sit on the bed. You, sit between us." The translator relayed this order, and squatted on his haunches between the administrator and the old men. The two elders moved over to make space for a fragile-looking old man; the rest stood and listened.

"I have come to you from Conakry, the big city on the ocean where the government is," the administrator began. "Today, we are on a mission our Supreme Leader has called the Demystification Program. What is this thing, this demystification? It is our mission to eradicate all the superstitions and all the backward practices that are keeping our country behind. It is a warning, a command to all those who live off the ignorance of others by tricking them with their deceitful and superstitious practices. From today onward, there will be no more of the secret societies—No Poro!—Do you understand?" When the young man finished translating, they nodded gravely, and said in unison, "*Owe.*"

"No witch doctoring; if someone is sick, you will send them to the hospital of the state. The people's state. Do you understand?" Again they assented.

"Those of you who have real knowledge in using medicinal plants will soon be given papers from the government. We will give you further training, and also ask you for your expertise in helping to cure many diseases. The knowledge contained in this country—even in this room—is very great, but with each generation we start from nothing, because we do not write this knowledge down, we only transmit it to one or two people; many sages take their secrets to the grave. This will change, and we will show the other countries of the world the true knowledge that lies in Africa. But first, we must rid ourselves of all superstitions! Of all mystifications! Do you understand?" Again, they grunted in unison.

"From today, there will be no more initiations. We know what you do in your sacred forests. These barbaric practices must stop immediately. These young people must be available to work, to build the new nation. They can no longer be sequestered off for years at a time. And as you know, many of them die in the bush. Of infections. Of untreated illnesses, because they can not be brought out to the hospitals. All of this must stop. Along with it, the divinations, the sacrifices of human beings, it must all stop! Have you understood?"

"*Ge meniga.*" They replied. Yes, we have heard.

"Then," continued the administrator, with a slight smile, "you will not object to indulging me with a demonstration of your comprehension. Tonight, my colleague, from the ministry of culture, will arrive in the village. He is presently in the neighboring town. You will organize all the young men and women to perform this village's dances of initiation. You will also bring out every mask owned by the men's societies, and they, too, will dance tonight. They will be displayed to the women, to the children, and to me. At the end of the demonstration, every mask will be burned before the village. That is, unless there is anything especially fine that my colleague chooses to save for the national museum. Have you understood everything I have said?"

This time, there was no response whatsoever.

"Very well then. Monsieur Moribah, you will lead my men to the place where the masks and fetishes are kept, and they will guard it until nightfall."

SIX

Personae: Demystification and the Mask

> Legibility is a condition of manipulation. Any substantial state intervention in society—to vaccinate a population, produce goods, mobilize labor, tax people and their property, conduct literacy campaigns, conscript soldiers, enforce sanitation standards, catch criminals, start universal schooling— requires the invention of units that are visible. The units in question might be citizens, villages, trees, fields, houses, or people grouped according to age, depending on the type of intervention. (Scott 1998, 183)

The interlude above is an imaginative recreation that brings together several published descriptions (Rivière 1971; Bellman 1984; Beavogui 1998; Højbjerg 2002a, 2007) and other verbal ones—always fragmentary and halting, because they described events that were both painful and governed by laws of secrecy—that were offered to me during my fieldwork in Macenta Préfecture. This iconoclastic drama, called the "Demystification Program," played out in hundreds of villages in this out-of-the-way corner of the country in 1961, under the socialist government headed by Sékou Touré.[1] In the second half of this book, I am interested in using the Demystification Program as a prism for thinking through the ongoing struggles over identity, power, and personhood between a marginal region and the precolonial, colonial, and postcolonial states that sought to encompass it from c. 1880 onward.

In the first decade after its 1958 accession to independence, Guinea's single party, the Parti Démocratique de Guinée, undertook sweeping changes that affected every aspect of citizens' society, culture, and politics. In the realm of marriage, it became illegal for young women to marry before the age of seventeen. Differences of more than twenty years between the ages of husband and wife were outlawed. Husbands could no longer take second or third wives.[2] In social relations, men and women who worked as serfs for noble families whose ancestors had taken their ancestors captive in war were freed—not just in name, as the French had done, but in the context of sweeping policies that sought to promote former captives in education and the political hierarchy and to simultaneously demote their erstwhile masters.

In the realm of fashion, the government distributed white muslin, encouraging the population to dress in pure white, especially at public celebrations, while such fashions as mini skirts, tight trousers, and extravagant hairdos were punishable by public censure or even jail time.[3] Sexuality, too, was regulated, and schoolgirls underwent an examination known as "la visite" at the beginning of every academic year. Nurses checked to see if the girls had lost their virginity since the last year, and if so, whether they had become pregnant. If the answer to either question was "yes," they were first coerced into revealing the name of the man or boy responsible, then both were publicly humiliated in front of the rest of the school, with pregnant girls barred from classes until the next year. Prostitution was severely punished, and Guineans say it virtually disappeared during this period.

In the arts, the state conscripted young people from all over the country into folkloric troupes that performed "animations politiques" in the form of politically themed dances, theatrical pieces, and choir songs (Straker 2007, 2009). As described in the vignette, young people from the forest region were forced to (folklorically) perform music and dances considered both secret and sacred, and now outlawed in their ordinary setting. In tandem with this folklorization, state-sponsored orchestras played every night in Conakry, recording songs praising the Party, its "Supreme Leader," Sékou Touré, and resistance heroes from the past, such as Almamy Samory Touré.

Interregional trade, with a history more than one thousand years old, was taken out of the hands of individuals. Their practices of buying cheap and selling dear were criminalized, while the state imposed prices it deemed fair and enforced them through its *Police Economique*. Regional merchant circuits—organized around sets of succeeding market days in neighboring towns—were short-circuited, as the state decreed that market day in every town and village would be Sunday. Crime evaporated under the menace of draconian punishments. In certain parts of the country it became common practice to kill petty thieves by pulling gasoline-soaked tires down over their shoulders and setting them alight. Murder was usually punished by the hanging of a person who had been accused, tried, and convicted within twenty-four hours.[4]

Religion also experienced many changes. In a country whose c. 80 percent Muslim majority was almost entirely Sufi, the government denounced and largely dispossessed the powerful marabouts, those Sufi ritual specialists who combined elements of African and Muslim practice and who often acted as intermediaries and teachers to ordinary Muslim farmers. French Catholic clergy were expelled from Guinea in 1967 and the church "Africanized." Finally, the c. 10 percent of the population that continued African religious practices and espoused no world religion—called "fétichistes" by both colonial and socialist states—came in for radical suppression and discipline. State officials went from village to village in the Demystification Program, burning masks used in initiations and village sacrifices. The initiations themselves were banned, and the state enjoined its citizens to choose a monotheistic faith. State surveillance of these practices was harsh, and even crossing the border into Liberia to undergo initiation was an imprisonable offense. These policies continued until Sékou Touré's death and the change of government in 1984.

These undertakings were strong, and most used some degree of coercion. This was not the inexorable, subtle work of Foucauldian governmentality but the radical and violent rupture characteristic of social engineering. No one familiar with the parallel histories of socialist politics—in Eastern Europe, China, or Cuba, for instance—will feel too disoriented in reading these brief descriptions. In Guinea, however, these programs take on a particular poignancy because there were so many other things to do. Thanks to the debilitating French educational policies,[5] Guinea had only eleven African functionaries with university education at the moment of independence. Infrastructure was minimal, health care was abysmal, and the French government spitefully punished the Guinean government, especially in the realm of banking and foreign exchange, for the people's having voted "No" to its 1958 referendum proposing continued, semi-autonomous colonization.

This chapter attempts to identify the structural and intellectual underpinnings of the Demystification Program. The interlude above depicts the way an authoritarian high modernist state (Scott 1998) violently intervened in local ritual, social, and political affairs. Such interventions had some precedents (see chapter 5), but this was part of an imagined project that was far more ambitious than anything that had preceded it in the region. It has been the argument of this book all along that complex events like Demystification can be explained neither by isolated reference to internal dynamics within Loma society, nor to external national or international dynamics. It is their interplay that tells us most about how these events played out.

In this chapter, I focus on some of those external dynamics, and the argument moves in consequence from the ethnographic to an analysis of historical, macropolitical, and discursive factors. My argument is that through contact and interaction with a variety of systems of thought, many Guineans in the 1950s and 1960s came to the conclusion that there were universal principles that could and should organize Guineans' participation in the modern world. The two most important of these systems were world religions, particularly Islam, and a modernist political ideology, namely Marxism.

In his novel, *The Comedians*, Graham Greene captures the relation between universalist religion and universalist political ideology in the following exchange:

> But Communism, my friend, is more than Marxism, just as Catholicism— remember I was born a Catholic too—is more than the Roman Curia. There is a *mystique* as well as a *politique*. . . . Catholics and Communists have committed great crimes, but at least they have not stood aside, like an established society, and been indifferent. . . . I implore you . . . if you have abandoned one faith, do not abandon all faith. There is always an alternative to the faith we lose. Or is it the same faith under another mask? ([1966] 2005, 308)

This passage inserts us at an oblique angle into the problem of belief, ideology, and social action in Guinea's history, particularly the history of its socialist period. A principal goal of this chapter is to explore the "structure of the conjuncture" (Sahlins 1985) between such internal dynamics as interethnic and intergenerational conflict and external forces such as world religions and political ideologies. This chapter argues that changes in notions about personhood—a concept intimately linked to masks, both etymologically and conceptually—parallel changes in notions about political participation. For this reason, masks and masquerade provided a powerful metaphor for what political subjectivity should *not* be in the context of a Marxist-modernist state such as Guinea.

In understanding such cultural struggles, we may find a key to understanding one of the logics of political culture within the Guinean nation-state. Policies like the Demystification Program were not epiphenomenal to "real" politics. Indeed they were often the sites where political practice was first theorized and codified. In a sense, the Demystification Program was Guinea's first purge. This purge was followed by others, which focused their attention on people rather than objects. The notion of a "permanent plot" articulated by the PDG government was the justification for the murder of ten to thirty thousand Guineans between the mid 1960s and 1984 (Kaké 1987; McGovern and Arieff forthcoming).

The cultural and aesthetic facets of statecraft often lead rather than follow those practices more typically studied by political scientists.[6] They are also a rich site for examining the interaction of rulers and ruled. Demystification was (among other things) a dramatic performance of the power and capacity of the state. The dramatic burning of masks and the folkloric performances of the same sacred objects were politics as theater and theater as politics. Whole populations often participate in such cultural struggles, while at the level of elections and party politics, those who have exited the political process become invisible by virtue of the categories of analysis.

The narrative of universal historical progression adopted by postcolonial states squares well with anticolonial nationalist theories of politics and economics, but it arrives at an impasse in the case of "backward" cultural practices like Loma "fétichisme." This is one of the contradictions within Guinean Marxism that prepared the way for Demystification, a program like those undertaken in many communist countries in the name of suppressing retrograde cultural and religious practices. The resulting stridency of Guinean Marxism dovetails with the regional history of Islamic conversion and iconoclasm in unexpected ways that I trace below.

In both cases, the local permutations of universalist ideology are characterized by what I call "double double consciousness," adapting DuBois's famous analysis of African American identity. This "sense of always looking at one's self through the eyes of others, of measuring one's soul by the tape of a world that looks on in amused contempt and pity" ([1903] 1994, 2) is to this day an important part of the way that Guineans talk about their relation to the wider (especially the Euro-American) world. But at the same time that Guineans express a piquant self-consciousness of their racial and civilizational "otherness" in the international scheme of things, they have nurtured their own stereotypes of an indispensable Other—the Forestiers. The group to whom I am imputing this "double double consciousness" includes people like Game Guilao, a Loma speaker educated and living in France, and several Loma informants who had been high-level functionaries in the Guinean state.

As I argue in the last part of the chapter, the Demystification Program was not only a means of bringing modernist political subjectivity to a supposedly backward people. It was also an exercise in national culture-building, in which Guineans demonstrated to themselves (and by implication to those skeptical, even racist others looking on in "amused contempt and pity") who they *were* (modern, monotheistic, politically unified) by delineating a useful Other that represented who they *were not* (traditional, "animist," parochial). This situation is by no means particular to Guinea, as the writings of Corinne Kratz (1994), Mary Margaret Steedly (1993), Anna Tsing (1993), and others have demonstrated.[7] Thus this analysis of Guinea's Demystification Program may be generalizable to contradictions within other postcolonial settings.

Changing Notions of Personhood in Modernist Political Discourse: Personae, Masks, and Mystification

The socialist state under Sékou Touré tried to engineer new forms of modernist political subjectivity that would make people feel and act as Guineans rather than as members of an ethnic group, a religion, or some other interest group. This was a monumental task, and it required, in the government's view, the eradication of many local institutions and formations, such as the men's power association in the forest region that includes Macenta Préfecture. Modernist anxieties grew in the context of what Guinean elites knew to be racist stereotypes about a savage continent, incapable of self-governance. This anxiety can be understood as interacting with notions of personhood, which Fortes has described as the question of how "the individual, as actor, know[s] himself to be—or not to be—the person he is expected to be in a given situation and status" (1987, 251). In decolonizing African states, the dissonance between who or what one is expected to be and who or what one experiences oneself as being operated at several levels. This dissonance, and the anxiety caused by it, was part of the motivation behind projects like the Demystification Program. The process is distinct from (yet related to) the simple extension of the dialectic of enlightenment, as Karp argues in quoting Carlos Fuentes: "it is one thing to write from within a culture that deems itself central and another to write from the borders of eccentricity—an eccentricity defined by the central culture's claim to universality" (2002, 97). Karp continues: "In encounters organized by the discourse of development, a space is set up in which different concepts of personhood and agency are put forward, and some actors, at least, experience considerable discrepancies between who they think themselves to be and how they find themselves defined" (99).

That dynamic also characterized the independence era, and in that context, demonstrating modernity became a type of self-justification in relation to existing nation-states. This was true even in Guinea, a country whose intellectuals were aware of the ways that racist common sense carried over from the colonial era, and who insisted on forging unique and culturally authentic types of modernity that did not copy European norms. This is a testament to the pervasiveness of the European model of modernity. However much Sékou Touré and his close associates were able to articulate the critique of a culturally specific (European) ideal of modernity, their model of progressive national culture and its importance to the state's political program shared a great deal with theories of national culture in capitalist and communist Europe. The power associations of the forest region "were from that point onward perceived as simply [representing] ethnocentric and obsolete values, incompatible with the exigencies of the creation of a modern, developed and united nation" (Beavogui 1998, 254).

The situation becomes more complex when one remembers that Northern Mande culture had until very recently been as profoundly connected to the power associations that controlled dangerous *nyama* ("power" or "capacity"), as had the Southwestern Mande societies of the forest. "Malinke" culture, effacing internal divisions among Maninka, Soninke, Diallonke, Koniyanke, Manya, and Kuranko, was the culture of Guinea's new president, Sékou Touré, and it became the implicit national culture. Especially in the face of Fulbe claims both to longer-standing Muslim piety and greater achievement in the colonial educational system, it was important for Touré and "Malinke" people more generally to jettison the traces of the animist past.[8] Thus the Demystification Program was partly a product of the set of distinctions among ethno-religious groups that long predated colonization, and partly the result of Guinean national double consciousness (which explains why Loma and other Forestier elites also participated). This process, like many others undertaken by the Guinean state, was violent and coercive, and it was only partially successful: many Loma speakers, like their Kpelle-speaking and Mano-speaking neighbors, simply crossed over into Liberia to perform initiations. Still, twenty-six years of modernist policies, supported by a strong, coercive state, did mark many Guineans in a lasting way.

In his 1938 essay, "Une categorie de l'esprit humain: La notion de la personne, celle de 'moi,'" Marcel Mauss chronicled the history of the legal, social, and psychological statuses of the person and the self, as they changed in (mainly) European settings from classical Rome to the twentieth century. As he points out, the etymology of the term "person" is from the Latin *persona*, which originally meant mask, later came to take on the sense of dramatic role, as in *dramatis personae*, and only recently came to be associated primarily with a sense of monadic individuality. Mauss's methodology and argumentation were an eclectic mix of etymology, classical scholarship, and ethnology, and through them he raised a critical analytic point by historicizing, and thus denaturing, the notion of an autonomous self. That is the same self assumed in much (enlightenment-derived) political theory to have the ability to exercise free will and to constitute the basic atomic particle of liberal-democratic political practice.

Mauss's deconstructive and historicizing work continues to influence both structuralism and poststructuralism in the fields of anthropology, and literary and art criticism, but has had less influence in the study of politics. This is surprising inasmuch as Mauss's narrative, which one commentator has glossed as his "suggestion that the story leads from a start in pure role without self, to a finish in pure self without role" (Carrithers et al. 1985, 220) would potentially raise all sorts of questions about both political subjectivity and the imaginable forms of political agency.[9]

In its links to the visible and potentially deceptive aspects of the persona, the mask is a trope par excellence of mystificatory work. Sometimes such mystification is intended, as when masked carnival revelers hide their identities in order to indiscriminately enjoy the pleasures of the flesh, even across the boundaries of class and race. In a different context, doctors and researchers talk of secondary symptoms "masking" the true causes of illness. Such unintentional "masking" has potentially deleterious consequences. Standing ambivalently between the two poles, many of the key notions of psychoanalysis (e.g., projection, transference, the symbolism of dreams) and Marxism (false consciousness, the agency and importance of superstructure, hegemony) raise complex questions about the relation between appearance and reality, surface and depth.[10] The power of masks derives from their ability to point clearly to a category, idea, or persona at the same time that they draw attention to the discrepancies between that category and the true identity of the mask's wearer. Masks index the dialectic between the hidden and the revealed.

In his 1986 book, *Masks, Transformation and Paradox*, anthropologist David Napier claims that modern ambivalence towards masking runs contiguous with the ambiguities that have developed around modern definitions of identity: "By identity, we may admit not only the 'absolute likeness of two or more things,' but also a 'sameness with self; selfsameness; oneness.' In the first case, the term refers to things that are equitable, referential, and class-oriented. In the second, it suggests something innate, indivisible, and unique—an entity that is called the self" (Napier 1986, 2-3). He thus links the development traced by Mauss of the "self," a notion whose origins lie in distinction from the multiple senses of the Latin term *persona*, with modern anxieties over the problem of identity.

Recent events from the former Yugoslavia to Rwanda and beyond have emphasized the fact that slippages between these two senses of "identity" have more than just academic interest. As Bayart (2005), Mbembe (2000), and Chabal and Daloz (1999) have recently pointed out, one of the primary strategies of modern African politics is the "re-traditionalization of society."[11] One may *appear* to be a member of a race, a gender, a political party, but one is also an indivisible and autonomous entity. As such, one is capable of harboring beliefs and desires that do not square with one's personae. In the modern era, the potential for contradiction between person and self is ever present.[12]

This is the paradox that, according to sociologist Karl Mannheim ([1936] 1955), causes the problem of identity to become eminently political. With the rise of the Christian era, the preeminent theological and political problematic is to bring belief and action into line with one another. This was a recurrent preoccupation of twentieth-century Communism, as the title of Sheila Fitzpatrick's 2005 book, *Tear off the Masks! Identity and Imposture in Twentieth-Century Russia*, suggests. Just as in Guinea, Soviet Russian society took general anxieties about identity and imposture and most frequently affixed them to the figures of internal minorities. In Russia, those minorities might be Jews, while in Guinea they were likely to be Foresters. In both cases, the early practice of seeking untrustworthy elements within the body politic metastasized, leading to more general and more lethal purges of the general population.

In the context of these worries that things may not be what they seem to be, indoctrination and socialization become the preoccupation of clerics and politicos precisely to the extent that the self is posited as having an internal life separate from a person's roles, statuses or, we may say, masks. There is some disagreement over exactly how one should periodize this history and which variables might be isolated as centrally important in its development. My interest here is to highlight the shift of political idiom from one in which a group (Roman, early Christian) with self-consciously shared interests seeks consensus on a particular point—the means of this process being rhetoric—to one in which organizations such as the political party seek to foster "those tendencies which enable us to make decisions on the basis of *a prior total orientation*" (Mannheim 1955, 183; my emphasis), in the context of acknowledged competition for political goods. Here the means are not just rhetoric but indoctrination. The model shifts from conviction to conversion. The conversion model was extremely important in socialist Guinea.

As his administration matured, Sékou Touré became increasingly explicit in linking Islam to the Guinean revolutionary experiment. One of the modes of this connection was the requirement that every political gathering open with al-Fatiha ("the Opening"), the first sura of the Quran, which is an integral part of prayer in Islam and is for Muslims more generally a profession of faith, assuring the clear conscience and good intentions of the speaker. In the context of writing about al-Fatiha in his book *L'Islam au service du peuple*, Touré stated:

> From day to day, militants of the party come to the Presidential Palace to request an audience with the head of state.[13] In general, these people dress properly for the circumstance and take care to comb their hair.

However, certain people who take great care in their appearance before presenting themselves to the president sometimes nourish more sinister sentiments:

> The boubou[14] one wears to meet the President is clean, but the heart one hides from him is all black, full of malicious intentions against the same President and against the People he represents and defends. (Touré 1977, 65–66)

This passage gives the reader a glimpse of Touré's messianic paranoia, his predilection for a Manichean rhetoric of good or bad, and his elision of his own person with the person of "the People" (cf. Barry 2002). Most importantly, it indicates his concern to distinguish appearances from reality. As with so many other aspects of its political development, such seemingly idiosyncratic orientations are not particular to Guinea. Writing about Indonesia, Mary Margaret Steedly observes, "never has the political project of religious intervention been so systematically undertaken or so successfully implemented [in Indonesia] as by Suharto's New Order, in which nonadherence to a world religion ("atheism") is equated with communism, and independent religious associations are seen as dangerous sites of potential political mobilization" (1993, 74).

Monotheistic faith in Guinea as in Indonesia came to stand for a kind of reliability, as if Touré and Suharto would thus be able to consult God to look deep into the souls of their citizens. Today, Guineans talk of the imposition of the Fatiha as one instance of Touré's "magic," which he used to esoterically discover his enemies.[15]

People living in the area that became Guinea had experienced a variety of monotheist challenges to pre-Islamic notions of personhood even before the French extended their control over the region. Islamization was highly uneven, and, as the material I presented in chapter 2 shows, many Northern Mande speakers who moved toward the forest during the colonial period were not Muslims. Nevertheless, most were probably aware of the general tenor of Muslim arguments over doctrine and and especially over the form of legitimate contact between believers and God. The role of the marabout for Sufi Muslims as a spiritual intermediary is not unlike that of the Loma *zowei* or ritual specialist. The shift that Demystification legislated away from these "charlatans" (this was the language the Guinean government used) presumes individual responsibility for one's own salvation. Yves Person argues that Samory Touré first promoted individualism of this kind in the region in the late nineteenth century.[16] This shift, and everything it implies about the alignment of belief, identity, and action, lends itself to the modernist sensibility regarding political affiliation. This is one of the reasons why the Northern Mande notion of portable identities prepared Northern Mande speakers to better negotiate the colonial and postcolonial state than Southwestern Mande speakers. The latter's ideology of mutable identity contradicted the modernist assumptions about subject formation and, by extension, political participation. We see a similar situation in the case Donham examines, in Maale, southern Ethiopia. There, it was primarily the small number of Maale Christian converts who became the core of the community's revolutionary cadres at the time of Ethiopia's Marxist revolution (Donham 1999).

The evidence for the link between religious and political imaginations is not simply a matter of historical analogy. The practices and techniques of the Guinean revolution sometimes borrowed directly from the religious idiom, as the use of the Fatiha indicates. Nowhere was this more evident than in the party's attempt to politically educate the newly independent "masses." A demonstrative text is the PDG's *Seminaires hebdomadaires de janvier-février, 1960*.[17] It was evidently intended as the beginning of a series of seminars to be given by local political officials during weekly meetings that all citizens of a village or a neighborhood were required to attend.[18] These Friday afternoon meetings continued throughout the twenty-six years of Touré's rule, though they became, over the years, moments for delegating unpopular but necessary tasks and fighting over the small goods the state provided.[19] In towns and cities, this was also the moment when the Party and its various organs distributed food rations to Guineans.

Early on, however, the notion was that these meetings would be the site of a kind of consciousness-raising. Those with more education and greater understanding of the mechanics of imperialism and capitalism would bring the peasantry into full consciousness of their situation. The mode of the "Seminars" is important: they are written in the form of a catechism, a series of questions, each followed by a fixed response. A few examples will illuminate the technique:

> **Question 29**, Is colonialism a form of government or the nature of a regime?
> **Response**: Colonialism is a form of government that comes out of the nature of a regime, the capitalist regime.
> In effect, the concentration of production and of capital in the capitalist regime leads to the formation of monopolies that dictate, each one to its state, a politics of exportation of capital and of the carving-up of the world, from which come colonial conquests in order to find markets and sources of primary materials and of high-profit investment.
> From that point on, colonialism takes on the character of a form of government based on exploitation, to the profit of the imperialist monopolies, on racism, and on the disqualification and depersonalization of the colonized, which are the conditions of their exploitation. (1962, 27)

> **Question 244**, What is the base of the Guinean state?
> **Response**: It is the *Parti Démocratique de Guinée* that authentically expresses the will of the people. (158)

Amidst all the prescribed responses, it is the following, lone exception that proves the rule about the type of political indoctrination envisioned in the "Seminars":

> **Question 239**, Explicate this passage: "This is why no regionalist spirit, no strict nationalism could know how to stop the universalist thrust of Guinean politics, a politics that culminates directly in the meeting point of humanity's positive values in order to eliminate the causes of injustice, exploitation and oppression in order to rehabilitate it in all its general ideals and in all its legitimate aspirations."
> **Response**: *Liberté de réponse.* (Free response.) (158)

Such "liberté" is nowhere else repeated in the book. A last example indicates the thoroughly didactic nature of this catechistic endeavor:

Question 25, According to you, what causes social contradictions?
Response: The principle causes of social contradictions are inequality, unjust differences in life conditions, different conceptions of how a society should be oriented, and the unequal distribution of the riches produced by social activity. (26)

It is the evident disjunction between the "According to you" ("D'après vous") and the carefully wrought, ideologically constrained response that mark the poignancy of this undertaking. As with the Catholic Church, another producer of catechisms, the PDG's orthodoxy did not brook dissent and for that reason was allergic to free interpretation. Once catechized subjects had begun to show mastery of and faith in the doxa, they might be given increasing leeway, and, if this did not lead to untoward results, they might rise up the hierarchy. The insistence by most Loma speakers on maintaining the autonomous political/ritual sphere delineated by their power associations clashed with the Guinean state's attempts to achieve national hegemony by demanding each citizen's *inner* allegiance.

The comparison to the Catholic Church and its *Baltimore Catechism* might seem an obvious parallel to the PDG's Seminars for North American readers. However, there is also a strong resemblance between the PDG's pedagogical system and that of West African Islamic instruction. In his book on the Malian Sufi teacher Cerno Bokar Saalif Taal (a great-nephew of El Hajj Umar Tal, described in the last chapter), Louis Brenner (1984) discusses some of the forms of Islamic education among West African Fulbe. In addition to memorizing the suras of the Koran, as Muslim children throughout the world do, the Fulbe utilize a dogmatic indoctrination called *kabbe* in Fulfulde. According to Brenner, "Although based on written Arabic texts, the *kabbe* was transmitted orally; it developed through several stages of increasing complexity, and concluded with an 'initiation' into a body of esoteric religious knowledge" (1984, 73). Brenner continues: "[Cerno Bokar's] personal version of an Islamic catechism in theology, which came to be known as the *ma'd-din* (Arabic for 'What is religion?') was also taught orally in Fulfulde" (73).

These teachings are derived from *al-Aqidat al-Sughra* (The Lesser Catechism) of Maghrebin scholar Mohammed bin Yusuf al-Sanusi (d. 1490). This book, used over the centuries in North and West Africa, states in its opening paragraph that "it is incumbent upon every legally competent adult that he know what is necessary, impossible or contingent with respect to our great and powerful Master. It is also incumbent to know the same with respect to the prophets" (quoted in Brenner 1984, 80). In this case, the PDG's techniques for educating and indoctrinating new Guinean citizens appear to have built upon practices familiar to many of Guinea's Muslim majority. As we saw in the last chapter's description of precedents to the Demystification Program, the line between religion and politics in the region that became Guinea has been blurred since at least the late eighteenth century. The two are often linked by the themes of renewal and purification, which have often been enacted through iconoclasm.

Contradictory Cosmopolitanism: Marxism and the Modern Person

Cosmopolitanism is a way of belonging to a sphere larger than the local or the national. An inquiry into cosmopolitanism may thus yield insights into the cultural politics of Demystification and how it is linked to Guinean imaginings of these larger spheres. In Guinea, postcolonial life has been characterized by a deep mistrust of outsiders, as they have been variously defined. Nevertheless, Guineans have known themselves to be part of a wider world. One of their cosmopolitan affiliations has been through Islam. The other primary mode of belonging to the wider world during the 1958–84 socialist period was through Marxism.

Theoretical Entanglements

One of the enduring tensions in Marxism is its aspiration to global communitas—"workers of the world, unite!"—countered by the necessity of operating within the national political-economic sphere. As Benedict Anderson has suggested, "nationalism has proved an uncomfortable anomaly for Marxist theory and, precisely for that reason, has been largely elided, rather than confronted. How else to explain Marx's failure to explicate the crucial adjective in his memorable formulation of 1848, 'The proletariat of each country must, of course, first of all settle matters with *its own* bourgeoisie'?"(1991, 3–4).

This tension has proven at least as acute in Africa, where nations-to-be inherited colonial languages and arbitrary frontiers and also became independent at different times. As a result of this unevenness, African socialist countries have often had more concrete political and economic links to the socialist countries of Europe and Asia than to some of their neighbors on the African continent. This has had the effect of fostering longstanding cultural, political, and educational exchanges. Many Guineans pursued their university educations in the U.S.S.R., Yugoslavia, Bulgaria, and Romania; and teachers from these countries, Cuba, and China taught in Guinean universities and technical schools. The exchange fostered by educational policies had the effect of allowing Guineans, at least in theory, to see themselves as part of a wider world defined not by color or place but by political affiliation. That this latter possibility was incompletely realized was partly the result of individual Guineans' experience of racism in Eastern Bloc countries. Nevertheless, Guinea is the only African nation to choose to place the face of a European on its currency—that of Josip Tito, the Yugoslavian socialist leader, who graced the 10,000 syli note.

Guinean Marxism, however, met an enduring contradiction: at the time of Sékou Touré's accession to power in 1958, there were virtually no capitalist relations of production, and the working class was a fraction of one percent of the national population. Not only was there no originary dispossession of workers against which to organize and militate, the government found itself in the strange position of *forming* the nation's first bourgeois elite (functionaries and party apparatchiks), as Claude Rivière has argued (1978). Thus, the symbolic and rhetorical weight of the Guinean "revolution" was shifted away from transforming the relations and means of production and towards "modernization," and "progress."[20] In this context, the allure of a socialist revolution is its promise of skipping forward right "over" industrial capitalism and directly into a modernist egalitarian future. This brand of Marxism eschews much of the actual mechanics of Marx and Engels' theory and espouses instead Marxism's most modernist aspect.[21]

Marxism and the Modern Person

In their attempts to account for differences in "development," colonial and postcolonial states have frequently subscribed to unilineal models of progress while arguing for opposed causal variables. In the colonizing nations' narrative, underdevelopment and backwardness are caused by the colonized societies' internal characteristics (lack of political hierarchy, ambition, gumption), while progress arrives thanks to qualities introduced from the outside (honesty, work ethic, propensity to save). The mirror image, elaborated in dependency theory, Pan-Africanism, and other decolonizing and anticolonial models, attributes underdevelopment to exogenous factors (Atlantic slave trade, expropriation of raw materials, destruction of indigenous institutions of education and religion), while postcolonial cultural evolution is seen as having the potential to grow from the genius of ancient indigenous traditions. In this process, culture is first reified, then turned into a rich symbolic resource. In application, each of these discourses has been parasitic on the other. Such parallelism is facilitated by the common shape and teleology of the two narratives. It is this set of shared assumptions that sets the scene for one of postcolonial socialism's great internal contradictions.

In his essay on "Development and Personhood," Ivan Karp (2002) writes about a financially successful women's cooperative in Kenya whose success has been attributed by a National Public Radio reporter to the supplemental "social training" that a Norwegian development agency attached to the technical training offered to the women. The Kenyan state newspaper, on the other hand, attributes their success to qualities innate, typically African, and implicitly "freed" by the activities of the Kenyan state. Karp writes:

> Both accounts of the labor cooperative are confident that Mathare Valley is a scene of economic and spiritual poverty, and both are equally confident that its economic success is the product of alterations of internal states [in the women]: NPR predicates an internal change in moral attitudes derived from without [i.e., the development agency], while the *Kenya Times* celebrates the innate personal qualities that enabled the women to transcend the conditions of their existence, which makes them different from their sisters. (Karp 2002, 91)

There are two explanatory schemes in play here, which in their ideal typical forms are diametrically opposed. In what we might call (neo-)colonial developmentalism, what is indigenous to a place like Guinea is negative, what is good has been imported (which does not necessarily imply that *everything* that has been imported is positive). In what we may call the nativist anticolonial scheme, that which is indigenous is valued as good, while that which is bad has been imported (again, not necessarily everything imported is bad). The nativist scheme (an ideal type) encompasses to a greater or lesser extent a variety of actual historical stances—from Léopold Senghor's Negritude to Cheikh Anta Diop's Afrocentricity to Sékou Touré's or Kwame N'Krumah's Pan-Africanism. It also has affinities to a wider range of African and Asian postcolonial rhetorical stances. This discursive constellation is by no means simply reactive to its colonial opposite. It originates from an empirical critique of the material and moral conditions of colonization.

In considering the "cultural politics of catching up" in the Guinean context, we must examine how the tropes of masks and unmasking interact with the tropes of progress, development, and evolution.[22] Crucial to this model is the assumption that progress moves in only one direction, and that at any given moment differing communities can be located on the graph of historical development, their relative positions open to comparison. On such a graph, the Forestiers were unambiguously represented as history's laggards. Describing Guinean hierarchies of civilization, Rivière writes, "The contempt of Islamized people for the *Forestier* is well transposed in the suggestive designation assigned the Soviets by [Muslim] Guineans: 'The Russians are the Guerzes [Kpelle] of the Whites,' that is: Europe's savages" (1971, 81).

While the developmentalist and nativist narratives share a common notion of progress, the question of whether the sources of progress may be universal and thus easily introduced, or local and particularistic, is their most crucial difference. It also has very real political ramifications. Anthropologist Edwin Ardener points out the affinities between certain universalist religious and political creeds as he writes about such disagreements in the context of theories of cross-cultural difference:

> Thus cultures were "relativistic" in detail, but there was some kind of limit to their arbitrary, reality-shaping powers. Some went so far as to argue that at a common sense level, cultural differences were greatly exaggerated, and that the major differences were mystifications deriving from ritual specialists (Bloch 1977). For people with any idea of universal truth to be taught to all mankind, the exact nature of cultural difference is a serious question. Thus at times both missionaries and historical materialists have led violent attacks on the merest hint of cultural relativism. . . . If there are self evident truths that are to be taught, these truths cannot themselves be subject to any law of cultural relativism. (Ardener 1989, 164)

This passage, in combination with the one before by Karp, is helpful in explicating the internal contradictions of a revolutionary modernist political program carried out in the anticolonial context.[23] While the paradigm of Marxist revolution offers the enticing possibility of a sudden political and economic leap "forward," it radically undercuts—because of its unilineal and universalizing structure—the possibility of blaming any hints of local cultural backwardness on exogenous forces such as colonialism. It offers a set of possibilities with one (world historical) hand, but takes these back with the other.

It has been easy for formerly colonized nations to equate colonial domination with capitalist political economies and thus to blame colonizers for disastrous political and economic legacies. This is not so easy when referring to an otherwise objectified and glorified ancestral culture. Revolutionary states like Guinea's may have felt constrained to quickly suppress the examples of a potentially embarrassing cultural "behindness." This is the necessary preparation for bringing anticolonial nationalism in line with high modernist Marxism—the figurative several steps back one must take before a great leap forward.

There was and is in Africa an intense awareness that both colonialism and Marxism assigned Guinea and other African societies a specifically backward position on a trajectory leading toward modernity, civilization, and a classless society. This paradox is well documented in Donham's (1999) book on the Ethiopian Marxist revolution initiated in 1974. In the "backwater" area where he conducted his research, divine kingship—rather than masks—was the target of this type of cultural slate-cleaning. The renunciation entailed in the revolutionary promise of moving "forward" is one of the motives behind the violence of the Demystification Program.

Modernist Anxiety and Double Double Consciousness

I have argued in this chapter that the Demystification Program was partly the result of the postcolonial state's attempt to shape Guineans into new types of persons who could be useful national citizens. It was also partly the crystallization of a set of stereotyped distinctions about Forestiers that were in play in twentieth-century Guinea. These two are inseparable to the extent that Forestiers came to represent everything that was pathological and unacceptable in the ideal national citizen. Demystification was a programmatic attempt to expunge the savagery embodied in Guinea's minority populations.

At the same time, it is important to emphasize that the bigotry enacted by the Guinean state and espoused by many Guineans operated in the shadow of European racist stereotypes. While Demystification drew on distinctions promulgated by West African Muslims who denounced polytheistic practices, even those "civilized," Islamicized Guineans knew that from another point of view, all Africans were stereotyped as an undifferentiated savage Other to European civilization. Sékou Touré's form of Marxist Modernism drew on these two legacies in his attempt to forge the conscience of a people—a unitary national identity that everyone knew to be a novelty. He chose the route that many European and Asian nations chose in the nineteenth and twentieth centuries, which was to legislate, then impose, national norms, and to attempt to engineer a common sense of of national identity.

The internal contradictions I have described within the forward-looking universalism of Islamic and Marxist ideologies in Guinea fed into this modernist anxiety and into the "double double consciousness" that exists in Guinea and elsewhere. That is to say that the dialectic between denigrated and lionized, savage and civilized, is in play within the Guinean national context, as it is in the American or any other. In this dialectic, Guinea's Foresters play something like the role played by African Americans in the United States—filling what Trouillot (1991, 2002) has called the "savage slot." DuBois's description, however, applied to a nation that considered itself "civilized" in relation to other nations and that was technologically and economically advanced. As a result, he didn't frame his notion of double consciousness within the second dialectic I suggest here, in which nations, too—even continents—relate to one another in similar terms, "this sense of always looking at one's self through the eyes of others."

I do not think Loma rice farmers spend too much time worrying about their place in the international scheme of things, although they are well aware of it. Most of the time, this second degree of double consciousness is the special burden of a poor nation's elites. Guinea's nationalist elite was in much the same position as Bengal's, as described by Partha Chatterjee: "[It] was simultaneously placed in a position of subordination in one relation and a position of dominance in another. The construction of hegemonic ideologies typically involves the cultural efforts of classes placed precisely in such situations" (1993, 36).

The situation Chatterjee describes is specifically colonial, and the same held true for the (much smaller) Guinean elite during the colonial period.[24] But it would be a mistake to assume that this structuration of consciousness ended with independence. Guineans continued to live in a world of distinctions. Knauft, ed. (2002, 28) writes of "the classification of persons into ranked categories by the bleached authority of an ostensibly objective scale of social and moral development. Now as before under colonialism, the local subject is viewed as inert material to be transformed through new forms of discipline." In other words, the work that national elites do on "backward" populations may not be intended simply to bring them up to speed with their more "advanced" compatriots but also to bring the nation *as a whole* "forward" on the supposedly "objective scale of social and moral development." In the next chapter, we turn to the sociology and micropolitics of how this process took place in Guinean villages and towns. As we shall see, Demystification was only the most dramatic of a range of authoritarian high-modernist interventions into people's lives.

SEVEN

Unmasking the State: Making Guinea Modern

The demystification campaign is finished. The children have made themselves the educators of their mothers and fathers; they have broken in their hands those nefarious playthings and thrown them in the fire. The fetishes have entered the void from which they came. . . . And so, mortally wounded, paganism realizes that it has no more chance of survival; it expires, but slowly, with those for whom it was significant: those people of the dusk who hear of a dawn they will not see and who seem to say: "What are we going to do?" rather than, "What are we going to become?" These are the people turned toward the past, who are interested less and less by the future. (Guilao 1967, 237)

The temporal emphasis of high modernism is almost exclusively on the future. . . . The past is an impediment, a history that must be transcended; the present is the platform for launching plans for a better future. (Scott 1998, 95)

Gebusi say they are exchanging their past for their future. In saying this, they use the same concept that they use for direct and reciprocal exchange in marriage, feasting, or killing. (Knauft 2002, 38)

So far, we have seen some of the ways that the socialist state intruded into its citizens' lives. Its changes to land tenure rules (chapter 4) were part of its broader attempts to reengineer relations between different categories of person: landowning nobles and landless ex-captives. The unintended result of this policy was to contribute to hardened ethnic identities. Policies aimed at reengineering gender relations and marriage had mixed outcomes for Guinean women. Guinea's Cultural Revolution, like China's, took the gerontocratic privileges of Guinean elders and turned them on their head, transforming youths from subalterns into despots.[1]

The revolutionary state's push for "the normalization of relationships of every kind, governing, at the heart of every collectivity, individuals among themselves" (Kouyaté 1996, 123) was a more general aspect of the PDG's approach to postcolonial governance. In this chapter, we will see how the Guinean socialist state attempted to realign the relations between elders and youth, and between men and women. We consider first the Demystification Program, justified in part as an attempt to eradicate the exploitation of youth labor by elders, and then look at changes in the laws regarding marriage introduced so as to give women more voice in this matter.

In the case of Demystification, it would be simplistic and misleading to pretend that this was simply a technocratic adjustment intended to release a little more productive capacity from the nation's youth and increase the Gross National Product. This chapter is a continuation not only of chapter 4's focus on state interventions and their consequences but also of chapter 5's focus on the importance of ethno-religious rhetoric in the legitimation of the state. Foresters became useful national stereotypes as counterexamples to proper modern citizenship. I have already discussed how the anxiety surrounding the recently fétichiste identities of Manya-speaking converts to Islam gave these stereotypes an especially strident tone.

It is, then, the combination of these two factors—the will of the authoritarian high modernist state (Scott 1998) to refashion social relations of every kind, and the somewhat manic energy invested in the construction of a stereotype of Foresters as a savage foil to the modern national subject—that gave the Demystification Program much of its momentum. It is also the combination of these two factors that make Demystification a privileged site for thinking about the dynamics of postcolonial state-making, attempts to legislate new forms of sociality, and indeed the state's attempts to inculcate new forms of subjectivity in a population it deemed lacking in certain necessary qualities.[2]

Plans to mould a new national citizenry were the product of complex and often contradictory forms of consciousness on the part of national elites.[3] They also produced different forms of complex consciousness of religious, ethnic, regional, and national identities among ordinary Guinean citizens. During the 1990s and 2000s, this resulted in complex formations and sometimes in violent politics. We should also tie this problematic back to the earlier chapters in which I have presented the dynamics of ethnogenesis in the Macenta area. What has Demystification to do with ancestral sacrifice, the Koivogui-Kamara corridor, and *kɛkɛ–daabe* relations?

There are two separate strands to a possible response. First, it was the very particularism and "traditionalism" of Forestier cultural and political practice that marked them for a socialist makeover. The power associations, their use of *sale* including masquerades, their initiations and magical beliefs were all among the ostensible targets of Demystification. At another level, these objects and practices were also symptoms of an underlying dynamic, one that I sketched in chapter 5: many Forestiers' preference for carving out small islands of autonomy rather than attempting to achieve hegemonic control of bigger spheres (e.g., empires, states). To put it in different terms, Forestier political practice was based almost entirely upon struggles to claim and control the prerogatives that flowed out of autochthony and first-comer status. These prerogatives were highly localized by definition and involved the establishment and maintenance of relations between the living and the dead, invisible spirits and living humans, and the use of *sale* and other powerful objects like lineage spears or swords. By contrast, those who characterized the Forestiers as "backward" aimed at a higher level of political control—the empire and later the nation-state—and legitimized those claims through ideologies that were predictably grander and more universal in their claims: noble descent, universal religious faith (Islam), or universal political faith (Marxism). From this angle, Demystification was part of a wider programmatic attempt by the state's elites to organize everyday life around the sign of the nation, which would encompass all less significant distinctions, like ethnic or regional origins, but which still imposed certain prerequisites for full citizenship, including monotheism.

This difference in the scale of political ambitions mapped onto the distinction I have made more generally between an ideology of portable identities (Northern Mande speakers) and one of autochthony (Southwestern Mande speakers).[4] Here the second strand comes in, which is what we might call the "second Dyula revolution," borrowing a phrase from Person (1968). From this angle, Demystification as it was practiced was part of a wider set of struggles taking place specifically along the forest–savanna frontier, during which the gradual process of ethnic assimilation that had been necessary for turning migrants, refugees, and conquerors into "autochthons" had been short-circuited by Manya speakers seeking to gain political control *without* assimilating to Forestier culture. This refusal drew on a number of sources, including the model of Mande empire (including the first Dyula revolution, during which Samory Touré and other Muslim dyula of his generation decided to wrest political control from their "Malinké fétichiste" hosts) and the later mise en valeur laws introduced by the PDG.

That these dynamics were intertwined is one of the things I hope to show in this chapter. But we should also not forget the Loma speakers, who were certainly not passive victims of the state's (or their Manya-speaking neighbors') depredations. One of the great strengths of Sékou Touré's political sensibility was his understanding of alliances. He recognized that if he could gain the support of the small but vocal groups of workers and intellectuals in Conakry, add to them most of Guinea's women by offering them advances from the status quo, and add to them the youth by promising them, too, a more equitable stake in formerly gerontocratic settings, he could effectively bypass the elder men who might oppose him (Schmidt 2005). This chapter shows, too, how the PDG worked in conjunction with women and youths, sometimes in explicit partnerships (e.g., Forestier youth participation in Demystification) and sometimes indirectly (e.g., by choosing not to ban the women's initiations). To the extent that Demystification was successful (a question I address at the end of the chapter) it could only have been so because the state, pursuing its program of modernization, found allies, and worked synergistically with Loma youth and Forestier intellectuals. After beginning with an overview of Demystification, the chapter looks at those factors internal to Loma society that shaped the way that the policy progressed on the ground. At the end of the chapter, I compare the state's alliances with youth to its alliances with women by exploring some of the changes made in marriage laws and comparing them to Demystification.

Demystification, the Forest Region, and the Guinean Nation

> There were marabouts who exploited the believers. Fétichistes who lived off of the ordinary people's mystification. There were in that country [Guinea] tree gods, mountain gods, gods in jars in front of which men would come to kneel down, sacrifice cola nuts, confide their secrets and wait [for a solution], with crossed arms. . . . We have crossed swords with every form of mystification. (Touré 1982)

Sékou Touré initiated a Demystification Program to modernize Guinea and to diminish the political influence of religion and religious leaders in the country. In the early stages of this program, Catholic schools were closed (1961), then nationalized; both Muslim imams and Guinean priests were prohibited from expressing independent political ideas in their sermons (from 1961); and later, French priests were expelled from the country (1967). The brunt of the Demystification Program's energies, however, was directed at the small percentage of Guineans practicing indigenous religions (c. 10 percent of the national population), and not Islam (c. 80 percent) or Christianity (c. 10 percent).[5]

The Demystification Program was oriented by late 1961 toward the thin coastal strip inhabited by Baga, Nalou, and Landuma speakers (Lamp 1996; Sarró 2009) and the southeastern rainforest region of the country inhabited by Kissi, Loma, Kpelle, Kono, and Mano speakers (Rivière 1971, Højbjerg 2002a, 2007). In the forest region, nearly all men and women were initiated into the Poro (*Pologi*) and Sande (*Zadegi*) power associations as the normal rite of passage into adulthood. Non-initiates have called these power associations barbaric because of their alleged practice of human sacrifice.[6] I interpret the Guinean state's opposition to the power associations as a reaction both to their role as fierce defenders of "tradition" (and thus impediments to modernization) and as the foundation of an autonomous political system.

Loma people with whom I have spoken about this period recall it as a time of considerable violence. Typically, agents of the Guinean state would enter villages and demand masks, statuettes, and other ritually powerful objects. These were most often burned, typically in the kind of public bonfire described in the interlude preceding chapter 6. Ritual specialists were bound, often beaten in front of their communities, and placed under arrest, sometimes until they relinquished ritual objects. Sometimes they were arrested and brought to the préfectoral seat simply because of their status as important "féticheurs." One teacher described how the death of a young man in the Dopamai/Sedime[7] initiation camp in 1964 caused the authorities to claim he had been sacrificed in the sacred forest.[8] They arrested the elders, beat them, and jailed them in Macenta town. It was also illegal for Loma speakers to pursue their ritual business in Liberia, although many people did so (Bellman 1984). In 1971-72, a group of people who had gone to Liberia to be initiated were thrown in jail for three months.[9] A teacher I knew had led a group of young men into Liberia for initiation in the 1970s, and was arrested upon his return. Other teachers told me he had been tortured so severely during his detention that he had gone mad for several years.

In addition to confiscating and/or burning wooden objects such as masks, government representatives gathered those power objects known as *sale* in Lomagui, and as *fétiches* or *grigris* in French. Some consist of a conical white kaolin clay base with powerful substances mixed in, and others are animal horns that have been filled with powerful plant and animal products. They may also include such powerful materials as cowry shells, iron, and animal bones. During some of my visits with him, the curator of the forest region's museum (in N'Zerekore) showed me boxes filled with hundreds of these power objects, gathered up from all over the forest region in 1961–62, which had sat in the museum's storeroom for forty years.[10]

This chapter enlarges on the picture of Demystification already offered, though it is important to note the degree to which the program has eluded both the documentary record and the archive of what Guineans are willing to discuss. Although I argue that the program was crucial to the development of the modern Guinean state, it was barely mentioned in the state newspaper during the time it was taking place.[11] The sole, cryptic reference I found in the national newspaper, *Horoya*, referred to "a schedule of informative tourneys in the interior of [the Macenta] region," and also, "placed [the party's] militants[12] on alert against the enemies of the Guinean people who, under religious pretexts, attempt to rupture national unity and create foyers of trouble" (*Horoya*, August 31, 1961).

After working for months in the national archives, I could locate no government documents on the planning or execution of the program. At the other end of the country, Loma people were exceptionally uncomfortable talking about Demystification, and they generally spoke about it only briefly and when they were sure that no one else would overhear them. Another anthropologist who works in the Guinean Loma-speaking area wrote:

> During an extended period of fieldwork among the Loma, I constantly had the impression that questions relating to the iconoclastic practices of the not-too-distant past had an embarrassing effect on those subjected to such events. Because of this, I rarely addressed the issue directly in my conversation with informants. When I finally chose to do so, the following short and precise account of past events was entered in my notebook: Everybody in the neighborhood was told to assemble on the village playground. We were watched over by the police and the gendarmerie who forced us to follow the event. The first mask to come was called *luwi*. The mask started to sound the horn and it was ordered to undress. The authorities then called on *afui* which was also placed on the ground. Next followed the women's mask *bowoi* and their "great song" *gouelai*. The last one to be presented and undressed was *onilegagi*. Hereafter all the masks were told to speak simultaneously. After a short while they were ordered to be quiet and one of the local authorities, a Fulani, explained to us that men had no right to possess more masks than women—that masks did not in any sense provide men with superiority. When an elder tried to explain why men have many masks, he was beaten by the gendarmes. They then prepared to burn the masks. But before putting

them on the fire, they told the women to come forward and play the instruments of *luwi* and *afui*. (Højbjerg 2002a, 59)

As Højbjerg indicates, research in southeastern Guinea poses a particular set of problems. On the one hand, local communities are largely structured around the power associations. Proper adult behavior is judged on the basis of discretion. This norm, based not only on a sense of propriety but also on a hierarchical notion of the ownership of knowledge, discourages most people from discussing even those topics that might seem innocuous but that might risk veering into the territory of protected knowledge. Thus, in conversations about the Demystification Program and period, it is common to be met with either the claim that one's interlocutor has no knowledge of such an event (in this case the law of *gele boga*, " it must not be spoken,"[13] that applies to the Poro society's rites is applied, at second hand, to the state's attempt to destroy those secrets), or that he claims to be too young to know anything about such a subject. This discourse of youthful ignorance may be invoked even by those who were in their twenties or thirties at the time when a particular event occurred.[14] As Bellman (1975, 109) has pointed out, privileged knowledge in the region is strongly linked to notions of ownership. On the other hand, some who were clearly old enough to have witnessed everything say without hesitation, "We can't talk too much about that time. Every time we start discussing it, we want to cry" (A.B., Siγipɔlɔzu, April 30, 1999).

Nevertheless, with patience, I came to understand many aspects of the Demystification Program. As I had first guessed, it offered a useful entry point for understanding the changes in Loma speakers' lives over the course of the twentieth century, though the aspects were often quite different from what I had expected them to be. One of them was the tension between elder and younger men in Loma and other Guinean gerontocratic societies, like the Kpelle and the Baga (Sarró 1999).

Part of the genius of Sékou Touré's political strategy in the late 1950s and the 1960s was to have tapped into the already existing intergenerational tensions in Guinea. This was perhaps nowhere so true as in the forest region. Elder men exerted control over male youth through the men's power association. In numerous interviews, Loma men and women specified the fact that no Loma-speaking woman would engage in sexual relations with an uninitiated male. Because just two generations ago, male initiates were generally 17–25 year olds, and their seclusion could last several years (within living memory, men's initiations are said to have lasted seven years, the women's, three), older Loma speakers say it was not uncommon to find thirty-year-old male virgins and forty-year-old men who had never married. Wealth and success within the subsistence economy of this region are based on two factors: access to women and thus the (re)production of children, and access to the spirit world, mainly through the medium of sacrifice. Both of these forms of capital were entirely blocked from most men in their teens and twenties. In the matter of sacrifice, the Loma case is similar to that described by Fortes for the Talensi in *Oedipus and Job in West African Religion* (1959). If a man has not outlasted his father, father's brothers, and older brothers, he remains in some respects a social minor, despite the fact that he may be in his sixties or seventies, with many children and grandchildren. Their structural marginalization made violent upheaval attractive to youths as well as to any other entrepreneurial man who was otherwise excluded from power by the existing configuration of autochthonous rights and lineage politics. In this chapter, we will see the ways that iconoclasm could be made attractive for similar reasons.

The friction between gerontocratic privilege and an entrepreneurial ethos through this region is systematically muted, even denied by actors. Yet entrepreneurial capture (McGovern 2011, 31–65) represents a primary means of shifting status. The recent wars in Liberia and Sierra Leone cannot be properly understood without paying attention to this dynamic (cf. Fanthorpe 2001; Richards 1996; Utas 2003). The preponderance of young combatants in the contemporary regional war is not only the result of frustrated, Rambo-film-watching young men acting on the impetus of stored-up testosterone. Nor is it just a matter of young people who resent their marginalization from Western-style education, electricity, or paved roads. It is also a case of youth trumping the power of elders. Many of the men who claimed esoteric powers in the arts of war during my own fieldwork (at the time that the Liberian/Sierra Leonean war came into Guinea) were in their late teens or twenties. Having proved the efficacy of their *sale* (often said to have been revealed in dreams by long-dead, famous war chiefs), they suddenly acquired a level of status and power greater than most elders. This dynamic is comparable to, and must be understood alongside, the intergenerational dynamics of the Demystification Program, when youth participated in unveiling secret knowledge, disempowering elders, and raising themselves up through their alliance with the state. The process Guilao describes in the epigraph to this chapter, through which "the children have made themselves the educators of their mothers and fathers," continued under the Touré regime beyond the Demystification Program. It was central to Guinea's Cultural Revolution, started in 1968, just two years after (and modeled on) the Chinese Cultural Revolution. As in China, this period was characterized by a kind of dictatorship of the youth (rather than the proletariat), who gained the state's support in stripping their allegedly reactionary parents and grandparents of power. The Cultural Revolution is not my focus here (though it deserves a lengthy study of its own), but I mention it as it is a continuation of a project that began in the forest region with Demystification and that continued throughout the twenty-six years of Touré's rule.[15]

There are three aspects of the Demystification Program worth emphasizing at this point: First, it was undertaken with an unusual fervor. French colonists had not meddled with practices such as initiations, secret societies, and masquerades. By contrast, the independent Guinean government made this complex of institutions one of the first targets of its postcolonial administration and pursued the policy—always declared a success, but always in need of renewed efforts[16]—with the jihadist zeal that had (nearly) eliminated masks from the Islamicized Northern Mande region of Guinea in the nineteenth and early twentieth centuries.[17] In chapter 5, I made explicit links between some of the historical precedents in Guinea of this type of iconoclastic movement and the Demystification Program.

Secondly, there was vital local participation by some Loma speakers in the region where I have done research. In his 1969 essay, "Fétichisme et démystification: l'example Guinéen," Claude Rivière describes some of the mechanics of the process as he heard about it in Guinea in the 1960s. Referring to one of the ritual specialists who assisted the members of the expedition that led to the film *Forêt sacrée* and to Pierre Gaisseau's book of the same name,[18] he writes: "Voné, called to Conakry to unveil the secrets of his pharmacopoeia to the director of the national pharmaceutical body, wrote to his friend in adventure, Virel [one of the members of the expedition on whose experiences the book was based], in Paris: 'The féticheurs are defeated'" (1971, 247).

Sometimes government officials, teachers, or Christian converts, these local iconoclastic collaborators were usually young, initiated into the power associations, but simultaneously modernist in their outlooks. Not only did they know where ritual objects were hidden and who was a ritual specialist, they also understood the structures of the power associations that organized the ritual, political, and expressive lives of most of the inhabitants of the forest region. Rivière describes one such instance in detail:

> But the zeal of a PDG neophyte, a [Loma] son of the country and a Catholic, gave the *coup de grace* to the retrograde traditions. The *chef de poste* [local administrator] of Bofossou (in the north of the Macenta region), no longer believed in fétichisme. He attacked it with a particular ardor and technique.

Let us allow a Toma witness to describe the events:

The first custom targeted was that of initiation. Since the democratic spirit reigned everywhere and had to justify all acts, it was decided in a general assembly of the regional PDG to vote on the suppression or conservation of this custom. The majority voted for its suppression, after having heard various arguments. One of the most important was this one: a young illiterate peasant made it known to everyone that he regretted having gone to be initiated (which lasted up to six or seven years) instead of going to school. He had separated from a childhood friend to go into the initiation camp at the same time his friend went to school. His friend's current social standing was well above his own, which made it clear to everyone that he, an initiated peasant, had followed the wrong path. After the vote of the general assembly, [the administrator] had carte blanche to accomplish his task of demystification. There was no violence. The ground was first prepared psychologically. [The administrator] first brought the youths around to the new ideas, and, using propaganda, they spread out across the country, in the name of the R.D.A.,[19] and of progress, the idea that fétichisme, pernicious to the society, had to disappear. They gained people's ears. [The administrator] began to collect masks and fétiches. One of his first profanations was to unveil the great secret of the *Afwi* to the women. They showed them the instruments used as the voices of this supreme mask, and further explanations completed the revelation. The *Afwi* was now familiar to the women.

This was a harsh blow to the older generation who forced themselves, nonetheless, to conform their will to that of the R.D.A. Once that seemed to be the case, it was necessary to prove it [their change of heart] by giving up all the fétiches. And so we saw the renewal of a gesture that only Protestant converts had made until then: each one throwing his [or her] fétiches or masques on the fire. Some of them did it laughing so as to make the pain supportable. There were some who refused, like the féticheur of "the black face," called *dogbomaigi*, that *Afwi* reputed for its magic and its gift of divination. He went to seek refuge in L., a Toma village in Liberia. At Bofossou, one house was filled with masks and filthy, mildewed fétiches. According to [the administrator], they smelled so terrible that one day it was necessary to light a great fire and burn them. The elders were left astounded by this spectacle, which will mark people's memories for a long time. They waited for reprisals by the dead and the spirits. But the only one was the fruit of a tall tale. Throughout the Toma country, the word went out that [the administrator], the man who had burned the fétiches, had received his chastisement, because periodically the *Afwi dogbomaigi* sang in his belly. . . . Others interpreted his accusation of embezzlement and his reassignment to Upper Guinée as the vengeance of the féticheurs. (1971, 247–49)

This passage contains a number of interesting elements buried within it. The "zealous" administrator was, Rivière notes, a Catholic. There was a strong affinity between Christian and Muslim monotheists in their opposition to the Forestier power associations. The administrator also oriented his attempt to eliminate the Poro within a discussion about youth, and in this regard, posed the relation of initiatory and Western-style education as a zero-sum equation. However, by that time, school-goers already attended truncated initiations over the summer vacation period, and there was no either/or decision forced upon young men or women. Another significant point is that the "Toma witness's" account of the undertaking is considerably less violent than the other versions I have encountered. We have no basis for guessing at this person's ideological orientation, but in reading this passage against the grain, we do see some of the kinds of euphemisms that appear in Loma settlement histories where instances of violent conquest are subtly acknowledged in ways likely to be passed over by those not looking for them.[20] The witness writes that the administrator "began to collect masks and fétiches." Given the descriptions I have heard, the use of the term "collect" ("collecter" in the original French), as well as the emphasis on the optional nature of the program, seem likely to be euphemisms for a coercive reality. Similarly, the description of the older generation, "who *forced themselves*, nonetheless, to conform their will to that of the R.D.A.," seems likely to be a transposition of the actual lines of force. The vast majority of the fragmentary descriptions of the Demystification Program I have encountered (and this includes Rivière's 1971 essay, taken as a whole) portray a situation similar to the one in Tanzania described by Scott, in which it was thought that "the shock of lightning-quick settlement [in Ujamaa villages] would have a salutary effect. It would rip the peasantry from their traditional surroundings and networks and would put them down in entirely new settings where, it was hoped, they could then be more readily remade into modern producers following the instructions of experts" (1998, 235).

Such tactics were the norm, though there was variation from village to village. In the Demystification Program, men's masks were exposed to women and uninitiated children. This act, which—according to Loma custom—should have caused death, sterility, or madness, was imagined by state ideologues and local modernists alike as the supreme catalyst of Demystification. Though some elders apparently did die immediately or soon after such shocks, most villagers continued with their everyday lives, had children, and experienced more or less the same good and bad health they had known beforehand. Modernists assumed that with secrets revealed and mystical punishments averted, the "backward" institutions of these societies would be short-circuited. In this paradigm, villagers would quickly come to see masks simply as "bois" (wood), which is just what the Muslims who trade them on the international art market typically call them (Steiner 1994).

Gamé Guilao, a Christian Loma speaker educated in France, wrote the fascinating 1967 essay "La mort des fétiches."[21] He describes a visit to his natal village in 1961, immediately after the Demystification campaign had swept through the area, and his attendance at an ancestral sacrifice. On the way back from the sacrifice, he encounters a Catholic missionary priest still in the region. He writes:

> I walked quickly to meet him, with a big smile, and in encountering him said, "Congratulations, father. Things have changed a lot (he automatically understood that I made allusion to demystification). Was it you who rendered a service to the government, or the government that rendered a service to you?" He responded, smiling, "Each one worked from his own side. These practices will no longer have anything but a folkloric interest." (1967, 244)

Thus the Catholic priests (there were few Protestant missionaries in this region at the time) may also have played a role in identifying the sites targeted by the government. We see here the formation of a coalition between the government and a cluster of local actors—Christians, Western-educated modernists, and youth. In many cases, key actors appear to have been all three.

Thirdly, the demystifying missions cast an objectifying gaze over their subjects and frequently folklorized the very practices and objects they outlawed. As in the case described by Herbert (1991, 150),[22] Forestier masks were gathered to be burned in the center of a village, but the best one might be saved to be taken to the national or regional capital and placed in a museum.[23] As noted above, the contents of the forest region's museum, in N'Zerekore, were largely expropriated during the Demystification Program. Rivière notes:

> In the Kissi country, a *chef de poste* took the initiative to gather all the fétiches confiscated in the region in one building: clay jars, horns, cowries, masks,

cult objects, and attached to each one the name of its village of origin and its owner. About half were taken back, and some féticheurs came nightly to consult their fétiches. The rest rotted or were eaten by insects before an ethnographic mission, sent at the insistence of Suret-Canale,[24] came to recuperate what remained. (Rivière 1971, 250)

Demystification: An "Inside Job"?

Minuit, c'est . . . les plaintes désespérée du féticheur aux abois sous la rigueur des dieux.

—"Minuit," *Bembeya Jazz National*

One of my interests in the Demystification Program was that while it was easy for the state to espouse such a program on ideological grounds, carrying it out *sur le terrain* would seem to present insurmountable difficulties. The task of moving from village to village, rooting out superstition, lecturing to peasant villagers, and locating and destroying ritual objects was both logistically overwhelming and up against every possible strategy of Loma dissimulation and concealment. The aesthetics and mechanics of discretion are highly developed in this part of the world.[25] I soon realized that to the extent it succeeded at all, Demystification had to be an "inside job." This was supported by a few textual references like the passages cited above from Rivière and Guilao. Would anyone still living in Macenta Préfecture in the period around 2000 admit to such a thing? Over the years, I found several interlocutors willing to speak on this subject.

One day, I asked a friend about the mechanics of the undertaking. He said, with a certain amount of looking-over-his-shoulder secrecy, that Forestier intellectuals in Conakry informed the government—even Sékou Touré in person—of Poro/Sande goings-on, and that they named places, people, and times where powerful people and objects could be found. They remained anonymous, allowing the government delegations to go and do the demystificatory work in the villages. He seemed quite sure that this was how the process worked, but he didn't want to tell me how he knew. In his essay on Demystification, Rivière also recounts, "Three months after independence, a delegation of young Forestiers came to demand that the government suppress the sacred forests" (1971, 256). When talking to another key informant who was a political figure and in his twenties and thirties during the revolution, I asked him *who* had provided the kind of detailed information necessary to root out ritual specialists, locating caches of sacred objects, and so forth. He replied, "Of course it was us, *la classe politique!*"

"Did you go into the villages? Were you directly involved?" I asked.

"No, of course not. We would have been killed."

"By the *zoweiti*?"

"Yes. Or any of the *traditionnistes*."

But it was what emerged next that was most surprising.

"So you helped the government demystify the *Pologi* and the *Zadegi*?" I probed.

"No!" He cried. "Are you kidding? We wouldn't mess around with the old women—we were afraid of them."

This was not the first time I had heard this claim, but in the hushed, brief conversations I had had on the subject, I had received conflicting reports about the effects of the Demystification Program on women. Rivière (1971), who simply mentions once that Sande leaders in 1959 had protested the diminution of the female initiation period to three months, implies that the Demystification Program was applied equally to men and women. While providing no evidence about the women, he lets the attacks on the men's Poro stand for the experiences of both men and women. However, during some discussions when women talked about the revolutionary period with me, several were quite explicit in specifying that there had been no major disruption of their normal practices.[26]

This discrepancy was a turning point for me because I recognized, on carefully rereading published references, my own fieldnotes, and Guinean students' theses, that they had also been men speaking to men, all operating on the assumption that men's experiences were perfectly adequate to "cover" the parallel experiences of women. That this is false is obvious,[27] but the actual process of seeking women out, convincing them to speak for themselves to an outsider, and understanding their analyses of public events discursively controlled by men was a long and torturous one.[28]

In this case, a man who had been involved in the actual undertaking of the Demystification Program corroborated hints I had gleaned from women's accounts. More importantly, he gave an explanation that clarifies the operative fault lines in the competition between modernist (male) youths and Loma traditionalists: Youth, threatened and excluded by elders' esoteric knowledge, were obvious demystificatory allies of the government. In many respects, the Demystification Program presented young Forestier men the same opportunities as making war has done over the past one hundred fifty years or more (McGovern 2011, 31–66). It was yet another opportunity for entrepreneurial men to "jump ahead" in line, just as warfare had been in the precolonial period. Straker describes the actions of JRDA youths, often not students, and considered shiftless and lacking strong work ethics by their co-villagers. These village good-for-nothings, he quotes Loma speakers saying, garnered money and the ability to coerce young women into having sex with them via "the further betrayal of co-villagers through the transmission of 'inside' knowledge to external authorities bent on cracking local defiance of state authority" (2007, 221).[29]

Moreover, in the competition between older men and younger ones to attract wives, young men had the same interest as the PDG in attracting women rather than alienating them. This issue is complex, because in many respects elder women and men were aligned against younger women and men in terms of those who had stakes in the continuation of the Poro/Sande system. In other respects, women had shared interests across the generations, as the socialist state sought to equalize rights and representation across the gender line.[30] Unlike the situation described by Berliner (2005), in which women became the guardians of the customary patrimony, for Loma speakers this was not necessary. Half the Loma-speaking population lived just across the border in Liberia, where they could practice their religion as they chose. Guinean Loma women received significantly less interference from the state, and Guinean men always had the option of crossing into Liberia to conduct their ritual business, a practice that was as common as it was dangerous.

Some of these issues come out more clearly in the last section of this chapter, where I compare the Demystification Program to the socialist state's reengineering of the laws surrounding marriage. Though in many other spheres, Touré was able to win women over to his side, in this case most women had nothing to gain from Demystification. Except for the small number of girls in school, women's work, knowledge, and authority in the forest region were embedded in the practices sanctioned and organized through the Sande society. By proceeding through the stages of the Sande and other power associations, women could attain a degree of power considered by Loma women and men to be equal to, though quite separate from, that of powerful men. This was a promise Sékou Touré never dared to make to those girls entering Guinea's school system, and which has yet to be realized in Guinea.[31]

By 1962 (within a year of undertaking the program), the government had claimed total victory over the "superstitions" of their fétichiste populations. Paradoxically, at the instigation of several dramatic events, the just "victorious" government began the search for masks and occult practices all over again. The prime event in 1962 was the alleged ritual murder in Zooulomai (a Loma village near the Liberian border) of a pregnant woman in order to consecrate an important new Poro mask. This sacrifice, mentioned by Rivière (1971, 249),[32] and to Beryl Bellman (1984) by his Liberian informants, was verified to me by several Loma men, one of whom claimed to have gone to the village where the sacrifice took place the day after the killing.

A Loma intellectual who had served as a functionary in the Touré government described his opposition to such practices in this way: "Traditions are fine. They are very good. All that is important. But when it is tied to these kinds of acts, this savagery, no. That is not acceptable. It was savagery and it had to be stopped." He went on to tell me that prior to the beginning of a Poro initiation, one of the village's young men would be killed in the bush. His body, left in the bush to decompose, would be consulted by the elders to see if it were eaten by red or by black driver ants. If the red ants, then the tidings were auspicious and the initiation could go on. If black, the initiation would be postponed a year. The purpose of using ritual murder in Poro initiations, he claimed, was to develop total psychological domination over the initiates, creating a kind of mutually shared culpability that was shrouded in secrecy and organized by a strict age hierarchy. Thus the death of certain members of the community served as an implicit threat to anyone stepping beyond the boundary of the law of the secret societies. From the colonial period onward,[33] it bound all power association members together in a system they knew to be pathologized and illegal in the eyes of the wider, encompassing society.

I should emphasize that this particular informant was a member of a small, distinctive group of Forestier intellectuals. He held strongly to many Loma traditions, but had never been initiated into the Poro. Thus, the extent to which his knowledge was accurate is difficult to say, though he acted as if he were certain of his knowledge. Like many Guineans from other regions, he used the rhetoric of "savagery."[34] This term is often launched as a kind of free-floating accusation against Forestiers, but the ambiguity of the term also stems from the modernist ambivalence (shared by some modernist Loma speakers) discussed in chapters 5 and 6. These were practices that had to be condemned and halted by the state, yet at the same time they could not be named because they pointed to an embarrassing artifact of Africa's "behindness." At the end of his account of having attended an ancestral sacrifice near Macenta,[35] Gamé Guilao recounts the following exchange:

A few days later, one of my friends, an influential member of the PDG, told me in confidence, while adding that I didn't need to worry about it: It had been reported to them with indignation that I had participated in the ancestral sacrifice on the mountain, and even that I had been the one to request it, *"I, whom they had considered civilized."* In that time of suspicion, any person coming from outside, and especially any student, had on his heels at least one spy, benevolent or not. But that still didn't prevent me from leaving Guinea again [for France]. (1967, 244; my emphasis)

Guilao's description helps us to see the set of presumed equivalences that had emerged around the time of independence and that were crystallized in the Demystification Program. In this implicit set of equivalencies, the distinctions are set out in table 7.

Clearly, not every supporter of the PDG was prepared to convert to Christianity or Islam, nor were most Forestier youths interested in attacking the traditions of their parents and grandparents. Yet the presumption that each of these dispositions or identities should entail the others was central to the PDG's attempts to create new kinds of citizens in Guinea. Thus, during the Demystification Period, the government *demanded* that all Guineans take up a monotheistic faith.

Policies like Demystification thus constituted themselves as a double sociological wedge: dividing civilized and uncivilized ethno-linguistic communities, while also dividing Loma-speaking communities themselves along generational and to a lesser extent along gender lines. This was partly a manifestation of preexisting contradictions in the Loma socio-political system, and partly the result of the new nationalist worldview that was espoused primarily by younger people. Intergenerational tensions continued on long after Guineans had lost the strong faith in the promises of independence that characterized the late 1950s and the 1960s. In fact, such tensions played themselves out in the village of Giziwulu while I was there in

Table 7. Socialist-era distinctions

Youth	Elders
Modern	Traditional
Monotheistic	Polytheistic (fétichiste)
Western educated	Educated in sacred forest
Nationalist	Tribalist (raciste)[a]
PDG	Ethnic particularist politics

[a] Touré used this term primarily to refer to ethnic particularism or nepotism and attributed the attitude mainly to Guinea's Pulaar speakers, secondly to the Forestiers.

ways that were eerily similar to some descriptions of the Demystification Program. The iconoclastic conflict was now between Christian and non-Christian Loma speakers, and ironically, the elder anti-Christian "traditionalists" I encountered in 1999 were the young firebrands of the 1950s and 1960s (McGovern 2004, 450–73).

The Cultural Politics of Catching Up: A Comparison

Here it will help to compare Demystification with another policy that is reflective of the PDG's cultural politics. The comparison will give a better understanding of the state's modernist orientation, which was directed not only against masks and the power associations. The following description of changes in laws surrounding marriage offers a parallel history of the socialist state's coalition with women, who (like youths) had also been politically marginalized up to the moment of anticolonial mobilization (Schmidt 2005). These strategies parallel the moves made by the state to change land tenure laws, as described in chapter 4. I argued there that one of the major goals of those changes was to give people of servile origin rights to land use that were equal to those of citizens of noble descent (although the laws had rather different effects in the forest region). This comparison underlines the fact that Guinea's modernist elites did not necessarily act with malice in applying their policies of social engineering, no matter how painful the outcomes. Askew makes the same sort of argument in her analysis of Tanzania's socialist period (2002, 157–95). The Nyerere government's attempts to legislate more modern and "civilized" forms of dress, marriage, and burial were often well intentioned, even if they did not often achieve their intended results.

In Guinea around 1961, optimism about dramatic change was high, at least within the intelligentsia, and in rural areas people were happy to be rid of the specters of forced labor and conscription into second-class units of the French army. The PDG government's experiments in social engineering, like the Demystification Program, took place in the context of such optimism and the kind of orientation toward the future noted by Guilao, Scott, and Knauft in the epigraphs to this chapter. At the same time, the Demystification Program shows that Guinean elites had deep ambivalences toward certain aspects of ordinary Guineans' quotidian lives, like masquerades and polygyny. Guinean elites' self-consciousness about the need to modernize their country in light of their understanding of Africa's status as a "backward" continent was a central component of such "authoritarian high modernist" (Scott 1998) interventions. Not all changes were as violent as Demystification, but there are family resemblances among them.

Guinean Legislation on Marriage, 1961–68

I have so far discussed some of the ways that the PDG's policies appealed to youths. In the case of Demystification, this refers to male youths who existed in a competitive and structurally contradictory situation in relation to their male elders.[36] This contradiction could emerge as conflict in the realm of warfare, or again in ephemeral irruptions such as the Demystification Program, or in many other instances. In addition to support from youth, the PDG had tremendous support from Guinea's women across the country, including in the forest region. One anecdote recounted by Elizabeth Schmidt is illustrative. Describing the general strike called by Sékou Touré and the PDG against the colonial government in 1953, she writes that women

> ostracized strike-breakers, refusing to allow male scabs into their homes. Obeying the appeals of strike leaders, they boycotted European-owned stores. Market women refused to sell chicken, eggs, and milk to French colonialists. They sent pointed messages to opponents of the strike. Amara Soumah, the RDA renegade, was a particular target, perhaps because he was once so esteemed by the market women. It was during the 1953 strike that they renamed their wares to suit the political situation; cut-up chunks of bread, symbolizing ethnic and regional factionalism, were touted as *pain* Amara Soumah, while the whole loaf, representing national unity, was called *pain* Sékou Touré. (Schmidt 2001, 32)[37]

From the late colonial period described here through most of his career, women threw their support behind Touré. Touré and the PDG strove to maintain that support, organizing an autonomous women's arm of the party (alongside the JRDA youth wing) and supporting women's education and promotion in politics and the civil service. Even aside from their coalition with the PDG, young Loma men had little to gain by alienating women. In one instance I observed in Pelema, Loma and Manya women together, angry that their sacred spring had been desecrated by a Manya father and his son, had killed the father and rendered the son impotent according to the son's own testimony. Several men commented during the ensuing court case that any man intent on opposing himself so openly to the wishes of the community's women was foolhardy and could only lose in the end.

If younger men were interested in breaking the hold that hyperpolygynous big men had on marriageable women,[38] they had little to gain in attacking the women's Sande society. This leads us to look at some of the broader aspects of the state's attempts to engineer a new type of society. Among the most striking changes were those made in marriage laws, as radical a break from customary law as were the changes made in land tenure, discussed in chapter 4.

Pierre Gulphe's "Réflexions sur la législation guinéenne en matière de mariage," begins with the paradox:

> Of all the countries that made up the federation of French West Africa, Guinea has undoubtedly placed the greatest distance between itself and the former colonial power in the political realm.
>
> However, in the area of private law, and especially regarding marriage, the laws it has passed since independence appear singularly close to the French civil code. (Gulphe 1970, 5)

As in other arenas of culture, the socialist state here intruded into Guineans' lives with the explicit intention of modernizing them. The implicit model for modernity seems to have been French mid-twentieth-century bourgeois society. The PDG's discourse surrounding marriage in Guinea in the 1960s and 1970s revolved around women's status, their rights, and the development of their full potential. One former PDG cadre justified the party's banning of polygyny by arguing that the government sought to "leave to marriage its character as a freely achieved union based on reciprocity of sentiment, concerted choice, and commonality of interests" (Kouyaté 1996, 106). In addressing these topics, the party focused on two related topics: polygyny and "forced" marriages.

The discussion of polygyny was complicated by the fact that some 80 percent of the national population was at least nominally Muslim, and that under Muslim law and custom, a man could take up to four wives.[39] Sékou Touré thus had to convince his fellow Guinean men that the Quran only allowed multiple wives under exceptional circumstances rather than encouraged or enjoined good Muslims to marry several women, which was the preferred interpretation among many Muslim Guinean men. Touré focused on the Prophet's precise instructions that the husband be fully capable of supporting all wives equally and well, in addition to the children that issued from these marriages. In a poor country, Touré argued, it was difficult for a man to look after one wife and her children properly, let alone several. In the new modernist sphere, it was the definition of "properly" that would make all the difference.⁴⁰

There were two Guinean laws passed in relation to marriage. The first, number 52 AN/62, passed on April 14, 1962, made two important changes in the laws regarding marriage that had essentially been carried over from the colonial period. First, both spouses had to be legal adults and to consent to the marriage before it was undertaken. Second, every Guinean citizen was enjoined to marry in a civil ceremony. Moreover, the civil ceremony had to precede any religious or customary ceremonies in order for the marriage to be valid. Gulphe (1970) underlines the social significance of this law by comparing it to the Senegalese laws concerning marriage at that time. In the Senegalese case, the customary marriage could, and usually did, precede any civil ceremony (if such a ceremony ever took place), and only at that point was the couple "required to seek registration with the state after personal appearances by both spouses who, a posteriori, solemnly swore to having consented to the marriage" (Gulphe 1970, 6). The significant point here is that even if the civil ceremony was often bypassed by citizens in both countries, in principle Senegal gave precedence to the realm of customary law, while Guinea effectively denied customary law any legal status.⁴¹

This choice by Guinea was the result of two factors. First, Touré made it clear that he wanted to promote the rights of women, particularly in regards to marriage practices. One of the primary manifestations of the $k\epsilon k\epsilon-daabe$ relation in Loma society was the relation between a wife-giver and a wife-receiver. Decisions about marriage partners were ideally made among men, and in the Loma-speaking region it was not unusual for a girl to become betrothed *in utero*.⁴² In other parts of Guinea, Fulbe, Maninka, and other ethnic groups similarly gave women little overt choice in marriage decisions. The Guinean law, by demanding that a woman verify her acceptance of the marriage partnership before *any* ceremony took place, favored women's equal rights within marriage more than the Senegalese law, which only asked women if they consented after the situation was effectively a fait accompli.

The Guinean authorities had a further inclination to subordinate the "customary" marriage laws to those of the secular state: The PDG recognized early on that a key tension in the postcolonial political realm would be the legacy of colonial separation of citizens from subjects.⁴³ The Senegalese legal code gave separate and relatively autonomous statuses to customary and secular national laws. It thus reinscribed the colonial distinction between the legitimate, modern state, and the separate but unequal status of African societies, each with its own quaint and particularistic practices. Gulphe notes that among the several dozen marriage customs on the Senegalese books, even the customary practices of Guinean Fulbe, who were frequent emigrants/refugees to Senegal, were listed. The Guinean government, in its persistent striving for modernization, rejected this logic. European nations had long since rejected the legitimacy of regionally or ethnically particularistic customs, imposing national forms of language and law on every citizen within their territory. From the Guinean point of view, the logic of customary law drew not only on the colonial attempt to use indirect rule to ease the difficulties of *commandement*. It also helped the French to evade their promises that colonial subjects could eventually accede to full rights as French citizens by assimilating to French society and culture.[44]

Guinean changes in marriage laws thus manifested much of the same logic as the Demystification Program. This helps explain Sékou Touré's constant harangues against ethnic particularism and what he called "racisme," which in the Guinean context meant ethnic groups sticking together and promoting a group agenda ahead of a national, multiethnic one (see especially Touré 1977). Touré saw early on that the problem of ethnicity was not only an issue of interest groups that could potentially unseat him but also the legacy of the colonial distinction between citizens and subjects, or between universal and customary laws or practices. The impetus to regularize one national law paralleled the struggle to institute a national culture. The regularizing impulse was also expressed above by the former PDG functionary who sought "the normalization of relationships of every kind, governing, at the heart of every collectivity, individuals among themselves" (Kouyaté 1996, 123).[45]

The 1962 law had a significant, if not immediate, effect on Loma marriage practices. In my interviews, both male and female elders constantly remarked upon the fact that in the 1960s, there began to be cases of girls promised by their fathers in marriage who simply, when the day of their marriage arrived, stated that they did not consent. Such willfulness on the part of a daughter was shocking at first, and it must have required exceptional courage on the part of the young woman. These women's mothers, after all, were of the generation that had been subjected to colonial forced labor for similar refusals.[46] As one elderly woman told me in an account of her life, "Our daughters tell us, today, that we were slaves to our parents. They say that they will not be slaves to us."[47] By the 1980s, parents' ability to choose a husband for their daughters had all but dissolved, Loma speakers told me almost unanimously.

These changes were compounded by another law, number 4/AN/68, passed on February 5, 1968. The 1962 law had "prohibited a man who could not support himself, or whose first wife vegetated in misery [as a result of poverty], from marrying another woman" (Gulphe 1970, 6). This was a fairly direct reproduction of the Quranic injunctions I have cited above. However, the 1968 law stated:

> The practice of polygamy is hereby prohibited to any person of Guinean nationality, and remains prohibited within the whole territory of the Republic [i.e., applying also to non-citizens living in Guinea], under threat of five to ten years imprisonment and a fine of 500 to 500,000 francs, incurred by both the spouses and the officer of the state [who marries them]. (1970, 6)

The law allowed existing polygynous households to remain so, making it clear that a man could not divorce one of his wives so as to take a new one. The only exception made was for "grave cases having the character of circumstances beyond one's control, and verified by competent medical authorities" (1970, 7). Ostensibly, this refers to situations in which an already married man impregnated a single woman. The 1968 law also strengthened a woman's right to unilaterally seek a divorce from her husband.

The laws passed by the socialist government in 1962 and 1968 thus strengthened the hand of those women brave enough and well-informed enough to use them in the face of societal disapproval. It is important to remember in this context that this was a time of massive social upheaval, and those who had formerly been relatively dispossessed—captives, youths, and women—were encouraged to turn the tables on their former oppressors. One also notes, however, the heavy-handedness of these policies: the five to ten year jail sentence and the heavy fine. This was typical of the Touré regime's attempts at social engineering. They reached a decision, claimed it was the "people's" decision, and then imposed it with ferocity.

The changes in Guinean laws regarding marriage had an uneven effect. While Loma women described significant changes in the routes they followed toward marriage, my colleague Rebecca Furth has told me the laws had relatively little effect among ordinary Pulaar speakers. They did make it embarrassing for a member of the literate, modernist "classe politique" to maintain polygynous households. As if to compensate for this, the party institutionalized easy access by male party cadres to concubines, partly through the *théatre* system through which local practices such as those banned by the Demystification Program were folklorized. Foresters often told me that their daughters had been turned into concubines and even raped by the men who ran these troupes. The party also maintained a nationwide network of "misses." These were most often attractive schoolgirls who were pressed into service as hostesses when important delegations came to visit a town. As these descriptions indicate, women were not necessarily as emancipated by the party as the party claimed, but the socialist government had given Guinean women something that could never be taken back: the egalitarian ideal that, even when not met, established qualitatively new rights and responsibilities for men and women in their various roles.

In comparing the Demystification Program and 1960s changes in marriage laws, we can discern two interlinked dynamics. First, women and male youth had comparable, contradictory positions in Guinea's patrilineal, gerontocratic societies.[48] Women's statuses in patrilineal societies are characterized by the "patrilineal puzzle" described by Karp (1987). Although they are the bearers and the primary caretakers of the patrilineage's children, they are outsiders, excluded (in Loma communities) from their husbands' lineage sacrifices, and often not fully trusted within the households where they live and raise their children.[49] Male youths, too, are both necessary and marginalized. Their labor and ability to defend the community in warfare are integral to the community's survival, yet it can be difficult for them to gain access to the benefits (wives, children, wealth) of the system they support. In the precolonial and colonial scheme of things, both groups were largely excluded from political participation in the public sphere.

The PDG grasped the potential of this situation, and their social engineering of the Guinean scene amounted to a true revolution. The promise they offered to youth, to women, and to the descendants of captives was the chance to "exchange their past for their future" (Knauft 2002, 38). This shift was based on a process of separation, individuation, and the replacement of the old *rites de passage* with new ones that provided access to a different (national) community. The shift required was nothing less than a change in personhood. Women, ex-captives, and especially youth had a special status in this formula. Adults, socialized in the old system, were already "spoiled." In the modernist imaginary, youths were a blank slate with no vested interest in the status quo. As women had been deprived of the right of overt political participation during the old regime, this same "purity" could be extended to them. Ex-captive peasants might not have been so ripe for transformation within the developmentalist model, but they filled the role of an oppressed socio-economic class. In many ways, reforms of land tenure and marriage laws and the banning of Poro initiations operated according to the same logic. Only Demystification, however, focused to such an extent on the cultural "pathology" of one region.

A Convergence of Reasonings

The Demystification Program drew on a surprising alignment of motivations and logics. Gerontocratic Loma social and ritual organization had built-in a tension between elders and youth. As with the tensions between men and women, or nobles and captives, Sékou Touré had a canny understanding of the kinetic possibilities of setting these contradictions in motion, given that in most cases the disadvantaged greatly outnumbered the more privileged. At the same time, Touré and his government tapped into the common embarrassment of the literate class about those cultural proclivities that could be classed as savage or backward. The Poro, especially in its alleged connections to human sacrifice, constituted the apotheosis of a culturally "backward" formation that had to be eradicated in order for the nation to move into the modern realm of coequal states. This modernist self-consciousness linked to a third logic, one that existed both before and during the colonial presence: the Islamic discourse of iconoclasm and renewal. This justification, which was integral to the establishment of such precolonial empires as Umar Tal's and Samory Touré's, was also important in anticolonial Islamic movements where youth played an important role, such as those of the Wahhabiyya in Mali, Guinea, and Côte d'Ivoire. The impetus to cleanse and renew the individual body as well as the body politic had already been applied in Guinea's coastal region in the 1950s in an attempt to eradicate fétiches, and it seems to have been at the root of eliminating the pre-Islamic masking traditions of the Maninka. It found an ideal target in the culture and practices of the Forestiers—"ceux qui mangent n'importe quoi,"[50] as they are often described by other Guineans. Finally, as the Poro constituted what Mauss refers to as a "total social fact" (1966, 274), organizing ritual, medical, political, as well as aesthetic activities, it posed a real threat to Sékou Touré's ambitions to control the political lives—and consciousness—of all Guineans.

Each of these four rationales, however, carried within it a set of contradictions. Youth-elder tensions were undercut by the fact that every youth knew himself to be an elder-in-the-making, one who, if he survived long enough, would benefit from the same system that now oppressed him.

Guinea's modernists were faced with an even more difficult contradiction, in that they claimed also to be Pan-Africanists and wanted to validate African culture. This use of and simultaneous resistance to the categories of Eurocentric cultural and historical hierarchies was to continue throughout Guinea's revolutionary period, and it was by no means specific to Guinea. The Marxist-modernist strain ultimately won out over the particularist, Pan-Africanist one, I argue, because it coincided with the preexisting Islamic logic of purification and renewal.[51] Yet even this iconoclastic logic, seemingly rigorous and inflexible, had its own internal contradictions. The shadow of "savagery" hung low over the historical horizons of many of the West African Muslims who prosecuted jihad against their neighbors. Many were the most recent of converts,[52] and the existence of pre-Islamic impurities was a constant threat even within the boundaries of the supposedly "faithful."

Finally, Touré's government had to come to terms with the fact that in its relations with these marginal communities it could claim monopoly of political control within its own borders, but that Forestier peasants (like some two million other Guineans by the 1970s), could also vote with their feet, crossing international borders to take care of their ritual business, just as they crossed the same borders to sell their agricultural goods at a price far higher than the artificially low one set by the Guinean state.

The fact that so many Guineans "opted out" of the socialist state's program for personal and national renewal leads one to ask how effective the Demystification Program was. On the one hand, there is no question that the practices of initiation have changed significantly, but this process was already well underway during the colonial period. The twentieth century saw a gradual diminution in the period of initiation. While boys once spent seven years isolated in the bush, girls three years, both initiation periods now rarely exceed the three months of "summer" vacation from school, and never exceed a year. The age of initiates has also decreased: while girls typically entered at 12–17 years, thus exiting the sacred forest at the ideally marriageable age of 15–20, they now usually enter and leave at the age of 7–13. Boys during the colonial era entered at 17–22 years, according to most informants, thus exiting in their early-to-mid-twenties (by the 1940s, the initiation period had diminished to one to four years). Now, most boys are initiated at seven to ten years old. There is a pervasive sense among elders in Loma-speaking communities that it would be impossible to initiate older children, as even those in their early teens now regularly refuse to go, or leave the isolated initiation to go see boy/girlfriends or carouse with their friends who are not being initiated. "They are no longer afraid," many elders say. Consequently, inasmuch as the Poro and Sande were partly institutions of social control (Harley 1950), or of increasing elder women's power by giving them control over the allocation of Sande graduates' sexual and domestic services,[53] they are no longer so powerful.

Women, left to their own devices during the revolution, are under increasing pressure today from the post-socialist state to abandon the practice of clitoridectomy, central to the girls' initiation. Men returned to their practices after Touré's death. When the military junta took power in 1984, they immediately gave the green light for the resumption of all ritual practices that had been outlawed by the PDG. Guineans, terrified that Touré was not in fact dead, but using his supposed death as a ruse to discover more "counter-revolutionaries," did not act immediately. But in 1985, Loma elders called all PDG cadres and other non-initiated men together in order that they be initiated, under threat of a kind of ethnic excommunication. Very few refused.[54] At that moment, some of those who had been involved in the Touré regime's administration found themselves in grave danger. As one Loma-speaking functionary told me, "those who were most brutal and most completely implicated in carrying out Sékou's policies (especially the *normes* and *theatre*) could not stay in their villages after Conté came to power. They died young in many cases—from poisoning—or at other times went to live in big towns. Macenta town (about 30,000 in population) might be big enough, but Seredou, for instance (about 10,000), would not be."

In a recent article and book, Christian Højbjerg (2002a, 2007) has argued that "the religion of the Guinean Loma has apparently remained immune to deliberate attempts to extirpate it" (2002a, 57). He refers to Loma religion's "immunity" to demystificatory practices. I think the term is rather too strong. Loma initiations went from seven years in duration to just a few months (or even a few days) during the twentieth century. Moreover, the extent to which Demystification affected Loma speakers' daily lives varies from one context to another. When I inquired of a friend in the Loma cultural organization, *Gilibaye*, to estimate the religious affiliation of the organization's members in Conakry (the national capital), he said that 90 percent were either Catholic or Protestant.[55]

These are the men and women who take an interest in Loma identity and the politics of Macenta Préfecture within the national context. Many are professionals with university educations, but many others have less European-style education. As a group, they have largely adopted world religions.[56] I cannot guess at their inner motivations, but I think that it is clear that the modernist thrust of the Touré regime's politics (of which

Demystification was the opening salvo) has had a lasting effect on many Loma speakers' views of the world. Modernist, professional Loma speakers in Guinea's capital (and in Macenta town and other large towns and cities around Guinea) seem to have a double consciousness about their place in Guinean society (DuBois [1903] 1994, 2-3). They are justifiably proud of Loma culture and traditions at the same time that they have an investment in national culture and politics. While they may maintain Loma traditions, most fully participate in the world of "modern" monotheism. This is a common situation across the African continent, but traditionalist elders in a village like Giziwulu would eye such hybrid identities with suspicion.

In the next chapter, we turn to the hybrid actors who lived in two worlds at once—Loma-speaking intellectuals who held roles of importance in the Touré administration. The suspicion of villagers was based not only on the fact that some of these elites were probably involved in the destruction of the sacred forests of their own villages. It was also because of the fundamental opposition between the principles of discretion cultivated within the power associations and the principle of legibility promulgated by the socialist state, which reached its apotheosis in the Demystification Program.

By the 1990s, many elites from the forest region had returned to the fold defined by a politics of discretion. The practice of politics through these networks—operating parallel to the state—combined with a new sense of ethnic identity that emerged in the 1990s as a result of experiences that included the Demystification Program.[57] The denigration of the ancestral culture of Loma speakers and other Forestiers was of central importance in the set of distinctions that facilitated the establishment of a Guinean national culture. At the same time, it contributed to the development of a unified sense of Loma cultural nationalism. This "sense" was not, however, a mysterious, disembodied state of mind that settled over the population of Macenta Préfecture. It is perhaps best understood by looking at the particularities of Guinea's culture industry (which objectified and re-presented the Forestier customs the state had banned) and the lives and words of Forestier intellectuals who were part of the socialist state apparatus.

EIGHT

Performing the Self, Performing the Nation

To this point, the reader has encountered the Demystification Program as a strange, Quixotic, and contradictory undertaking. I have tried to say something about its importance in making Loma speakers into Guinean citizens, and in contributing to an already hardening sense of ethnic difference between Loma speakers and Manya speakers. Yet to fully understand the power of the Guinean state policies surrounding the "secret societies" and other supposedly backward practices, we must also address the process of folklorization and performance that followed their banning. This chapter also allows me to say more about the intentions, aspirations, and strategies of Guinean elites, especially Loma-speaking elites, than I have done so far.

When I read Kelly Askew's superb book (2002) on Swahili music and the Tanzanian nation,[1] I was convinced that, like she had, I needed to engage actors in the national culture industry. Jay Straker's insightful work on Guinea's revolutionary period (2007, 2009) also drew significant portions of its insights from his discussions with Loma-speaking intellectuals. Thus, in 2008–9, I spent four months conducting further research, mostly in Conakry and focused on socialist-era elites from the Forest Region. This research gave me a heightened appreciation of the ways in which the cultural politics of the socialist state in Guinea was oriented toward capturing the aesthetic and political benefits of portable identities and the *griot* praise-singer culture that accompanied them. This contributed to the state's own legitimation, and, at least in those regions of the country where such practices had a centuries-old tradition, the fact that the independent state would mobilize such cultural capital was considered normal. I also better understood the ways the state mobilized the potent idiom of religious iconoclasm in the name of state-organized transparency. Demystification was only the most dramatic instance of this orientation. From the point of view of the forest region, both the principles of portable identity and of iconoclastic ground-clearing clashed with the aesthetics and habitus of discretion cultivated in Loma society within the power associations and everyday life. This set the forest region on a collision course with the socialist state.

At the same time that this was true, there were many Loma and other Forestier intellectuals who served the socialist state and did so successfully. Although none said so explicitly, my own analysis was that the attitudes and practices that allowed many of them to succeed in the bureaucracy and the society that grew around the socialist state rested in important ways upon their own practices of reticence, reserve, and discretion. In other words, the very qualities that defined Forestier otherness and that the Touré administration actively sought to extirpate may have been among the most important for mid- and upper-level socialist bureaucrats who sought to rise or at least to survive in a system that repeatedly promoted ambitious individuals only to kill them off. I thus begin the chapter with a discussion of the politics and aesthetics of discretion. I move on to describe the ways that formerly discreet practices and rituals from the Forestier sacred forest became integral parts of the socialist culture industry, and the consternation this caused many Forestiers. I then describe the ambiguous position this placed many Forestier intellectuals in, trapped as they were between two seemingly incommensurable cosmological and political systems. I finish by describing, mostly in their own words, the different ways that socialist-era elites found to thrive and survive during the dangerous and unpredictable times of the Guinean revolution.

The Aesthetics of Discretion and the State

I have already introduced some of the cosmological notions surrounding personhood and power that both link and separate Northern and Southwestern Mande speakers. In short, both have a notion of power as a set of capacities centered on potentially dangerous energy—*manye* in Lomagui and *nyama* in Mandekan—that must be cultivated and controlled, and that can be channeled. Such channeling takes place through the use of objects and medicines called *sale* in Lomagui and *basi* in Mandekan. In his 2007 book, Christian Højbjerg has given us the most comprehensive analysis to date of Loma ritual and masquerade seen through the lens of the category of *sale*. Though he worked in the northern Loma region of Macenta Préfecture and I worked in the south, the majority of his observations apply to the area I describe. (The reader interested in greater detail about the polysemic category of *sale* should consult his book and also chapter 3 of McGovern 2004.) These objects range broadly from masks to individual or collective protective talismans to medicines used to cure everyday illnesses.[2] Figures 4 and 5 show two typical types of *sale* object. In Lomagui, *sale* also refers to the different power associations that teach, control, and promulgate the use of specific types of *sale: gbosale* for "thunder medicine/society," *kalisale* for "snake medicine/society," or *kolisale* for "iron medicine/society."

In order to enter any of these subsidiary societies one has to first be an adult member of one's community, thus a member of the men's or women's initiatory societies, known generically as the Poro for men (*Pologi* in Lomagui) and Sande for women (*Zadegi* in Lomagui). The Poro and Sande are gateways into adulthood and also into the privilege to join other more specialized societies where more powerful esoteric knowledge is owned and promulgated. As Bird and Kendall have written about the Northern Mande speakers described in the famous epics of old Mali: "Because *nya* and *nyama* can be controlled, augmented, or diminished by manipulation, it follows that the devices associated with this manipulation,

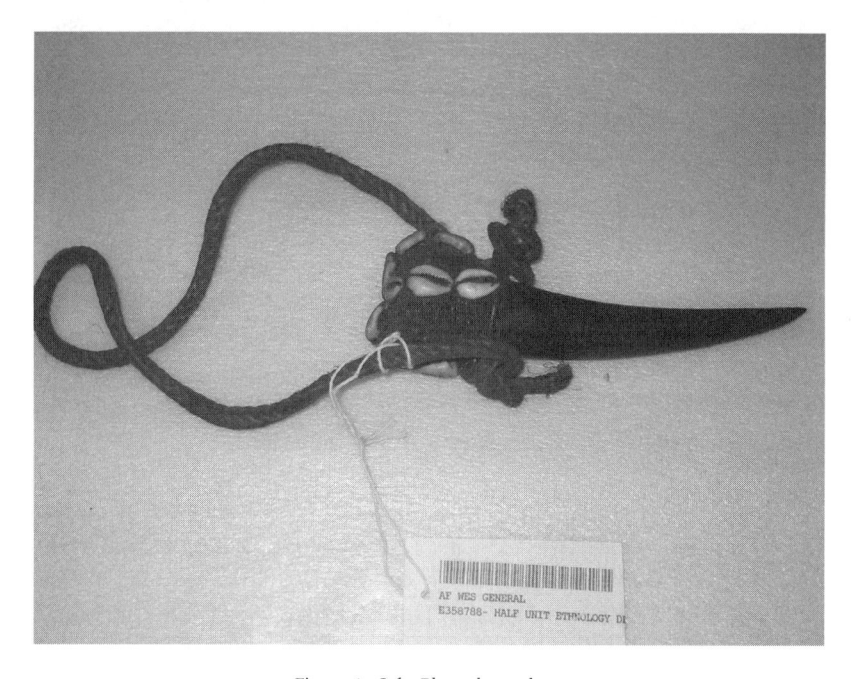

Figure 4. *Sale*. Photo by author.

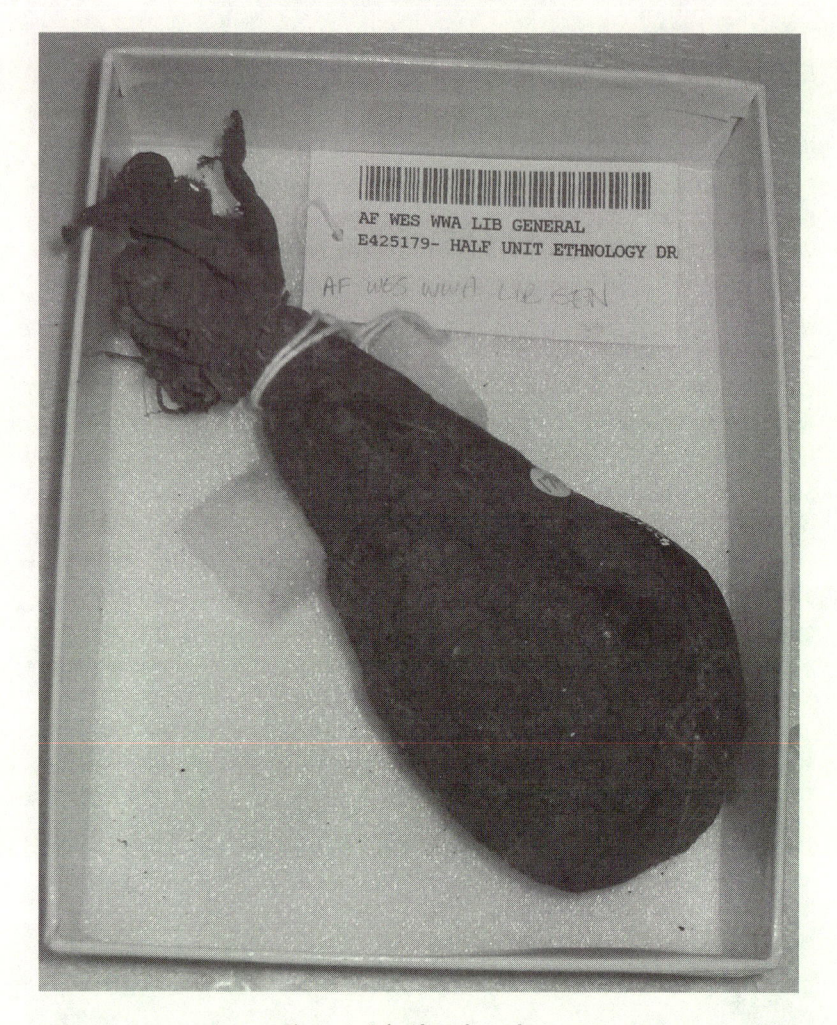

Figure 5. *Sale.* Photo by author.

dalilu, should be kept secret. . . . The hero, seeking every means possible to distinguish himself, cloaks himself and his instruments of action in great secrecy" (1980, 17).

In the Southwestern Mande-speaking societies characterized by almost universal initiation into the Poro and Sande power associations, the nexus of *manye, sale*, and the power associations forms an anchor for local conceptions of power and personhood. This nexus is paralleled in the Northern Mande-speaking world by the relation among *nyama, basi/dalilu*, and the Northern Mande power associations such as the *Jon, Ntomo,* and *Komo.* The introduction of Islam into most Northern Mande-speaking areas has complicated—though not effaced—the importance of this nexus as what Mauss (1966) called a "total social fact."

The work of blacksmiths, midwives, hunters, warriors, and the leaders of the power associations releases tremendous quantities of *manye/nyama* that must be controlled through the esoteric knowledge of those trained in the use of *sale/basi/dalilu*. One's capacities in such work become integral to one's statuses, rights, and responsibilities within a Mande community, and thus to one's social personae. However, this entire edifice is shrouded in an aesthetics and hermeneutics of opacity to which we now turn. The subject of secrecy and discretion is inherently interesting and worthy of our attention, but it serves another purpose as well: it may help us to tease apart some of the separate strands of the strategies of discretion—aesthetic, political, religious—so that we better understand how they are woven together in practice.

My analysis here of Loma cultural style moves from an emphasis on "secrecy" toward one on "discretion." As those scholars who argued for the use of the term "power association" in place of "secret society" have pointed out, "secrecy" is probably a poor choice of terms when discussing initiations that involve (even today) virtually every member of an ethnolinguistic population.[3] The fact that Poro and Sande split these populations into gender moieties still does not seem to justify the use of the term, for despite the very strong rhetoric about the punishment of those who do not respect the other gender's rules of secrecy, it is clear to anyone who has lived in these regions that many things are "open secrets." What is more important than knowing or not knowing is knowing what can and cannot be discussed openly (Bellman 1984; Murphy 1990; Zempléni 1996). As Georg Simmel emphasized (Simmel and Wolf 1950, 330–55), it is not so much the content of secrets as the social practices surrounding them that are culturally and politically significant. These practices are embodied in the injunctions *gele boga* (Lomagui) or *ifa mɔ* (Kpellewo), meaning "we cannot speak it." (cf. Bellman 1975, 1984). In order to make this distinction clear, I will use the term "discretion" to refer to these social practices and ideals, as separate from the content of the secrets themselves.

Virtually all descriptions of initiation into the power associations of the Mande world emphasize that initiates take a vow of secrecy (Bellman 1984; Harley 1941; Schwab 1947). Breaking this vow is explicitly punishable by death. Among Poro practitioners in Guinea, the Loma are reputed to be the most severe in punishing any breaches of secrecy. Ironically, the word that Loma-speaking Christians use to translate the term "sin"—*kɔɔtui*—is originally the term for the worst infractions within Loma society, namely the breaking of power association oaths of secrecy. Schwab describes the town of Kolon-wi, in southern Guinea, where the first man to reveal Poro secrets fled, and where, he writes, "even today, Kolon-wi is a refuge for offenders against the laws of the Poro cult" (1947, 24).[4] The town's name means, in Loma, "sinner person," or "person who has broken his/her oath."

In Guinea, the cultural emphasis on discretion that is so pronounced in Forestier societies was compounded by the culture of paranoia cultivated by Sékou Touré's government.[5] The problems in doing research on a topic shrouded in two layers (local and state) of secrecy begin as methodological ones. Only patience and long periods of time spent in Guinea have allowed me to construct a fairly clear picture of these events. Eventually, these difficulties point toward the most interesting conceptual aspects of the problem. How do political systems—like the Loma one—based on the principle of discretion deal with ruptures of secrecy?[6] How does a modernizing state that nonetheless wants to valorise African "culture" deal with those practices it deems backward? And in the midst of these negotiations, how does the postcolonial state come to delineate the categories of art, folklore, and national or regional culture?

While writers such as Harley (1941) focused on the topic of secrecy and gory talk about the painful deaths awaiting those who break their vows, Loma speakers' ideals and comportment most of the time are a more complex mixture of dignity, discretion, reticence, and ambiguity. Proverbs such as, "When the goat is thirsty, he remains quiet before the water," and "Where the guinea fowl hides, there will not be any signs of her presence," teach Loma speakers, young and old, that there is more to be gained by watching, listening, and considering, than by talking. Glossing this as secrecy is an injustice to Loma speakers and to the educational system that still ensures that most Loma adults exhibit these qualities. Stuempges puts the point well:

> Among the Loma, secrecy depends upon two things: an official concealing agent, like night, a door, a fence, the forest or a mask: and an agreement by the people not to penetrate this secret. When the ladies are covered with white chalk [kaolin clay], the Loma do not know them. If a Loma has his eyes lowered or closed, it is as if he or she is not there. Therefore, although everyone knew that the girls had gone and actually where they were, no one would acknowledge the fact. (Stuempges 1972, 25)

The Poro and Sande societies handle many responsibilities in the forest communities where they operate. They are involved, like most individuals, in attempting to control boundaries around persons and communities. Their control of the flow of potentially dangerous persons could be punitive in those cases where strangers refused to respect the restrictions placed upon their movements by their hosts. The members of a trade mission, led by Frenchmen Bailly and Pauly in 1897, were killed by their Loma hosts at Zolowo (just outside N'Zapa) when they insisted on continuing their journey despite their hosts' demand that they stay put (Beavogui 1991; Bouet 1911). African-American missionary explorers Seymour and Ash likewise found themselves captured and sold into slavery when they insisted on continuing toward Musadu without permission from their Loma hosts (Fairhead, Geysbeek, and Leach 2003).

The Poro also concerned itself with such economic matters as the regulation of markets and the fixing of the value of *koli* iron money (Brown 1937, 9; Beavogui 2001, 57). In addition to these economic flows, the Poro and other power associations were primarily involved in the regulation of flows of knowledge, and of the potentially harmful energies inherent in the spaces they manipulated between the visible and invisible worlds.

The control of these flows required, above all, the discretion and self-control of those involved. The majority of children's instruction in discretion took place in the Poro and Sande bush schools. Paul Germann wrote in 1933 about socialization in the Poro sacred forest: "The ability to keep a secret, to keep one's mouth shut and to be of an even disposition are considered to be virtues of the men. These traits all indicate a good upbringing and one that can be singled out almost as easily as scarification marks" (1933, 110). I found this to be just as true sixty years later.

The aesthetic of reticence, discretion, and reflection that forms Loma ideals of proper behavior is perhaps best represented in Loma sculpture. Most masks and figures in the Loma sculptural tradition, such as the *nyanγbai* shown in figure 6, have no mouths. Another Loma masquerade, called *onilegagi* (figure 7), the "bird man," dances in utter silence, only rattling the metal bells that are attached to his ankles. Though this is not the case in the photo pictured in figure 7, when I have seen this masquerade dance, the *onilegagiti* had folded leaves in their mouths, held between their teeth. When I asked why this was so, I was told, "It shows that they never open their mouths, never speak." Indeed, even in the case of those secular masquerades that do speak, such as *kpakɔlɔgi*, the speech is otherworldly and the mask is accompanied by a translator who renders the mask's speech intelligible to those assembled. Sacred masks that do speak cannot be seen

Figure 6. *Nyan%bai*. From Gaisseau 1954.

by non-initiates, who must remain closed in their houses with all doors and windows shut. Thus as Murphy has emphasized, following Simmel, the secret must always announce itself in order to construct itself as the basis of social and political power:

> More important than the actual secret content, however, is the skill with which one can convey the impression of having dangerous secret knowledge, especially by a demeanor that implies that something is hidden inside the

Figure 7. *Onilegagi*. From Gaisseau 1954.

abdomen. The ideal Kpelle face, like secret society masks, creates this demeanor by drawing attention to the act of concealment and its dangerous significance. (Murphy 1981, 670)

Despite the complex transactions that have helped Loma and Kpelle elders to turn control of secret knowledge into political power, I argue (against the more materialist bent of some of Murphy's writings on Kpelle and Mende societies) that discretion was an important value in itself for Loma speakers I knew in places like Giziwulu. Further, such discretion did not always have instrumental value in the micropolitics of village life. In an account of the aesthetics of *sowo-wui* masks used by the Sande society of the neighboring Mende, Sylvia Ardyn Boone noted:

> Mende are not casually loquacious people. . . . Only in the most intimate, secure circumstances do people chat freely. Consequently, the mouth of the mask is deliberately deemphasized. Sowo's mouth is small, pursed, inalterably shut. . . . The Sowo, like Sowei, is a conservative, serious person; . . . The mouth on the sowo-wui head is what a mouth should be: an image of ideal, perfect silence. (Boone 1986, 170–71)

Loma speakers, often described as more taciturn still than Mende-speakers (Dennis 1972), would appreciate this interpretation.

The aesthetics Boone describes for the Mende are part of a regional ideal of propriety and discretion. However, just as descriptions that fetishize secrecy can be misleading in their emphasis, Boone's emphasis on aesthetics is unbalanced to the extent that it portrays these preferences as purely "cultural." The combination of aesthetic and practical training in discretion is also a political one. As Murphy (1980, 1981) and d'Azevedo (1962b) argue, discretion is sometimes part of a set of micropolitical strategies through which landowning lineages and elders maintain their advantages over newcomers and youth. Another aspect of discretion's political importance emerges in the context of persistent warfare, where loose talk poses a real danger to the survival of the community. This is an area of discussion that is highly gendered, and in a way that is contested (at least among Loma speakers)—a fact one would not immediately glean from Boone's idealized descriptions. Loma men describe women as having insufficient control of their speech and emotions, causing them to put the whole community at risk through their lack of discretion. Women dispute this fact, often noting that drunk men are far more uncontrolled than any women. Melissa Leach has described an identical set of contested notions surrounding secrecy, discretion, and gender among Kɔ Mende (1994, 161–64), and notes "a more general view, widely ascribed to by men and elderly women, that female talk is uncontrolled. The idea is evident in the symbolic link between tongue and clitoris (both *nɛɛ*), and the symbolic restraint which clitoridectomy at initiation thus puts on talk as well as sexuality" (164).

Along the same lines, Loma speakers often talk about the ability or inability of individuals to rein themselves in. Those who cannot are described as *ziigbadie*, or "hot hearted." Such people are described as being like uninitiated children, who are incapable of exercising restraint. Two men I knew well in Giziwulu had a tendency to become uncontrollably *ziigbadie* when they had drunk too much.[7] At such times, I saw them speak resentfully to friends and relatives, and to try to start fights. I was told that one of them had even stripped naked once when drunk, and had exposed himself to a number of the powerful elder women of the village. This behavior was treated as simultaneously humorous, embarrassing (for everyone involved), and potentially dangerous. Because such people were so lacking in self-control, they were unlikely to gain access to powerful *sale*. At the same time, they were considered more likely to use whatever power they gained spitefully or out of immediate resentment.[8] Any time such behavior escalated to the level of physical violence or words that directly threatened such an attack as poisoning, the guilty party would find himself at the center of a village moot the next morning and would probably be levied a heavy fine.[9]

Most of Loma childrearing from the age of seven or eight years is oriented towards teaching children to become emotionally self-contained and discreet. This process culminates in the Poro and Sande's work, but similar work is done on children all the time in many different settings. Donald Cosentino (1982) has described the ways that Mende-speakers use *domesia* (stories) as cautionary folktales. The Mende, who seem to have a highly developed sense of anti-aesthetic (against the idealized *sowo* mask rests the ugly *Gonde* mask, and the misshapen *Gongolei* mask), tell stories exemplifying what one should not do. In one example, a defiant maid marries a stranger from the spirit world. Falling too easily in love and refusing to listen to any warnings, she accompanies him to the netherworld and ultimately to the destruction of herself and her whole family. The audience sees the results of a headstrong young woman's actions, and they are warned away as a consequence.

William Murphy has noted that "pragmatic secrets are sometimes overlooked by scholars in favor of the supposedly exotic traditional secrets" (1980, 203). By contrast, African scholars writing on the Poro and Sande (Bilivogui 1984; Goepogui 1990; Sakou 1983), and Africans who are intellectuals and Poro/Sande initiates, tend to emphasize its educational functions. For a long time, I considered this emphasis to be a strategic misrepresentation of Poro and Sande that drew attention away from the esoteric aspects of the power associations.[10] However, at a certain point, I came to realize that in my conversations with Guinean Forestiers about the postcolonial period, middle-aged and older people were making a set of interlinked distinctions that shed light on the issue of education. I came to realize that they made a distinction in Lomagui between the terms kɛlagi and tɔɔgi,[11] which correspond to the French terms "enseignement" and "éducation." Though "education" in English refers primarily to schooling, for Loma speakers, *éducation* and *tɔɔgi* meant primarily out-of-school socialization, or the broad project of forming moral and social persons that we call "upbringing" in English. Conversely, *kɛlagi* was the formal schooling organized by the state and done by the teacher or *kalamoi*, a loan word from the Mandekan *karamoko*, or Islamic scholar and Quranic school teacher.

Proper upbringing (*tɔɔgi*) instills the discretion that allows people to control their desires, emotions, and speech in such a way that they are prepared to deal with life's hardships, including hunger, the physical pain of childbirth or injury during hunting or farming, and the emotional pain of losing children, spouses, and relatives to disease and accident. During fieldwork, I found the degree of stoicism Loma-speaking people showed in the face of hardship to be extremely consistent. This was true not only in comparison to Euro-American societies but also to those of their West African neighbors. Against this, Loma children were as rambunctious, uncensored, and indiscrete as any other children I have known.

In his thesis on Loma proverbs, Akoye Zoumanigi states that every Loma male initiate is told, *zunui ɣaga ta levhebai, faala zunu vaizu ewula ziilɔi wolu*, or "man is diminution; there is nothing in a man's life but courage" (1989, 11). As he explains it, this phrase, enunciated as the initiate crosses the threshold of the sacred forest, refers both to the surgical operations that will be performed there to transform his body into that of an adult, through which he will lose blood and flesh, and to the various forms of psychological and social diminution that will be imposed upon him. Up until the point of initiation, the boy has been given carte blanche. He has been considered wild and not subject to reason or to the laws that govern adult life. Initiation is a time when his submission to his elders is demanded, and where he will be made to undergo trials that will teach him about his body's stamina and his mind's endurance.

Loma education in discretion does not, however, happen only in the initiation camps. I have already mentioned the aesthetics of Loma sculpture, in which the mouth is often effaced. There are many Loma proverbs encouraging prudence and discretion, for instance: *Kɛlkoi woinvhɛ teɣagima kɛlɛ golai lale*—"The rat likes peanuts, but not those out of the shell," or *Koi nɛzɛveɛ kɛlɛ paa zuai maazu*—"The panther eats meat, but only from an animal it has killed." Such prudence relating to food and drink is a central tenet of proper Loma behavior because of the perceived need for constant vigilance against poisoning. *Nu ladhaga kpalaga vhele lɛɛga wonni*—"You don't show the bird the way to your rice farm," and *Dha buuzanu zalena evhila a anza wolu dhaga ediama*—"When you cure an impotent man who is chasing your wife, you have given him the OK" (Zoumanigi 1989, 17–21) are more lighthearted. The combined wisdom of these proverbs and much exemplary behavior is: watch and listen, say little, and consider carefully before acting. Be slow to trust, and never reveal more than absolutely necessary.[12]

I have so far touched on some of the aesthetic aspects of discretion, especially as they pertain to the work of turning Loma-speaking boys and girls into men and women. To conclude this section, I want to lead the analysis back to the political exigencies of discretion in the context of long-term insecurity. Ferme argues that her "premise is that the domain of secrecy is essentially political at multiple levels" (2001, 6). As a result, "a person who communicates directly what she or he desires or thinks, or who draws unmediated inferences from sensory data and texts, is considered an idiot or no better than a child. Instead, ambivalence is prized. Great value is attached to verbal artistry that couches meaning in puns, riddles, and cautionary tales and to unusual powers of understanding that enable people to both produce and *unmask* highly ambiguous meanings" (2001, 6–7; my emphasis).

It is not coincidental that Ferme, who uses a photograph of a Loma mask on the cover of her book and discusses the maraboutic Arab inscriptions on the inside as one of her first examples of the hermeneutics of secrecy, would use the term "unmask" to describe the work of decoding undertaken by Mende people in everyday life.[13] The work of unmasking took on different but related connotations in the "authoritarian high modernist" (Scott 1998) project of Sékou Touré's government. Yet we should use the tension between these two kinds of unmasking—one interpretive, the other iconoclastic, both political—in order to consider the politics of ambiguity in the Macenta region.

Facinet Beavogui, in an article entitled "Le Poro, une institution politico-religieuse ouest africaine: le cas de la Guinée forestière" (1998), argues that in the precolonial period the Poro served three main purposes for the men of the region that became Guinée forestière, Liberia, and Sierra Leone: first, "the Poro and Sande [were] the principal origins of citizenship" in such forest societies as the Loma (1998, 250). Secondly, the internal hierarchy instantiated in the Poro facilitated "the ruling classes of the different Forestier cultures to succeed in orienting all the youth into their military activities" (252). Thirdly, he argues:

Certainly, it was the systematic violence caused by slave-raiding that oriented powerful social actors in the West African hinterland to protect themselves against the arbitrary acts of a minority among them. The Poro thus became the privileged instrument of the democratization of power. Transposed into modern language, the articulation of power around the Poro already translated the notion of checks and balances, pluralism of expression, control of power by the majority, and the primacy of customary law. (252–53)

Beavogui thus raises the interesting possibility that the kinds of depredations Rosalind Shaw (2002) has described landowning chiefs practicing against their own people (including selling them into slavery on trumped-up witchcraft charges or to settle small debts) could be gainsaid by the authority of the Poro.[14] But later in the article, Beavogui describes a still more intriguing dynamic. Describing the contemporary migration of Manya- or Koniyanke-speaking Muslims into the forest region as a sort of "invasion," he writes:

In these conditions, the Poro has transformed itself into a kind of Masonic organization organized in resistance to the invader, that is to say a place where one may debate in total discretion and quiet questions vital to the ethnic group whose answers are imposed on the entire collectivity. The Poro has become again [since the socialist government's Demystification Program ended] the formidable means of regulating political life that it was for centuries, in the hands of some of the forest region's elites. A whole network of solidarity thus criss-crosses the forest region thanks to this institution. . . . [T]he Poro has transformed itself into a very effective means of mobilization. . . . Youths are recruited and militarily trained in the strictest discretion. (256)

What is fascinating here is to see how, in the course of a few pages, Beavogui describes the intersection of citizenship and discretion such that they first combine to allow communities to fight back against powerful chiefs who sell their own subjects into slavery, and later to push back a perceived "invasion" by another ethno-religious group.

Aestheticization, Folklorization, Re-presentation

That "invading" group was the Manya speakers, and I have already described in the first half of the book how disputes over land, differing ways of reckoning identity, and the interventions of the colonial and the socialist states helped to shape the process of ethnogenesis in the Macenta region.

How was this ethnogenesis intertwined with the work of iconoclasm exemplified by Demystification? In the last chapter I described how initiations were outlawed, but the demystificatory mission, sometimes accompanied by an ethnographer or a representative of the Ministry of Culture, would ask the villagers to perform initiation dances so that the best young dancers could be recruited for local, regional, and national theatrical troupes. Some of these young dancers became members of *Les Ballets Africaines*, the Guinean troupe that toured internationally from the 1960s to the present. Thus the cultural practices considered anathema by the state were simultaneously aestheticized and made part of the folklore and the public culture of the nation.

This move was part of the dramaturgy of state power by which the PDG asserted its control over rural populations by reifying and re-presenting their culture to them in folkloric form[15] (just as its representatives had confiscated their crops and used their daughters as concubines). That was not the only thing the state achieved with its folkloric performances, however. Loma men and women, now in their fifties, told me of their experiences on entering theater troupes and PDG youth militias. In many cases, they were taken out of their villages and sequestered away from the community. They were tested and trained, and their parents were asked to provide the food that would nourish them in their seclusion. They learned new songs, dances, and slogans; the militias learned to march and to carry weapons. The process resembled in every respect the initiation of boys and girls in the sacred forests that had formerly been undertaken by the elders of the community through the Poro and Sande societies. The elders were now held at arm's length and the work of initiation became the responsibility of party cadres. Just as in "traditional" Loma initiation, they entered the initiation camp[16] as one sort of person and came out as another, fully-socialized person. The PDG appears to have consciously attempted to supplant the Poro as an institution of youth education.[17]

Both by shattering the discretion that Loma speakers had so carefully cultivated in their young people and by usurping the socializing function of the sacred forest bush camp, the PDG government sought to replace the Loma power associations. The trump card in the socialist government's deck, however, was the use of theater to recreate and re-present an imagined world of primitive Forestier secrecy. In the morality plays acted out by Guineans all over the country, Forestiers were able to (indeed forced to) see themselves as the savage counterexample of proper Guinean modernity. As Straker (2009) has described, the performer-audience relationship here was in no way simple. As I have already demonstrated, many of the "civilized" monotheists in the audiences were only just recently converted from polytheistic practices nearly identical to those that were being banned and performed on stage. Moreover, the new dispensation opened privileged spaces for young men and women to assert themselves against their elders, tainted as they were by "tradition." In this, Guinea was much like Tanzania, China, and other socialist countries during their Cultural Revolutions (Askew 2002, Siu 1989). Lastly and most interestingly, the formerly sacred and discreet rituals of the sacred forest now being performed by local, regional, and national dance troupes were a source of wonder and admiration both to Guineans from outside the Forest Region and also for Forestier young people and women who were able to see the masquerades formerly monopolized by adult men (Straker 2007).

What, then, were the ramifications for revolutionary-era cultural production? First, the government came to evaluate all cultural production in instrumental terms. For theater, the only meaningful criterion was a piece's potential service to the revolution. To quote Touré:

> To be revolutionary, theater must, necessarily, have the qualities of instruction and transformation. BECAUSE THE REVOLUTION IS NOT ONLY THE VALORIZATION OF THE PAST AND THE PRESENT, BUT ALSO AND ESPECIALLY THE REALISATION OF THE SUCCESSFUL FUTURE OF THE SOCIETY. And so, with each representation, before even choosing the scenario, or writing the piece, it is necessary to ask, "Of all the objectives of the revolution, which is the one or ones that must inspire and push forward the work in progress through dance, music or chorale?" (1969, 347)

The stakes in this project were very high. Touré justified the enlistment of art as a weapon of the revolution through the following logic: "[T]he revolution is devoted to acting on the people so that they come back to themselves [*pour qu'il revienne à lui-même*], to their personality, to their originality" (1969, 351). This paradoxical locution captures the ambivalent posture of the government when faced with the actually existing "traditions" of Guinea. The revolution, through such institutions as the theater, sought to reinstate organic links between the Guinean people and "themselves, their personality, their originality." This is a prime example of Touré's empty speech, speech so vague that it becomes impossible to define the referents of the words he utters. The intent of the passage seems to assert (without evidence) that colonization depersonalized (a favorite term of Touré's) and deracinated Guineans. Because he was undisputedly the major figure in

Figure 8. "Art is not the diversion of a dilettante, but the expression of the aspirations of the people." From *L'action politique du Parti Démocratique de Guinée en faveur de l'émancipation de la Jeunesse guinéenne.*

Guinea's decolonization movement, the implication is that by halting this process, he became the country's savior.

In this scheme, culture—a reified "Guinean" culture, and not a Fulbe, or Maninka, or Loma one—is called upon to restore to Guineans that which was taken away from them by the French. Touré openly admitted that the Guinean state existed before the Guinean nation (and was thus required to call that nation into being). However, he never explained how national culture, by definition a hybrid product of the arbitrary boundaries imposed by the French, and transmitted through the colonial language, could return Guineans to the hypostatized precolonial wholeness that preceded the existence of any territory called "Guinea." That Touré did not intend for Maninka to return to precolonial Maninka life and Fulbe to return to precolonial Fulbe life is clear from nearly every policy and pronouncement of the government.[18] The prime example of the fact that he did not intend for Forestiers to return to their precolonial lives is the Demystification Program. Some of the masks banned and the dances prohibited by Demystification were salvaged by representatives of the Ministry of Culture for later display in museums and on stage. The simultaneous prohibition and folklorization of the same practices were two aspects of an overarching policy for demystifying them. A second consequence of the contradictions within Guinean Marxism was that Sékou Touré himself increasingly became the sole arbiter, and in the case of poetry, the primary producer, of Guinea's artistic output. It is clear that the one-party state, with its centralized institutions and pyramidal structure in every realm, aided in the development of a Stalinist cultural policy as well as Stalinist policies in other realms. Much of the shaping of cultural production in Guinea took place during the *Quinzaines Artistiques*—the "Artistic Fortnight" festivals. This was a process that began with the recruitment of artistic troups at the level of the Pouvoir Révolutionnaire Local (PRL) (several villages or a neighborhood in a town). PRLs competed among themselves and victors advanced, competing against other troupes at local and then regional levels. The process culminated in the Quinzaines, held in June every other year from 1961 onward. About these performances, Touré wrote: "The party's national directorate is effectively satisfied by the revolutionary content of these artistic representations, as well as by the talent of the young actors and the immense progress realized. . . . The artistic festival organized each year at the regional and national levels is a solemn occasion for our artists to reaffirm their fidelity to the correct political line of the party" (1969, 340–44).

The effects of such rhetoric and policies are predictable. At first, Lansiné Kaba has written, the interest taken in the arts by the state led to positive results: "it is not an exaggeration to speak of a cultural renaissance" (1976, 207). As time went on, however, Jean-Paul Alata described the outcome: "They found, in fact, a way to put the people's creative possibilities under the yoke. Very quickly, sections and federations competed in zeal and platitude. Their choirs sang nothing but the praises of the Party and its chief [Touré], the theater had no objective other than to show the errors of colonization, denounce the counter-revolution, and to exalt the new order" (quoted in Kaba 1976, 593).

Touré asserted colonization as a radical break and decolonization as an equally radical one. This was an ideologically loaded (though generally accepted) periodization of African history that is contradicted by Loma rice farmers, who describe the socialist period as essentially coterminous with the colonial. Touré nevertheless proposed a return to African practices, knowledge, and values through culture. He wrote: "Drawing support from themselves and assuming their responsibilities, the people of Africa must, to provoke this divorce [from colonial mentalities] without ambiguity, undertake *their own reconversion* through the conscious expression of their liberty, the manifestation of their will to progress, the deliberate return to African culture, its values and its virtues" (Touré 1969, 195; my emphasis).

The primary manifestation of this move to rediscover, indeed to *reconvert*, the population to African values and virtues was the Quinzaine Artistique. Operating from the grass roots upward, these cultural manifestations became increasingly organized around sycophantic ideological concerns. In the Loma-speaking region, with the Poro and Sande associations and their panoply of masks, peasants resisted the theater for several reasons. First, the local PDG cadres recruited young people forcibly (Straker 2007). Not only did children have to go against their will, but parents were also robbed of their children's productive capacities. Secondly, it was common for party representatives who were connected to the theater troupes to take the pubescent girls and use them as concubines, sometimes raping them, sometimes impregnating and abandoning them, and sometimes giving them sexually transmitted diseases (Rivière 1971, 261; Straker 2007). Finally, these politicos often demanded that the troupes dance sacred masks in this secular, state-controlled setting. Many families hid their children or allowed them to run away (often over the border to Liberia). In this case, the parents had to go to the grueling practice sessions in place of their children.

As Facinet Beavogui has argued, "the theatralisation of the Poro" was an integral part of "the systematic destruction of a multisecular cultural order, the foundation of the identity of several populations" (1998, 254).

We should thus consider it both as part of the Guinean state's attempts to engineer a national folkloric culture out of the diverse, particular traditions of its various ethno-linguistic groups and at the same time as an extension of the Demystification Program. Alongside these attempts to desacralize sacred masquerades, the theater performances and the administrative apparatus that surrounded them were a performance of state power. In choosing theater troupe members, the government reminded people of its ability to count them, locate them, and intrude into their lives, forcing them to perform acts they did not want to. With the build-up every other year to the Quinzaine Artistique, Guineans were reminded of this capacity, and thus state power was dramatized in the theater at the same time that the theater was a product of state power.

Ballet

It was in the realm of ballet that many of the banned masquerades were re-presented to a national audience that included Forestiers. Building on the success of Fodéba Keita's 1950s *Ballets Africains*, many of these productions incorporated elements of African dance, European stagecraft, and a heaping dose of fantasy. Figures 9 and 10 show a *Ballets Africains* depiction of the *Forêt Sacrée*. While the *onilegagi* in both photos is easily recognized as a "real" Loma masquerade, the second mask visible in figure 9 is a fantasy, closer to one of the Mende anti-aesthetic grotesqueries than anything actually carved and danced in Guinea.

The re-presentation was of masquerades, dances, and sounds that would normally have been seen and heard only by initiates. Strangely, it included an orientalist aesthetic that systematically included the appearance of bare-breasted young women. While in Guinean villages at this time many women still went about their daily activities uncovered from the waist up, the "ethnoporn" aesthetic promulgated by the Guinean dance troupes and its links to forms of unwelcome sexual advances were topics of discussion, at least in the forest region. As my female research colleague stated, "When girls got to the age of fourteen, fifteen, sixteen when their breasts grew, families would often send them over the border to live for several years. Once they had met a man and had a child, it was all right. After nursing, the shape of their breasts changed, and they were no longer sought after for the ballets."[19]

A last point worth noting is that although the post-socialist government immediately withdrew its financial and administrative support for the arts, the objectification and re-presentation of sacred objects continued

Figure 9. "La Forêt Sacrée" with onilegagi. From Ensemble national de la République de Guinée, *Les Ballets Africains*. 33 rpm.

nonetheless. This was of course the case in the National and Regional Museums, where formerly confiscated objects were displayed. Those who did not want to see these objects could of course stay away from these institutions. Not so in the case of Guinea's money which, from shortly after the 1984 coup d'état to the present, depicts masks like the *Nyanybai* and the Baga *D'Mba* (better known as Nimba) on banknotes.

Orchestre

Every region of Guinea was called upon to produce an "orchestra" that would typically play a hybrid style of Sahelian jazz that brought together elements of West African music, Cuban and other Afro-Latin styles, and jazz, rhythm and blues, and later funk influences from the U.S. The best-known band of this era is Bembeya Jazz National. The group originated

Figure 10. «La Forêt Sacrée» with *onilegagi* and fantasy mask. From From Ensemble national de la République de Guinée, *Les Ballets Africains*. 33 rpm.

from the forest–savanna frontier region of which Macenta is a part, and indeed the intellectual mastermind of the band is Sékou Legrow Camara, the band's trumpeter and one of their composers. Legrow is a Manya speaker from Macenta. The peculiarity of his trajectory into music gives a window onto the kinds of changes the Guinean revolution ushered in to post-independence society:

> I was in Macenta as the assistant Secretary General of the JRDA. The Youth of the African Democratic Revolution. I was recommended to become Secretary General of the Beyla office of the JRDA. In my role as a teacher and in my role as a member of the youth committee of the JRDA, I was charged with guiding those youths who were interested in music. . . . [W]ith my mandate as a political guide to the youth, I was interested in these [musical] activities, but I was not a musician at that time. So, naturally I was interested in playing

Figure 11. Guinean 25 franc (post-socialist) banknote depicting two different *nyaγbai*. Photo by author.

an instrument, and there was a university student in Beyla who was a trumpeter. He gave me his trumpet, and said that if I was interested in buying it, I could give the money to his mother. (Camara, December 13, 2008)

Thus not only was Camara not of the occupational griot group, at the age of twenty-one, he didn't even know how to play music. His interest in music as a medium came first from his appreciation of its ability to serve as a vehicle of political consciousness-raising.

As several authors have emphasized (Camara 2005; Counsel 2006; Eyre 2000), the Sahelian "jazz" sound perfected by Bembeya Jazz, Horoya Band, Balla et ses Balladins, Keletigui et ses Tambourinis, Camayenne Sofa, and Les Amazones de la République[20] was the crowning glory of Guinea's culture industry. Only dance and the orchestras survived the post-Touré transition, and while Bembeya Jazz continues to tour worldwide, playing

Figure 12. "Music can and must furnish a positive support to the Revolution." From *L'action politique du Parti Démocratique de Guinée en faveur de l'émancipation de la Jeunesse guinéenne.*

essentially the same music they perfected in the 1960s, both the political economy and the aesthetics of Guinean dance have changed dramatically.

What the best performers in both genres understood was that the harsh didacticism of the Guinean revolution would not by itself draw in their fellow citizens. As Sékou Legrow said, the purpose of music was to

> sensitize [people] about the ties that should unite citizens and reinforce national unity. It was toward that end, let's say, that the content of our songs

was politicized. But [although] musicians were forced to do this, we didn't want to always be lecturing people. We also needed to find those social and moral things that would let us influence, let's say, citizens' characters and allow them to have fun at the same time, yes. . . . Back then it was Otis Redding, James Brown, etc. So we played James Brown's big hits. (Camara, December 13, 2008)

It is this aspect of the Touré years—the enjoyment that many Guineans experienced even during times of real political repression—that drops out of many accounts of this period. However, without such an understanding, it becomes very difficult to explain how Guineans accepted the Touré administration for twenty-six years.[21]

A Sociology of Ambition

In writing about "double double consciousness" and the ways that "modernist anxiety" played a role in motivating Demystification, I have attributed these states of mind to various actors sometimes in terms they themselves would not recognize. Certainly, most Manya Muslims in the forest region did not to my knowledge openly talk about the recentness of their own or their families' conversion to a monotheistic religion. Some Forestier intellectuals, like the high-level civil servant quoted in the last chapter describing Loma practices in the sacred forest as "savagery," were more forthcoming. Others were more measured, but as I conducted more and more interviews with socialist-era intellectuals, certain patterns became evident. Many were acutely aware of the marks of their own difference that they quite literally wore on the surface of their skin, had they been initiated prior to the ban on Poro initiations in the Forêt Sacrée. State policy went further, dramatizing this ban as one of the central battles of nation-making and modernization of the young Guinean state. This dramatization was part of a didactic process undertaken by state-employed elites in order to socialize and educate proto-citizens very similar to the one described by Abu-Lughod (2004) in her analysis of Egyptian television programming.

One area in which this was particularly true was in talk about eating. As discussed in chapter 2, both Loma speakers and Mandekan speakers have strict totemic limitations on the things they can and should eat. In addition, Guinean Muslims observe the food taboos of their religion, which includes pork, snakes, dogs, and other animals like monkeys. Here it is important to note that even successful socialist cadres from the forest region have recounted to me experiences of schoolyard fistfights and other clashes with Muslim Guineans who openly expressed their disgust and disdain for Forestier eating habits and more broadly their culture, which they characterized as uncouth.

This is a necessary backdrop to any discussion of the life and career arcs of Forestier intellectuals. Many Loma-speaking friends and colleagues who have spoken with me about the socialist years occasionally become resigned, angry, or resentful as they describe aspects of those years.[22] For the length of the socialist period, the trajectory toward social, economic, and political success took place by definition within parameters defined and overseen by the state.[23] The early independence era was a time of radical possibility for ambitious young men and women in Guinea. Guinea had chosen a difficult but exhilarating path of early independence (Goerg et al. 2010) and worked hard to maintain real independence by rejecting satellite status in the Cold War. The French who had served in various roles in the colonial administration left suddenly upon Guinea's 1958 "No" vote for immediate independence, and, as noted in chapter 6, Guinea had only eleven university-educated government officials at the moment of independence. Those Guineans with any level of education within the colonial system were immediately put to work from the moment of independence. Socialist and Pan-African fellow travelers also came to Guinea from all over the world, including Frantz Fanon, Stokely Carmichael, Miriam Makeba, and Louis Béhanzin. For most ambitious young Guineans, the path toward success began with attending state-run schools (within a few years after independence, the government had banned private or religious schools) and joining the party's youth wing (the JRDA). The most brilliant students competed for foreign scholarships, especially in the Eastern Bloc countries including Hungary, Romania, Bulgaria, and of course the USSR, with its Patrice Lumumba People's Friendship University in Moscow. Continuing their education as far as they could, the ambitious would likely seek some sort of salaried job working for the state. The only alternative to this was to work as a subsistence farmer, not a glamorous or "modern" occupation, despite the state's pro-agricultural rhetoric.

State salaries were very low, but most Guineans recall that they were always enough to survive. An ethos of shared sacrifice pervaded city dwellers' lives during those years. A Japanese diplomat who had served his first overseas tour in Conakry during the Touré years recounted how most houses were wired for electricity, and each was outfitted with a single twenty-five watt bulb hanging from the ceiling of the living room. This allowed the Guinean officials to rightly state that all citizens in Conakry had access to electricity without having to specify how modest that access actually was.

State employees and all residents of Conakry and a handful of other main towns were entitled to weekly or monthly rations of meat, sugar, oil, milk, and such household items as cloth, soap, and kerosene. Those looking to rise most quickly would probably join the party, though membership in the party's women's and/or youth sections could be just as effective.

Though citizens in the city and towns received many small perks during the socialist years, the situation in the countryside was often the inverse. Loma-speaking peasants consistently state that the socialist period was the only time in anyone's memory that Loma rice farmers had experienced famine. The reason was that farmers typically had one third to one half of their crops expropriated by the state in the form of in-kind taxes known as *normes*. The ostensible purpose of collecting the normes was to be able to make the free food distributions of foodstuffs to the city and town dwellers. However, many Guineans point to competition amongst socialist-era elites as the cause of excess confiscation of crops. In their attempts to outdo their colleagues, local and regional bureaucrats often collected more than the state was able to redistribute. Many Loma farmers told me ruefully of instances where their rice had sat rotting in warehouses in regional capitals while their families went hungry.

Aside from the question of how ambitious Guineans might strategize their rise in socialist society, there was a more delicate question of how to survive once they had started to succeed. The greatest limiting factor was that the same regime that promoted bright and ambitious administrators, teachers, and trade unionists also regularly imprisoned, tortured, and killed them. Sékou Touré began to clamp down on the possibilities of dissent in 1961, when the so-called Teachers' Plot became the first major event in a long line of claims by the state to have discovered a "permanent plot" to sabotage and overthrow the Guinean revolution. Remaining blameless in the eyes of the state was not simply a matter of respecting the written and unwritten laws of the country. It also had to do with maintaining a sufficiently innocuous profile so that one would not become the target of others' envy, resentment, or anger.

A comprehensive discussion of the series of plots and purges that characterized the Touré years is beyond the scope of this book, but I have discussed it elsewhere (McGovern and Arieff forthcoming). Suffice to say that estimates of the number of Guineans killed by their own government for real or perceived betrayals of the revolution range between several thousand and fifty thousand. Most estimates range between ten and thirty thousand. Far greater was the number of those imprisoned without trial, tortured, and sometimes forced to sign prewritten confessions with often fantastical details[24] and accusations of still other innocent citizens. During this period, more than two million Guineans—a full third of the population—left the country to live in exile.

One of the characteristic patterns of the Touré years was that mid- to high-level civil servants would be arrested with little notice. The most famous of these was Telli Diallo, formerly Guinea's representative to the United Nations and the first Secretary General of the Organisation of African Unity. Thousands of other civil servants met the same fate as Diallo, while many others were imprisoned, tortured, but later released. There are many theories about why this took place. Some blame Sékou Touré himself, while other blame those around him, especially his half-brother Ismael and his nephew Siaka. While some claim that Touré was intent on eliminating all those who might challenge him, others say that intellectual insecurity on the part of Touré, the family members who surrounded him at the top of the state apparatus, or both, was to blame. According to this version, Touré, who had a ninth-grade education, and his family members, some of whom were illiterate yet held ministerial posts, actively hunted down and eliminated those who were better educated or more competent because of the perceived threats they posed. Lastly, a small number still hold that most arrests and executions were the justified reactions of a Marxist Pan-Africanist state that was perpetually under siege by reactionary and imperialist forces from within and without. For these defenders of the revolution, even if some individuals were wrongly accused, the general premise on the basis of which the state had acted was sound.

For a socialist-era civil servant, the justifications and the motivations behind the acts were of secondary importance. Regardless of what might have really been going through the minds of Sékou or Ismael Touré, everyone knew by 1971 that they could receive a knock on the door in the middle of the night and be taken away to face the process that usually began with five days detention without food or water known as the *diète noire*, passing to interrogation, usually to torture and then signature and recitation of a prewritten confession, followed by further imprisonment, execution, or release. The level of randomness that characterized this process was so great that every Guinean knew he or she might meet this fate. What did individual Guineans do to manage such insecurity and to try to minimize the possibility of falling afoul of the powers that be?

Discretion turned out to be a key strategy. As Tolo Beavogui, a socialist-era Education Ministry official (and Guinean ambassador to the U.S. and Germany under the post-socialist Conté government) described: "Once I arrived in Conakry, I realized that I could not fulfill my functions as an educational inspector and as a member of the Bureau Fédéral at the same time.²⁵ So, I resigned without resigning. Since at that time, one could not frontally resign, I just stopped attending the meetings of the Bureau Fédéral of Conakry II" (Beavogui, December 13, 2008).

Such discretion was common sense, but at other times keeping a low profile went against the dispositions of some civil servants. As another Education Ministry official, Felix Faber, described:

> You had to keep your head on your shoulders, you see? You know the story of Camp Boiro and all that. . . . I have the impression that back then they were against the [educational] elite, because a lot of them went away [were killed]. Of those that were left, there were not a lot who escaped; all the rest were crushed by the revolution. But, at that time, those who wanted to make themselves seen, they socialized with the people who were at the summit of politics. That was their mistake. Because [if] you socialize with me, and I come to realize that you want to be higher than me although I am now higher than you, I just liquidate you. That much is clear; that's how we lost a lot of our cadres. . . . I never went to visit anyone. I went to a few friends' houses, but those who were above me, I did not socialize with them. (Faber, January 22, 2009)

In the intimate world of post-independence Guinea where Conakry was still, in the words of many Guineans, "a big village" and where citizens visited and ate meals with Sékou Touré almost daily, Faber's unwillingness to socialize was highly unusual.

Many Guineans described a kind of trap that Touré laid. Particularly in the case of those intellectuals who had supported the *Bloc Africain de Guinée* (BAG), a moderate political party that had supported continued semi-autonomous colonization in 1958 when Touré and the PDG had pushed for immediate independence, Touré eventually invited many of these intellectuals to take up administrative positions in the state apparatus. Perhaps the archetype of this fate befell Diawadou Barry, a Guinean politician from before independence who defeated Touré in a 1954 election for a seat in the French National Assembly. Though he later joined the PDG and served in Touré's post-independence government, he was arrested on what are widely considered trumped-up charges as part of the "Kaman-Fodéba" Plot of 1969. He was reportedly shot with his co-accused²⁶ after they had been forced to dig their own graves.

One friend's father had been a BAG supporter and colonial-era intellectual who was later invited by Touré to join his government. After the Nth time he had turned down an important administrative post, Touré went through his wife, who was a friend of the man's wife. Finally, he sent back this message to Touré: "Tell Andrée [Sékou's wife] to tell her husband that I will not be his prey. I am staying here with my students. [He was a teacher in Macenta.] I'll die with my chalk in my hand, and it is my students who will bury me here." Several Guineans who heard this story agreed that he had correctly analyzed the situation. Former BAG supporters were generally safe when they stayed out of politics. Many had been educated at the elite William Ponty Lycée in Senegal, and Guinea needed their skills as doctors, teachers, and mid-level civil servants. Their problems would begin when they allowed Sékou to draw them into politics in a seeming gesture of magnanimity. Of those who were so drawn, most fell, one by one.

Socialist-era travel presented cadres with both exciting opportunities and a minefield of potential dangers. Guinea's socialist government strove to perform an international and cosmopolitan aesthetic of membership in a larger world. As Sékou Legrow Camara of Bembeya Jazz put it:

> At FESTAC 77, the World Festival of Black Arts, Stevie Wonder's manager heard our concert [of *Régard sur le passé*] in English, and asked the Guinean delegation to allow us to go to New York with a contract to play the concert in a lot of universities there. But it was the revolution then, and the bosses said that if we let Bembeya go over there they won't come back, so we didn't get to go.
> MCGOVERN: So you never went to the US during that period?
> SLC: Ah, no, no. Never during the revolution. It was imperialism. . . .
> MCGOVERN: And in reality, would you have taken the opportunity to leave?
> SLC: Not at all, not at all, not at all, not at all. (Camara, December 13, 2008)

Even travel closer to home still posed potential problems. As former Minister of Youth and Sports Diao Baldé described:

> In 1972 I went with the [Guinean] football team to Abidjan. We played and we were so afraid that we decided to let it be a 0–0 tie. We were a much better team, but we left it a 0–0 tie so we wouldn't be killed by the crowd [at the time, relations between Guinea and Côte d'Ivoire were extremely strained]. After the match, President Houphouët invited us to Yamoussoukro, and he received me along with the team. I remember his words. He said, "My children cannot come to find their father in his plantation and leave without their share of the bananas." So, he gave us each an envelope. It was money. He said this was the portion belonging to Hafia [Guinea's premier football

club and three-time African champions] and to his children. It was their portion of the bananas. And I tell you, I was really afraid to take that money. I did not want to offend a head of state, the president of the republic. And back in Conakry, here, when the radios announced that we had received these envelopes, everyone wondered, will he take it or won't he take it? What is he going to do? In any case, if he takes it, when he gets back it's sure that he'll go to Camp Boiro. So, I got back to Abidjan, and I asked the Ivorian Minister of Youth and the football federation, and I said, "This is our portion of the bananas, and we will share this portion with the Ivorian youth! Thus, we invite you to a banquet at the Hotel Ivoire, where our team is staying, and the two teams will now have a banquet together, financed by that money. So we ate together and I came back without any money. (D. Baldé, February 10, 2009)

Guinean civil servants and even ordinary citizens had to invest considerable energy in guessing what would get them into potentially fatal trouble, and what would keep them safe. As one saying has it, totalitarianism is any system in which one doesn't know how to follow the law even if one wants to. That certainly applied to Guinea, especially in the late 1960s and the 1970s. The theories surrounding the logic behind the Touré-era arrests and executions sometimes became positively Byzantine. In one version, Sékou and Ismael Touré would have a public dispute. They would then wait to see who took Sékou's side against Ismael. They would be arrested or demoted. It took many years for the ordinary bureaucrats to catch on. Finally, when one cadre protested to Sékou about the ill treatment of Ismael, he received a promotion, thus validating this theory. Ambitious cadres during the Touré period had to navigate ever-changing circumstances, react nimbly to them, and above all, refrain from appearing ambitious.

Surviving Authoritarianism

Regardless of the theory explaining the inner workings of the Touré regime, it is clear in retrospect that the most prudent and successful strategy was one of discretion. Performing competently but not so brilliantly so as to become a threat to a key political figure; refraining from building a personal patronage network; keeping secrets and revealing little about one's own state of mind—these were all, in the end, successful strategies for navigating this violent and perilous "grey zone" (Levi 1989). The record of Loma and other Forestier intellectuals attests to an unusually successful ability to prosper under these difficult circumstances.

The list of important ministers from the forest region is long. Lansana Beavogui was Sékou Touré's longtime protégé and his Prime Minister at the time of Touré's death. Galéma Guilavogui was Minister of Education for eleven years, also until Touré's death. Forestiers were especially well-represented in the army and the education ministry. They were overrepresented as students in higher education. Moreover, they seem to have done a better job than most other groups, in aggregate, at "keeping their heads on their shoulders." The lists of those imprisoned and killed at Camp Boiro contain an underrepresentation of typical Forestier names.

This is not conclusive proof: many Forestiers, as mentioned already, changed their family names to the Northern Mande equivalents, especially as they entered the formal school system or the military. Moreover, there is no comprehensive accounting of all who were imprisoned, tortured, and killed by the Touré administration. Still, I would challenge Charles's (2010) contention that Forestiers were severely disadvantaged under the revolutionary government. He shows approximately 9 percent of Sékou Touré's ministers and 11 percent of his governors to be Forestiers. The estimation that Forestiers make up 17–18 percent of the population makes this seem like an underrepresentation, but most scholars, like most Guineans, would place the Forestier proportion of the population lower, at around 12 percent. Further, it is not clear whether or how Charles accounted for those Forestiers who had changed their names to the Northern Mande equivalents, yielding names like that of Guinea's third president, Moussa "Dadis" Camara, a Kpelle with a Northern Mande name.

In any case, one further point bears emphasis: Forestiers may have been more successful than any other group at being successfully "recycled" from the highest levels of the Sékou Touré state apparatus to those of the Lansana Conté government that succeeded it. Even figures like Galéma Guilavogui, who was initially imprisoned by the Conté government along with other high-level Touré officials, eventually returned to government to serve as the Sécretaire Générale of the University of Conakry, and later to serve a second stint as Minister of Education. The perception that Forestiers were simultaneously impartial and loyal to those in power helped them to navigate the tumult of changing regimes. Again, discretion was a successful strategy, even for those Forestiers who had traveled far from the world of their rainforest villages, their rice fields, and their forêts sacrées.

CONCLUSION

Double Double Consciousness in an African Postcolony

In the preceding chapters I have explored the interrelationships of iconoclasm, ethnogenesis, and the emergence of Guinea's postcolonial state. I have tried to show the ways iconoclasm worked on people; the ways it turned Forestiers into negative examples, stereotypes of savagery, yet at the same time shaped them into modernist national citizens. Looking at the situation in Macenta Préfecture, we saw that the socialist government's policies and discourse pulled people in opposite directions. For Forestiers, the socialist period did not create but it did cement their sense of ethnic separateness, thus unity among themselves. At the same time, their use as exemplary (national) Others was part of a nation-building process that affected Forestiers just like other Guineans, and it developed in many of them strong feelings of national identity. They were in effect "hailed" (Althusser 1971) by the very state that objectified them as the nation's backward others.

This is not a dynamic that existed only in Guinea, and thus the Demystification Program serves as a useful window on a wider set of phenomena, which I believe is quite common across postcolonial countries in Africa, Asia, and beyond. As an ethnography of a particular socialist postcolonial state, I hope the analysis of how this complex set of dynamics played out in one part of Guinea provides food for thought for those working to understand comparable situations in other places. Guinea's particular combination of a strong socialist state that also had Pan-Africanist aspirations and a desire to build a national culture industry was somewhat unique. However, the ways that an ethnic minority group such as Loma speakers came to experience the state was comparable to similar dynamics between minority groups and socialist states around the world. I conclude by focusing on the emergence of new forms of ethnic solidarity, national identity, and the ways these could be experienced sometimes as contradictory and sometimes as complementary.

The First Legacy: Denigration into Ethnic Solidarity

> The underrepresentation of the Forestiers is general. One notes the rarity of Kissi-Toma-Guerze in regional administration, and their absence in the category of [political heads of the] souspréfectoral administration. But the weak sense of their own solidarity [*faible prise de conscience de leur solidarité*] renders these distortions of lesser consequence. . . . "Whatever the reasons, we come away with at least one conclusion: there is a 'special policy' toward the Fulbe[1] that may have provoked the accentuation of their ethnic particularism. For the Forestiers, the conclusions are even more marked, if they consider themselves a solidary group." This solidarity remains to be seen. (Rivière 1971, 69–72)

The passage above comes from Claude Rivière's 1971 essay on Guinea, "L'Integration des ethnies" ("The Integration of Ethnic Groups"). In it he discusses the push and pull between national and ethnic identities in Guinea in the 1960s. In interpreting the underrepresentation of Fulbe and Forestiers in the Guinean civil service, he notes the "weak sense of their own solidarity" that distinguishes Loma-, Kpelle-, and Kissi-speakers from the Fulbe. He does not go on to explain this "faible prise de conscience." In the early chapters of this book, I have argued that for several centuries, pre-colonial strategies for dealing with insecurity caused Loma speakers (like their Forestier neighbors) to seek tiny spheres of political autonomy while forgoing the kinds of self-narration and solidarity that contribute to fixed identities. This is a strategy almost identical to the one described by Scott (2009) as "the art of not being governed" for highland Southeast Asia.

As I also argued in chapter 5, this process of non-consolidation has a functional explanation inasmuch as it is one way for mini-polities and those who live within them to maximize flexibility, keeping their options open so as to facilitate their abilities to deal with unexpected and often violent events. It is also intertwined as both cause and effect with the work of narrative. For reasons that are both cultural and sociological, some societies in the region that became Guinea had both the will and the institutions to tell the story of who they were, how they were different from their neighbors, and why they were fit to rule over others. This was the case amongst both Northern Mande, who in the Guinean postcolony have often referred to themselves under the umbrella term "Malinke," and amongst ethnic

Fulbe. As recently as the period when Rivière was writing, it was much less true amongst Loma speakers and their Forestier neighbors.

I have argued that the pursuit of autonomy was an advantage in the context of the violence and insecurity of the slave-raiding period, c. 1500–1900. In the context of the modern nation-state, however, it was a serious handicap, and it contributed to Loma speakers' further denigration, marginalization, and relative impotence as Manya-speakers used the apparatus of the state to solidify their claims to land in Macenta Préfecture and elsewhere in the forest region. However, this situation began to change during the Touré years and into the period of Lansana Conté's administration (1984–2008). Loma-speaking intellectuals saw the ways that politics worked in the capital, and an increasing number of literate Loma speakers were able to face Manya-speakers as equals in the courtroom or administrative offices.

The eventual Forestier "prise de conscience" of their group solidarity resulted partly from the disjunction between how Loma speakers saw themselves and how they were portrayed in widespread, denigrating stereotypes. However, nothing solidified Loma-speaking men's sense of ethnic solidarity like a series of interethnic massacres that took place in the forest region in the 1990s. This is a subject I will analyze in detail in another book. The 1990s saw the growth of a robust and sometimes aggressive ethnonationalist sensibility amongst some Loma speakers. This sensibility emerged in part from exchanges between Liberian and Guinean Loma speakers, and from exchanges between Loma speakers in Conakry and those back home in Macenta Préfecture.

Thus, at just the moment when in some parts of the world, such as Rwanda and ex-Yugoslavia, cultural nationalism's reputation was tarnished by the violence it had spawned and justified, it was taking its first real steps in parts of Guinea. This was the period when the Loma cultural nationalist organization, *Gilibaye*, was formed (see Højbjerg 2007). During the same period, the Guinean government initiated the *Radio Rurale* broadcasts in the local languages of the forest region, including Lomagui. These were important steps toward codification of the forest's languages and cultures in Guinea, begun for some Loma speakers during the sixteen years (1968–84) of socialist-era primary school instruction in national languages.[2] I still remember the visit of a Loma priest to my Loma family's home in Pelema one evening. A young girl was there, speaking to some of the family members, and I followed little of her conversation. I was tired, and didn't feel like trying too hard, and simply chalked it up to the fact that my Lomagui wasn't good enough to understand people with unusual accents (I had sometimes had trouble in interviews with elders, trying to understanding "toothless Lomagui"). When the girl left, her speech became the subject of a good ten minutes of laughter and analysis. I felt much better when the priest announced, "I didn't understand more than three or four words she said!" What was surprising is that she came from a village only twenty-five kilometers from where we were sitting.

The precolonial autonomy of Loma chiefdoms, combined with the fact that each place was the product of different kinds of interethnic mixing, was a historical factor that worked against a unified sense of identity.[3] The fact the colonial-era Catholic missionization took place primarily in French and that the socialist government did not welcome missionaries from the 1960s onward left many Loma still split into numerous mini-groupings. The major policy move feeding ethnic self-consciousness in the colonial period was the logic of partition used to decide disputes over canton chieftaincies (as discussed in chapter 4). The most significant unifying policies of the socialist state were the imposition of mise en valeur land tenure policies and the ways they changed the political economy of autochthony; dramatic portrayals of Forestier backwardness, as in the case of the Demystification Program; and the use of local languages in all primary education between 1968 and 1984. For this purpose, one dialect of Lomagui was used throughout Macenta Préfecture. Each of these policies contributed to the gradual emergence of a sense of ethnic identity and unity.

The 1990s saw a convergence of several factors in Macenta Préfecture that accelerated this gradual process. The introduction of the first-ever experience with democratic political participation brought with it the mobilization of the ethnic group as ready-made political constituency. The opening of markets increased competition amongst groups whose occupational niches were often mapped onto ethnicity. An increase of violence and lawlessness took place as the strong socialist state dissolved into a laissez faire postsocialist one. The influx of refugees who were fleeing wars in Liberia and Sierra Leone introduced a different set of experiences and attitudes to Guinea. Finally, increasing pressure on land and water resources resulted from population growth and refugee presence. These combined with the culturally objectifying work of the Loma cultural organization *Gilibaye* and of *Radio Rurale*, broadcasting in Lomagui, as well as that of Protestant missionaries translating the Bible and other texts into Lomagui. These factors contributed to the development of new forms of ethnic identity that were characterized by many Loma speakers' sense of themselves as being part of a community of suffering. In this narrative, they had been victimized both by the Manya-speaking minority among them and by the series of states that had in many cases underwritten and supported this form of internal colonization.

The Second Legacy: Embattlement into National Solidarity

> Immediately after independence (gained by the ballot box), the obsession [*la hantise*] of the PDG was to see the Guinean state paralyzed in its mission to create a Guinean nation by racism. The battle to eradicate racism was not simply (or only) limited to the juridical realm; it suffused every activity of the society—politics (elections), school, the promotion of national languages, the world of work, productive activities, even marriage. Every manifestation of racism was considered not only as an infraction, but as a veritable scandal. (Louis Béhanzin in Camara 2007, 64)

Louis Béhanzin, a French-educated Beninois, came to Guinea at independence and remained one of the chief ideologues of the PDG until Sékou Touré's death. In Guinea he met his wife, a Martinican teacher who had come for similar reasons, as did Stokely Carmichael, Miriam Makeba, and other politicized blacks from around the world. Béhanzin stated that he considered it one of the greatest challenges of the PDG administration to overcome the racist presumptions Guineans themselves had internalized during colonialism. He wrote:

> Colonization undergone cannot be reduced to the legal submission of an entire nation by some foreign state, which thus does as it pleases with the soil, the mineral wealth, the ocean, the flora, the fauna, and the people who become its subjects; it goes all the way to colonize the souls of those subjects. And that is why the deformations thus caused persist, often in very malignant ways. For us, the PDG judged it necessary to apply an appropriate and variegated therapy. (Béhanzin in Camara 2007, 61)

The paradox for many people living in Macenta Préfecture during the socialist period is that although they were in many ways the exemplary Others against whom Guinean national culture defined itself, they were also profoundly influenced by that same national culture. This is a counterintuitive assertion, and I would never have been able to reach such a conclusion on my own, so strong was my sense over the years of the grinding denigration of the Forestier minority by members of Guinea's larger ethnic groups. I assumed that this must have had a deeply alienating effect on Forestiers' attitudes toward the Guinean nation. However, a number of my experiences during fieldwork convinced me that I was wrong.

The arrival of Loma-speaking Liberian refugees caused Loma-speaking Guineans (and other Forestiers who had ethnolinguistic "cousins" across the border) to confront the differences between themselves and the Loma-speaking Liberians seeking refuge with them. These differences lent themselves to a controlled comparison of the two national cultures—Liberian and Guinean—that overlay whatever complex of practices, values, and styles we might define as "Loma culture." The differences noted by Guineans and those noted by outsiders like me were sometimes congruent, sometimes not, but they were the subject of lively discussion (McGovern 2012). Once Liberians settled in the forest region, they, too, began to analyze the differences between themselves and their hosts.

Guineans and Liberians often talked about differences in comportment and style: Liberians dressed more casually. Women wore trousers and even shorts, something still rare in Guinea, even in the capital. Liberians were said to have more "exotic" sexual practices, and both Guinean men and women describe many Guinean men seeking out refugee women as junior wives. To the outsider's eye, the most striking difference was the refugees' ease in undertaking entrepreneurial projects. Where refugees lived, restaurants, bars, hair salons, and other shops suddenly sprang up. The Guineans displayed a cautiousness born of the socialist period, when anyone who bought zinc roofing for his or her house was investigated by the economic police to find out how they were able to afford such a luxury. Refugees turned sleepy Guinean towns in the forest region like N'Zerekore and Guekedou into boomtowns, and Guineans at first looked on as if observing events taking place in another country.

However, the biggest difference between the Guineans and the refugees was the degree of national unity that organized each group's identity. Guineans regularly defined themselves against Liberians and Sierra Leoneans as people who valued peace and unity above individual gain. They thus put a moral valuation on the Liberians' predilection for entrepreneurship, making a connection between entrepreneurial maneuvers and destabilizing violence. To my surprise, national culture really mattered: Guinean Loma speakers talked about themselves as primarily Guineans, while Liberian Loma speakers from just a few kilometers away talked about themselves as primarily Loma.

This difference, I have tried to show, was largely the product of state policy and rhetoric. The Guinean state was mobilized by the concerns expressed by Louis Béhanzin above and Sékou Touré, whose claim that "the revolution is devoted to acting on the people so that they come back to themselves [*pour qu'il revienne à lui-même*], to their personality, to their originality" (Touré 1969, 351) opened this book. In consequence of these concerns, the state worked constantly to inculcate a sense of national identity and unity into its citizens. It carried out this work in schools, through sport, during mandatory Friday afternoon party cell meetings, through political rallies, and during the biannual Quinzaines Artistiques, when Guineans theatrically re-presented their march toward liberation and modernity to themselves. It is easy to be skeptical about whether such undertakings had a lasting effect, but most Guineans I know would insist that they did. This set of approaches to creating national unity and identity were buttressed by the discourse of the "permanent plot," which insisted that Guinea was under constant threat of violent overthrow by the forces of imperialism and neocolonialism.

Violence, Marginality, and Divided Consciousness

I have written elsewhere about the ways in which this work to create a sense of national identity paid unexpected dividends in 2000, sixteen years after Sékou Touré had died. At that time, Guineans in the Forest Region were faced with Liberian warlord/President Charles Taylor's attempts to export the regional war from Liberia and Sierra Leone into Guinea. As his emissaries to Guinean Loma speakers argued, the fog of war would give villagers the opportunity to expel Manya speakers they considered usurpers of their land and wealth. They also tempted the more ambitious with the possibilities of unseating Lansana Conté's deeply unpopular government. Despite many cross-border attacks and the initial success of the rebels, who seemed to be marching toward Conakry, Guineans, including many Loma speakers I knew, rejected these arguments, frequently stating a phrase that came directly from the socialist period: "We are Guineans first and members of ethnic, religious, or regional groups only second" (McGovern 2002, 2004).

Still, the rhetoric of national unity that underpinned many Loma-speaking Guineans' arguments against violence was itself the product of a field of socialist-era distinctions that claimed to separate the healthy from the diseased parts of the body politic.[4] This work of distinction often operated by creating, finding, and defining difference in ways that were symbolically or physically violent. As two passages quoted earlier in this book have stated, "modernity is a geography of imagination that creates progress through the projection and management of alterity.... Notions of progress provoke paradoxes and creative struggles that highlight the power of imagination in the face of violent interactions, deferments, and disillusionments" (Knauft ed. 2002, 18–35).

And, "Legibility is a condition of manipulation. Any substantial state intervention in society . . . requires the invention of units that are visible" (Scott 1998, 183). Guinean modernity was born partly out of the violence of such interventions as the Demystification Program, which imposed legibility on forest societies that had previously sought autonomy through obscurity and the "hermeneutics of suspicion" (Ferme 2001). Through such legibility, Loma speakers came to know themselves as a unified group rather than as a congeries of largely autonomous chiefdoms and confederations. In the words of W.E.B. DuBois, Guinean Loma speakers entered a disenchanted space, "which yields him no true self-consciousness, but only lets him see himself through the revelation of the other world. It is a peculiar sensation, this double-consciousness, this sense of always looking at one's self through the eyes of others" ([1903] 1994, 2).

Yet Guinean Forestiers were insiders at the same time that they were outsiders. Though they were singled out for certain types of ridicule and denigration, they also shared in the collective suffering of a national citizenry denied the ability to express itself freely, practice its chosen religion without constraint, keep the fruits of its labor, or freely choose its political leaders. If the rhetoric of Marxist modernism partially separated fétichiste Forestiers from the dominant monotheistic culture, the rhetoric of betrayal and siege by neighboring countries, emigrants, imperialists, neocolonialists, and even internal traitors (the "fifth column") made them full-fledged members of a national citizenry that also knew itself to be what it was "through the revelation of the other world." Much like the situation described by Anna Tsing, where "Meratus marginality in the Indonesian nation cannot be divorced from Indonesian marginality in international rankings" (1993, 17), the Guinean situation consisted of a doubling of double consciousness. Guinea's "civilized" populations still knew themselves to be "savages" in the eyes of much of the rest of the world, "a world that looks on in amused contempt and pity" (DuBois [1903] 1994, 3). Thus, at the level of relations among nations, Loma speakers were united with their compatriots.

One might ask why this ambivalent, partial belonging would result in a positive outcome, such as choosing to reject the path of large-scale violence. To quote Ernest Renan:

More valuable by far than common customs posts and frontiers conforming to strategic ideas is the fact of sharing, in the past, a glorious heritage and regrets, and of having, in the future, [a shared] programme to put into effect, or the fact of having suffered, enjoyed, and hoped together. These are the kinds of things that can be understood in spite of differences of race and language. I spoke just now of "having suffered together" and indeed, suffering in common unifies more than joy does. (Renan [1882] 1990, 19)

There is no question that, over the course of the twentieth century, Loma speakers moved from what Berman and Lonsdale (1992) call "moral ethnicity" to "political ethnicity," and that this shift accompanied a bittersweet set of interactions with encompassing states epitomized by the Demystification Program. In Tsing's poetic words, "Marginals stand outside the state by tying themselves to it; they constitute the state locally by fleeing from it. As culturally 'different' subjects they can never be citizens; as culturally different 'subjects' they can never escape citizenship" (1993, 26).

Still, the narrative of national unity and modernist progress is suffused with hope and a set of expectations of the future that can be both articulated and envisioned as being achieved in a step-by-step process. Politically and imaginatively, this can be a very powerful antidote to marginal ambivalence. The two legacies of the socialist period I have described here—a heightened sense of ethnic identity *and* a strong sense of national identity—continue to play central roles in the political and social life of Guinea's forest region. For these reasons, Guinea almost slid into the kind of civil war that plagued almost all of its neighbors—Liberia, Sierra Leone, Guinea Bissau, Côte d'Ivoire—yet managed several times to pull back from the brink.

One of the key questions that carries over from this book on the 1958–84 Touré period and the kinds of divided consciousness it produced is whether the forms of coercion that representatives of the socialist government visited upon their compatriots may have had some salutary effects over time. Most discussion of the Touré government's abuses draws from a language of trauma and fear. However, I would argue that it is also worthwhile trying to understand what may be the bracing, almost homeopathic effects of some types of state-organized violence on citizens. Such violence results in negative effects, but there may also be positive sequellae—as a reminder of the stakes and sacrifices involved in politics and as a source of solidarity through communities of suffering.

APPENDIX 1

Kɔkɔlɔgi/zu and their Dominant Clans, according to Beavogui and Person[1]

Chiefdoms (*zuti*) located between the Niando/Diani/St. John's River and the Ziama Mountains

Kɔkɔlɔgiti	Clan(s)	
2. Bhuuzu	Grovogui	Beavogui notes that this chiefdom became part of Buzie canton in 1925.
3. Woima/ Wymar/ Koima/Domar	Koivogui [Bilivogui][2]	
4. Vɛkɛma	Pivi [Guilavogui][3]	
5. Ghainga/ Niankan	Pivi[4]	A Kpelle *kɔkɔlɔgi* on the right bank of the Diani

1. Numbers refer to Beavogui's "Carte Politique" (fig. 10), which forms the basis of fig. 6 in this book. Dominant clans listed according to Beavogui (1991) first, according to Person (1968) in brackets.
2. According to my own research, Person is correct here and Beavogui mistaken—the Bilivoguis are dominant through these villages.
3. According to my research, it is the Pivis who are actually dominant in Vɛkɛma. Person probably refers to several Gilavogui villages within the colonial administrative unit that was known as Vekema, considerably larger than the precolonial *kɔkɔlɔgi* (including part of Bhilu as well as Akae, neither of which are mentioned in Person's text).
4. This dominant clan is listed in neither Beavogui nor Person, but comes from my own research.
5. Southern Loma speakers agree that Gizima was and is actually a portion of the larger Bhilu *kɔkɔlɔgi*, dominated by the Grovogui. Gizima, under Gilavogui leadership, built the im-

238 / Appendix I

6. Akae	Bilivogui/Grovogui	Incorporated by the French into Vɛkɛma canton.
7. Gizima	Gilavogui[5]	
8. Bhuliyema/ Briama	?	Kpelle/Loma chiefdom in present-day Liberia.
9. Ziama	Beavogui [Beavogui, Guilavogui, Koivogui,	Bilivogui][6]

Chiefdoms (*zuti*) located between the Ziama mountains and the Manwana/Makona River

Kɔkɔlɔgiti	Clan(s)	
10. Famoila-Kpetea	Koivogui	Became part of Buzie canton.
11. Famoila	Koivogui	Became part of Ziama canton.
12. Yala	Koivogui	Became Kunukoro-Toma canton.
13. Kunukɔrɔ/ Konokoro	Kamara	Became the core of the Kunukoro-Malinke canton.
14. Muidu	Kamara	Became part of Kunukoro-Malinke canton.
15. Mandugu	Kamara	Became Mandugu canton
16. Bhode/Bonde	Kamara	This *zu* became Bonde district in Liberia.
17. Oniguamɛ	Kamara	As of 1922, this chiefdom formed the core of the Koadu canton.
18. Koemɛ	Beavogui/Koivogui	As of 1922, this chiefdom formed the core of the Koodu canton.

portant trading and war towns of N'Zapa, Koyama, and Zorzor, among others, and especially in Liberia the memory of their relation to Bhilu seems to have been effaced. Gizima's claim to autonomy was supported by the French colonial administrative divisions, which erased Bhilu, tacking about half its territory onto Vɛkɛma canton, and making the southern half into the autonomous canton of Gizima.

6. According to my own research, Person seems to be mistaken in claiming that other clans have the same stature as the Beavogui within this *kɔkɔlɔgi*. This is probably because he is referring to the colonial administrative unit of Ziama, which swallowed some of the smaller, neighboring precolonial chiefdoms such as Famoila, which was Koivogui-dominated.

List of Kɔkɔlɔgi/zu and Their Dominant Clans / 239

19. Weybhalaga	Gilavogui (with important) later dominance by Kamaras in some areas	During the colonial period (in 1919, to be exact), the French colonial authorities split Weybhalaga into two cantons, one called, Kolibirama-Toma, and the other Kolibirama-Malinke.
20. Ugbemɛ / Wubomai	Koivogui [Koivogui]	This *zu* became the Liberian Wubomai district.
21. Fasalɔ / Fasalor	Zumanigi / Koivogui [Zumanigi / Koivogui]	The French split this chiefdom into two cantons called Dulama-Malinke and Dulama-Toma.
22. Manzama	Zumanigi / Keita / Kamara / Kane [Gilavogui / Beavogui]	The French also split this chiefdom into two cantons called Dulama-Malinke and Dulama-Toma.

Chiefdoms (*zuti*) to northwest of the Manwana / Makona River

Kɔkɔlɔgiti	Clan(s)	
23. Ninibu	Koivogui, Gilavogui, Zumanigi [Zumanigi]	In 1919, this chiefdom was separated from Mandugu, and became Ninibu canton.
24. Keleɣelega / Gerengerenka	Koivogui / Gilavogui [Gilavogui / Goepogui]	
25. Davhabu / Dawabu	Onivogui	
26. Wulukoza	Onivogui	
27. Anamay / Anamai	Onivogui / Beavogui [Onivogui]	Became the canton of Baizia.
28. Woijama	Onivogui / Inapogui / Bhavogui / Sovogui / Gilavogui	
29. Wotume	Beavogui [Sovogui]	
30. Wulome / Ulyamay	Zumanigi [Zumanigi]	

31. Wotame   ?

32. Abuγalɛa /   Onivogui [Onivogui]
    Apawarya / Apouaria

33. Vighinɛmɛ /   Onivogui / Zumanigi /
    Viginamay   Gilavogui / Bhole
                          [Onivogui]

APPENDIX 2

Agricultural Production in Giziwulu, 1999

Below is a chart showing some agricultural patterns in "Giziwulu," the village where I did much of my fieldwork. The data comes from a 1999 survey, and market prices are based on early 1999 prices, when the exchange rate between the Guinean franc and the U.S. dollar was about 1,500/1.

A few things will be immediately obvious. Rice is the main crop for Loma speakers, but not everyone has a rice field. The survey results were partly skewed in this respect because we only surveyed people from twenty-five-years old upward. On average, respondents stated that they had planted their own first fields at thirteen years of age, so a sizeable chunk of the active farmers in the community were not part of the survey at the same time that the elderly, who no longer farmed, brought the average down. Perhaps more interesting is the number of farms per household figure. Because husbands in many polygynous households make farms for each wife, and in monogamous or polygynous households the husband and wife may have separate farms, the number is close to two farms per household. I discuss the changing links between domestic units and agricultural production below.

As for cash crops, it is clear that cola and cocoa are men's crops while peanuts are women's. The difference in their profitability is also striking. The average Loma coffee farmer with trees in production could look forward to the equivalent of $233 in 1999. The average cocoa farmer with trees bearing fruit could expect $139. Meanwhile, the average (female) peanut farmer only made $49. As I have mentioned above, it is my understanding from interviews and participant observation that women do not own coffee or other perpetual fruit-bearing trees. The ten women who harvested coffee ostensibly obtained use rights to producing coffee trees, perhaps belonging to husbands working in the capital. It remains interesting to note

Table 8. Agricultural production in Giziwulu, 1999

	Men (184)	Women (195)	Total (126 households)
Rice farms (upland rice)	131 (71%)	88 (45%)	219 (1.74 farms/household)
Average size[a]	0.95 hectares	0.78 hectares	
Average fallow	7.39 years	6.00 years	6.81 years
No. of old-growth forest farms[b]	28 (21.4%)	13 (14.8%)	
No. of paddy rice farms	2 (1.5%)	4 (4.5%)	6 (2.7%)
Coffee (c. $57/sack)[c]	156 (84.8%) (31 not yet yielding)	9 (4.6%)	165
Average yield[d]	4.09 sacks/year	1.25 sacks/year	3.27 sacks/year
Cola (c. $4/basket)	31	1	
Average yield	1.89 baskets/year	1 basket/year	
Cocoa (c. $47/sack)	107 (58.2%) (34 not yielding)	0	
Average yield[e]	2.96 sacks/year	N/A	2.02 sacks/year
Bananas	39	14	
Average yield	3.96 sacks/year	2.07 sacks/year	
Peanuts (c. $16/sack)	0	115 (59%)	
Average yield	N/A	3.07 sacks/year	
Other	N/A	Beans—4 Taro—2	

[a] Size was calculated by asking respondents how much rice they had planted. I had already calculated with informants' help that one long sack of rice seed planted approximately one hectare. Of the Temne of Sierra Leone, Littlejohn notes, "There is no way whatsoever of measuring area. The area of a farm is the only one ever estimated and that is done by estimating the number of bags of rice it ought to yield" (1967, 332).
[b] These plots had never been planted before in living memory.
[c] The price of coffee in Guinea fell by half the next year (early 2000) and dropped again the next. Worldwide coffee prices have dropped to a point where most Loma farmers will probably not continue to grow the crop.
[d] Yields for coffee are measured in "long sacks," used to store and sell rice, and equivalent to about 60 kg of dried coffee berries, a similar amount of dried cocoa pods, and about half that weight in dried, unshelled peanuts. Plantains are transported in long sacks, but sold by the piece. Their selling price depends on the season, but most importantly, on the distance from the forest. They cost four to six times as much in Conakry, the capital, as in the forest. The first figure subtracts those coffee plantations not yet yielding. The second includes the thirty-one unproductive plantations.
[e] The first figure gives average yield for those plantations that had entered the productive phase, the second figure factors in the thirty-four plantations not yet yielding any fruit. Amelonado cocoa trees, most common in West Africa, take at least seven years to begin bearing mature fruit (Berry 1975, 54). The fact that many plantations did not yet yield anything in 1999, and that many other yields were still miniscule (if one subtracts the two biggest plantations, with yields of 90 and 15 sacks, the average yield drops to 1.04 sacks/year), is a legacy of the Touré years, when such cash crops were mostly confiscated by agents of the state. Most Loma farmers abandoned cash cropping at that time, and it took a long time after the 1984 change of government before they returned to crops like cocoa and coffee.

that in the cases of both coffee and bananas, where men and women both harvest the same cash crop, the men's yields are significantly larger than women's. Men harvested almost twice as many bananas as women, and about three times as much coffee per person. I believe this is a result of women's limited and tenuous access to land for production other than rice and garden vegetables.

NOTES

CHAPTER ONE

1. Rivière (1971) states that the Demystification Program started in 1959, while my interlocutors in the southern part of Macenta Préfecture consistently stated the year was 1961. Højbjerg sometimes uses Rivière's 1959 date, but often leaves some ambiguity about the actual start date of the program. Since it was not directly publicized in the Guinean press and the archives are not publicly available for this period, it is difficult to determine an exact start date, although, as I detail in the second half of the book, there are several events that caused the policy to be resuscitated, and Loma speakers remember their dates.
2. The Guinean government was coercive and quite violent in suppressing polytheistic "fetishism" (the term actually used by the government), but totally noncoercive when it came to choosing between Christianity and Islam. Although converting to Islam might have yielded some social advantages given its majority status, most people in the southeastern forest region of the country chose either to resist the prescribed conversion or converted to Christianity, thus maintaining a sense of cultural-religious distinction from the majority culture.
3. Part of the reason for this is that several excellent books have recently appeared on how iconoclastic movements were experienced and managed by people both along the coast and in the rain forest region. See Sarró 2009 and Højbjerg 2007.
4. The people refer to themselves as "Loma," though in Guinea most non-Loma use the French ethnonym "Toma" to refer to them. The language is called "Lomagui," a term I sometimes use to make clear that I am talking about the language, not the people, but I often substitute "Loma" when it is obvious I am talking about the language. This is especially the case in my use of the term "Loma speakers," a phrase I pointedly use in preference to "the Loma" in order to underline the fact that language, culture, and population groups have not mapped on to one another in a one-to-one fashion. This is an argument that I develop throughout the first half of the book.
5. All initiates into the men's Poro society receive cicatrizations as part of their initiation. They are thus permanently marked, and in certain instances over the last twenty years (including interethnic massacres) these markings on the body have been subject to close examination.

6. Loma men's Poro initiation in the precolonial and early colonial periods lasted seven years. It has progressively shortened to the point where today it typically lasts anywhere from a week or two up to several months.
7. Translating from possession to the affective orientation to objects, "exorcism" would be similar to iconoclasm and "adoricism" to idolatry. There is an interesting essay to be written about the relationship between possession and iconoclasm. The former turns persons into things; bodies that become vessels to be emptied of their everyday inhabitants' persons and replaced by the possessing deity or personality. If possession turns persons into things, then iconoclasm conversely turns things into quasi-persons, attributing powerful forms of agency to them. It is this very aura that calls forth the iconoclast's attempts at erasure.
8. Not to mention Frazer's sympathetic and contagious magic.
9. The essays in Pietz and Apter's 1993 *Fetishism as Cultural Discourse* attempt to untangle the many intertwined meanings originating in seventeenth-century Luso-African trade and amateur ethnographic observations and the Freudian and Marxist uses of the term that build upon this substrate to construct uses of the term that sometimes seem twinned and at other times incommensurable.
10. The iconoclasts were often converts (in the Guinean case, as in Donham's). Whether to Christianity or Islam does not seem to matter.
11. The secret societies/power associations that used these objects are simultaneously ritual, aesthetic, and political institutions. The masks could thus be seen as troubling indexes of a form of parallel political sovereignty that would be threatening to a new nation whose sovereignty was under symbolic and even material attack from the beginning.
12. Loma speakers have concepts and terms close enough to anxiety that I don't think it is too far a stretch to talk about this, and, for many of the other concepts (not least fetishism itself), the linguistic and cultural setting was and is self-consciously hybrid, the product of five hundred years of Euro-African cross-cultural interaction that at this moment was often phrased in the idiom of postcolonial nationalism and international socialist solidarity.
13. The classic anthropological distinction between the two is that witchcraft operates without the witch's knowledge, while sorcery is a conscious act. Højbjerg (2007) makes a few mentions of what he calls "witchcraft" (*motai* in the northern dialect of Lomagui). My understanding of what speakers of southern Loma dialect call *matalai* is that it is always a set of techniques consciously put into action to drain another (often a baby or child) of its life force, and thus I call it sorcery.
14. Brecht theorized the *verfremdungseffekt* which has been variously translated as an alienation or distancation effect, but is probably best translated as "estrangement effect" (cf. Bloch 1962). In his writings on Brecht, Fredric Jameson (1998) has opted not to translate the term, shortening it to "V-effekt." Brecht argued that it is essential to break the trance-like naturalness of the theater audience's suspension of disbelief by breaking through the theatrical "fourth wall," using a variety of techniques, as when an actor breaks out of character to address the audience directly. It is not incidental to my interests in this book that the metaphorical template for most of these techniques is that of the actor taking off her or his "mask" for a moment. The discussion of the V-effekt also returns to our earlier discussion of the power of images inasmuch as it is based upon Brecht's argument for the need to shatter the aura of the diegetic *mise en scène*. Laura Mulvey (1989, 25) has put the argument even more powerfully in a gendered critique of the dream world of feature films, in which "cin-

15. Again, the parallels to the coastal Baga Sitem and Bulongic as described by Sarró (2010), Berliner (2010), and others are striking.
16. This is an insight that emerged from many discussions with Paul Richards, Ramon Sarró, and James Scott.
17. This is not to say that they fled easily or without consequences. As I describe later in the book, people were beaten, jailed, and occasionally killed by Guinean security forces for either trying to "escape" to Liberia, or upon returning.
18. It is also why the most vivid depiction of what a demystificatory event probably looked like is rendered as the fictional interlude that opens part 2 of this book.
19. See McGovern (forthcoming) for a description of Loma peasants' subaltern historiography and their comparisons of different historical periods from the late precolonial through the postsocialist.
20. One of the most eloquent rejections of this aspect of Marxism's racial-cultural blind spot is Aimé Césaire's 1956 "Open Letter to Maurice Thorez." Thorez was the head of the French Communist Party, which had not opposed the French war in Algeria, despite its opposition to the French government on domestic issues.
21. The anthropological discussion of belief has a long history, and many analyses use Evans-Pritchard's 1937 *Witchcraft, Oracles and Magic Among the Azande* as their touchstone. I have also found Sperber's 1985 discussion very useful.

CHAPTER TWO

1. Jacques Germain was a French colonial administrator in Guinea's forest region, and an amateur historian of the area.
2. These groups, calling themselves and called variously Manya, Mandingo, Koniyanke, and Kuranko were the southern fringe of the large population of speakers of Mandekan, only recently converted to Islam. In Macenta Préfecture, Guinea, they are called "Manya," while in adjacent Lofa County, Liberia (where the other half of Loma speakers live), they are called "Mandingo."
3. This claim is supported by such travelers' accounts as Anderson's (1870), who describes most major towns in present-day northern Liberia and southeastern Guinea as multilingual, cosmopolitan centers.
4. Kankan is the biggest town of the savannah "Upper Guinea" region to the north of the Forest Region. I use the term "Maninka" to specify speakers of Maninkakan from the core Mande heartland of present-day northeastern Guinea and southwestern Republic of Mali, some of whom have a centuries-old history of Muslim practice. While Manya, Mandingoes, and others I call "peripheral Mandekan speakers" also spoke Maninkakan, the biggest distinction between them and the Maninka is the historical depth of their Muslim practice and their links to the medieval Sahelian empires such as the empire of Mali.
5. This was not the primary motivation of the Liberian war more generally.
6. Presented in these terms, I think few of the authors I cite below would disagree with my thesis. The problem comes when aspects of the model are reproduced in subtle ways that ultimately pull the rug out from under the anthropological truism that no identity is primordial. One consequence of this shift is that the researcher must treat oral histories with considerable care.
7. E.g., F. Beavogui (1998), who described contemporary uses of the Poro society as a bulwark against "foreign invasion."

8. This is the argument that Vail and the authors in his *The Creation of Tribalism in Southern Africa* (1989) make. However, the imposition of colonial rule can only explain part of that process in the area that became Guinea. As I argue in this chapter, the categories used in Guinean colonial censuses both reified ethnolinguistic identity and provide evidence for its fluidity. Conversion to Islam was at least as important a factor in fixing ethnic identity in the Macenta region as ethnolinguistic identity.
9. Fairhead and Leach (1996) have probably come closest to the position I am advocating in their work on Kissi- and Kuranko-speaking farmers in Kissidougou Préfecture, Guinea.
10. Linguists have been ambivalent about the classification of such Mande languages as Mano and Dan, whose populations lie at the point where Liberia, Côte d'Ivoire, and Guinea meet. The most recent publications (Vydrine 2002) class these in a small, separate group as "southern," or "southeastern" Mande languages. They are culturally close to their neighbors, the Kpelle, Mano, and Loma. An important ethnographic difference is that they have Poro but not Sande societies.
11. Again, excepting the southernmost corner of the coastal area, which was probably populated by speakers of Kruan languages.
12. Hill (1972) and Jones (1981) argue that Kono and Vai were probably mutually intelligible dialects of the same language. Kono speakers, in Eastern Sierra Leone, and Vai speakers, in coastal Liberia, are today separated by some one hundred miles where Mende is the lingua franca. However, as David Dalby has noted (1963), this region is where a language called "Dama," similar to Vai and Kono, was spoken. Dama-speakers only abandoned their own language (in favor of Mende) in the twentieth century.
13. These are the Makona, the Loffa, and the Diani (called the St. John in Liberia).
14. Jones (1981) and Person (1971) have argued that this elite was Vai-speaking. The evidence indicates that these armies moved through what was then and is now Vai-speaking territory, but this seems insufficient evidence for the claim.
15. Galaty (1993) points out that ethnic identities are both fluid and structured. His use of the concept of "shifters," borrowed from linguistics, emphasizes the situational nature of these negotiations.
16. It is an interesting coincidence that the Liberians United for Reconciliation and Democracy (LURD) rebels, who controlled much of northern Liberia between 2000 and 2003, were also based in Bopolu.
17. Without going into undue detail that would make all but the most dedicated regional specialist's head spin, we should note the key points that have been gleaned from this passage in conjunction with other data:

   (1) There is general agreement (Hair 1967; Jones 1981; Massing 1985; Person 1971; Rodney 1970) that the "Konde-Quoja" were the present day Kono's ancestors; the "Quoja" and also the "Vey" were the present-day Vai's ancestors; and the Gala were the present-day Gola's ancestors.
   (2) There is very little interpretation of the "Manoë," though I believe Rodney correctly identifies them as the ancestors of today's Mano, who live in roughly the area Dapper indicates: to the northeast of the Gola, along the present-day border between Guinea and Liberia (and to the east of the Landoyo-Loma-Bandi-Mende area I argue made up the Hondo population).
   (3) Few have had much to say about the "Dogo," encompassed, Dapper writes,

by the Hondo confederacy. Person (1971, 682) and Hair (1967, 56) suggest, somewhat tentatively, that they may be the Loko. Not speaking the relevant languages, they miss an obvious fact. In the Southwestern Mande languages, initial consonant change applies for a handful of phonemes, and one of the most common substitutions is D = L. Thus "Dogo" and "Logo" are the same word, the pronunciation varying according to the tone of the last syllable of the preceding word.

With this base, we see a connection to two present-day ethno-linguistic groups, the Loma and Loko. Loma speakers use the terms "Lomagui" and "Loγoma" interchangeably to describe "the Loma people" (Labouret 1934). The Loko do not in fact call themselves Loko, but Landoγo. Given that the "γ" sound, a voiced velar fricative, is pronounced like a "G" in the back of the throat, it has been written as "G" or sometimes "K" by Europeans unaccustomed to the sound. Taking Dapper's ethnonym "Dogo," and effecting the initial consonant change we get Dogo = Logo. With the confusion between the locally pronounced "γ" and either "k" or "g," we get Dogo/Logo = Doko/Loko = Doγo/Loγo. The various transformations show that in local phonemic terms, the word written "Dogo" could represent an earlier form of either "Loγo-ma," (Loma), or "Lan-*doγo*," (Loko). The fact that Landoγo is mutually intelligible with Bandi, and that both languages are extremely close to the Mende and Loma languages, indicates that this group was probably—in the fifteenth and sixteenth centuries—a relatively undifferentiated ethnolinguistic population.

18. Some accounts of the Mani invasions describe the rank-and-file of the invading forces as the "Sumbas," a group sometimes described in these versions as cannibals. I basically agree with Person that the so-called Sumba were Southwestern Mande speakers, but am suspicious of his seemingly a priori interpretation, accompanied by no further explanation except the implicit ones that (1) the Malinke are/were glorious conquerors, and (2) the Mano were purported, in the twentieth century during which Person worked, to eat human flesh.

19. This intensification was also the result of the growth of the Samorian empire, which emerged in the 1860s and 1870s, and participated actively in the raiding and selling of slaves.

20. After I wrote this chapter, Robert Leopold sent me a copy of a conference paper written by Weisswange (1976), in which she analyzes village histories she collected in thirty Loma-speaking villages and thirteen Manya-speaking villages in Lofa County, Liberia. She effectively came to an identical conclusion: "The last great overwhelming immigration evidently was that of the koeiwogui [Koivogui]—the leopard taboo group, the people of Kamara or Joomani. It may have been during the entire nineteenth century, starting perhaps earlier but became intensified toward the end of it. . . . In this area the koei [Koivogui] people, though powerful in gaining control of the land, had to subject to local tradition, and assimilated themselves within the last three generations. A number of [Loma] people for instance in Bokeza are known, whose grandfathers were considered Mandingo and who spoke that language. In the Nyaameε part of Gbooni the reverse was told. People along the Lofa all spoke Loma until about 1920 and then adopted the Manya-kan very likely together with the Islam" (1976, 11–12).

21. Throughout the Mande-speaking region, a clan is defined as the maximal unit practicing marriage exogamy. Men and women inherit their clan identity from their fathers, and in Guinea, both men and women use their clan names throughout their

lives as family names. Each clan is identified with a totemic plant or animal which the member of the clan must never kill or eat.

22. In Liberia, chiefdom maps and general parlance recognize "Gizima" and sometimes "Bhuliyema" as separate chiefdoms or confederations. Gizima, however, was part of Bhilu. Interviews in N'Zapa, the seat of the Gizima sub-federation of Bhilu, confirmed this. Because N'Zapa was a powerful town in the late nineteenth and twentieth centuries, far outshining Sibata (the seat of Bhilu), the recognition is grudging, and in some sense only pro forma. Bhuliyema, again a semi-independent sub-federation, was actually part of Ziama, whose seats were Bhusɛme [Boussedou] and Sɛdime, in present-day Guinea.

23. This contradicts Weisswange (1969), who writes that the relationship is that between *kekɛ* and *daabe*, or mother's brother to sister's son. This is the dominant kinship idiom of Loma social and ritual life, and more strictly hierarchical than the *die–dɛye* (elder brother–younger brother) relation. Every time I discussed the *kɔkɔlɔgi* in the Guinean southern Loma area, I was told, unprompted, that they stood in a *die–dɛye* relation to one another.

24. One of Beavogui's informants, referring to the links between the passage of the *kɔkɔlɔgi* and the extension of the Poro said of the term's etymology, "the symbolic usage made here [of the piece of thick bark] refers to the idea of a shield, of a shell used to protect oneself from the view of inquisitive outsiders" (Beavogui 1991, 121).

25. Germain (1984) notes that Kpelle speakers also claim to have moved to their current location in southeastern Guinea and northern Liberia via Musadu.

26. This map uses Beavogui's approximations of the chiefdom boundaries, but is not meant to give the exact boundaries in a way that could settle, for instance, contemporary land disputes.

27. Beavogui, for reasons he does not explain, does not consider the Ziama mountains as a significant geographic barrier, and thus groups these chiefdoms in such a way that the clear patterns I am presenting here do not stand out (he uses the categories of the "valleys of" the Diani, Loffa, and Makona rivers, deceptive geographical boundaries especially in the southern Loma region, since both banks of the Diani—from N'Zebela to the Guinea-Liberia border—have been settled by Kpelle speakers). However, the importance of the mountains as a cultural and geographical breaking point is exemplified by the fact that the northern and southern dialects of Lomagui can generally be located on either side of the mountain range. Southern Loma speakers refer to northern dialect-speakers as the *giziwululomagui*, or literally, "the Loma behind the mountain." As the Ziama range tails off at about the Guinean-Liberian border, there is not the same kind of sharp geographic division between northern and southern Loma speakers in Liberia. Nevertheless, southern Liberian Loma speakers (clustered around Zorzor) live within Bhilu/Gizima and Ziama *kokologiti*, both having their seats in present day Guinea (to the south of the mountains), and recognize a distinction between themselves and those Loma speakers who live in Bonde and Wubomai chiefdoms (clustered around Voinjama) to the north.

28. See the case of M. Traoré in the next chapter for a description of this dynamic.

29. It is significant in this regard to note the fact that the small Loma-speaking chiefdoms north of the Makona were "the only Toma areas which remained independent during the Samorian period," along with the westernmost villages in the Gbunde region, surrounding Pandemai (Massing 1978–79, 56).

30. The history of Kwanga is significant in the region, and is the subject of chapter 4's case study, but is not as crucial to the history of Kamara migration and conquest.
31. The South Windward Coast is the coast of what is today Liberia, but the region he discusses is the same as that defined as the Central West Atlantic region by d'Azevedo (1962a).
32. The point at issue here is not simply the backward extrapolation of ethnoreligious identities that have become hardened in the last fifty years, but also a conception of the dynamic of conversion and faith that has often smuggled a series of Eurocentric assumptions about belief, personhood, and religious experience into its argumentation. Attempts to approach the problem from an African perspective have ranged from Horton (1971, 1975) to Peel (2000). For Guinea, Berliner (2002, 2005), Højbjerg (2002a, 2007), and McGovern (2004) have all addressed this issue.
33. I describe how such transformations have taken place in several Loma chiefdoms over the last one hundred fifty years in McGovern 2012.
34. The instance cited above of the Komara lineage accepting Poro initiation and being granted access to farming land is one step in this process.
35. As Corinne Kratz has remarked to me on this point, it is not just individuals who would have "crossed the line" between two fixed groups, but the groups themselves would have been changing over time. This aspect of the interaction between individual allegiances and group identities comes out most clearly in chapter 4, where I emphasize the growing importance of religion in both ethnic and national identities in twentieth-century Guinea.
36. Some of these dynamics *preceded* colonialism and others gained momentum in the *postcolonial* era. While I agree that the colonial period was a significant period of ethnogenesis, especially because of the intersection of chieftainship politics and changes in land tenure norms occasioned by the introduction of cash crops (topics explored in chapter 3), one should not exaggerate the efficacy of colonial categories.
37. My female research colleague's maternal grandmother was a Manya-speaking captive purchased and married by her grandfather, a Loma-speaking canton chief.
38. *Niei* is the term Gamory-Dubourdeau uses for the totemic prohibition that I call *gẽ*. This term in Maninkakan is *tana* (see also Jackson below, who notes *tana* as the Kuranko term). *Diamu* is the term for the totemic clan name in Maninkakan.
39. The Kuranko, like the Dyula, Manya, and Koniyanke, are part of the southern periphery of Mandekan speakers, less directly attached to the centralized Mande states and generally not Islamicized until the twentieth century.
40. I once described the translatability between Manya and Loma clan names to an American Peace Corps volunteer who lived in a Manya-speaking town in Macenta Préfecture. I said that Kamara and Koivogui are the same name, as both respect the leopard as their totem. She said: "Oh, I understand . . . my Guinean name in the town is Fanta Kamara, and Nathan's [the American living in the nearest Loma-speaking town] Loma name is Koivogui. People used to tease me that he was my 'husband,' until they heard his Loma name. Then they said, 'oh, you two can't be married after all—he's a Koivogui and you're a Kamara.' I didn't really understand what they were talking about." This joking plays off the fact that totemic clans for both Loma and Manya speakers are exogamous, and one should never marry a person respecting the same totem. This fact is taken into consideration in interethnic marriages between Loma and Manya, or Loma and Kpelle speakers.
41. Translated into their Mandekan equivalents.

42. Not only does this linguistic diversification indicate the first step in the process I have described of Northern Mande speakers "becoming" Loma, it also parallels a situation noted throughout the region. Holsoe has noted that "many of the so-called 'Vai' lineages were originally Gola" (Holsoe, 1980, 97); Richards has noted that the Kpa Mende were mostly Mel-speaking Banta people who adopted the Mende language (Richards, p.c., May 2002); Dalby (1963) has noted that speakers of Dama, a northern Mande language similar to Kono and Vai, gradually adopted Mende over the course of the nineteenth and twentieth centuries to the point where the Dama language became extinct. Hair (1967) and others have made the same argument generally about the Mani/Sumba invaders remarked by sixteenth-century European traders and missionaries: though outsiders, many remained in present-day Sierra Leone, intermarrying and adopting the language of the Mel speakers they had conquered. Amselle's researches (1990) in the Wassoulou region of Guinea/Mali/Côte d'Ivoire have yielded similar entanglements of language, ethnicity, and religion amongst Maninka/Bamana/Fulbe.

43. In villages, this had much to do with Malinke families having their children initiated in the local men's or women's society groves, and then deciding to stay and farm rice, rather than being involved in trade. The case study at the end of chapter 4 describes the specific case of a family that switched identities in the other direction. The situation in Macenta town, with *tirailleurs*, Muslim *dyula* traders, and imams from further north (and virtually no Loma speakers), created a different dynamic.

44. One exception was centers such as Kwanga, where a sufficiently large number of non-Muslim Manya was cause for instituting two separate sacred groves.

45. This figure is not equivalent to the percentage of the Guinean population that speaks Lomagui. Macenta Préfecture is home to sizeable numbers of Pulaar, Kpelle, Kissi, and especially Manya speakers. There are also Loma speakers living in the other regions of the country, including a sizeable number in Conakry, the capital. However, this latter group is relatively small in comparison with the number of "non-Loma" (primarily Manya) living in Macenta Préfecture. Loma speakers probably make up 3 to 4 percent of the national population.

46. I retain the French terms *fétichiste* and *fétichisme*, roughly equivalent to the English "animist" and "animism," throughout the book, because they capture an important and partly untranslatable aspect of francophone African talk about religion, identity, and modernity, namely its derogatory attitude toward indigenous religion.

47. As the Liberian joke goes: "Liberia is a country that is 70 percent Christian, 30 percent Muslim, and 100 percent animist" (cf. Ellis 2001).

48. See McGovern 2004, 83–174.

49. While this wealth has been reckoned by Loma speakers and their strangers primarily in terms of plentiful, fertile land in a region receiving a lot of rain, twentieth-century discoveries of gold and diamonds below the surface of this land complicate the situation, as does the contemporary presence of timber companies, who are now clear-cutting their way across Macenta Préfecture.

50. For further details about the ways that the idiom of mother's brother/sister's son relations conditioned the process of assimilation, see McGovern 2004 and 2012. It is important to stress, as both these essays do, that the work of assimilation often fails. The comparison I suggest here is not between an idealized precolonial "before," when people lived happily together, and an anomic "after," when they adopted crude, hardened identities for instrumental gain. Rather in the period through the

1920s, and possibly as late as the 1950s in parts of Macenta Préfecture, there was not a well-articulated language for rejecting the principle of stranger-host reciprocities.
51. Marx and Engels (1848) 1992, 21; cf. Berman 1988.

CHAPTER THREE

1. I treat the topic more extensively in McGovern 2004 and 2012. See also Højbjerg 1999 and Leopold 1991.
2. These are the terms used by Hubert and Mauss in their 1898 essay on sacrifice. Translator W. D. Halls defines the *sacrifiant* as 'the subject to whom the benefits of sacrifice accrue . . . or who undergoes its effect" (Hubert and Mauss 1964, ix). The *sacrifiteur* is the person who performs the sacrifice.
3. In this regard it is interesting to note that Loma speakers use the idiom to talk about the deep history of population movements discussed in chapter 2. In this context, Loma speakers acknowledge ethnic Kissi as being their *keke*, while they identify Manya as being their *daabe*.
4. Indeed, Manya speakers in the Macenta area have broken the rules in ways so offensive to their hosts that this betrayal became the primary justification for intercommunal violence in the 1990s.
5. Although it is worth noting that in the local context this aspect of the object's importance was a distant third to its other two meanings.
6. In this respect, Zoumanigi is mistaken, I think, to say that Loma speakers do not actively seek such mobility during certain periods of their lives.
7. Gamory-Dubourdeau makes reference only to the fact that young men came to realize once they were *forced* to earn money for taxes that they could *choose* to bypass many of the onerous aspects of the subservient period of bride-service work by gathering together enough money to buy bridewealth gifts with money (a direct cash substitution remains unacceptable to the present in the Loma bridewealth system with its small, largely symbolic gifts). This combination of bridewealth monetization and youth mobility was a phenomenon common to most of Africa from the colonial period onward (Guyer 1995; Parkin and Nyamwaya 1987).
8. This is ironic, as Northern Mande speakers are often sedentary farmers, while Guinea's other biggest ethnic group, the Fulbe, are historically West Africa's best-known nomadic herders. In Guinea, although many Fulbe do tend cattle, the majority are sedentary farmers, merchants, and bureaucrats. The Northern Mande living in the forest region have traditionally been mobile *jula* traders, and are thus known among Loma and Kpelle speakers for their mobility.
9. This is the most frequently-used term in the southern Loma dialect. Leopold uses the northern Loma term *kaalai* (1991, 96).
10. It happens rarely that two members of the same totemic clan marry. In my own interviews and surveys, I heard of one such instance. It immediately became the subject of lively discussion, and several people present said it might be acceptable in the case where each partner's secondary totem was different. Secondary totems are highly negotiable: some Loma speakers say the first child inherits his or her mother's totem in addition to the father's (while subsequent children do not); other people say that all twins must respect snakes as a secondary totem; and many lineages also share a secondary totem. Nevertheless, even while discussing the one anomalous case, people made it clear that they were attempting to give an ex post facto explanation for the embarrassing "mistake" that the interviewee and her husband had

made in marrying (the interviewee was a woman, and refused to comment on the situation). Leopold gives the impression that intraclan marriages are more common (though still rare) in Liberia. He writes that "Loma have no unanimous opinion about the propriety of intraclan marriages per se" (1991, 125). The fact that Loma speakers use their totemic names as family names in Guinea but not in Liberia may keep clan identity at the forefront of the Guineans' awareness.

11. *Daabenui* literally means "sister's son person," but in its broader connotations can also mean wife-receiver, stranger, or newcomer.
12. Average household size in Giziwulu was 7.06 people, but a household can be spread across two or more adjacent houses.
13. Unlike many West African societies, Loma speakers do not enclose the lineage or extended family compound with a wall. Thus, if the lineage grows, new houses are added wherever space permits. If it stagnates, older houses are left to fall into disrepair. The *kwi* thus takes on a kind of amoeba form, transforming and changing shape around the nucleus of the ancestral tomb.
14. The status derived partly from the fact that their lineage elder had become Giziwulu's first Western-educated intellectual. Attending colonial schools, he learned to read and write, and entered the civil service immediately after independence. Through his position in the public works department, he was in 1960 able to commandeer a bulldozer and carve out the first-ever dirt road to the village. He also built a large stone house and used his wealth to see that his many children were well educated.
15. Victims of "bad deaths" like drowning, snake bite, lightning strikes, or death during childbirth are buried unceremoniously in the bush, away from civilized space. Most villagers are buried with varying degrees of ceremony (usually depending upon the power associations to which they belonged) in the burial space located in the sacred ring around the village that also includes initiation groves and many medicinal plants.
16. People in Giziwulu today have created a new, hybrid category in this semiotic system, by erecting concrete tombs over the graves of several elders who are buried in the ordinary cemetery spaces just outside the village. On the one hand, these tombs resemble the politically significant ones found inside the village, while on the other, their location outside the village prevents them from taking on the same sort of political-spatial significance as landowners' tombs. I knew several families that talked regularly about saving the money to buy enough cement to construct such tombs for a deceased lineage elder. In addition to the political undertones of such an undertaking (the graves were in all cases located beside the bush paths leading to the lineage's farming land), the fact that it was often younger lineage members (in their thirties and forties) who aspired to making these monuments led me to believe that the Catholic burial styles they encountered in bigger towns could also have influenced them.
17. Contrary to my American assumptions, there was no offense inferred from sitting on the tomb, nor was it a more powerful spot from which to speak than the immediately surrounding area. While it spatially anchored important political discussions, it was not invoked during them in the way it would be during lineage sacrifices.
18. Personal, lineage, and funeral sacrifices continued as normal. Everyone, Muslim, Christian, animist performed them, even during the socialist period. However, major Loma sacrifices—for a whole village or a big chief—required more accoutrements, and would-be sacrificers were handicapped as a result of the Demystification Program's restrictions. Some big sacrifices, for instance, required the presence of a

particular mask, which was banned. From the Loma point of view, doing an incomplete sacrifice would only anger the ancestors and would thus not be effective. People either abandoned them or went over the border into Liberia to do them. Sacrifices were not directly suppressed, but the suppression of the Poro undercut the fulfillment of many sacrifices. Sacrificial practices are still under attack by some Loma-speaking Christian converts, who denigrate such shrines as backward.

19. According to Guilao, the only interest the sacrifice holds for these freshly demystified villagers is the feast provided by the immolated bull and chickens. Although the sacrifice is on behalf of an entire chiefdom and performed on a mountain, he never mentions the *inegiti*, but specifies that the sacrificers address themselves to a blacksmith/war chief named "Massawoi." Guilao describes a debacle: the bull breaks its tether, and they spend most of the day chasing it through the bush. Ultimately, they shoot it in the bush and drag it back to the sacrificial site, rather than cutting its throat and letting the blood run in honor of the landowning ancestors.

20. Although he seems to disregard it, Guilao presents the resolution of the very problem he himself has posed: when someone suggests that they shoot the animal where it is found and drag the carcass back to the site of the sacrifice, he recounts, "That would ruin the benefit of the sacrifice, said several sticklers in a low voice; the bull must be slaughtered live. That's not important, since it wouldn't be the first time it's happened like this, said the more accommodating ones, who were trying to find a way out of the fix" (1967, 241). By the time the bull is dragged back, "It was as if it were a victory. It was prohibited to say he had been killed. One had to say that he had simply been seized, and the ceremony took place as if on a living bull" (241–42). Anyone familiar with rituals in Africa will recognize the compromise struck here between ideal forms passed down from past instances and the ad hoc improvisations necessary for meeting the contingencies of the day. Two excellent discussions of these dynamics are Evans-Pritchard (1956, 203) and Kratz (1993).

21. Loma speakers in Guinea often refer to one another interchangeably by the totemic clan name ending in "-vogui," which means "does not eat," or by the name of the totemic animal itself (e.g., "Bea" instead of "Beavogui"). With certain clan names, such as Tupu (horned viper), the full form (Tupuvogui) is rarely used.

22. George Schwab describes the same process from his 1927 research:

    In Loma and Gbunde, before the final leaving of an old for a new town, the bones of a chief whose "presence" the diviner may have found necessary for prosperity are exhumed, carried to the new site, and there reinterred. Whether this is done or not, one or more objects, such as "irons" (Kissi pennies), knives, copper or iron bracelets, and the like, which had belonged to the dead leader, and had been put under his shroud before burial, are always taken to the new town with the petition that the corpse allow its spirit to enter the object. Some said that if for any reason, such as war, these sacred heirlooms had been lost, an "iron" from a grave may be substituted. (There are always small iron replicas of axes, knives, and so on, on an important grave.) In this event, the spirit of the person in the grave must first be coaxed to enter into the iron. Unless such objects are taken along there will be misfortune in the new settlement: people will be bitten by snakes or killed by falling from oil palm trees, children will die, and other calamities will follow, until the neglect is repaired. (1947, 36)

23. Another ceremony through which such hierarchies are enacted is funerals, vividly described and analyzed by Leopold (1991, 192–203; cf. Bunot, 1950, 153–58; Gamory-Dubourdeau 1925, 310).

24. While Loma speakers use divination to find out the truth about illness, death, or misfortune (and as such it is an important complement to the practice of sacrifice), they do not, to my knowledge, use divination with any regularity in the area of legal process.

25. In extreme cases (e.g., of poisoning or major theft), Loma speakers have recourse to the ordeal as a form of verification. All those accused are lined up and forced to undergo the same test. These ordeals have become rare. I never witnessed one, but several Loma speakers have described them to me. These descriptions are close to those by Gaisseau (1953), Harley (1941), and Schwab (1947), and include *bewɔgi*, one test in which each suspect grabs a metal ring out of pot of boiling oil. People I have asked had not seen a sasswood ordeal but had heard of it. In this test, those under accusation would drink a deadly poison distilled from the bark of the sasswood tree. As with medieval witchcraft ordeals, the innocent would vomit up the poison in time to save his or her life, while those who died proved their guilt. One Liberian Kpelle acquaintance told me of another test: heating a piece of metal until it was red hot, letting it cool, then rubbing it over the arms of the accused, at which time it would cause the actual culprit's arm to burst out in flames.

26. They are common across the region, as Paulme notes for the Kissi, where they are called *tumbye*: "*Tumbyes* almost always derive their power from their association with the cult of the ancestors: one takes an oath on the tomb of the latter (*mandu*), on a *yallo* (that is, an altar that concentrates the vital force of the entire group), on a 'prohibited mountain,' *luandɛ sola*, on a rock or on any other object respected as the legacy of the founder" (Paulme 1948, 5).

    See also Littlejohn (1973) for a description of the similar Temne *ansassa*: "Sometimes one has to affirm unequivocally one's adherence to the moral imperatives of one's society. Thus sometimes in Temne court cases litigants or witnesses swear to tell the truth, and in doing so must touch an instrument called ansassa with the right hand" (1973, 292–93).

27. Or doesn't. Many narratives of oath-taking end in the guilty claimant, afraid for his or her life, "giving up" and admitting guilt just before having to take the oath. More than anything else, such instances indicate the degree to which Loma speakers believe in the efficacy of *kpelɛgiti*.

28. Several people in Giziwulu surmised that elder *zoweiti* opposed the opening up of the village, as much of their symbolic power derived from the isolated and "traditional" reputation of the village. In the end, the road was redone, and the village inaugurated a weekly market.

CHAPTER FOUR

1. This shift was accompanied and compounded by the introduction of cash crops in the 1920s.

2. Cooper (1993) has made a similar argument in a slightly different vein by arguing that a Foucauldian model of "capillary" power may not accurately describe the exercise of power during the colonial period. I am suggesting that the argument holds in the postcolony as well.

3. Since economic liberalization in the 1990s, Guinean Loma-speaking farmers almost universally buy Brazilian steel machetes that are relatively inexpensive (about $3 equivalent), strong, pliable, and hold an edge. Until this time, they used machetes (*kpiligayeti*) made by local blacksmiths. These tools, made of iron like the rebar rods

4. As is the case throughout this book, these names are pseudonyms.
5. In the case of primary forest, undergrowth is usually relatively sparse, so the heaviest work was chopping down the massive hardwood trees that grew there.
6. Men have a shorter period (about five months) between the end of the harvest and the arrival of the rainy season in which to prepare the fields for planting. Because much of this preparation requires the assistance of controlled brush fires, the farmer who is late in completing his tasks may ruin the yield of his crop.
7. The exact status of this "ancient forest" is a highly contentious issue. Some areas beyond the typical ring of sacred flora with its tall iroko and mahogany trees are also sacred, considered the homes of lineage or village ancestral spirits. These areas, where sacrifices take place, are likely never to have been cultivated, at least not during the lifetime of the current village. Other areas, like the Ziama forest reserve that bisects Macenta Préfecture, are protected forest that was once partly cultivated. The status of the rest, formerly assumed to be ancestral forest never before cultivated, has been thrown into question by James Fairhead and Melissa Leach, whose work on the forest–savanna frontier region has marshaled historical, sociological, and even photographic evidence to support the claim that areas now heavily forested were savanna less than a century ago. They have shown this to be true in the Macenta area, along the plateau running between the Ziama mountains and the Diani river (1994), as they also showed it to be true of the Kissidougou region directly north of Macenta (1996). This groundbreaking work throws much of the common sense understanding about humans' interaction with the environment in the region into doubt. I thus use the phrase "not cultivated in living memory" to indicate that while the farmers themselves say that the land has never been cultivated, the longue durée status of such forest is ambiguous.
8. Because population density was so low in many villages, their territory still contained many sections of old forest. Clearing this forest is far more arduous work than reclearing fallow regrowth, so the initial clearing gives moderately strong personal rights of usage for that piece of land to the first person who has farmed it. It is common for a man who has cleared large trees from an upland rice farm plot to give rights of usage to a friend, relative, or stranger-client, but this form of weak ownership reverts to him after the plot has been replanted (in other words it does not pass on to the most recent user, since that person did not clear the large trees).
9. In McGovern 2012, I also describe the ways that the actual first settler *tiyizamayati* lineage may not have the more politically significant title of *zukenui* "owners of the land," in cases where the latter title was conceded to powerful warlords and their families who were reinscribed into the village history as its fictional autochthons.
10. In principle, the trees could be dug up and transplanted. I have never heard of this happening, although I am aware of several instances in which trees were cut down by people other than their owners, and it was decided in village moots or in government court proceedings that the owner had to be reimbursed for the value of the trees.
11. The significance of this crop in regional economic history is indicated by the Northern Mande name for the forest region: *worodugu*, or "cola-land." See Brooks 1980, 1993; and Goerg 1986.

12. Both trees produce palm wine. However, southern Loma speakers prefer the wine of the raffia palm. In the Northern Loma-speaking region, people drink both types of wine.
13. The French did not even claim to control the Loma-speaking region that became Macenta until 1908, and the Kpelle, Mano, and Kono-speaking regions still further south until the next year. The Kpelle rebellion of 1911 showed just how tenuous their foothold was, and it was not until the region was shifted from being a "zone militaire" to the "cercles" of Macenta, Beyla, and N'Zerekore (1918) that the colonial administration began to "normalize."
14. Currens (1979, 82) states that in the Liberian northern Loma village of Lawalazu, "there is no allocation of land by the 'owners of the land' or anyone else nor are there traditional divisions of the area according to group filiation." However, both Carter (1970, 43–45) and Weisswange (1969, 52) observed the same sort of lineage divisions of the land I describe in their research in the southern Loma-speaking region of Liberia.
15. Ironically, when Leopold went to do fieldwork in Lofa County, Liberia (in 1985) he reports that he had

    speculated that when land in a subsistence economy assumed a commodity value, a region's first settlers would be better placed, both socially and economically, than "stranger" groups: these first settlers were, after all, called the "owners of the land." In short, I was prepared to discover that the land-owners had a comparative advantage that might "really" be an incipient descent-based class system.

    He found this not to be the case, largely because "land is neither scarce nor commoditized in the Loma region" (Leopold 1991, 9–10). I am arguing, effectively, that he was right in his intuition that this was an incipient dynamic once cash-cropping was taken up. By the 1990s in Macenta Préfecture, at any rate, it had become an important enough economic dynamic to take on political significance, although as I argue below, it was not necessarily the landowners who came out on top.
16. In the colonial system each larger unit—"cercle"—was subdivided into smaller "cantons." Thus Macenta cercle contained several dozen cantons. During the Touré period (1958–84), former "cercles" were called "régions," and "cantons" became "arrondissements." Finally, during the Conte years and after (1984–present), "régions" became "préfectures," and "arrondissements" became "souspréfectures."
17. As I have described, members of the Guilavogui clan, for instance, could be landowners in one village and newcomers in another, nearby village.
18. Summers and Johnson attribute the social and political flux of the 1920s and 1930s to the return of former captives who had been conscripted into the French Army to fight in World War I and who later spurred other former captives to disperse: "Where slaves withdrew, chiefly power was weakened. As resources grew scarce, competition must have increased, and perceptions of social status changed. The interwar years saw an endless series of tugs-of-war over chieftaincies in the Forest and Upper Guinea: almost certainly a related phenomenon" (1978, 34).
19. Called Sivilisu by Loma speakers, Kuankan by the French, and Kwanga by the resident Manya speakers.
20. This was the Manya name for the chiefdom known as Weybhalaga in Lomagui.
21. Archives Nationales de Guinée, dossier 2D120.
22. I thank Eddy Bay for pushing me to develop this point.
23. This is especially true in the "Koivogui-Kamara corridor" I describe in chapter 2.

24. There are two contributing factors to the French interpretation of the situation. First, many of their "Malinke" interpreters and soldiers were from the Northern Mande heartland of upper Guinea and Mali, and although they had a shared language with the Northern Mande speakers of the forest–savanna frontier, they were not products of the same hybrid socio-political situation. As information was channeled through these subalterns, they may have imposed their own notions about Northern Mande identity on the situation. Secondly, the French themselves were, in the early twentieth century, still cognizant of the political and administrative work required to *impose* national language, identity, and habitus on all people living within the frontiers of European nations. The work involved in enforcing a uniform national language and culture on hybrid spaces within the nation (for instance in the French Basque, Breton, or Alsatian regions) may have informed the French impatience to do the same in West Africa.
25. It may be useful to think of their relation in terms of the residual/dominant/emergent relation proposed by Raymond Williams (1977, 121).
26. This process ran parallel to the solidification of the nation-state in the Americas and Europe as described by Anderson (1991), who emphasizes the importance of such instruments as the census and the map in concretizing the idea of a congruity between people and territory.
27. *Décrets* 025/PRG du 10 janvier 1962; 170/PRG du 5 avril 1962; 127/PRG du 25 avril 1974; 237/PRG du 2 mai 1983.
28. The land tenure laws promulgated by the Parti Démocratique de Guinée (PDG) raise a paradox in relation to the principle of autochthony. Loma ethnic identity, particularly to the extent that it has come to be formed in contrast to Manya (i.e., non-autochthonous) identity, makes claims to Loma speakers' authochthonous political legitimacy. While the thrust of the PDG's policies was toward creating a consciousness of national unity by downplaying ethnic identity, the attacks on autochthonous land tenure rights directly contradicted the PDG's own raison d'être, which was to decolonize Guinea by claiming that it was Guineans who, as the nation's autochthonous population, were the only people who could legitimately rule the territory. This argument was ultimately accepted by the French and is taken as the most basic common sense by many Guineans (like other formerly colonized people). But the Loma experience of state intervention raises the question: if such a logic were applicable to the nation as a whole, then why not to each portion of the national territory?
29. This was especially true in the Futa Jallon region, the Pulaar-speaking region of Guinea. Touré's government was particularly aggressive in attacking "feudalism" in this region (Barry 2002; Sow 1989).
30. The state under Touré attempted to convert Forestier rice farmers to cultivation of irrigated paddy rice, use of tractors, and other techniques of modern agriculture. Chinese and Vietnamese experts worked in Macenta for many years as technical consultants on this other form of "conversion," which had virtually no impact on Loma agricultural techniques. Given the low population density of most Loma villages, the absence of fertilizer to support intensive agriculture, and the lack of roads to transport surplus yields, Loma hesitancy in the face of such innovations seems to have been quite sensible.
31. The term Dioula simply means "trader" in the Northern Mande languages. Like Malinke, it is sometimes used as an ethnonym, especially in Côte d'Ivoire.
32. Rivière bases his analysis of ethnicity and political influence partly on the statistical

data in the doctoral thesis of Bernard Charles, "Cadres guinéens et appartenances ethniques" (1968). Rivière argues that while there was a more-or-less proportional representation of the various ethno-linguistic groups at the highest levels of the administration, the middle level of officials who controlled the day-to-day flow of politics at the local level were overwhelmingly Malinke. Schatzberg (1988) has made a similar case for the structures of domination in Mobutu's Zaire.

33. Conté fostered ethnic particularism and explicitly promoted the logic of autochthonous landownership in the forest region, even suggesting that "Malinke" who came into the forest region during the Touré years should go back to their homeland.

34. Rivière (1971, 309) gives a cercle-wide figure of 12.8 percent Muslims for Macenta in 1945. Assuming nearly all of these Muslims were Manya speakers, and that the Manya-speaking population made up some 30 percent of the cercle's total, that gives a rate of slightly over 40 percent Islamisation among Manya speakers in Macenta just thirteen years before independence.

35. Five years later, Diaby and Keita were accused of being the authors of a mutiny by the parachutists in Labe. This "complot Kaman-Fodeba" was just one of three "discovered" by the government in 1969, each one allowing Sékou Touré to eliminate more of the figures he considered untrustworthy or threatening. Many Guineans still comment on the ironies surrounding Fodeba Keita's demise. Born in Siguiri and educated at the Ecole William Ponty, Keita was a poet and the director of the Ballets Africaines, Guinea's premiere dance company. After shifting from the artistic to the political realm, he became Minister of the Interior. He and Diaby died in the Camp Boiro concentration camp (Touré 1989). Had Mamadi continued to work with them, he would surely have met the same fate.

36. Though miniscule in the context of a serious plantation economy, like Côte d'Ivoire's.

CHAPTER FIVE

1. This explanation is in no way mutually exclusive from one that focuses on the interplay between the levels of logical principles, cultural idioms, and behavior. The most difficult task of social analysis, in my view, is steering between the Scylla of a methodological individualism that would portray actors as perpetually strategizing (often guided by an instrumental reason that we wrongly attribute to them) and the Charybdis of Durkheimian intellectualism. I will not rehearse the arguments here, which are as old as the discipline of anthropology. I hope that the book, taken as a whole, will be read as an argument for the possibility (indeed the necessity) of doing an analysis that draws from both traditions.

2. Why did they not, for instance, inherit the legacy of "the people who could not hold an empire together"?

3. Nor is there any indication of the notion of "prenatal destiny" in the ethnographic literature on the Loma or their culturally similar neighbors (Kpelle, Bandi, Mende).

4. Many Guineans would read their national history in such a way as to see Sékou Touré as such an "agent of disequilibrium."

5. The most significant form of inheritance is birth into one of the endogamous occupational groups (*nyamakalaw*). *Jelilu* are genealogist praise singers, *numulu* men are blacksmiths, *numulu* women are potters, and *garankew* are leather workers. No Northern Mande person from outside these groups is permitted to practice these professions, and they are not allowed to intermarry with ordinary farming clans

(McNaughton 1988; Conrad and Frank 1995). Among Loma speakers, the sons of blacksmiths are encouraged to take up their fathers' work but are not obligated to do so, and blacksmiths intermarry with other clans. There is no role similar to the *jeli* in Southwestern Mande life.

6. In Giziwulu, the members of the Pivi clan were recent arrivals and thus junior to almost every other clan in the village. In the nearest village, just nine kilometers away, they were the landowners. Such hierarchies are constructed on the basis of highly localized claims about autochthony, not about transcendental relations between the clans or some historical personages within each clan. The actual order of arrival of different Loma clans may not be the order indicated within the contemporary symbolic economy of autochthony. Histories and genealogies are often recalibrated to meet the realities of power politics (Murphy and Bledsoe 1987). Nevertheless, at the level of argumentation, the idiom of autochthony is the one that Loma speakers invoke.

7. Recruitment may take place against the individual's will, especially by trickery: sorcerers (*matalai*) invite the person to a meal and, after he or she has eaten, reveal that the meal consisted of human flesh. The new sorcerer is now obligated to "repay" the debt with a fresh victim, but from this point onward operates in cognizance of the situation. One daybreak, I listened to a Loma woman declaring her refusal to join sorcerers who had invited her to dine with them in a dream the night before. She went on, at the top of her voice, for forty-five minutes, declaring publicly that she wanted nothing to do with their cabal.

8. Or alternatively, to reject it. This is the source of a controversy that still surrounds Salif Keita, the "Golden Voice of Mali," who was born into the same royal Keita clan that produced Sundiata, but chose to become a singer, a profession as prohibited to nobles as it was prescribed for the *jeli* clans of Kouyatés, Tounkaras, Sangares, Sissokos, and Diabates. Keita was disowned by his family and did not speak with them for many years.

9. The *nyamakala* groups are in principle endogamous.

10. Cf. Fairhead and Leach 1996 for an empirically and theoretically rich analysis of the forest–savanna frontier zone between Kissi and Kuranko speakers.

11. His mother was Loma; he spent much of his early adulthood as a *dyula* trader in the Macenta area, trading in cola nuts, salt, and slaves; and he retreated to the Loma-speaking area when under attack early in his career as a warlord, c. 1865.

12. The term "Malinke" that Ellis uses was used as an umbrella term by the French, and was subsequently appropriated by peripheral Northern Mande speakers like the Manya in order to "trade up" their identities. "Mandingo" is often used the same way in Liberia. When referring to the "core" Northern Mande people from the Kankan-Kouroussa-Siguiri-Kangaba region in this book, I use the term "Maninka."

13. An exemplary study of such a "short-lived social formation" is Wendy James's series of books and articles on the Uduk (1979, 1988, 1997). Always a self-consciously heterogeneous grouping of people of disparate origins, they were resident in eastern Sudan when she began her research. They are now almost entirely relocated to Western Ethiopia, where most live in refugee camps.

14. It is especially important to describe this context given the relative ease with which Touré can be relegated to the category of megalomaniac or brutal dictator. When the decision to undertake the Demystification Program was taken, there is little evidence that he was either of these things. Moreover, it allows us to see the context in which Demystification was interpreted by most Muslim Guineans.

15. Importantly, historical states such as the Mali or the Samorian empires were portrayed as prefiguring the postcolonial state.
16. On other facets of Touré's discourse, see Barry 2002; McGovern 2002; and McGovern and Arieff forthcoming.
17. These people, known as Torodbe in what is now Senegal and Tukulor/Toucouleur in present-day Guinea, are of Fulbe or mixed Fulbe-Mande origin, and came from the Futa Toro region of Senegal's Upper Senegal River floodplain.
18. The Tijani brotherhood was founded by Ahmad al-Tijani (1737–1815) in the Maghreb and had started to influence some West African Muslims shortly after 1800.
19. The Masina empire was based at Hamdullahi, founded by the warrior-cleric Sékou Amadou.
20. The best-known jihadist in West Africa was Shehu Usman Dan Fodio. A Fulbe Islamic scholar, he led the armed struggle against the Hausa State from 1804 to 1812 that decapitated the autochthonous ruling dynasties and replaced them with a class of Fulbe cleric-warriors. Shehu Usman passed the jihadist flag of the Sokoto Caliphate to Seku Ahmadu, who conquered the Masina area and established the Islamic state of Hamdullahi. Fulani jihadists carrying one of Usman's flags also attacked the Borno empire, which also came under the rule of warrior-clerics.
21. Willis (1989, 95). This attempt to grab political power at the end of his formative six-year stay in Sokoto on the way back from Mecca was one of the first signs of his interest in combining worldly with spiritual agendas.
22. Segou, like the part of the forest–savanna frontier I write about, resisted Islamization until very late. According to Arnoldi (1995, 28), French documents indicate that 44 percent of the Segou region's inhabitants were still "fétichiste" in 1940.
23. Muslims are enjoined in the Qur'an not to wage jihad (of the sword) against other Muslims. Umar's rhetoric thus had to shift to an accusation that Masina practiced an illegitimate form of Islam, which called for purification. This line of reasoning was hard to justify in the case of Masina, which had been the site of one of the major regional jihads only forty years before. Umar's argument was that the Tijani brotherhood was the only correct form of Islam. One might suspect his sincerity. Was it just a land grab with a flimsy theological justification? That seems almost impossible to tell from the available evidence (Robinson 1985), although it is clear that there was a longstanding dislike between Umar and the Masina caliph. Umar's jihad killed many of both his followers and his enemies, and his huge army, which did not cultivate its own food, had to be fed from local peasants' stocks that were already diminished by the fighting that had disrupted the now-subjugated populations' agricultural cycles. These depredations caused a major famine in the large region of his jihad. As David Robinson has written, "Umar was aware of the dangers of expanding the size of his community and directly entering the sphere of military political action. His calling, his ambition, and his sense of the growing Dar al-Islam of the Western Sudan brought him, at some cost, to jihad" (1985, 136–37).
24. Martin Klein has described the parallel case of the Wolof *tyeddo*, warrior slaves who came to dominate their masters (1977, 344).
25. In the northern Mande languages, "Jula" (spelled Dyula by the French) means trader. In this peripheral zone that stretched into northern Côte d'Ivoire, the term became and ethnonym as well as a vocational description.

26. In addition to Person 1968, see Goerg 1986 and Brooks 1980.
27. The Dyula revolution thus presaged the move by Manya newcomers fifty years later (around 1910) to take over political control of much of Macenta Cercle as the French colonial administrators carved the territory up into chiefdoms.
28. This was the title of the theocratic rulers of the Futa Jallon.
29. It is ironic that the Saudi state, which has derived its political legitimacy from its connection with the puritanical Wahhabi strain of Islam has, in turn, been accused of moral laxity, particularly to the extent that it has accepted the status of a U.S. client state. Wahhabist forms of political Islam have emerged in Saudi Arabia, Egypt, and more recently Pakistan and Afghanistan, with the intention of pursuing their own renewal movements, as in the case of Afghanistan's Taliban and Egyptian Islamic Jihad. This internal contradiction, now driving many political developments in the Muslim world, is not an innovation but an echo of the many renewal movements that have preceded it.
30. West African reformists are known as "Les bras croisés," referring to their manner of praying with their arms crossed over their chests, as opposed to hanging at their sides (Kaba 1974, 37). For more on the Ivorian side of this story of religious renewal, see Miran 2006.
31. In many respects, the Wahhabi challenge to Sufism resembles that of the Protestant Reformation, which attempted to return to the "true" Christianity by stripping Catholicism of its worldly accretions. It is not accidental that both renewal movements abhor icons, saints, and shrines, which they consider polytheistic.
32. Soudan and Western Sudan were colonial names for the territory that became the Republic of Mali.
33. Kaba writes: "Every Subbanu member was required to withstand the disruptiveness of French influences and strive for the reinforcement of Islamic values and the emergence of a political system more concerned with Muslim interests" (1974, 127).
34. The French colonial Archives d'Outre-Mer, in Aix-en-Provence, contain a massive stock of dossiers documenting French colonial espionage, analysis, and fretting over the threat posed by various forms of political Islam in the 1940s and 1950s.
35. Indeed Sarró (1999, chap. 5) reveals that one of the primary motivations of some of his then-young informants' turn to Sayon's message was the fact that the elders had autocratically banned certain types of Fulbe music from youth *soirées* in the months before Sayon's arrival. This music, which contained flutes, was considered by the elders to be sacrilegious, as flutes were strictly ritual instruments for Baga traditionalists. The disgruntled youth thus joined Sayon's iconoclastic Islamic movement.
36. The logic of jihad meshed quite easily with the model of communist social engineering available from Europe and Asia.
37. Although I point to Islam here, it is only because it became the predominant monotheistic religion in Guinea. Forestier Christians have exhibited exactly the same kinds of anxiety, and I would argue that it emerged out of the same contradictions. An extensive literature on charismatic Christianity (Harding 2001; Knauft 2002; Marshall 2009; Piot 2010; Robbins 2004) bears this out. Marxism's teleological form of argumentation exerted a similar pressure.
38. Leopold described the same situation in Lofa County, Liberia: "Though Loma scoff at the suggestion that their language is derived from Mandekan (the language of their Mandingo neighbors), they recognize a linguistic affinity with the other Southwestern Mande speakers" (1991, 40).

39. The process resembles the forms of segmentary opposition described by Evans Pritchard in *The Nuer* (1940).

CHAPTER SIX

1. Several anthropologists have published on the Demystification Program in Guinea. Claude Rivière's chapter "Mutations socio-religieuses: Fétichisme et Démystification" (in Rivière 1971) gives a general description of the movement, while Christian Højbjerg's 2002 article and 2007 book inquire into the "cognitive puzzle" of how a "secret society," once demystified, continued to exist.
2. This law was later loosened to allow for polygyny—widespread through this part of West Africa—only if the first wife explicitly accepted it.
3. Such matters of morality were overseen by the youth wing of the party, named the Jeunesse de la Révolution Démocratique Africaine, or JRDA.
4. Although Guineans now look back at the low crime rate of that period with nostalgia, the possibility that many people died for crimes they did not commit leaves one less enthusiastic about justice that proceeded so rapidly. Ironically, one of the paradigmatic revolutionary Guinean poems—Fodéba Keita's "Minuit"—deals precisely with the unjust execution of a Guinean accused of murdering a French colonial officer after a rushed twenty-four-hour judicial process (Miller 1990, 54–55).
5. For most of the colonial period, there was only one *lycée* (high school) for all of French West Africa's eight countries.
6. Thus it is not surprising that fledgling African nation-states invested so much energy and money in cultural programming. Leopold Senghor, Sékou Touré's opposite number in Dakar, is said to have spent over one third of the national budget on "culture" in the early years of Senegal's independence (Jules-Rosette 2002, 1).
7. As Joan Scott has pointed out in her writings on the headscarf controversy in France (2005, 2010), women can and do serve this function of "internal others" in most polities, even when gender difference is only referenced implicitly, as in the headscarf debate, which is ostensibly about minority culture and universal freedoms.
8. This is a vitally important point, but it lies beyond my competency to adequately explore, as I have not done research on Mande-Fulbe relations or politics. However, it is important to note that attempts by Malinke elites to outflank Fulbe elites may have been an indirect cause of attacks on Forestier culture. Not only did Forestier culture instantiate the disowned past of Malinke culture, it was also something against which Malinke and Fulbe (as good Muslims), could define themselves.
9. This topic was of prime importance to the Frankfurt School (e.g., Adorno and Horkheimer 1972). If political scientists have generally been silent on this topic, it has been a major preoccupation of political philosophers, especially those with an interest in the intersection of Marxist and poststructuralist theories: e.g., Chantal Mouffe and Ernesto Laclau (1985) on hegemony, Judith Butler (1990, 1997) on identity and subjectivity, and above all, Slavoj Žižek's (1999) multifaceted investigation of the political subject (cf. Butler, Laclau, and Žižek 2000). It is, I would argue, Žižek's experience of the Yugoslavian socialist state's attempts to create new types of political subjects that gives him particular clarity in his meditations on the subject.
10. Anthropologists familiar with Victor Turner's work will recall his section on "Status Reversal: The Masking Function" in his book *The Ritual Process* (1969). In the course of six pages, his discussion of masks moves effortlessly from American children's Halloween masks, to structuralist analyses of myth, to psychoanalysis. He describes

one aspect of Kayapo myth as "a kind of mask that both reveals and conceals a process of structural realignment" (1969, 173).
11. Interestingly, the first chapter in Chabal and Daloz's book (1999) dealing with this re-traditionalization is entitled "Of Masks and Men: The Question of Identity."
12. See also Raymond Williams's cultural etymologies of the terms "Individual" and "Personality" in his *Keywords* (1985).
13. Touré remains famous for granting audiences to ordinary Guineans throughout his tenure as president.
14. The boubou is the West African robe worn by both men and women.
15. The efficacy of such techniques is also linked to the existence of parallel practices in Guinean society, such as the use of oaths discussed in chapter 3.
16. In this way the Islamic renewal movements, like the Wahhabiyya described in chapter 5, resemble the Protestant reformation of European Christianity, both in their iconoclastic thrust and in emphasizing the personal relationship between God and each believer (cf. Goody 1997).
17. Weekly Seminars for January–February, 1960.
18. This series was never continued beyond the first volume.
19. See Donham 1999, chap. 7, "The Revolutionary State at the Grass Roots: Modernist Institutions in Maale during the 1980s," for an attentive ethnographic description of similar dynamics in Ethiopia.
20. This has been a recurrent dynamic in actually existing Marxism, from the time of the Russian revolution. Donham writes of the parallel situation in Ethiopia: "while Ethiopia had little capitalist production within its borders, nonetheless, its placement within a stratified global system—the outlines of which Ethiopian actors were intensely aware of—provided the essential ground on which local notions of the 'modern' were constructed" (2002, 251).
21. Touré combined his Marxism with a form of Pan-Africanism. He was a friend and associate of Kwame N'Krumah, and pushed hard, with him, for the formation of a United States of Africa. After N'Krumah was deposed in 1966, Touré made him honorary co-president of Guinea, and he spent most of the next six years in Guinea, until his death. Shortly thereafter, Miriam Makeba and Stokely Carmichael sought refuge in Conakry from the South African and U.S. governments respectively. They married for a time, and Carmichael, who changed his name to Kwame Touré, remained in Guinea until his death in 1998.
22. I consider it significant that two of the major contributions to the literature on the Upper Guinea Coast region—Stephen Ellis's 1999 *The Mask of Anarchy* and Mariane Ferme's 2001 *The Underneath of Things*—both use the term and the metaphor of "unmasking" throughout their texts to refer to the politics and aesthetics of secrecy in relation to the states that encompass Poro/Sande practitioners. The currency of this trope, despite the fact that both the Liberian and Sierra Leonean states they write about co-opted rather than attacked the power associations (as the Guinean state did), points to the immanent tension between Poro/Sande and modernist political practices.
23. See also Miller's discussion of this tension throughout his 1990 book, *Theories of Africans: Francophone Literature and Anthropology in Africa*.
24. Analyses of southern African elites by Manchester school anthropologists use the term "intercalary" to describe the position of these chiefs, translators, teachers, and supervisors (e.g., Mitchell 1956, 16). See also Nancy Rose Hunt's analysis (1999) of

what she calls "middles," roughly the same class of persons in the Belgian Congo. Guinea's nationalist "elite," as I call them here, were mostly "middles," intercalary figures like Touré himself (a trade unionist who had attended school to ninth grade) who became elites in the true sense of the term only after independence.

CHAPTER SEVEN

1. Siu (1989) presents a view of the multiple facets of the Chinese revolution as it was experienced in a rural commune of Guangdong Province in southern China that is remarkably similar to many of the elements I have presented here, despite the differences in colonial experience and the role of religion.
2. See Fairhead and Leach (1996) for a superb study of how this dynamic played out in Guinea in the realm of agriculture, and Karp (2002) for a definitive discussion of this form of developmentalist discourse.
3. It is exactly this sort of contradictory postcolonial modernist subjectivity that has been the subject of much writing in postcolonial studies, including Bhabha (1994), Chatterjee (1993), Fanon [1961] (1963), [1952] (1991), and Mani (1990). Such work commonly draws on psychological (often Freudian/Lacanian) models of contradictory consciousness, but also draws on notions such as DuBois's "double consciousness" (1994 [1903]) and Bakhtin's heteroglossia (1981).
4. It is not, however, limited to them. Other internal minorities, such as the Baga, Nalou, Coniagui, and Bassari, were structurally in much the same position as the Forestiers, and Muslim Soso and Pulaar speakers were also in much the same position as all those who came under the umbrella term "Malinke."
5. These numbers are approximate, and there were certainly many who combined their monotheistic faiths with various of their grandparents' polytheistic practices.
6. Cf. Harley 1941.
7. Two Guinean Loma villages next to the Liberian border.
8. In fact, it was relatively common for boys and girls to die in the camps. The everyday mortality rate was high in the first place, with people regularly dying of malaria, meningitis, dysentery, and other illnesses. Initiates could also die of blood loss, tetanus, or infection resulting from the surgical procedures they underwent or accidents resulting from their training in dangerous adult tasks. Families of initiates who had died in the sacred forest found a broken pot left on their doorstep in the middle of the night (Harley 1941; Schwab 1947).
9. Interview, S.O., September 4, 2000.
10. The curator was himself a Forestier (though Muslim) and told me that as he began the Demystificatory work, he became seriously ill. He attributed this illness to powerful energy (Loma: *manye*) released from the confiscated objects, and possibly also from the invisible agency of powerful féticheurs. In the middle of the Demystificatory work, he returned to his natal village, where he convalesced for several months and was specially "washed" so as to protect him from any further problems. He had experienced no further problems during the intervening forty years.
11. In his important source for the reconstruction of this period, Claude Rivière, a French anthropologist who was resident in Guinea from 1964 to 1968, gives a possible explanation for such gaps in documentation. In describing a case of alleged human sacrifice in the town of N'Zerekore in 1968, Rivière writes: "Living vestige: During the interrogations, one elder admits having eaten human flesh 17 times during his life. Reasonable discretion: For the honor of Guinea, the newspaper and the radio silence the affair" (1971, 266–67).

12. It is worth noting that here as elsewhere in the party's publications and Touré's discourses, the French for "militants" reads, "les militants et militantes." Even today, such explicit reference to gendered subjects (commonplace now in English) is rare in French. This is one of several indices of the PDG's consistent concern with including women in the public sphere, a subject I explore at the end of this chapter.
13. For a discussion of the parallel injunction of *Ifa mo* among the neighboring Kpelle, see Bellman 1975, 1984.
14. This aspect of Forestier discourse has interesting ramifications for the definition of "youth" in the region. This topic becomes especially complex in the context in which adults (even into their forties) claim the status of youth. This claim may signal either a disinclination to discuss the matter at hand, or a lack of authority to discuss it. Moreover, the same person may hold "major" status in one realm (for instance lineage politics) and minor status in another (for instance, power association business). See the last section of this chapter for a discussion of shifts in the age at and duration of initiation, and their effects on the definition of youth.
15. In both the Guinean and Chinese cases, we see the ways that these movements work through a series of substitutions: although the revolution is overtly characterized by class oppositions, different groups can stand in for the classic Marxist proletariat when needed: youth, women, peasants. These substitutions have to do not only with the paucity of proletarian workers in many of the countries where actually existing Communism took root, but also with the social ontology of these movements, which leaned heavily on the process of finding subjects who were less "tainted" by the old order, and thus were closer to being "tabulae rasae" available for resocialization in the new order.
16. This makes a definitive dating of the Demystification Program impossible. While there is some question as to how early it began (Rivière states 1959, my informants in the southern Loma-speaking region all said 1961, Højbjerg states 1959), there are instances cited throughout the 1960s in Rivière's 1969 essay on Demystification, despite the fact that he accepts the government's claim that the program was successful. My informants also indicated that attempts to demystify them continued sporadically right up to Sékou Touré's death in 1984.
17. But see El-Dabh 1979 for the chronicling of certain puppetry and masked dancing traditions in the Maninka-speaking region of Guinea in the 1970s. These traditions seem to have survived for two reasons. First, they were framed as Islamic manifestations (rather a contradiction in terms), and second, they seem to have been entirely owned and performed by local jelilu praise singers who were a central pillar of support for the PDG state, and perhaps were able to gain a "free pass" from the rigors of Demystification.
18. Pierre Gaisseau's *Forêt sacrée* was a sensational (though fairly accurate) exposé of the Loma men's power association, the Pologi. Loma *zoweiti* decided to allow four Frenchmen to be initiated on the basis of their promise never to reveal the secrets told them, but soon changed their minds. They were right to have had misgivings, as Gaisseau, the leader of the French explorers, returned home and immediately published his tell-all book.
19. The RDA, or Rassemblement Démocratique Africain, was the regional anticolonial party in francophone West Africa, founded in Bamako, Mali, in October 1946. The Parti Démocratique de Guinée came out of the RDA. Touré later muddied the waters by appropriating the acronym anew, referring to the Révolution Démocratique Africaine. This was largely a stab at Félix Houphouet-Boigny, who had founded the

RDA with Touré in Bamako. As president of Côte d'Ivoire, he had gone on to follow a policy of engagement with France that Touré considered neocolonial and a betrayal of the anticolonial ideals of the original RDA. Because of these multiple links, the terms "RDA" and "PDG" were often used interchangeably in Guinea under Touré.

20. In one such history I recorded, the narrator described one ancestor's leaving an arrow behind after drinking another man's palm wine in the bush, rather than openly discussing the conquest of the second man's territory by the first.

21. In chapter 3, I quoted a passage from his description of what he interpreted as a botched village sacrifice.

22. Herbert (1991) describes a particular form of missionary salvage ethnography in which the missionaries carefully document exactly those elements of Polynesian culture they are working to eradicate. In Guinea, this impetus was combined with the dramatization of state power.

23. According to Manthia Diawara, this system soon found outlets in the international art trade: "Many marabouts saw the revolution as a chance to increase their power beyond the mosque to the rest of their village or even their province, by denouncing the powerful founders and local leaders whom they could not entirely convert to Islam during the colonial era. Their whistle-blowing led to corruption and bribery, as the same marabouts soon became rich traders of African masks and statues in New York, Paris and Geneva" (Diawara 1998, 182). This thesis is supported by Ramon Sarró, whose work on the Demystification Program in the Baga-speaking region of coastal Guinea indicated that Asékou Sayon, who undertook a major iconoclastic jihad in the area in 1956–57, was selling the "evil" objects he was supposed to destroy. One of his lieutenants told Sarró, "He burnt some of them [ritual objects], but many of them we would put in a van and he would take them to Kindia, where his master Sékou Boubacar would then sell them to the whites" (Sarró 1999, chap. 5). Rivière makes the same claim (1971, 250).

24. Jean Suret-Canale, the French Marxist historian and PDG fellow traveler, lived for many years in Guinea, and was one of the intellectuals who promoted research on Guinea's historical and material patrimony in the 1960s.

25. In this context, Demystification should be seen as one moment in a long line of violent disruptions against which Guinean Forestiers had to mobilize much the same techniques as during "ordinary" periods of instability. This argument for continuity underpins Højbjerg's excellent analysis of Loma religion (2007), seen through the category of *sale*.

26. The disruptions had come, they said, with the post-socialist Conté regime, which was always telling them that the clitoridectomy they performed during girls' initiations (circumcision is performed on boys of about three years, and is thus not part of male initiation) was a bad practice, and went so far as to say it had become illegal. Nothing of the kind had occurred during the socialist years, they said.

27. See Edwin and Shirley Ardener's essays in Ardener 1978.

28. It would have been impossible for me to do this on my own, and I thank my research assistant Alamako for all of her hard work to this end.

29. Siu (1989, 213–15) describes a comparable situation during and immediately after the Cultural Revolution in southern China. She points out that members of the Party Youth League who were recruited into the Party in the early 1970s fractured the socio-political landscape and rendered the negotiation of state power by older local cadres less likely. Cadres at all levels found themselves subject to destabilizing

and potentially dangerous denunciations and accusations and thus had to apply party rules and policies "by the book." The combination of crude bravura, rapid empowerment, and mobility of JRDA youth members in Guinea had a similarly polarizing effect on village-level politics in Guinea's forest region.

30. Young women were, however, far more likely to benefit from these policies than elder women.
31. By the estimation of literate men and women in Guinea today, the Touré period afforded women significantly more influence and visibility than did the Conté regime (1984–2008). Just one example of the rolling back of socialist era attempts to promote women's concerns is the fact that President Lansana Conté had three wives as opposed to Touré's one.
32. Rivière notes that part of the furor surrounding this affair had to do with the fact that the woman was related to a government functionary.
33. Indeed, this shared consciousness might well have originated from the first time Poro members came into contact with Muslims, though my informant specified the colonial period.
34. See Ellis 2001 for an account of the parallel change over time in both terminology and purported practices surrounding human sacrifice in Liberia.
35. This is the same account discussed in chapter 3's section on autochthony and ancestral sacrifice.
36. Indeed, it is worth asking the question, what is the gender of youth? In the Guinean situation, as I suspect in many others, the category tends to stand for young males, excluded from power because of their social age. In such categorizations of the oppressed and excluded, young women tend to be women before being youths. In settings like Guinea, this is partly the result of the fact that females often become social adults through their roles as wives and mothers at an earlier age than males. The same bias is evident in many studies of youth in Cultural Studies, which produced many of the ethnographic studies of youth culture. See Powell and Clarke's "A Note on Marginality" in Stuart Hall and Tony Jefferson's edited volume, *Resistance through Rituals* (1975).
37. This last detail is taken from Morgenthau 1964, 229.
38. The colonial-era canton chiefs continued many of the practices of the precolonial chiefs, including hyperpolygyny.
39. The forest region, with most of Guinea's non-Muslims, continues to have a lower incidence of polygyny than any other region. According to a 1992 survey, 41.2 percent of Forestière women lived in polygynous households, while women of other ethnic groups ranged from 49.4 to 53.7 percent. Moreover, among women in polygynous households, 28.4 percent of Forestière women had more than one co-wife, while other ethnicities ranged from 33.4 to 39.9 percent (*Direction Nationale de la Statistique et de l'Informatisation* 1994, 73–75).
40. While Touré outlined his thoughts on the role of women in the independent nation in "La condition humaine de la femme africaine" (1967, 283–94), the fullest expression of these views can be found in his essay, "La femme dans la société," in the 1978 tome, *Informer et former pour transformer* (1978, 265–345).
41. Again, the parallel with the state's changes in land tenure laws should be clear.
42. Because polygynous elder men married so many of the marriageable women, a young single Loma man would often reach an agreement with a friend that if his pregnant wife should give birth to a daughter, she would be his future wife. The pregnant woman would in this case wear a special bracelet letting everyone know

that her unborn child was already "spoken for." If the baby should turn out to be a boy, the friend would have to start again from scratch.
43. Mamdani (1996) has identified this as the biggest obstacle for postcolonial African states.
44. In Senegal, the historical legacy was quite different. Since residents of the *quatre communes* (Dakar, St. Louis, Gorée, Rufisque) had French citizenship, along with the fact that a relatively large group of people were of mixed parentage, the notion that Europeans were citizens while Africans were subjects did not always hold true. The fact that the seat of the French West African colonies was in Senegal, along with the region's only *lycée*, meant that the prospects for (and the benefits to be derived from) assimilation were quite different for Senegalese than they were for Guineans. It also added to the naturalization of the notion that, in Senegal, some Africans would have access to citizenship, modernity, and universal law, while others would remain in the world of tradition and customary law.
45. This puts a slightly different spin on the international dynamic of "authoritarian high modernism" that I have cited several times from James Scott's 1998 *Seeing Like a State*. Taken in the context of the problematic Mamdani poses for the African postcolony, it appears as a simultaneously necessary and disastrous step for African states to take.
46. This was the case for two elderly women I knew in my second fieldwork site, Pelema.
47. M.G., May 18, 2000.
48. In many respects, Guinea's other ethno-linguistic groups, such as the Fulbe, Soso, and Maninka, can probably be said to be more patriarchal than the Loma and other Forestiers, whose women are empowered through the Sande and other power associations.
49. See Ferme (2001) for a sensitive analysis of the gendered dynamics of the ever-changing personnel in Mende households. Her description applies in almost every detail to Loma family life.
50. "Those who eat *anything*."
51. The fact that the Islamic heritage in Africa (as opposed to, for instance, the Christian tradition) has been naturalized and cleansed of its own ethnocentric and indeed racist encumbrances is one of the ironies of Africanist historiography. For an incisive critique, see Chinwezu 1988.
52. The same is true of the most militantly iconoclastic Christians that I know personally. Those who come from second or third generation Christian families are far more likely to limit their spiritual concerns to their own souls.
53. At the time when girls were initiated at a later age, they typically married upon leaving the sacred forest. Carol MacCormack (1974) points out that marriage negotiations involved the Sande elder women as much as the family of the young woman, and that Sande elders derived monetary and political capital from these "transactions."
54. Interview, S.G., June 1999.
55. Thanks to Jay Straker for relaying both the question and answer for me.
56. A fair number of Loma speakers have also converted to Islam, but because of the politics of religion in Macenta Préfecture, many of them probably do not participate in the *Gilibaye* organization.
57. This consciousness did not hatch full-formed. It developed gradually over time,

partly, as Beavogui has argued, out of the ethnic partition of Macenta Préfecture around 1918, partly over the material tensions introduced through mise en valeur laws, and partly through the denigrating stereotypes and practices of which Demystification was a part. That Loma cultural nationalist politics did not emerge until the 1990s is largely an artifact of the extent to which the Touré regime had crushed all forms of civil society organization during the socialist period. Højbjerg (2007) gives an excellent analysis of these dynamics in chapters 8 and 9 of his book.

CHAPTER EIGHT

1. The title of this chapter is a tip of the hat to Askew's *Performing the Nation*.
2. See Højbjerg 1993 for an excellent discussion of the polysemic aspects of the term *sale* in Lomagui.
3. This discretion is a historically constituted practice having to do with Loma speakers' uncertain relations with neighbors and encompassing states. In this context, I suggest the reintroduction of the term "secrecy" to refer to outsiders' objectification of Loma discretion, while reserving the term "discretion" for the practices themselves.
4. I believe Schwab refers to Kotonhoui, in Yomou Préfecture. The equivalence of the letters "L" and "T" in initial consonant shifts in the SW Mande languages makes the two names, Kolon-wi and Kotonhui, phonemically equivalent.
5. While this suspicion was actively directed toward Europeans, it also targeted Africans from other countries, and with the development of a rhetoric of suspicion directed at an internal "cinquième colonne" (fifth column) of Guinean traitors, it turned neighbors against neighbors, parents against children, and spouses against one another.
6. Højbjerg (2007) gives an excellent account of how Loma speakers dealt with these breaches in Guinea. Sarró (2002) does the same for the Baga of Guinea.
7. A certain amount of "macho" aggressiveness was allowable, especially among men in their twenties who had been drinking. One young male friend of mine whom I call "Taanu" in McGovern 2004 was known to sometimes become *ziigbadie*, but often over points of honor or principle. Such behavior was never preferred over consultation and compromise, but it was considered manly as long as it was not canalized into the realm of personal resentment. As one of the *ziigbadie* men I have mentioned above once said to me, " I have a man's heart," and he later contrasted himself to another man he said had a "woman's heart—he'll forgive any wrong done to him." Again, Leach's description of Mende society notes an identical set of ideas around gender and "hot hearts" (1992, 162).
8. Compare this talk again to Mende men's talk about gender: "male hunters feared to give women guns in case they shot the men who displeased them" (Leach 1992, 162).
9. See Turner ([1957] 1996, 95) for a similar case among the Ndembu.
10. This is also Murphy's point of view in his "Secret Knowledge as Property and Power in Kpelle Society: Elders Versus Youth" (1980).
11. Although *tɔɔgi* can be used to mean something like upbringing or instilling values and proper behavior, its literal meaning is "the law." Guilavogui (1968) derives the ethnonym "Toma" (as Loma speakers are called by their Northern Mande and Kissi-speaking neighbors) from this term, offering "the people of the law" as an etymology.
12. Although it would draw this chapter out to extreme lengths to follow the thread

fully, I recommend to the reader Zahan (1960, 1963) and Jamin (1977, chap. 2) for analyses of parallel Mande ideas about and practices of secrecy and discretion among the Bamana and Senufo, respectively.

13. The term recurs in the writing of William Murphy (1980, 1990), and features as well in the title of Stephen Ellis's 1999 book on the Liberian civil war, *The Mask of Anarchy*.

14. I am not entirely convinced by this argument (but see Schwab [1947, 167], who makes a similar claim). The regional war of the 1990s has shown that at least in the present context, one must introduce into such an equation the agency of powerful warlords who bridged the idealized complementary system of autochthonous political rulers and ritually powerful Poro heads.

15. This calls to mind Geertz's study of the Balinese theater state. While his focus on "the ordering force of display, regard and drama" (1980, 121) is quite applicable to the Guinean context, the Balinese case presents so many profound differences (at the cultural, economic, and especially the political levels), that I hesitate to draw the comparison. In a later work, I hope to expand on this problematic by showing some of the specific ways that Mande expressive traditions were reinvented in a Negara-like manner. The complicating factor in the case of Demystification is the extent to which the colonial culture (actually, its representation of itself) seems to have been the primary model for the postcolonial obsession with rationalization. Askew (2002) describes a similar set of challenges in the context of Nyerere's Tanzania.

16. This process seems to have developed over time, and the training of youth militia members seems to have been the site of the most obvious parallels to Poro/Sande initiation. Another site of revolutionary socialization was the school, especially after 1968, when secondary schools were renamed "Centers of Revolutionary Teaching" (see Straker 2004 for a full discussion of this aspect of Guinean cultural politics).

17. Here I refer to education in the broadest sense (Loma: *tɔɔgi*), meaning the inculcation of proper adult dispositions like patience, forbearance, the ability to manage pain, hunger, and thirst, and most importantly discretion.

18. Not least of them the dismantling of the precolonial feudal relation between noble and servile populations in both Maninka and Fulbe regions.

19. Interview, A.O., May 4, 2000.

20. Les Amazones was a band made up entirely of female police officers. Like several of the other groups, they toured internationally during the Touré years.

21. This is an aspect of the 1958 to 1984 period that Mohammed Saliou Camara (2005) and Jay Straker (2009) have been keen to explore without falling into the hagiographic rhetoric of those who portray the revolutionary period as being without problems. Askew (2002) proposes a similarly nuanced interpretation of cultural policy in socialist and post-socialist Tanzania, and, in a non-socialist but autocratic setting, Bob White (2008) has done the same for music in Mobutu's Zaire. For a parallel analysis of visual pleasure in Stalin-era Soviet cinema, see Kaganovsky 2006.

22. See Straker 2007, 222–24, for a sensitive reading of one such account by a Forestier man who was still incensed as he recounted an event that had taken place thirty years prior.

23. Fitzpatrick (2005) describes the comparable trajectory of success in Stalinist Soviet Russia: peasant birth, which facilitated entrée into the category of proletarian youth and created the possibility of eventual promotion to white collar status. Though the Guinean revolution was less concerned than the Soviet or Chinese ones in ascertaining citizens' class origins, many Guineans today emphasize the ways in which

the socialist state leveled the playing field so as to allow brilliant and ambitious youths of modest background gain access to education, scholarships, and positions of influence. The general feeling was that the post-socialist period had reneged on this advance.
24. After the "Portuguese Aggression" of 1970, many Guineans were forced to confess that they were part of a network organized by the Nazi SS. The addition of this admission to the more plausible (though still coerced) admissions of involvement with the CIA or European secret services came in part from the fact that Hermann Siebold, a technical coopérant who worked in Kankan and was arrested in 1971 for involvement in the Portuguese attack, had in fact been an SS member. A Czech advisor to Sékou Touré who had been imprisoned by the Nazis during World War II apparently also advised Touré to utilize this accusation against the alleged members of the internal fifth column.
25. The Bureau Fédéral was the party-state's political decision-making body one level down from the national level.
26. They included Fodéba Keita, the founder of the *Ballets Africains* who later earned infamy by enthusiastically participating in purges and arrests before falling prey to his own practices.

CONCLUSION

1. In other words the Touré government, despite its claims to be inclusive, was favoring Malinke and discriminating against Fulbe and Forestiers in the 1960s. Rivière notes that this was especially true in the realm of regional administration in the hinterland, a point I have made in regards to questions of land tenure in Macenta under the Touré regime. Every group was represented at the ministerial level, but Rivière implies that this was a form of tokenism.
2. These were processes that began in the nineteenth century (usually under the impetus of missionization) in other parts of West Africa, such as among the various people who came to be known as the Yoruba (Peel 2000).
3. See Berliner 2010 on the Bulongic's explanation of the introduction of their language by a spirit, allowing the ethnically heterogeneous maroon community that had formed on that part of what became the Guinean coast to communicate with one another. Among Bulongic much more than Loma speakers, the unintelligibility of language across small distances is embraced as "proof" of a historical experience of survival in a multiethnic shatter zone.
4. As described by Barry 2002.

WORKS CITED

Abraham, Arthur. 2001. "Who Were the Mende?" Paper presented at African Studies Association Annual Meetings, Houston, TX.
Abu-Lughod, Lila. 2004. *Dramas of Nationhood: The Politics of Television in Egypt*. Chicago: University of Chicago Press.
Adam, Jérôme. 1951. "Noms de clan en pays toma (Guinée française)." *Comptes rendus: Première Conférence internationale des Africanistes de l'Ouest* 2:149–52.
Adorno, Theodor and Max Horkheimer (1947) 1972. *Dialectic of Enlightenment*. New York: Herder and Herder.
Althusser, Louis. 1971. *Lenin and Philosophy and Other Essays*. London: New Left Books.
Amselle, Jean-Loup. 1990. *Logiques métisses: anthropologie de l'identité en Afrique et ailleurs*. Paris: Editions Payot.
Amselle, Jean-Loup, and Elikia M'Bokolo. 1985. *Au cœur de l'ethnie: ethnies, tribalisme et état en Afrique*. Paris: Editions de la Découverte.
Anderson, Benedict R. O'G. 1991. *Imagined Communities: Reflections on the Origin and Spread of Nationalism*. New York: Verso.
Anderson, Benjamin J. K. (1870) 1971. *Narrative of a Journey to Musardu, The Capital of the Western Mandingoes*. London: Cass.
Anderson, Benjamin J. K., James Sims, and George Seymour. 2003. *African-American Exploration in West Africa: Four Nineteenth-Century Diaries*. Bloomington: Indiana University Press.
Appadurai, Arjun. 1996. *Modernity at Large: Cultural Dimensions of Globalization*. Minneapolis: University of Minnesota Press.
———. 2006. *Fear of Small Numbers: An Essay on the Geography of Anger*. Durham: Duke University Press.
Ardener, Edwin. 1989. *The Voice of Prophecy and Other Essays*. New York: Blackwell.
Ardener, Shirley. 1975. *Perceiving Women*. New York: John Wiley and Sons.
Arnoldi, Mary Jo. 1995. *Playing with Time: Art and Performance in Central Mali*. Bloomington: Indiana University Press.
Askew, Kelly. 2002. *Performing the Nation: Swahili Music and Cultural Politics in Tanzania*. Chicago: University of Chicago Press.
Bakhtin, M. M. 1981. *The Dialogic Imagination: Four Essays*. Edited by Michael Holquist and Vadim Liapunov. Austin: University of Texas Press.

Barry, Alpha Ousmane. 2002. *Pouvoir du discours et discours du pouvoir: l'art oratoire chez Sékou Touré de 1958 à 1984*. Paris: L'Harmattan.
Barth, Fredrik. (1969) 1998. *Ethnic Groups and Boundaries*. Long Grove, Ill.: Waveland Press.
Barthes, Roland. 1973. *Le plaisir du texte*. Paris: Editions du Seuil.
Bayart, Jean-François. 1993. *The State in Africa: The Politics of the Belly*. London, New York: Longman.
———. 2005. *The Illusion of Cultural Identity*. Chicago: University of Chicago Press.
Bayart, Jean-François, Stephen Ellis, and Béatrice Hibou. 1999. *The Criminalization of the State in Africa*. Oxford: International African Institute in association with James Currey; Bloomington: Indiana University Press.
Bazin, Jean. 1974. "War and Servitude in Segou." *Economy and Society* 3 (2): 107–45.
———. 1985. "A chacun son Bambara." In *Au cœur de l'ethnie: ethnies, tribalisme et état en Afrique*, edited by J.-L. Amselle, 87–127. Paris: Editions de la Découverte.
Beavogui, Facinet. 1991. Contribution à l'histoire des Loma de la Guinée forestière de la fin du XIX siècle à 1945. Doctoral thesis, Université de Paris VII.
———. 1995. "Place et rôle de Game Guilavogui dans la naissance d'un nationalisme Loma pendant la colonisation française." *Histoire et anthropologie* 11:138–45.
———. 1998. "Le Poro, une institution politico-religieuse ouest africaine." In *Des historiens africains en Afrique: logiques du passé et dynamiques actuelles*, edited by Odile Georg and C. Coquery-Vidrovitch, 245–58. Paris: L'Harmattan.
———. 2001. *Les Toma—Guinée et Libéria—au temps des négriers et la colonisation française: XVIe–XXe siècles*. Paris: L'Harmattan.
Beidelman, T. O. 1986. *Moral Imagination in Kaguru Modes of Thought*. Bloomington: Indiana University Press.
Bellman, Beryl Larry. 1975. *Village of Curers and Assassins : On the Production of Fala Kpelle Cosmological Categories*. The Hague: Mouton.
———. 1984. *The Language of Secrecy: Symbols and Metaphors in Poro Ritual*. New Brunswick, NJ: Rutgers University Press.
Berliner, David. 2002. "'Nous sommes les derniers Bulongic': sur une impossible transmission dans une société d'Afrique de l'Ouest." PhD diss., Université Libre de Bruxelles.
———. 2005. "An 'Impossible' Transmission: Youth Religious Memories in Guinea-Conakry." *American Ethnologist* 32 (4): 576–92.
———. 2007. "When the Object of Transmission is not an Object: A West African Example." *RES Anthropology and Aesthetics* 51:87–97.
———. 2010. "The Invention of Bulongic Identity." In *The Powerful Presence of the Past: Integration and Conflict along the Upper Guinea Coast*, edited by J. Knörr and W. Trajano Filho, 253–72. Leiden: Brill.
Berman, Bruce, and John Lonsdale. 1992. *Unhappy Valley*. 2 vols. Oxford: James Currey.
Berman, Marshall. 1988. *All That Is Solid Melts into Air: The Experience of Modernity*. New York: Viking Penguin.
Berry, Sara. 1975. *Cocoa, Custom and Socioeconomic Change in Rural Western Nigeria*. Oxford: Clarendon Press.
Bhabha, Homi. 1994. The *Location of Culture*. London: Routledge.
Bilivogui, Oua. 1984. *Monographie historique de Macenta des origines à l'intrusion coloniale*. Memoire de fin d'études, Institut Polytechnique Julius Nyerere.
Bird, Charles. 1970. "Development of Mandekan (Manding): A Study in the Role of

Extra-linguistic Factors in Linguistic Change." In *Language and History in Africa*, edited by D. Dalby, 146–59. New York: Africana Publishing Corporation.

Bird, Charles, and Martha Kendall. 1980. "The Mande Hero." In *Explorations in African Systems of Thought*, edited by Ivan Karp and C. Bird, 13–26. Bloomington: Indiana University Press.

Bledsoe, Caroline. 1980. *Women and Marriage in Kpelle Society*. Stanford, CA: Stanford University Press.

Bloch, Ernst. (1962) 1970. "Entfremdung, Verfremdung: Alienation, Estrangement." *The Drama Review* 15 (1): 120–25.

Boone, Sylvia Ardyn. 1986. *Radiance from the Waters: Ideals of Feminine Beauty in Mende Art*. New Haven, CT: Yale University Press.

Bouet, F. 1911. "Les Tomas." *Renseignements Coloniaux* 8, 9, 10:185–200; 220–27; 233–46.

Brenner, Louis. 1984. *West African Sufi: The Religious Heritage and Spiritual Search of Cerno Bokar Saalif Taal*. London: C. Hurst & Co.

Brooks, George E. 1980. *Kola Trade and State-Building: Upper Guinea Coast and Senegambia, 15th—17th Centuries*. Boston: African Studies Center, Boston University.

———. 1993. *Landlords and Strangers: Ecology, Society, and Trade in Western Africa, 1000–1630*. Boulder, CO: Westview Press.

Brown, Geo. W. 1937. "The Poro in Modern Business: A Preliminary Report of Field Work." *Man* 37 (3): 8–9.

Bruijn, Mirjam de, and Han van Dijk, eds. 1997. *Peuls et Mandingues: dialectiques des constructions identitaires*. Paris: Karthala.

Bunot, Raoul. 1950. *Forêts du sud et Brindilles de la forêt toma*. Mayenne: G.-G. Collet.

Butler, Judith. 1990. *Gender Trouble: Feminism and the Subversion of Identity*. New York: Routledge.

———. 1997. *Excitable Speech: A Politics of the Performative*. New York: Routledge.

Butler, Judith, Ernesto Laclau, and Slavoj Žižek. 2000. *Contingency, Hegemony, Universality: Contemporary Dialogues on the Left*. London: Verso.

Camara, Mohamed Saliou. 2005. *His Master's Voice: Mass Communication and Single Party Politics in Guinea under Sékou Touré*. Trenton, NJ: Africa World Press.

———. 2007. *Le pouvoir politique en Guinée sous Sékou Touré*. Paris: L'Harmattan.

Carrithers, Michael, Steven Collins, and Steven Lukes. 1985. *The Category of the Person: Anthropology, Philosophy, History*. Cambridge: Cambridge University Press.

Carter, Jeanette E. 1970. "Household Organization and the Money Economy in a Loma Community, Liberia." Ph.D. diss., University of Oregon.

Césaire, Aimé. 1956. *Lettre à Maurice Thorez*. Paris: Présence Africaine.

Chabal, Patrick, and Jean-Pascal Daloz. 1999. *Africa Works: Disorder as Political Instrument*. Oxford: James Currey.

Charles, Bernard. 1968. "Cadres guinéens et appartenances ethnique." Ph.D. diss., Sorbonne.

———. 2010. "Une désespérance de l'indépendance: l'unité nationale." In Goerg, Pauthier, and Diallo, eds., 2010, 133–58. Paris: L'Harmattan.

Chatterjee, Partha. 1993. *The Nation and Its Fragments: Colonial and Postcolonial Histories*. Princeton, NJ: Princeton University Press.

Chinweizu, ed. 1988. *Voices from Twentieth-Century Africa: Griots and Towncriers*. London, Boston: Faber and Faber.

Chretien, Jean-Pierre, and Gerard Prunier. 1989. *Les ethnies ont une histoire*. Paris: Karthala.

Cohn, Bernard. 1987. *An Anthropologist Among the Historians and Other Essays.* Delhi, New York: Oxford University Press.

Conrad, David C., and Barbara E. Frank. 1995. *Status and Identity in West Africa: Nyamakalaw of Mande.* Bloomington: Indiana University Press.

Cooper, Frederick. 1993. *Confronting Historical Paradigms: Peasants, Labor, and the Capitalist World System in Africa and Latin America.* Madison: University of Wisconsin Press.

———. 1996. *Decolonization and African Society: The Labor Question in French and British Africa.* New York: Cambridge University Press.

Cosentino, Donald. 1982. *Defiant Maids and Stubborn Farmers: Tradition and Invention in Mende Story Performance.* New York: Cambridge University Press.

Counsel, Graeme. 2006. "Mande Popular Music and Cultural Policies in West Africa." PhD diss., University of Melbourne.

Currens, Gerald E. 1974. "The Loma Farmer: A Socio-Economic Study of Rice Cultivation and the Uses of Resources among a People of Northwestern Liberia." PhD diss., University of Oregon.

———. 1979. "Land, Labor and Capital in Loma Agriculture." In *Essays on the Economic Anthropology of Liberia and Sierra Leone,* edited by V. Dorajohn, and Barry Isaac, 79–102. Philadelphia, PA: Institute for Liberian Studies.

d'Azevedo, Warren L. 1962a. "Some Historical Problems in the Delineation of a Central West Atlantic Region." *Annals of the New York Academy of Sciences: Anthropology and Africa Today* 96:512–38.

———. 1962b. "Uses of the Past in Gola Discourse." *Journal of African History* 3 (1): 11–34.

———. 1994–95. "Phantoms of the Hinterland: The 'Mandingo' Presence in Early Liberian Accounts." *Liberian Studies Journal* 14 (2–3): 197–242.

Dalby, David. 1963. "The extinct language of Dama." *Sierra Leone Language Review* 2:50–54.

Dapper, Olfert. (1668) 1686. *Description de l'Afrique, contenant les noms, la situation & les confins de toutes ses parties, leurs rivières, leurs villes & leurs habitations, leurs plantes & leurs animaux; les mœurs, les coûtumes, la langue, les richesses, la religion & le gouvernement de ses peuples. Avec des cartes des États, des provinces & des villes, & des figures en taille-douce, qui représentent les habits & les principales cérémonies des habitants, les plantes & les animaux les moins connus.* Amsterdam: Wolfgang Waesberge Boom & van Someren.

Das, Veena, and D. Poole, eds. 2004. *Anthropology in the Margins of the State.* Santa Fe, NM: SAR Press.

Dennis, Benjamin G. 1972. *The Gbandes: A People of the Liberian Hinterland.* Chicago: Nelson-Hall Co.

Diallo, Mamadou Saliou, Julie Fischer, et al. 1995. "Le foncier et la gestion des ressources naturelles en Guinée Forestière: une étude de cas du terroir de Nonah." Madison: Land Tenure Center, University of Wisconsin.

Diawara, Manthia. 1998. *In Search of Africa.* Cambridge, MA: Harvard University Press.

Dieterlen, Germaine. 1947. "Note sur le tere chez les Bambara." *Notes Africaines* 35:28.

Donelha, Andre. (1625) 1977. *Descricao da Serra Leoa e dos rios do Guine do Cabo Verde.* Lisbon: Junta de Investigacoes Cientificas do Ultramar.

Donham, Donald L. 1999. *Marxist Modern: An Ethnographic History of the Ethiopian Revolution.* Berkeley: University of California Press.

———. 2002. "On Being Modern in a Capitalist World: Some Conceptual and Comparative Issues." In Knauft, ed., 2002, 241–57.

DuBois, W. E. B. (1903) 1994. *The Souls of Black Folk.* New York: Dover.

Ebron, Paulla A. 2002. *Performing Africa*. Princeton, NJ: Princeton University Press.
El-Dabh, Halim. 1979. *Puppetry and Masked Dance Traditions of the Republic of Guinea: A Report of Field Findings Submitted to the Smithsonian Institution Foreign Currency Program, Smithsonian Institution Folklife Program and the Puppeteers of America*. Washington, D.C.: Smithsonian Institution.
Ellis, Stephen. 1999. *The Mask of Anarchy: The Destruction of Liberia and the Religious Dimension of an African Civil War*. London: Hurst.
———. 2001. "Mystical Weapons: Some Evidence from the Liberian War." *Journal of Religion in Africa* 31 (2): 222–36.
Evans-Pritchard, E. E. 1937. *Witchcraft, Oracles and Magic Among the Azande*. Oxford: Clarendon Press.
———. 1940. *The Nuer: A Description of the Modes of Livelihood and Political Institutions of a Nilotic People*. Oxford: Clarendon Press.
———. 1956. *Nuer Religion*. Oxford: Clarendon Press.
Eyre, Banning. 2000. *In Griot Time: An American Guitarist in Mali*. Philadelphia, PA: Temple University Press.
Fairhead, James, and Melissa Leach. 1994. "Contested Forests: Modern Conservation and Historical Land Use in Guinea's Ziama Reserve." *African Affairs* 93:481–512.
———. 1996. *Misreading the African Landscape: Society and Ecology in a Forest-Savanna Mosaic*. New York: Cambridge University Press.
Fairhead, James, Tim Geysbeek, Svend E. Holsoe, and Melissa Leach, eds. 2003. *African-American Exploration in West Africa: Four Nineteenth-Century Diaries*. Bloomington: Indiana University Press.
Fanon, Frantz. (1961) 1963. *The Wretched of the Earth*. New York: Grove Press.
———. (1952) 1991. *Black Skin, White Masks*. New York: Grove Weidenfeld.
Fanthorpe, Richard. 2001. "Neither Citizen nor Subject? 'Lumpen' Agency and the Legacy of Native Administration in Sierra Leone." *African Affairs* 100:363–86.
Ferguson, James, and Akhil Gupta. 2002. "Spatializing States: Toward an Ethnography of Neoliberal Governmentality." *American Ethnologist* 29 (4): 981–1002.
Ferme, Mariane C. 2001. *The Underneath of Things: Violence, History, and the Everyday in Sierra Leone*. Berkeley: University of California Press.
Fischer, Eberhard, and Hans Himmelheber. 1984. *The Arts of the Dan in West Africa*. Zurich: Museum Reitberg.
Fischer, Julie E. 1994/95. "Tenure Opportunities and Constraints in Guinea: Resource Management Projects and Policy Dialogue." *Land Tenure Center Newsletter* 72:1–7.
Fitzpatrick, Sheila. 2005. *Tear off the Masks: Identity and Imposture in Twentieth-Century Russia*. Princeton, NJ: Princeton University Press.
Fortes, Meyer. 1959. *Oedipus and Job in West African Religion*. Cambridge: Cambridge University Press.
———. 1987. *Religion, Morality, and the Person: Essays on Tallensi Religion*. New York: Cambridge University Press.
Fortes, Meyer, and E. E. Evans-Pritchard, eds. 1940. *African Political Systems*. London: Published for the International Institute of African Languages and Cultures by the Oxford University Press.
Freud, Sigmund. (1917) 1995. "The Uncanny." In *Psychological Writings and Letters*, edited by Sander Gilman, 120–53. New York: Continuum.
Furth, Rebecca. 2005. "Marrying the Forbidden Other: Marriage, Status and Social Change in the Futa Jallon Highlands of Guinea." PhD diss., University of Wisconsin.
Gaisseau, Pierre Dominique. 1953. *Forêt sacrée: Magie et rites secrets des Toma*. Paris: Albin

Michel. English translation, 1954: *The Sacred Forest: The Fetishist and Magic Rites of the Toma*. London: Weidenfeld and Nicolson.

Galaty, John G. 1982. "Being 'Maasai'; Being 'People of Cattle': Ethnic Shifters in East Africa." *American Ethnologist* 9:1–20.

———. 1993. "The Eye that Wants a Person: Where Can It Not See? Inclusion, Exclusion, and Boundary Shifters in Maasai Identity." In Spear and Waller 1993, 174–94.

Gamalo, Bamba Bakary. 2001. "Toma et Toma-Manian: de la querelle foncière au feu de la rébellion." *Le Lynx*, October 29.

Gamory-Dubourdeau, P. M. 1925. "Notice sur les coutumes des Tomas de la frontière Franco-Libérienne." *Bulletin du Comite d'études historique et scientifiques de l'Afrique occidentale française* 9 (2): 289–350.

Geertz, Clifford. 1968. *Islam Observed: Religious Development in Morocco and Indonesia*. New Haven, CT: Yale University Press.

———. 1980. *Negara: The Theatre State in Nineteenth-Century Bali*. Princeton, NJ: Princeton University Press.

Gellner, Ernest. 1983. *Nations and Nationalism*. Ithaca: Cornell University Press.

Germain, Jacques. 1984. *Peuples de la forêt de Guinée*. Paris: Académie des sciences d'outre-mer.

Germann, Paul. 1933. *Die Völkerstämme im Norden von Liberia: Ergebnisse einer Forschungsreise im Auftrage des Staatlich-sächsischen Forschungsinstitutes für Völkerkunde in Leipzig in den Jahren 1928/29*. Leipzig: R. Voigtländer.

Geschiere, Peter. 2009. *The Perils of Belonging*. Chicago: University of Chicago Press.

Geschiere, Peter, and Francis Nyamnjoh. 2000. "Capitalism and Autochthony: The Seesaw of Mobility and Belonging." *Public Culture* 12 (2): 423–52.

Goepogui, Dobo. 1990. "Monographie historique du Guizima (Macenta) des origines a l'implantation coloniale." Mémoire de fin des études, Université Julius Nyerere de Kankan.

Goerg, Odile. 1986. *Commerce et colonization en Guinée*. Paris: L'Harmattan.

Goerg, Odile, Celine Pauthier, and Abdoulaye Diallo, eds. 2010. *Le NON de la Guinée (1958): Entre mythe, relecture historique et résonances contemporaines*. Paris: L'Harmattan.

Goffman, Erving. 1959. *The Presentation of Self in Everyday Life*. Garden City, NY: Anchor Books.

Goody, Jack. 1997. *Representations and Contradictions: Ambivalence towards Images, Theatre, Fiction, Relics and Sexuality*. Oxford: Blackwell Publishers.

Greenberg, Joseph. 1955. *Studies in African Linguistic Classification*. New Haven, CT: Compass.

Greene, Graham. (1966) 2005. *The Comedians*. New York: Penguin Classics.

Guilao, Gamé. 1967. "La mort des fétiches." *Esprit* 9 (n.s.): 237–44.

Guilavogui, Galema. 1968. "La résistance à la pénétration française dans la région de Macenta." Mémoire de fin d'études, Institut Polytechnique de Conakry.

Guilavogui, Keletigui. 1987. "Les croyances religieuses en milieu traditionnel Loma." Mémoire de fin d'études, Université Julius Nyerere de Kankan.

Gulphe, Pierre. 1970. *Réflexions sur la législation guinéenne en matière de mariage*. Paris: Editions A. Pedone.

Gupta, Akhil. 1995. "Blurred Boundaries: The Discourse of Corruption, the Culture of Politics, and the Imagined State." *American Ethnologist* 22 (2): 375–402.

Gupta, Akhil, and James Ferguson. 1997. *Anthropological Locations: Boundaries and Grounds of a Field Science*. Berkeley and Los Angeles: University of California Press.

Guyer, Jane. 1993. "Wealth in People and Self-Realization in Equatorial Africa." *Man* 28 (2): 243–65.

Guyer, Jane, ed. 1995. *Money Matters: Instability, Values and Social Payments in the Modern History of West African Communities.* London: James Currey.

Guyer, Jane I., and Samuel M. Eno Belinga. 1995. "Wealth in People as Wealth in Knowledge: Accumulation and Composition in Equatorial Africa." *Journal of African History* 36 (1): 91–120.

Hair, Paul E. H. 1967. "Ethnolinguistic Continuity on the Guinea coast." *Journal of African History* 8 (2): 247–68.

Hall, Stuart, and Tony Jefferson. 1975. *Resistance through Rituals: Youth Subcultures in Post-War Britain.* London: Hutchinson and Co.

Harding, Susan. 2001. *The Book of Jerry Falwell: Fundamentalist Language and Politics.* Princeton, NJ: Princeton University Press.

Harley, George Way. 1941. *Notes on the Poro in Liberia.* Cambridge, MA: Harvard University Press.

———. 1950. *Masks as Agents of Social Control in Northeast Liberia.* Cambridge, MA: Harvard University Press.

Heald, Suzette. 1989. *Controlling Anger: The Sociology of Gisu Violence.* Manchester: Manchester University Press for the International African Institute London.

Herbert, Christopher. 1991. *Culture and Anomie: Ethnographic Imagination in the Nineteenth Century.* Chicago: University of Chicago Press.

Heusch, Luc de. 1971. *Pourquoi l'épouser?* Paris: Gallimard.

Hill, Matthew H. 1984. "Where to Begin? The place of the Hunter Founder in Mende Histories." *Anthropos* 79 (4–6): 653–56.

Hobsbawm, E. J. 1990. *Nations and Nationalism since 1780: Programme, Myth, Reality.* New York: Cambridge University Press.

Hoffman, Barbara G. 2000. *Griots at War: Conflict, Conciliation, and Caste in Mande.* Bloomington: Indiana University Press.

Højbjerg, Christian Kordt. 1993. "Fetish and Space among the Loma: An Examination of a West African Medicine." *Folk* 35:91–110.

———. 1999. "Loma Political Culture: A Phenomenology of Structural Form." *Africa* 69 (4): 535–54.

———. 2002a. "Inner Iconoclasm: Forms of Reflexivity in Loma Rituals of Sacrifice." *Social Anthropology* 10:57–75.

———. 2002b. "Religious Reflexivity: Essays on Attitudes to Religious Ideas and Practices." *Social Anthropology* 10:1–10.

———. 2007. *Resisting State Iconoclasm among the Loma of Guinea.* Durham, NC: Carolina Academic Press.

———. 2010. "Victims and Heroes: Manding Historical Imagination in a Conflict-Ridden Border Region (Liberia-Guinea)." In *The Powerful Presence of the Past: Integration and Conflict along the Upper Guinea Coast,* edited by J. Knörr and W. Trajano Filho, 273–94. Leiden: Brill.

Holsoe, Svend E. 1977. "Slavery and Economic Response among the Vai (Liberia and Sierra Leone)." In Miers and Kopytoff 1977, 287–303.

———. 1980. "Notes on the Vai Sande Society in Liberia." *Ethnologische Zeitschrift Zürich* 1:97–111.

Horton, W. Robin G. 1971. "African Conversion." *Africa* 41 (2): 85–108.

———. 1975. "On the Rationality of Conversion (Part I)." *Africa* 45 (3): 219–35.

———. 1976. "Stateless Societies in the History of West Africa." In J. F. A. Ajayi and M. Crowder, eds., *History of West Africa*. New York: Columbia University Press.

Hroch, Miroslav. 1985. *Social Preconditions of National Revival in Europe: A Comparative Analysis of the Social Composition of Patriotic Groups among the Smaller European Nations*. New York: Cambridge University Press.

Hubert, Henri, and Marcel Mauss. 1966. *Sacrifice: Its Nature and Functions*. Chicago: University of Chicago Press.

Hunt, Nancy Rose. 1999. *A Colonial Lexicon of Birth: Ritual, Medicalization, and Mobility in the Congo*. Durham, N.C.: Duke University Press.

Jackson, Michael. 1974. "The Structure and Significance of Kuranko Clanship." *Africa* 44 (4): 397–415.

Jackson, Stephen. 2006. "Sons of Which Soil? The Language and Politics of Autochthony in Eastern D. R. Congo." *African Studies Review* 49 (2): 95–123.

James, Wendy. 1979. *Kwanim Pa: The Making of the Uduk People: An Ethnographic Study of Survival in the Sudan-Ethiopian Borderlands*. Oxford: Clarendon Press.

———. 1988. *The Listening Ebony: Moral Knowledge, Religion, and Power Among the Uduk of Sudan*. Oxford: Clarendon Press.

———. 1997. "Names of Fear: Memory, History, and the Ethnography of Feeling among Uduk Refugees." *Journal of the Royal Anthropological Institute* 3 (1): 115–31.

Jameson, Fredric. 1998. *Brecht and Method*. London: Verso.

Jamin, Jean. 1977. *Les lois du silence*. Paris: Maspero.

Jones, Adam. 1981. "Who were the Vai?" *Journal of African History* 22 (1): 159–78.

Jules-Rosette, Benetta. 2002. "Leopold Senghor: The Strength of Contradictions." *African Arts* 35 (2): 1–4.

Kaba, Lansiné. 1974. *The Wahhabiyya: Islamic Reform and Politics in French West Africa*. Evanston, IL: Northwestern University Press.

———. 1976. "The Cultural Revolution, Artistic Creativity, and Freedom of Expression in Guinea." *Journal of Modern African Studies* 14 (2): 201–18.

———. 1989. *La Guinée dit "non" à de Gaulle*. Paris: Editions Chaka.

Kaganovsky, Lilya. 2006. "Visual Pleasure in Stalinist Cinema." In *Everyday Life in Early Soviet Russia: Taking the Revolution Inside*, edited by Christian Kiaer and Eric Naiman, 35–60. Bloomington: Indiana University Press.

Kaké, Ibrahim Baba. 1987. *Sékou Touré, le héros et le tyran*. Paris: Groupe Jeune Afrique.

Karp, Ivan. 2002. "Development and Personhood: Tracing the Contours of a Moral Discourse." In Knauft, ed., 2002, 82–104.

Klein, Martin A. 1977. "Servitude among the Wolof and Sereer of Senegambia." In Miers and Kopytoff 1977, 335–63.

Klumpp, Donna, and Corinne Kratz. 1993. "Aesthetics, Expertise, and Ethnicity: Okiek and Maasai Perspectives on Personal Ornament." In Spear and Waller 1993, 195–221.

Knauft, Bruce M. 2002. *Exchanging The Past: A Rainforest World of Before and After*. Chicago: University of Chicago Press.

Knauft, Bruce M., ed. 2002. *Critically Modern: Alternatives, Alterities, Anthropologies*. Bloomington: Indiana University Press.

Kopytoff, Igor. 1987. *The African Frontier: The Reproduction of Traditional African Societies*. Bloomington: Indiana University Press.

Korvah, Paul Degein. 1995. *The History of the Loma People*. Oakland, CA: O Books.

Kouyate, Mohamed Mancona. 1996. *Nous sommes tous responsables*. Conakry: Imprimerie Moderne de Kaloum.

Kratz, Corinne A. 1986. "Ethnic Interaction, Economic Diversification and Language Use: A Report on Research with Kaplelach and Kipchornwonek Okiek." *SUGIA: Sprache und Geschichte in Afrika* 7 (2): 189–226.

———. 1993. "'We've Always Done It Like This . . . Except for a Few Details': 'Tradition' and 'Innovation' in Okiek Ceremonies." *Comparative Studies in Society and History* 35 (1): 30–65.

———. 1994. *Affecting Performance: Meaning, Movement, and Experience in Okiek Women's Initiation*. Washington: Smithsonian Institution Press.

Labouret, Henri. 1934. "Les Toma, Loma ou Logoma." *Anthropologie* 44:723–24.

Laclau, Ernesto, and Chantal Mouffe. *Hegemony and Socialist Strategy: Towards a Radical Democratic Politics*. London: Verso.

Lamp, Frederick. 1996. *Art of the Baga: A Drama of Cultural Reinvention*. New York: Prestel.

Latour, Bruno. 1993. *We Have Never Been Modern*. Cambridge, MA: Harvard University Press.

———. 1997. "A Few Steps Toward an Anthropology of the Iconoclastic Gesture." *Science in Context* 10 (1): 63–83.

Leach, Edmund Ronald. 1954. *Political Systems of Highland Burma: A Study of Kachin Social Structure*. London: G. Bell.

Leach, Melissa. 1994. *Rainforest Relations: Gender and Resource Use among the Mende of Gola, Sierra Leone*. Edinburgh: Edinburgh University Press for the International African Institute London.

Leach, Melissa, and University of Sussex, Institute of Development Studies. 1992. *Dealing with Displacement: Refugee-host Relations, Food and Forest Resources in Sierra Leonean Mende Communities during the Liberian Influx, 1990–91*. Brighton: University of Sussex Institute of Development Studies.

Lefebvre, Henri. 1991. *The Production of Space*. Oxford: Blackwell.

Leopold, Robert. 1983. "Shaping of Men and the Making of Metaphors: The Meaning of White Clay In Poro and Sande Initiation Society Rituals." *Anthropology* 7 (2): 21–42.

———. 1991. "Prescriptive Alliance and Ritual Collaboration in Loma Society." PhD diss., Indiana University.

Levi, Primo. 1989. *The Drowned and the Saved*. New York: Vintage.

Lévi-Strauss, Claude. (1949) 1969. *The Elementary Structures of Kinship*. Boston: Beacon Press.

Littlejohn, James. 1973. "Temne Right and Left: An Essay on the Choreography of Everyday Life." In *Right and Left: Essays on Dual Symbolic Classification*, edited by R. Needham, 288–98. Chicago: University of Chicago Press.

MacCormack, Carol P. 1974. "Madam Yoko: Ruler of the Kpa Mende Confederacy." In *Woman, Culture and Society*, edited by Michele Z. Rosaldo and Louise Lamphere, 171–87, 333–34. Stanford, CA: Stanford University Press.

MacGaffey, Janet. 1991. *The Real Economy of Zaire: The Contribution of Smuggling and Other Unofficial Activities to National Wealth*. London: James Currey.

MacGaffey, Janet, and Rémy Bazenguissa-Ganga. 2000. *Congo-Paris: Transnational Traders on the Margins of the Law*. Bloomington: Indiana University Press.

Mafeje, Archie. 1971. "The Ideology of Tribalism." *The Journal of Modern African Studies* 9:253–61.

Mamdani, Mahmood. 1996. *Citizen and Subject: Contemporary Africa and the Legacy of Late Colonialism*. Princeton, NJ: Princeton University Press.

Mani, Lata. 1990. "Multiple Mediations: Feminist Scholarship in the Age of Multinational Reception." *Feminist Review* 35 (Summer): 24–41.

Mannheim, Karl. (1936) 1955. *Ideology and Utopia: An Introduction to the Sociology of Knowledge*. New York: Harcourt.
Marshall, Ruth. 2009. *Political Spiritualities: The Pentecostal Revolution in Nigeria*. Chicago: University of Chicago Press.
Marx, Karl, and Friedrich Engels. (1848) 1992. *The Communist Manifesto*. New York: Bantam Books.
Massing, Andreas. 1978-79. "Materials for a History of Western Liberia: Samori and the Malinke Frontier in the Toma Sector." *Liberian Studies Journal* 8 (1): 49-67.
———. 1985. "The Mane, the Decline of Mali, and Maninka Expansion towards the South Windward Coast." *Cahiers d'Etudes Africaines* 97 (25): 21-55.
Mauss, Marcel. 1966. *Sociologie et anthropologie: précédé d'une introduction à l'œuvre de Marcel Mauss, par Claude Lévi-Strauss*. Paris: Presses universitaires de France.
———. 1985. "A Category of the Human Mind: The Notion of Person, The Notion of Self." In Carrithers, Collins, and Lukes 1985, 1-25.
Mbembé, Achille. 2000. *De la postcolonie: essai sur l'imagination politique dans l'Afrique contemporaine*. Paris: Karthala.
McGovern, Mike. 2002. "Conflit régionale et rhétorique de la contre-insurrection: Guinéens et réfugies en septembre 2000." *Politique Africaine* 88:84-102.
———. 2004. "Unmasking The State: Developing Modern Political Subjectivities in 20th Century Guinea." PhD diss., Emory University.
———. 2011. *Making War in Côte d'Ivoire*. Chicago: University of Chicago Press.
———. 2012. "Life during Wartime: Aspirational Kinship and the Management of Insecurity." *Journal of the Royal Anthropological Institute*.
———. forthcoming. "The Morality of Liberty: Socioeconomic Transition and Bodily Comportment in the Republic of Guinea." *American Ethnologist*.
McGovern, Mike, and Alexis Arieff. forthcoming. "'History Is Stubborn': Talk about Truth, Justice, and National Reconciliation in the Republic of Guinea." *Comparative Studies in Society and History*.
McNaughton, Patrick R. 1988. *The Mande Blacksmiths: Knowledge, Power, and Art in West Africa*. Bloomington: Indiana University Press.
Middleton, John, and Edward Henry Winter. 1963. *Witchcraft and Sorcery in East Africa*. New York: Praeger.
Miers, Suzanne, and Igor Kopytoff. 1977. *Slavery in Africa: Historical and Anthropological Perspectives*. Madison: University of Wisconsin Press.
Miller, Christopher L. 1990. *Theories of Africans: Francophone Literature and Anthropology in Africa*. Chicago: University of Chicago Press.
Miran, Marie. 2006. *Islam, histoire et modernité en Côte d'Ivoire*. Paris: Karthala.
Mitchell, J. Clyde. 1956. *The Kalela Dance: Aspects of Social Relationships among Urban Africans in Northern Rhodesia*. Rhodes-Livingston Papers number 27. Manchester: Manchester University Press.
Mitchell, Timothy. 1991. "The Limits of the State: Beyond Statist Approaches and their Critics." *American Political Science Review* 85 (1): 77-96.
Mitchell, W.J.T. 1986. *Iconology: Image, Text, Ideology*. Chicago: University of Chicago Press.
———. 2005. *What Do Pictures Want? The Lives and Loves of Images*. Chicago: University of Chicago Press.
Morgenthau, Ruth S. 1964. *Political Parties in French-speaking West Africa*. Oxford: Clarendon Press.

Mulvey, L. 1989. *Visual and Other Pleasures*. Bloomington: Indiana University Press.
Murphy, William P. 1980. "Secret Knowledge as Property and Power in Kpelle Society: Elders versus Youth." *Africa* 50 (2): 193–207.
———. 1981. "The Rhetorical Management of Dangerous Knowledge in Kpelle Brokerage." *American Ethnologist* 8 (4): 667–85.
———. 1990. "Creating the Appearance of Consensus in Mende Political Discourse." *American Anthropologist* 92 (1): 24–41.
Murphy, William P., and Caroline Bledsoe. 1987. "Kinship and Territory in the History of a Kpelle chiefdom (Liberia)." In Kopytoff 1987, 121–47.
Napier, A. David. 1986. *Masks, Transformation, and Paradox*. Berkeley: University of California Press.
Neel, H. 1913. "Deux peuplades de la frontière libérienne: Les Kissi et les Toma." *L'Anthropologie* 24:445–75.
Niane, Djibril Tamsir. 1965. *Sundiata: An Epic of Old Mali*. London: Longman.
Parkin, David. 1978. *The Cultural Definition of Political Response: Lineal Destiny Among the Luo*. London: Academic Press.
———. 1991. *Sacred Void: Spatial Images of Work and Ritual among the Giriama of Kenya*. Cambridge: Cambridge University Press.
Parkin, David, and David Nyamwaya, eds. 1987. *Transformations of African Marriage*. Manchester: Manchester University Press.
Paulme, Denise. 1948. "Dénkongo, un rituel juridique en pays kissi." *Notes Africaines* 40:5.
Peel, J.D.Y. 2000. *Religious Encounter and the Making of the Yoruba*. Bloomington: Indiana University Press.
Person, Yves. 1961. "Les Kissi et leurs statuettes de pierre dans le cadre de l'histoire ouest-africaine." *Institut Français d'Afrique Noire. Bulletin* 23 (1): 1–59.
———. 1968. *Samori: une revolution dyula*. Dakar: IFAN.
———. 1971. "Ethnic Movements and Acculturation in Upper Guinea since the Fifteenth Century." *International Journal of African Historical Studies* 4 (3): 669–89.
Pietz, William, and Emily Apter, eds. 1993. *Fetishism as Cultural Discourse*. Ithaca, NY: Cornell University Press.
Piot, Charles D. 2010. *Nostalgia for the Future: West Africa after the Cold War*. Chicago: University of Chicago Press.
Powell, Rachel, and John Clarke. 1975. "A Note on Marginality." In Hall and Jefferson 1975, 223–30.
Prunier, Gérard. 1995. *The Rwanda Crisis: History of a Genocide*. New York: Columbia University Press.
Reno, William. 1998. *Warlord Politics and African States*. Boulder, CO: Lynne Rienner Publishers.
Richards, Paul. 1996. *Fighting for the Rain Forest: War, Youth and Resources in Sierra Leone*. Oxford: James Currey.
———, ed. 2004. *No Peace No War: Anthropology of Contemporary Armed Conflicts*. Athens: Ohio University Press.
Rivière, Claude. 1969. "Fétichisme et démystification: l'exemple Guinéen." *Afrique Documents* 102–3:131–68.
———. 1971. *Mutations sociales en Guinée*. Paris: M. Rivière et Cie.
———. 1978. *Classes et stratifications sociales en Afrique: le cas guinéen*. Paris: Presses Universitaires de France.

Robbins, Joel. 2004. *Becoming Sinners*. Berkeley: University of California Press.
Robertson, Claire, and Martin Klein. (1983) 1997. *Women and Slavery in Africa*. Portsmouth, NH: Heinemann.
Robinson, David. 1985. *The Holy War of Umar Tal: The Western Sudan in the Mid-Nineteenth Century*. Oxford: Clarendon Press.
Rodney, Walter. 1970. *A History of the Upper Guinea Coast, 1545–1800*. Oxford: Clarendon Press.
Sahlins, Marshall. 1985. *Islands of History*. Chicago: University of Chicago Press.
Sakou, David Pepe. 1983. "Histoire et civilisation Loma des origines à la pénétration coloniale étrangère." Mémoire de fin d'études, Institut Polytechnique Julius Nyerere Kankan.
Sarró, Ramon. 1999. "Baga Identity: Religious Movements and Political Transformation in the Republic of Guinea." PhD diss., University of London.
———. 2002. "The Iconoclastic Meal: Destroying Objects and Eating Secrets among the Baga of Guinea." In *Iconoclash: Beyond the Image Wars in Science, Religion and Art*, edited by Bruno Latour and Peter Weibel, 227–30. Cambridge, MA: MIT Press.
———. 2009. *The Politics of Religious Change on the Upper Guinea Coast: Iconoclasm Done and Undone*. Edinburgh: International Africa Institute.
———. 2010. "Map and Territory: The Politics of Place and Autochthony among Baga Sitem (and their Neighbours)." In *The Powerful Presence of the Past: Integration and Conflict along the Upper Guinea Coast*. edited by J. Knörr and W. Trajano Filho, 231–52. Leiden: Brill.
Schatzberg, Michael G. 1988. *The Dialectics of Oppression in Zaire*. Bloomington: Indiana University Press.
Schmidt, Elizabeth. 2001. "Africans into Frenchmen: Assimilation, the Overseas Labor Code, and the French West African General Strike of 1953: An Examination of the Guinean Code." Paper presented at African Studies Association Annual Meetings, Houston, TX.
———. 2005. *Mobilizing the Masses: Gender, Ethnicity, and Class in the Nationalist Movement in Guinea, 1939–1958*. Portsmouth, NH: Heinemann.
Schnell, Raymond. 1949. "Notes sur le folklore des montagnes dans la région forestière d'Afrique occidentale." *Notes Africaines* 41:3–4.
Schwab, George. 1947. *Tribes of the Liberian Hinterland*. Cambridge, MA: Harvard University Press.
Scott, James C. 1998. *Seeing Like a State: How Certain Schemes to Improve the Human Condition Have Failed*. New Haven: Yale University Press.
———. 2009. *The Art of Not Being Governed: An Anarchist History of Upland Southeast Asia*. New Haven, CT: Yale University Press.
Scott, Joan. 2005. "Symptomatic Politics: The Banning of Headscarves in French Public Schools." *French Politics, Culture and Society* 23 (3): 106–27.
———. 2010. *The Politics of the Veil*. Princeton, NJ: Princeton University Press.
Shaw, Rosalind. 1997. "Production of Witchcraft, Witchcraft as Production: Memory, Modernity, and the Slave Trade in Sierra Leone." *American Ethnologist* 24 (4): 856–76.
———. 2002. *Memories of the Slave Trade: Ritual and the Historical Imagination in Sierra Leone*. Chicago: University of Chicago Press.
Simmel, Georg, and Kurt H. Wolf. 1950. *The Sociology of Georg Simmel*. Glencoe, Ill.: Free Press.
Siu, Helen. 1989. *Agents and Victims in South China: Accomplices in Rural Revolution*. New Haven: Yale University Press.

Southall, Aidan. 1956. *Alur Society: A Study in Processes and Types of Domination.* Cambridge: W. Heffer.

———. 1970. "The Illusion of Tribe." *Journal of Asian and African Studies* 5 (1–2): 28–50.

Sow, Alpha Mohammed. 1989. "Conflits ethniques dans un état révolutionnaire (le cas guinéen)." In *Les ethnies ont une histoire,* edited by Gérard Prunier and J.-P. Chretien, 387–404. Paris: Karthala.

Spear, Thomas T., and Richard D. Waller, eds. 1993. *Being Maasai: Ethnicity and Identity in East Africa.* London: James Currey.

Speed, Clarke Karney. 1991. "Swears and Swearing among Landogo of Sierra Leone: Aesthetics, Adjudication and the Philosophy of Power." PhD diss., University of Washington.

Sperber, Dan. 1985. *On Anthropological Knowledge: Three Essays.* Cambridge: Cambridge University Press.

Steedly, Mary Margaret. 1993. *Hanging without a Rope: Narrative Experience in Colonial and Postcolonial Karoland.* Princeton, NJ: Princeton University Press.

Steiner, Christopher. 1994. *African Art in Transit.* Cambridge: Cambridge University Press.

Straker, Jay. 2007. "Stories of 'Militant Theatre' in the Guinean Forest: 'Demystifying' the Motives and Moralities of a Revolutionary Nation-State." *Journal of African Cultural Studies* 19 (2): 207–33.

———. 2009. *Youth, Nationalism, and the Guinean Revolution.* Bloomington: Indiana University Press.

Stuempges, Richard. 1972. "The Sande Secret Society in Northwestern Liberia (Wozi area): An Agent of Socio-Cultural Control." MA thesis, Duquesne University.

Summers, Anne, and R. W. Johnson. 1978. "World War I Conscription and Social Change in Guinea." *Journal of African History* 19 (1): 25–38.

Suret-Canale, Jean. 1963. "Les noms de famille Toma." *Recherches Africaines* 1963 (2–3): 33–34.

———. 1969. "Les origines ethniques des anciens captifs au Fouta-Djalon." *Notes Africaines* 123:91–92.

Tannenbaum, Nicola, and Cornelia Kammerer, eds. 2003. *Founders' Cults in Southeast Asia.* New Haven, CT: Yale University Press.

Taussig, Michael T. 1999. *Defacement: Public Secrecy and the Labor of the Negative.* Stanford, CA: Stanford University Press.

Taylor, Christopher. 1999. *Sacrifice as Terror: The Rwandan Genocide of 1994.* Oxford: Berg.

Touré, Ahmed Sékou. 1959. *L'action politique du Parti démocratique de Guinée.* Paris: Présence Africaine.

———. 1966. *L'Afrique et la révolution.* Conakry: Imprimerie du Gouvernement.

———. 1967. *L'Afrique en marche.* Conakry: Imprimerie du Gouvernement.

———. 1969. *La révolution culturelle.* Conakry: Imprimerie du gouvernement.

———. 1976. *Révolution, culture, panafricanisme.* Conakry: Bureau de presse de la Présidence de la République.

———. 1977. *Unité nationale.* Conakry: Bureau de presse de la Présidence de la République.

———. 1978. *Informer et former pour transformer.* Conakry: Bureau de presse de la Présidence de la République.

———. 1982. Press conference. Audiocassette. Paris: Radio Télévision Guinéenne.

Trouillot, Michel-Rolph. 1991. "Anthropology and the Savage Slot: The Poetics and

Politics of Otherness." In *Recapturing Anthropology: Working in the Present*, edited by R. G. Fox, 17–44. Santa Fe, NM: School of American Research Press.

———. 2002. "The Otherwise Modern: Caribbean Lessons from the Savage Slot." In Knauft, ed. 2002, 220–40.

Tsing, Anna Lowenhaupt. 1993. *In The Realm of the Diamond Queen: Marginality in an Out-of-The-Way Place*. Princeton, NJ: Princeton University Press.

Turner, Victor Witter. (1969) 1977. *The Ritual Process: Structure and Anti-Structure*. Ithaca, NY: Cornell University Press.

Utas, Mats. 2003. "Sweet Battlefields: Youth and the Liberian Civil War." PhD diss., Uppsala University.

Vail, Leroy, ed. 1989. *The Creation of Tribalism in Southern Africa*. Berkeley: University of California Press.

van Gennep, Arnold. (1908) 1960. *The Rites of Passage*. Chicago: University of Chicago Press.

Vydrine, V. F. 2002. "Mande Language Family of West Africa: Location and Genetic Classification." Summer Institute of Linguistics. Available at: http://www.sil.org/silesr/2000/2000-003/silesr2000-003.html.

Wald, Priscilla. 1995. *Constituting Americans: Cultural Anxiety and Narrative Form*. Durham, NC: Duke University Press.

Weisswange, Karin. 1969. "Feindschaft und Verwandtschaft: Konflikt und Kooperation im zusammenleben von Loma und Mandingo in dem ort Borkeza in Liberia." MA thesis, Johan Wolfgang Goethe Universität.

———. 1976 "Mutual Relations between Loma and Mandingo in Liberia according to Oral Historical Tradition." Presented at Liberian Studies Conference, Bloomington, IN.

Welmers, William. 1958. "The Mande languages." In *Linguistic Language Studies: 9th Round Table Meeting*, edited by W. Austin, 9–24. Washington DC: Georgetown University.

White, Bob. 2008. *Rumba Rules: The Politics of Dance Music in Mobutu's Zaire*. Durham, NC: Duke University Press.

Whitehouse, Harvey. 2000. *Arguments and Icons: The Cognitive, Social, and Historical Implications of Divergent Modes of Religiosity*. Oxford: Oxford University Press.

———. 2002. "Religious Reflexivity and Transmissive Frequency." *Social Anthropology* 10:91–103.

Williams, Raymond. 1977. *Marxism and Literature*. Oxford: Oxford University Press.

———. 1985. *Keywords: A Vocabulary of Culture and Society*. New York: Oxford University Press.

Willis, John Ralph. 1989. *In the Path of Allah: The Passion of al-Hajj Umar: An Essay into the Nature of Charisma in Islam*. London: F. Cass.

Zahan, Dominique. 1960. *Sociétés d'initiation bambara*. Paris: Mouton.

———. 1963. *La dialectique du verbe chez les Bambara*. Paris: Mouton.

Zempléni, András. 1996. "Savoir taire: du secret et de l'intrusion ethnologique dans la vie des autres." *Gradhiva* 20:23–41.

Žižek, Slavoj. 1999. *The Ticklish Subject: The Absent Centre of Political Ontology*. New York: Verso.

Zoumanigi, Akoye Massa. 1989. "Recueil et interprétation des proverbes en pays loma." Mémoire de diplôme de fin d'études supérieures, Université Julius Nyerere de Kankan.

INDEX

Page numbers followed by "f" or "t" refer to figures or tables, respectively.

Abd al-Wahab, Muhammad ibn, 128
aestheticization, 208–19
agriculture. in Giziwulu, 241–43; Loma, 85–86, 138–39. *See also* cash crops; coffee production; land tenure; rice farming
al-Aqidat al-Sughra (Yusuf al-Sanusi), 159
ambition, sociology of, 220–25
Amselle, Jean-Loup, 18
Anderson, Benedict, 129, 160
animism, 11
anxiety. *See* modernist anxiety
Appadurai, Arjun, 12
Ardener, Edwin, 163
Ardyn Boone, Sylvia, 204
Askew, Kelly, 195, 210
authoritarian high modernism, 125, 270n45
authoritarianism, surviving, 225–26
autochthonous landownership, 78–79
autochthony, 12–13, 49, 66–67, 112; as cultural resource, 67–70; fictive, 67, 84
autonomy, pursuit of, 229
L'aventure (mobility), 68–69

bad deaths, 79, 254n15
Baga, 31, 36, 173
Baga Islamic revival, 131–33
Baldé, Diao, 224–25
Balla et ses Balladins, 217
ballet, 214–15
Ballets Africains, Les, 209, 214–15, 273n26
Bandi, 32, 36
Barry, Diawadou, 223

Barth, Fredrik, 29
Beavogui, Facinet, 39, 41–43, 207–8, 213–314, 237–40
Beavogui, Lansana, 226
Beavogui, Tolo, 222–23
Béhanzin, Louis, 231, 233, 2120
Bellman, Beryl Larry, 17
Bembeya Jazz National, 136, 217, 215–18
Berliner, David, 15, 17
Bird, Charles, 116, 197
Bledsoe, Caroline, 39
Bloc African de Guinée (BAG), 223–24
Bolowologi, 124
"Bonfire," 143–45
Brenner, Louis, 159
Bulongic, 273n3
burials, 75. *See also* funerals

Camara, Moussa "Dadis," 226
Camara, Sékou Legrow, 218–19, 224
Camayenne Sofa, 217
Camp Boiro, 226, 260n35
canton chiefs, 95–98, 269n38
cantons, 93–97, 258n16
Carmichael, Stokely, 220, 231, 265n21
cash crops, 92
catechisms, 158, 159
Cercle, 258n16
Chatterjee, Partha, 165
civil servants, 222–25
clan names, interchangeable, 53, 54t
clans, defined, 249n21
clanship, 52–55
coffee production, 92

Conté, Lansana, 233, 260n33, 268n26
Cosentino, Donald, 205
cosmopolitan idioms, iconoclasm and, 5
cosmopolitanism, 160
cultural production, ramifications of revolutionary-era, 210–12
Cultural Revolution, of Guinea, 167–68, 174–75
Cumba (Mani), 36–37
currency, Guinean, 217f

daabe, 21,] 65, 66, 68, 250n23, 253n3. See also kekɛ-daabe
daabenui, 70, 71, 78, 254n11
dance. See Ballets Africains
Dapper, Olfert, 36, 37, 50
d'Azevedo, Warren, 17, 37, 204
decolonization, 133
de Heusch, Luc, 8
Demystification Program, 5–7, 13–14, 18, 113, 147, 235, 264n1; alignment of motivations and logics of, 191–94; beginning of, 245n1, 267n16; burning of masks and, 171–72; as double sociological wedge, 138; elites and, 184–85; fervor of, 175; forest-savanna frontier and, 169; Guinean modernity and, 234; Guinea's minority populations and, 164–65; as "inside job," 179–84; local collaborators and, 175–77; local participation of Loma speakers and, 175; Loma speakers and, 171–73; monotheism and, 183; as national culture-building exercise, 151–52; orientation of, 170–71; as purge, 150–51; swidden rice farmers and, 15; ideal typical distinctions within, 183t
developmentalism, 133–34
Diallo, Telli, 222
discretion, 17; civil servants and, 222–23; Loma cultural style and, 199–200; proper upbringing and, 206
Dogo, 37
Donham, Donald, 12, 164
double consciousness, 24, 153, 165, 194
double double consciousness, 20, 151, 164–65, 219
dry land rice cultivation, 87
DuBois, W. E. B., 20, 234
Dyula revolution, 121, 263n27; second, 169

eating, 219–20
elites, 114, 184, 220; Demystirication Program and, 184–85; Forestier, 153, 194, 208; Fulbe, 264n8; Loma-speaking, 133, 138, 195; Malinke, 264n8; modernist, 77; national, 168, 169; national (state), 5, 86, 124, 152, 161, 165, 266n24; Northern Mande military, 37; socialist-era, 196, 221; South African, 265n24; state-employed, 219
Ellis, Stephen, 121–22
ethnicity: anthropological studies of, 29–30
ethnicized territory, 85; logic of, 93–100
ethnic mediation, 52–55
ethnogenesis, 3, 14–19, 227

Faber, Felix, 223
Fairhead, James, 257
Fala Wubo, 45, 46
Fanon, Frantz, 220
Feren Kamara, 45, 46
Ferme, Mariane, 17, 207, 270n49
fetishism, 9, 245n2
fictive autochthony, 67, 84
firstcomer, 66
Fitzpatrick, Sheila, 155
Folgia, 37
folkloric performances, 209
folklorization, 208–19
forest bush camps, 209
Forestiers, 125, 151, 165, 273n1; as insiders, 234; ministers, 226; as national stereotypes, 168; treatment of, 226
Freud, Sigmund, 11–12, 134
Fulbe, 30, 36, 159, 228–29, 273n1
funerals, 255n23. See also burials

Germain, Jacques, 2147n1
Germann, Paul, 201
Gilibaye, 193, 229, 230, 270n56
Giziwulu, 204, 254n12, 254n16, 261n6; agricultural production in, 241–43
Gola, 31, 36
goveiti, 66, 71, 76, 79
Guilao, Gamé, 76–77, 151, 178, 255n19, 255n20
Guilavogui, Galéma, 226
Guinea, 3–5; changes in marriage laws of, 185–91; colonial system of administration in, 93–95; Cultural Revolution of,

Index / 291

167–68, 174–75; foci of iconoclastic attention in, 10–11; identity and, 235; Marxism in, 160–61; under Sékou Touré, 152; West African languages in, 32t
Guineans, Liberians vs., 232
Gulphe, Pierre, 186

Hair, P. E. H., 49
Hoffman, Barbara, 116
Højbjerg, Christian, 15, 17, 193, 196
Hondo, 37, 50
Horoya Band, 217

iconoclasm, 3, 227; as cosmopolitan idiom, 5–8; as making claim for equal membership in world, 19–20, 27; precedents, 123–25
iconoclasts, 246n10
identity: Guinea and, 235; unified sense of, 230
idols, 9, 10
image of the offending image, 10–11
images: power of, 8–9
imaginations, links between religious and political, 157
inegiti, 21, 66, 76, 78–80, 255n19
inherited clans, 3
insecurity, 112, 121, 207, 222, 228–29

Jackson, Michael, 52, 54
jelilu (praise singers), 116
joking relations (*sanankuya*), 116–17
Jones, Adam, 44–45, 49
jouissance, 9, 12–14

Kaba, Lansiné, 129, 212–13
kabbe, 159
"Kaman-Fodéda" plot, 223, 260n35
Kamara clans, 39–40
Kamara Diomande, 45–46
Kanté, Soumaoro, 32
Karp, Ivan, 162, 163
kɔkɔlɔgi, 40–41, 105; dominant clans, according to Beavogui and Person, 237–40
Keita, Fodéba, 273
Keita, Sundiata, 32
kɛkɛ–daabe, 66, 85. See also *daabe*
kɛkɛ–daabe relations, 112, 187
Kekoura Kaman Kamara of Kwanga, 95–96
Keletigui et ses Tambourinis, 217
Kendall, Martha, 116, 197

Kissi, 31, 36, 256n26
Knauft, Bruce, xv, 134, 165
Koivogui clans, 39–40
Koivogui-Kamara corridor, 39–40, 46–52, 47
kokolo, 45
koli, 72
Komara, 45–46
Komo society. See power associations
Kondo, 37
Koniyanke, 247n2
Kono-Dama-Vai, 32, 36, 248n12
Kopytoff, Igor, 122–23
kpakpagi, 53t, 72, 73f, 78
kpelɛgi, 81–83
Kpelle, 32, 36, 173, 203, 250n25
Kratz, Corrine, 152, 251n35
Kuranko, 247n2
Kwanga, 251n30, 252n44

Landoqo, 32, 36
land tenure, 85, 86, 89–92; changes in laws by PDG, 100–1; laws, 259n28
languages, West African, 32t
latecomer, 139
Latour, Bruno, 10
Leach, Edmund, 16
Leach, Melissa, 257n7
Les Amazones de la République, 217, 272n20
Liberians, Guineans vs., 232
libidinal objects: ways of relating to, 9
Limba, 31, 36
lineages, 69–70
Loma, 7, 32, 36, 245n4; fighting and, 51; totemic clan names, 53t
Loma agriculture, 85–86, 138–39
Loma childrearing, 205–6
Loma cultural style, 199–200
Loma proverbs, 206–7
Loma sculpture, 201–2
Loma speakers, 14, 27–28, 114, 246n12, 254n13, 255n22, 256n24, 256n25; Demystification Program and, 171–73; solidification of, 229
Loma-speaking chiefdoms, 40, 42, 43–45

Macenta Préfecture, 3, 14, 16, 18, 30, 39, 46, 93–94, 229, 247n2, 252n45; ethnic identity in, 230–31; French and, 258n13; Manya-speaking planters in, 99–100; 1908 census of, 55–60; paradox of people living in, 231–32

Makeba, Miriam, 220, 231, 265n21
Malinke, 55–60, 114, 228, 252n43, 261n12, 273n1. *See also* Mandingo; Maninka
Mamadi, story of, 106–9
Mande languages, 31–32, 248n10
Mandingo, 50, 121, 247n2, 249n20, 261n12. *See also* Malinke; Maninka
Mane invaders, 49
Maninka, 37, 261n12. *See also* Malinka; Mandingo
Mannheim, Karl, 155
Manya, 7, 51, 121–22, 247n2
Manya speakers, 27–28, 229
manye (nyama), 196–99
marriage, 60, 66, 68, 97, 117, 127, 147, 167–68, 181, 184; Guinean legislation on, 50, 185–91
Marxism, 5, 13, 19; Guinean, 160–61; modernization and, 133–34; modern person and, 161–64; nationalism and, 160
masks, 154; Demystification Program and burning of, 171–72; and figures, 201; masquerade and, 150
Massing, Andreas, 46, 49–50
Mauss, Marcel, 153–54
mawɛɛiti, 66
McNaughton, Patrick, 118
Mel languages, 32
Mende, 32, 36
mise en valeur laws, 100–3; effects of, on local politics, 103–4; interethnic tensions and, 104–6
Mitchell, W. J. T., 8–9
modernist anxiety, 134–35, 164–65, 219
modernity, Guinean, 234
modernization: Marxism and, 133–34
monotheism, 135, 156
moral ethnicity, 235. *See also* political ethnicity
Murphy, William, 202–4, 205–6
music, 215–19

Nalou, 31, 36
Napier, David, 154
Niger-Congo language family, 31
Ninibu chiefdom, 96–97
N'Krumah, Kwame, 265n21
Non-consolidation, process of, 228

Northern Mande societies, 114–17; inherited statuses and, 119; links with Southwestern Mande societies, 137–39; Southwestern Mande societies vs., 118, 119–20
Northern Mande speakers, 252n42
nyama (manye), 196–199
nyamakala, 118, 120, 260n5
nyanybai, 201, 202f

oaths, 80–84
"oil-and-water thesis," 29, 30, 39, 48–49
oral historians, 3
orchestras, 215–19
ordeals, 80–84

Pan-Africanism, 5, 13, 19, 265n21
Parti Démocratique de Guinée (PDG), 15; changes in land tenure laws and, 100; changes undertaken by, 147–49; eradication of masks and, 124; land tenure laws and, 259n28; seminars of, 157–59
patrilineal descent groups. *See* lineages
Person, Yves, 37–38, 49, 121, 127, 157, 237–40
personhood, 190, 196, 198, 251n32
political ethnicity, 235. *See also* moral ethnicity
Poro society, 14, 17, 41, 171, 197, 199, 201, 213, 245n5, 246n6
portable identities, 94, 109. *See also* personhood
Portuguese Aggression, 273n24
Pouvoir Révolutionnaire Locaux (PRLs), 212
power associations, 169, 171, 173, 175, 246n11
praise singers (*jelilu*), 116
prise de conscience, 229
purification, myth of, 125

Radio Rurale, 229, 230
Rassemblement Démocratique Africain (RDA), 267n19
La Région forestière, 19
Renan, Ernest, 234–35
rice farming, 87–89
Richards, Paul, 252n42
rites of passage, 14

Rivière, Claude, 161, 175–77, 228–29, 269n31

sacrifices, 70–72, 76–79, 254n18, 255n19
salayati, 72
sale (medicine, talisman, mask, or power of associations), 14, 169, 174, 196–199, 197f, 198f, 205, 268n25
Samory Touré, 3, 18, 95–96, 126–28, 136–37; empire-building period of, 121
sanankuya (joking relations), 116–17
Sande society, 14, 17, 171, 197, 199, 201, 213
Sarró, Ramon, 15, 94, 263n35
savage slot, 165
Sayon, Aseku, 131, 263n35
Schmidt, Elizabeth, 185
scientific socialism, 19
Scott, James, 16, 125, 207
Second Dyula revolution, 169
secrecy, 17; Loma cultural style and, 199–200
secret societies, 17–18, 246n11
Sehu Usman Dan Fodio, 262n20
Sékou Legrow. *See* Camara, Sékou Legrow
Seymour, George L., 50
Shaw, Rosalind, 208
Sherbro, 31, 36
Siu, Helen, 266n1, 268n29
slash-and-burn agriculture, 3, 15, 138–39
slave trade, 38–39
sorcery, 246n13
Soso, 32, 36
Southwestern Mande languages, 31–38
Southwestern Mande societies, 114, 117–18; links with Northern Mande societies, 137–39; Northern Mande societies vs., 118, 119–20
Steedly, Mary Margaret, 152
Straker, Jay, 195, 209, 210
Subbanu, 130

Taal, Cenro Bokar Salif, 159
Taussig, Michael, 10–11
Taylor, Charles, 233
Teachers' Plot, 221
Temne, 31, 36
tests, 80–81
Tijani brotherhood, 262n18
"Togba's Sword," 63
Toma, 245n4
Toma Manian, 59. *See also* Manya
Tomas, 55–56. *See also* Loma
Torodbe people, 262n17
totems, 9
Touré, Ismael, 222
Touré, Sékou, 3, 15, 113, 233, 265n21; as anticolonial hero, 123–25; arrests and, 222; changes in land tenure laws and, 100; as dictator, 261n14; intellectuals and, 223–24; linking Islam to revolution, 155–56; political skills of, 191
travel, socialist-era, 224–25
Tsing, Anna, 234

Umar Tal, El Hajj, 125–26, 262n23
uncanny (Freud), 11, 134

"la visite," 148

Wahhabism, 128–31, 263n29
West African Zomia, 16
West Atlantic languages, 31–32, 32t

Yusuf al-Sanusi, Mohammed bin, 159

zalabhaloe, 41
ziigbadie, 205
zomia, 16
Zoumanigi, Akoye, 206
zukenuiti, 66, 90, 97, 106, 257n9